Union Society

Minutes of the Union Society

being an abstract of existing records, from 1750 to 1858; comprising, also,

chronological lists of its officers, members and beneficiaries

Union Society

Minutes of the Union Society
being an abstract of existing records, from 1750 to 1858; comprising, also, chronological lists of its officers, members and beneficiaries

ISBN/EAN: 9783337849634

Printed in Europe, USA, Canada, Australia, Japan

Cover: Foto ©Andreas Hilbeck / pixelio.de

More available books at **www.hansebooks.com**

OF

THE UNION SOCIETY;

BEING AN

ABSTRACT OF EXISTING RECORDS,

From 1750 to 1858;

COMPRISING, ALSO,

CHRONOLOGICAL LISTS OF ITS OFFICERS,

MEMBERS AND BENEFICIARIES,

WITH THE

ANNIVERSARY ADDRESSES

OF

HON. T. U. P. CHARLTON, COL. HOWELL COBB, HON. ROBERT M. CHARLTON,
REV. WILLARD PRESTON AND COL. ROBERT H. GRIFFIN.

ALSO,

A HISTORICAL SKETCH OF BETHESDA.

SAVANNAH:
JOHN M. COOPER & COMPANY.
1860

EXPLANATORY.

THE main purpose in printing these transcripts has been to preserve from loss a portion, at least, of such of the records of this time-honored institution, the Union Society, as still remain; and to place in an accessible form, many interesting facts and details found therein. The minutes from which they have been taken are full and regular, from April 2nd, 1791, to November 7th, 1796; meagre and imperfect, partly mere memoranda, from this latter date to October, 1798; *Managers'* Minutes, containing no reports, or anything in relation to election of officers, or anniversary proceedings, from May 4th, 1815, to May 2d, 1820; minutes, full and regular, from April 1st, 1828, continuously. Efforts have been made to fill up the gaps from other sources; and through the aid of Mr. J. F. Cann, the meetings of the Society, &c., on pages 196 to 205, have been condensed from old files of the *Georgia Gazette*, in the Georgia Historical Society Library, and of the *Savannah Republican*.

The transcripts have been made literally, save when indicated by parenthesis, and the earlier minutes have been carefully followed, even in the punctuation, and use of capitals; also, the manner of the minutes, as near as practicable, has been followed as a rule rather than taste or style,—as, for instance, on pages 46, 47, 48, &c.: the whole giving, as far as it goes, a faithful and unvarnished record of the growth and operations of the Society, of the times, and of the men.

The list of officers and members presents the names of many worthy and benevolent citizens, who once occupied the places of those of to-day; and whose names, with theirs, will be handed down to their successors, and be often called to memory hereafter. Arranged as they are, as far as could be ascertained, in the year of their admission, these names tell something, also, of the progress of the institution, and of its history. The names of beneficiaries are also appended, as far as could be ascertained, and show, in part, the operations of the institution and what has been accomplished. These lists of members and beneficiaries have been obtained by a careful and repeated examination of every page of the minutes and other books in possession of the Society, and from other investigations. It is hoped they may yet be made more complete; they are paged separately with a view to their continuation.

With the missing records, the Society has also to regret the loss of its Seal, no legible trace of which has yet been obtained.

The new career entered upon by the Society, and the newly awakened interest felt by its members, since the location of the institution upon the grounds of the ancient Bethesda, upon the principle of a Farm-School, opens to view an extended field of usefulness, which may be limited in the future, it is hoped, only by the number of those who may need its shelter and support.

The address of Col. Howell Cobb, spoken of as lost, on page 92, has since been found, and with that of Hon. T. U. P. Charlton, recently presented to the Society, by I. K. T. M. Esq., will be found appended.

The Registry Book of Members, as on page 92, was dispensed with, the Book of Rules and Signatures of Members answering all purposes—it was not got ready until 1860. The Ledger, also, as described on page 92, opened in 18 9, was set aside for one opened in 1860, of a size and form more convenient and suitable.

SYNOPTICAL INDEX.

8

9

2

20

* Orations of Charlton, Cobb and Charlton are not in order as printed above; they follow Bethesda, its founders, &c.

SYNOPSIS

OF MEETINGS HELD. ADMISSION OF MEMBERS, OF RECEIPTS AND
EXPENDITURES

MEETINGS HELD AND MEMBERS PRESENT.

MEETINGS OF THE BOARD OF MANAGERS.

NOTE.—The Rules adopted 1821, require monthly meetings of the Board of Managers, and quarterly meetings of the Society, and provide fines for default; but from 1820 to 1828, there are no minutes, and meetings are not herein regularly recorded after that time.

MEETINGS OF THE SOCIETY, &C.

ciaux, David Gugel, John Grommet, John McCall. John N.
Brailsford, James Shaw, George S. Hull, Solomon Shad, John
Glass, Rev. Thos. H. McCaule, William Wallace, John Moore,
Thomas Young, John McKinnon, James McIntosh, Thomas
Netherclift and David Brydie Mitchell, being read, they were
ballotted for and duly admitted........................ 39—40

William Belcher, admitted under 7th Rule............ 43

1797. April 24. J. C. Smith, Wm. H. Lange, Thomas Pitt, and John Roberts admitted 48

1818. May 5. On second reading of Petition. Donald McLeod. John
Speakman, Moses Herbert. John Tanner and John J. Roberts,
were unanimously admitted............................ 77

1818. July 7. William H. Joyner, balloted for and unanimously admitted, 78—79

Aug. 5. Archibald Smith, admitted..... 79

Oct. 6. Samuel M. Bond, admitted........................... 80

Nov. 3. S. S. Williams, Worthington Gale and Joseph King, unanimously admitted...................................... 80

Dec. 1. Wm. M. Kelly, admitted 81

1819. Feb. 2. Thomas Wright and Charles Maual, admitted........... 82

J. P. Henry and James Hunter, *resigned*.................... 82

March 2. Edward F. Tattnall, Francis H. Welman, Joseph Clay
Habersham, Benjamin Howard. William Neff and William C.
Wayne, admitted...................................... 83

April 5. Thirty-one new members admitted.................... 84

June 1. Six new members admitted 86

Dec. 7. Michael Brown, admitted.. 88

1820. May 2. Lazarus Petty, admitted.......................... 91

[There are no minutes from 1820 to 1828, and after that time only leading and prominent facts from the minutes have been transcribed.]

MONEY RECEIVED.

1791. James Port paid Society on account, (April 23, 1791)	£ 5.	6s.	9d.	1	
Balance in hand at last Anniversary.............	69.	2s.	8½d.	1	
Received since last Anniversary.....	10.	12s.	3d.	1	
" from 29 persons for dinner on Anniversary.	13.	10s.	8d.	2	
" from Dr. Augustus Mayer, loaned him last Anniversary................	5.	19s.	5d.	5	
also, interest on same, to Nov. last............					
1792. April 23. Received on and since last Anniversary,...	109.	7s.	8½d.	6	
Received this day...........................	44.	3s.	11½d.	7	
1793. April 23. Received this year....................	52.	12s.	9½d.	10	
Received this day................£61. 8s. 6d.				12	
1794. April 23. Received from last to present Anniversary,	98.	13s.	10d.	16	
Received this day ....£84. 3s. 2d.				18	
1795. April 23. Received from last to present Anniversary,	147.	19s.	11d.	27	
Received from Mayor and Aldermen, donation..	6.	6s.	0d.	27	
" this day...........................	83.	11s.	2½d.	31	
1796. April 23d. Received from 23d April, last, to 4th in.st...... $566 50				38	
Received this day, April 23, 1796................. 397 40				40	

1797. April 23. Sundry amounts loaned and paid out during the
year (no regular report) and balance in hand 122 77¼ 47
Received this day 176 60¼ 47
1820. Collections in the Churches........................ 689 31 89
1802. April 23. Balance in hand of late President. M. McA. ... 135 44 92
" " Received from Sundry Members 166 35 92
1805. April 1. Legacy of Wm. Gibbons. Jr................. 100 00 . 94
1806. April 23. Received from Thomas Dechenaux........... 20 00 94
1819. June 8. Interest on two Exchange Certificates from City
Treasurer 48 00 96
1820. Jan. 1. Interest on two Exchange Certificates. from City
Treasurer 24 00 96
1821. Jan. 1. Interest on two Exchange Certificates. from City
Treasurer 24 00 96
(No minutes from 1820 to 1828.)
1828. April 23. Total receipts this year, $1498 35, with the bal-
ance from last year........................... 2273 12¼ 102
(Receipts and Expenditures not hereafter regularly given.)
1833. Bequeathed to the Society, by the late Thomas Young... 6000 00 104
Exchange Stock, redeemed by City, principal and in-
terest............................. .... 702 00 104
Donation from A. A. Suares, La................... 500 00 104
1834. Donation from John Bolton, N. Y.................... 20 00 106
18'6. Bequest from the late Robert Cooper.......... ...... 50 00 108
1839. Bequest from the late Wm. M. Evans, of West Chester,
N. Y., 4 Shares Planters' Bank Stock, $80 paid in.... 320 00 108
1841. Receipts the past year............................. 1883 81 109
Balance from last year 260 17 109
1850. Received the past year, from all sources.............. 2488 40 113
1853. Total Receipts. including $28 45, balance last year..... 3045 63 132
1854. Present Annual Income........................ 3466 00 136
1855. " " " (Bethesda purchased).......... 2782 00 142
1856. " " " 3746 00 156–7
Donation from the Mayor, out of the Collections of
1854 .... 75 00 158
1857. Donation from Mr. Andrew Low. a Land Warrant, 160
acres 167
1858. Bequest of the late Henry Haupt.................... 500 00 172
Income this year........................... ... 3981 99 172
Donation from an unknown friend 175 00 173
" " 37 ladies and gentlemen "upwards of". 2700 00 173
1840. Received from Orphan House Estate, on account....... 1085 02 184
1844. Voluntary Contributions from sundry persons 70 00 184

MONEY PAID OUT.

1791. James Port. Paid him for Schooling............ £13. 13s. 9d. 2
Paid last year for Schooling and other expenses.. 37. 0s. 7½d.
Mr. Brown, dinner for 30 persons, on Anniversary.. 14. 0s. 0d. 4
James Port, for Schooling..................... 5. 2s. 3d. 4

1792. John Hanarahan, Schooling, Jno. Warnock (also —)	18s.	8d.	4
1792. James Port, for Schooling	1. 4s.	0d.	5
Mrs. Lydia Myers, her account for Schooling			5
James Port, for Schooling and Stationery	3. 18s.	11d.	5
April 23. Paid out and loaned on interest since last			
Anniversary	101. 9s.	10d.	6
Mrs. Lydia Myers, for Schooling, six *dollars*	$ 6 00		7
Emblematical Copper Plate, and 100 Membership			
Certificates therefrom....	£10. 14s. 4½d.		8
Maj. Brown, balance for dinner, last Anniversary,	$20 00		8
Mr. Stephens, for Seal for the Society..........	£ 1. 9s.	4d.	9
1793. April 23. Expenses the past year..............	37. 3s.	2½d.	10
Messrs. Johnstons, the printers, for advertising..	2. 3s.	0d.	12
1794. Justus H. Scheuber, Secretary, salary...........	10. 0s.	0d.	16
Expended the past year.....................	69. 7s.	10d.	· 16
Lydia Myers, for Schooling	1. 19s.	8d.	19
James Casey, for advertising	0. 13s.	0d.	19
James Port, Schooling to 15th June	6. 2s.	11d.	19–20
Rev. Mr. McCaule, entrance money for David Mur-			
ray Washington.........................	$2 00		24
James Port, Schooling to 5th September.........	£ 6. 19s.	6d.	24
Sheriff's and Clerk's Fees, on eleven suits	7. 14s.	0d.	24
Mr. Clay, for three Suits, to be brought against ——	2. 2s.	0d.	24
City for seven years' ground rent, Lot 2	15s.	0d.	24
Lydia Myers, for Schooling to 23d October	3. 7s.	11½d.	24
1795. James Port, for Schooling to 22d March	17. 7s.	9d.	26
Rev. Thomas H. McCaule, for Schooling..........	3. 18s.	4d.	26
Mrs. Lydia Myers, for Schooling to 23d January...	2. 16s.	9½d.	26
April 23. Expended since last Anniversary.......	57. 13s.	11d.	27
Ordered paid for Advertising	1. 18s. 10½d.		28
" " for Secretary's salary	10. 0s.	0d.	28
Lydia Myers, for Schooling to 23d April last........	$ 10 27½		33
James Port, for Schooling and Paper to 15th June....	41 50		33
[Fines henceforth for not attending Meetings.]			
Lydia Myers, for Schooling, Aug. 10........	12 50		35
James Port, Sept. 23, for Schooling, $36 00, Books $1 37.	37 37		35
1796. " " Dec. 18, " "	32 06¼		36
Peter S. Laffitte, April 23.........................	26 00		36–7
James Port, for Schooling. March 21......	39 62½		37
Rev. Mr. McCaule for Schooling Mary Washington. ...	6 70		37
April 23. Since last Anniversary to 4th inst...........	373 53		38
June 6th, Mrs. Lydia Myers, to May 2d..............	12 50		41
June 26th, James Port, for educating children..........	43 25		45
August 3d, Lydia Myers for " "	8 00		45
1797. Feb. 6th, " " "	6 00		46
" " James Port " " "	40 00		46
April 26. " " " " "	42 25		47
" " " " for the use of his room.......			47
Corporation Account, Secretary, &c	85 87½		48

James Port, July 4th, $40 00; Sept. 29th, $35 25	75 25	50
" " Dec. 21st	35 00	50
Lydia Myers, May 21st, $6 00; Nov. 9th, $12 00	18 00	50
Peter S. Laffitte	67 62½	50
1802. April 23. Disbursements for Children	9 00	92
Contingent Expenses—Secretary's salary	60 00	92
" " Anniversary Expenses	82 50	92
Subscription for building Exchange	40 00	93
May 18. Disbursements for children—Clothing,	12 00	93
June 21. " " " Tuition, Paper, Ink and Quills	40 25	93
Sept. 15. Disbursements for children—Tuition, Paper, Ink and Quills	42 50	93
Oct. 29. Disbursements for children—Tuition	12 00	93
Disbursements for children		182
Dec. 20. Wm, F. Port, for Tuition	24 00	182
" " " " for Paper, Ink and Quills	2 00	182
1803. March 22. Disbursements for Children—Tuition	26 00	93
April 23. Mrs. Lydia M. Myers, for Tuition	6 00	182

CONTINGENT EXPENSES.

Peter S. Laffitte, Secretary, one year's Salary	60 00	182
April 28. James Johnston, printing 3 quires Summons	4 00	182
Lyon & Morse, Advertising	3 75	182
June 3. John Lawson, Steward	106 08	182-3

DISBURSEMENTS FOR CHILDREN.

June 16. Wm. F. Port, Tuition, Paper, Ink and Quills	25 62	183
Hazen & Kimball, posting books, &c	158 00	183
July 8. Seymour, Woolhopter & Stebbins, printing	36 52½	183
Sept, 19. Schooling $16 00; Paper, Ink and Quills, 37c	16 37	183
Nov. 4. Tuition, $9 00; John Lawson, Clothing $26 50.	35 50	183
1804. Feb. 16. Lawson for D. & C. Gugel, clothing John Randolph	21 00	183
March 22. Wm. F. Port, Tuition, $10 50; G. Tufts & Co., Shoes, 75c	11 25	183
July 2. Peter S. Laffitte, Secretary, one year's salary	60 00	183
" 18. Stewards, deficiency Anniversary dinner	52 62½	183
Lyon & Morse, and Seymour & Woolhopter, Printing	6 25	183
Dec. 27. Wm. F. Port, Schooling	67 50	183
John Lawson, Clothing	9 00	184
1805. Jan. 17. Subscription for building an Exchange	12 00	94
April 23. Contingent Expenses—Secretary's Salary	60 00	94
Disbursements for children—Clothing and Schooling	219 31½	94
March 30. Mr. Port, Schooling	37 50	184
1806. April 23. Contingent Expenses—Printing, Dinner &c	67 25	185
1807. April 23. Contingent Expenses—Printing, Ann Exp., Secretary's Salary and Certificates of Membership	159 12½	
Disbursements for children—Schooling, Clothing, &c	249 25	94-95

1808. April 23. Contingent Expenses, J. Johnston, Printing,
$12 00; Adam Cope, Steward, $33 75 .... 45 75 184
Disbursements for children—Schooling and Clothing.... 996 97¼ 95
Contingent Expenses—J. F. Everett, and Seymour &
Woolhopter, Printing 6 75 184
1809. April 24. McLean & Barnes, Everett & Evans, and James
Johnston..................................... 44 50 184
Peter S. Laffitte, Secretary, (October 17th, last)...... 20 00 184
Contingent Expenses—Secretary's Salary, two years.. 120 00 95
Disbursements for Children—Schooling, Clothing, &c.. 614 50 95
1810. April 23. Contingent Expenses—Anniversary dinner.... 50 00 95
Secretary's Salary, three years.................. 187 50 95
Printing, Recording Deeds, &c..................... 97 01¼ 95
Disbursements for Children—Clothing Schooling, Board-
ing, &c...................................... 1213 57 96

CONTINGENT EXPENSES.

1818. April 23. J. O. Gray, Secretary, one year's Salary 250 00 96
1819. May 20. James Morrison, Secretary, one year's Salary... 250 00 96
1820. April 3.   "   "   "   "   "   "   ... 150 00 96
1821-2-3. Lowell Mason, Secretary, three year's Salary....... 450 00 95
[*No minutes from 1820 to 1828, and receipts and expenditures not hereafter regularly included in transcripts.*]
1828. April 23. Total expenditure this year................ 1725 93 102
1841.   "   "   Expenditures this year.................... 2095 43 109
1850.   "   "   "   "   "   " 1841 98 113
1852. Total Expenditure for Wing of the Academy.. .... 3280 35 132
1853. Ordinary Expenditures the past year................. 1909 02 132
Extraordinary Expenditures the past year 1065 03 132
1855. Paid this year for the purchase of Bethesda........... 7200 00 140
1857. Total Disbursements this year 5184 42 165
1858.   "   "   "   " 4945 90 172

Minutes: Union Society.

At an Anniversary of the Union Society, (41st.) held at Mr. Brown's
Coffee House, in Savannah, on Saturday the
23d day of April, 1791.

Present—NOBLE W JONES Esq'r *President.*
JOSEPH CLAY Esq'r *Vice Presid't,*
DAVID MONTAIGUT *Secret'y,*
JUSTUS H SCHEUBER *Assist't.*

William Henry Spencer	James Bulloch
John Ruppert	Francis Courvoisie
Isaac Fell	Sir George Houstoun
George Millen	William Stephens
John Eppinger	William Bryan
Frederick Fahm	Joseph Habersham
William Lewden	John Habersham
Venebles Bond	William Gibbons Sen'r
John Herb	Edward Lloyd
William Gibbons Jun'r	John. G. Williamson
Josiah Tattnall	James Moore
Peter Deveaux	Samuel Stirk
John Morel	James. B. Young
James Port	(31 members.)

Mr. PRESIDENT reported that he had Received £5 6 9 on Accompt from James Port and that he had paid Mr. Port the balance of
his Acc't for Schooling Children on the bounty of the Society to the
15th of March last Amounting to £13. 13 9¼ which had been paid
at different times but which he observes has not been entered on the
Minutes.

Mr PRESIDENT laid before the Society his Account of Receipts and
payments at and since the last Anniversary.

ORDERED that Mr. Joseph Habersham Sir George Houstoun and
Mr. William Gibbons Jun'r be a Committee to examine the Presidents
Acc't's The said Committee Reported they find that at the last An-
niversary the Sum of Sixty Nine pounds two Shillings and Eight pence
half penny was paid into his hands by his Predecessor in Office, and
that the Sum of Ten Pounds Twelve Shillings and three pence has been
Received by him to this Day making together the Sum of Seventy-
Nine pounds Fourteen Shillings and Eleven pence half penny and that

the Sum of Thirty Seven Pounds and seven pence half penny has been paid for Schooling the Children and other Expenses of the Society for which satisfactory Vouchers are produced leaving the balance of Forty two pounds fourteen Shillings and four pence Exclusive of Monies received this Day which Report was agreed to.

THE PETITION of Doct'r James. B. Young was read the Second Time, and being ballotted for, was duly Elected a Member of this Society.

Account of Monies Received at the Anniversary, the 23d Day of April, 1791.

	£	s.	d.
Samuel Stirk in part	3	15	4
Justus. H. Scheuber in full		13	8
Noble. W. Jones in full	1	2	0
Venebles Bond in part (Note for ball'ce)	3	14	6½
John Ruppert in full	3	12	4
John Eppinger in full	2	4	4
William Lewden in full		15	—
Fredrick Herb's Estate in full		10	—
John Herb in full		17	
Stephen Millen's Estate in full			6
George Millen in full	1	7	6
Federick Fahm in full	1	14	7
William Gibbons Jun'r in full		19	7
Isaac Fell in full	1	4	8
Joseph Clay in full	1	13	—
George. B. Spencer's Estate in full		11	11½
William Hen'y Spencer in full	1	9	5½
Francis Courvoisie in part (Note for ball'ce)	3	8	—
Sir George Houstoun in full		16	—
William Stephens One Y'rs Int'st on Bond	2	17	9
Contributions and fines		17	6
Joseph Habersham in part	1	8	—
John Habersham in part	2	2	—
William Gibbons Sen'r in full		18	—
William Bryan, in full	1	1	7
John. G. Williamson in part (Note for ball'ce)	2	16	—
Edward Lloyd in part (Note for ball'ce)	2	11	4
James Moore in full		18	—
Josiah Tattnall in part	3	15	8
Leonard Cecil in full		18	11½
Peter Deveaux in full	1	7	1¼
John Morel in full for Int'st Contrib'n and fines	1	7	11
James B. Young in part	1	8	0
	54	9	11¼

RESOLVED, that One Child of John Warnock at Veruonburgh be Schooled on the Bounty of this Society in that Neighborhood. Also that John Riley son of John Riley deceased be Schooled with Mr Port on the said Bounty.

THE SOCIETY then proceeded to Elect Officers for the ensuing Year when Doct'r. NOBLE. W. JONES Esq'r was again Elected President JOSEPH CLAY Esq'r Vice President JAMES PORT was Elected Secretary MR. FRANCIS COURVOISIE and MR. JOHN EPPINGER Stewards.

RESOLVED that a Committee of Three Persons be appointed to Superintend the Schooling of such poor Children, as may be Instructed on the bounty of the Society, And that Mess'rs John Habersham, William Henry Spencer, and George Millen, be the said Committee.

RESOLVED that a Sum not exceeding Forty Pounds be and is hereby declared to be set apart as a fund for Schooling such Children.

That the President do pay to the Order of the said Committee or any Two of them, the Quarterage of said Children with such Incidental charges as may occur.

RESOLVED that the President be empowered and directed to let at Interest agreeably to the Rules of the Society a Sum not exceeding One Hundred Pounds payable on the next Anniversary, taking good and Sufficient Security for the same provided that the Sum already Voted for, be Reserved.

THE QUESTION being put on Col. Habersham's Motion, for altering the Anniversary, was not agreed to.

Mr. Stephens from the Committee presented an Emblem for a Certificate Copper Plate which was approved of, and the Committee was Requested to have the same Engraved.

RESOLVED That Notice be given to such Persons, as are in Arrears to the UNION SOCIETY. that unless their Acc'ts are Settled, to the Satisfaction of the President, and Vice President within Two Months, they will be placed in the hands of an Attorney at Law, to Recover the same.   N W JONES President

(Monthly Meeting, May 2d, 1791, at Mr. Brown's Coffee House present Noble W Jones Esq., Pres't, James Port Secre'y, William Lewden, Edward Lloyd, Frederick Fahm.)

(Monthly Meeting, June 6th, 1791, at Mr. Brown's Coffee House, present, the President. William Henry Spencer, David Montaigut, Justus Scheuber.)

(Quarterly Meeting, July 4, 1791, at Mr. Brown's Coffee House; present, Noble W. Jones Pres'dt, Joseph Clay V. P., James Port Sec'y, William Stephens, Sir George Houstoun. Samuel Stirk,

Peter Deveaux, John G. Williamson, William H. Spencer, William Gibbons, Jun'r, James Milledge, John Ruppert, William Bryan, John Eppinger, Benjamin Lloyd, Frederick Fahm.)

Mr William. H. Spencer one of the late Stewards reported that he had paid Mr Brown £14 for the Dinner of 30 Persons at the Anniversary and that 29 Persons had paid for their Tickets and that the Sum of 9. 4. was advanced by him for the Extra Charge.

ORDERED That the President do pay the said Sum of 9. 4D. to Mr Spencer.

Ordered That a Sum not exceeding £25 be appropriated for paying for the Seal and Certificate for the Society and that the President do pay such Bill or Bills as may within the above Sum be Certified by the Committee, directed to procure the said Seal and Certificate.

THE PRESIDENT reported that he had Loaned the Several Sums of £55 — — £15 — — and £5 19. 5. viz to the Church Wardens of C Church J H Scheuber and Doct'r Aug's Mayer agreeable to the Resolution of the Society.

THE PRESIDENT reported that Mr. Port's Acct for Schooling Children on the bounty of the Society to the 15th of June last Amounting to £5 2. 3. being Certified by the Committee appointed for that purpose he had paid the Same.

* * * * * * * * *

N W JONES President.

(Monthly Meeting, August 1, at Mr. Brown's Coffee House; present, the Sec'y, Montaigut, Fahm, Lewden, Schenber. President sent an Excuse that he was unwell.)

(Monthly Meeting, September 5, at Brown's Coffee House; present. the Presid't and Sec'y, Spencer. Lewden.)

(Quarterly Meeting, October 3, at Brown's Coffee House ; present Port Sec'y, John Herb, W H Spencer.)

(Monthly Meeting, November 7, at Brown's Coffee House; present, Pres't, V. P., Sec'y, Montaigut, Cecil, Young, Spencer, John Herb, Schenber.)

(Monthly Meeting, December 5, at Brown's Coffee House; 12 members present.)

Mr PRESIDENT laid before the Society an Acct of John Hanarahan for one Quarter's Schooling of John Warnock agreeable to an Order on the last Anniversary which he had paid, on a Certificate of Sir George Houstoun of the duty being performed Amt £18. 8. Commencing from April to July. Also another Acct of said John Hanarahan for Schooling the said John Warnock one quarter from July to October which he had also paid.

Mr PRESIDENT Informs that he has Received of Doct'r Augustus Mayer, the Amount of his Note for £5. 19. 5. with Interest to the —— of November last.

(Quarterly Meeting, January 2, 1792, held at Mrs. Barbara Eppinger's house, 15 members present.)

It appearing that Messrs John Habersham and George Millen Two of the Committee for Schooling Children from an apprehension that they had such powers had put two Orphan Children namely, Sarah the Daughter of the Widow Hershman, and Marlow the Son of the Widow Prior, to School with Mrs Lydia Meyers on the 24th of April last, but tho it does not appear that the Committee have such Powers, yet they are of Oppinion that the said Two Children ought to be continued to be Schooled on the bounty of the Society.

ORDERED that the President do pay for the same.

Mr President reported that he had paid Mr Port's Accompt for Schooling Children from 15 of September to the 15th of December Amount £4. 4. 0.

(Monthly Meeting, February 6, 1792, held at Mrs. Barbara Eppinger's house, present, Pres'dt, Sec'y, Fahm, Houstoun, Joseph Habersham, John Eppinger.)

(Monthly Meeting, March 5, 1792, held at Mrs. Barbara Eppinger's house, 12 members present.)

Mr President Inform'd the Society that he had paid Mrs. Lydia Meyers her Accompt Agreeable to the Order of January last.

ORDERED that Doctor Young, Mr Lewden, and Mr Scheuber be a Committee to inquire for a Suitable Room for the Society to meet in and that they Report at the next Meeting.

(No report on minutes.)   N W JONES President

(Quarterly Meeting, April 2, 1792, held at Major Brown's Coffee House, 13 members present.)

Mr President informs the Society that he had paid Mr Port's Account for Schooling from Dec'r 15th 1791 to March 15th follow'g Amount £3. 14. 3. also 4. 8D. for Stationary.

RESOLVED. That Dinner be provided for 30 Persons At two Dollars each, and that the President Invite the Clergy, Judges of the Superior Court of this State, of the Federal Court, and the Mayor and Aldermen of Savannah, to dine with the Society on the Anniversary.

ORDERED. That the following Notice be given in the Gazette

UNION SOCIETY

The Members of the Society are desired to meet at Mr. Brown's Coffee House on Monday the 23d Inst, precisely at 9 O Clock in the forenoon on the Usual Business of the Society and to Celebrate the Anniversary. The Business of the Society being Urgent, the Members are Requested to be punctual in their Attendance.

Doct'r Young and Mr. George Millen were appointed to assist the Stewards on the Anniversary.

N W JONES

(Forty Second Anniversary, April 23d, 1792, held at Mr. Brown's Coffee House, 25 present.)

Mr. President laid before the Society his Account of Receipts and Payments, at and since the last Anniversary.

ORDERED! That Mr. John Habersham, William ——, and Mr. Francis Courvoisie be a Committee to examine the President's Account,

The Committee to whom was referred, the Account Current of Noble W: Jones Esquire President, commencing on the last Anniversary and ending this day.

Report: That it appears, that he received the Sum of One Hundred and Nine Pounds Seven Shillings and eight pence half penny Sterling, and that he had paid and loaned on Interest on account of the Society One Hundred and One Pounds Nine Shillings and ten pence Sterling regular Vouchers for which accompany the said Account, consequently that a Balance of Seven Pounds Seventeen Shillings and ten pence half penny remained due to the Society which was accordingly paid by the President and deposited by the Committee into the Box.

Account of Monies received at the Anniversary, 1792.

		£ s. d.
Noble W. Jones Esqr President Contribution and fines		0 12 10
Joseph Clay Esqr Vice President	ditto	1 18 00
William Gibbons Junior	ditto	0 18 1
William Lewden	ditto	0 15 9
Frances Courvoisie	ditto	1 11 6
Sir George Houstoun	ditto	0 18 00
James B. Young,	Interest and ditto	2 4 11½
George Millen	ditto	1 00 4
Frederic Fahm	ditto	00 16 0
John Herb	ditto	1 00 1⅜
John Ruppert	ditto	00 16 6
John Eppinger In part for	ditto	00 14 00
William H: Spencer In part for	ditto	00 4 8
Leonard Cecil	ditto	1 4 2
Joseph Habersham	ditto	00 18 8

	£	s.	d.
Joseph Gibbons for Interest on his Account to this day	2	1	1½
William Stephens Interest on Bond from the Church Wardens	4	4	00
Same Interest on his own Bond and Contrib'n and fines	3	15	3
Josiah Tattnall Interest 4. 1. & Contrib: and fines from last Year	1	4	1
John Habersham in part	2	16	00
William Gibbons Sen'r Contribution and fines	00	19	00
Nathaniel Pendleton in full	3	10	0
Edward Lloyd in part	2	3	6
John Morell Interest and Contrib: and fines	1	8	00
Samuel Beacroft in part	2	19	3
James Habersham in part	1	12	8
Justus H. Scheuber in full including 23. Interest	1	19	6
John Richards gave his Note for Two Pounds Seven Shillings and ten- pence for Contribution and fines.			

£44 3 11½

Total cash received from the different persons aforementioned amounts to Forty four Pounds Three Shillings and Eleven pence half penny Sterling.

The Society then proceeded to the Election of Officers for the ensuing Year, when by counting the Ballots, it appeared, that

    JOSEPH CLAY Esquire was elected President

    JOSEPH HABERSHAM Esquire Vice President

    JUSTUS H. SCHEUBER Secretary

    EDWARD LLOYD Esquire and ⎱ Stewards.
    Doctor JAMES B: YOUNG ⎰

Mr John Richards, having given his Note for all arrears due, desired to be no longer considered a Member of this Society.

(Monthly Meeting May 7, 1792, held at Brown's Coffee House; present, Joseph Clay Esqr Pres., Joseph Habersham Esqr V. P., Justus H. Scheuber Sec'y, N. W. Jones, James Port, James Milledge, William Lewden.)

Resolved ! That the Members of this Society be requested to meet in future precisely at Sunset, that they may be enabled to get through their necessary Business, within the Time prescribed by the Rules.

(Monthly Meeting, June 4th, 1792, at Brown's Coffee House, 11 present.)

Mr. President reported that he had paid Six Dollars, to Mrs Lydia Meyers for the Schooling of Marlow Prior and Sarah Hershman, from 23d Jan'y to April 23d last, as per Certificate for schooling poor Children.

A Petition from Mrs Delphia Prior. Widow, praying that her Son John Prior, might be admitted, to be schooled, with Mrs Lydia Meyers, on the Bounty of this Society, was received and read.

Mr. Stephens from the Committee appointed, to procure an Emblematical Copper Plate, and Certificates for the Members of the Union

8

Society; Reported : That he had received the same from New York with one hundred Copies, which he delivered in, with an Account amounting to Ten Pounds 14s. 4½d. Sterling : duly certified by the Committee for the purpose.

(Account paid.)

(Quarterly Meeting, July 2d, 1792, at Brown's Coffee House; present, Pres't, Sec'y, Jones. Spencer, Ruppert, Milledge, Lewden, Port, Eppinger.)

The Members present, recommended the President, that he pay to Major Brown the Sum of Twenty Dollars, being the Ballance due him, for Thirty five persons Dinner provided by him on the last Anniversary; and that the Conduct of the Stewards, in that Matter, be inquired into by the Society.

The Petition of Mrs Delphia Prior, was again read;

Ordered ! that her Son John Prior, be Schooled, with Mrs. Lydia Meyers, at the Rate of Two Dollars per quarter; Such Schooling to begin from the fourth of June last.

(Monthly Meeting Aug. 6, 1792, at Major Brown's Coffee House ; 12 present.)

The Society took under Consideration, the Conduct of the Stewards at the last Anniversary, and are of Opinion, that they ought not to have contracted, with Major Brown, to provide for a greater Number of Persons, than they were authorized, to do, under the Resolution of the 2d of April last.—They are further of Opinion, that such Members as attended the Society at that Anniversary, and did not dine with them, Should pay the Sum of Two Dollars each, towards defraying the Expenses of that Day, and the Secretary is required to charge such Members, with that Sum.

JOS: HABERSHAM:

(Monthly Meeting, Sept. 3d, 1792, at Major Brown's Coffee House: present, Doctor William Bryan and Secretary Scheuber.)

(Assembled, Sept. 27, 1792, at Major Brown's Coffee House, to attend the Funeral of Leonard Cecil, Esquire, 20 present.)

(Quarterly Meeting, Oct. 1, 1792; present, Pres., Sec., Jones, Herb, Port, Milledge, Eppinger.)

No other Members attending, those present could not proceed to any Business.

(Monthly Meeting, Nov. 5, 1792; 9 present.)

Mr. Stephens, from the Committee appointed, to procure a Seal for this Society, presented the Same by Letter, with an Account, amounting to one Pound Nine Shillings and four pence. which Sum he requested might be written off his Bond.

ORDERED that **Mr.** Stephens have Credit on his Bond for the Sum of one Pound Nine Shillings & 4d. in full for the Seal as aforesaid.

A Petition from Ann Jones, a widow, dated the 8th of August last, praying that her Son John William Jones, might be schooled on the Bounty of this Society, was read ; Ordered ! That the same lie over for the next Quarterly Meeting.

(Monthly Meeting, Dec. 4, 1792; present, Pres., Sec., Jones, Lewden, Fahm, Port.)

(Assembled Dec. 14, 1792, (12 present) to attend the funeral of John Ruppert.)

(Quarterly Meeting, January 7, 1793, at Major Brown's Coffee House; 12 present.)

The Petition of Ann Jones, praying to have her Son John Wm. Jones Schooled on the Bounty of the Society, was again read, and thereupon

Ordered That the Prayer of the said Petition be granted, and that the Schooling of the said John W: Jones be paid for, from the thirteenth of August last.

A Petition from Joseph Clay junior Esquire praying to be admitted a Member of this Society, was received and read; Ordered ! to be read a Second time, at the next Monthly Meeting, and to be ballotted for, at the next Quarterly Meeting.

On Motion Ordered that Elizabeth Hays, the Daughter of Mrs. Lawingburg, be Schooled with Mrs Myers at the rate of Two Dollars per Quarter, on the Bounty of this Society.

(Monthly Meeting, Feb. 4, 1793, at Maj. Brown's Coffee House; present, V. P. Habersham, Sec. Schenber, Wm. Gibbons Sen'r, Lewden, Lloyd, Milledge.)

No other Members attending, no Business could be transacted 2s 4d in the Box

(Monthly Meeting, March 1, 1793, at Maj. Brown's Coffee House; 10 present.)

The Petition of Joseph Clay junior Esquire, to become a Member was read a Second time & ordered to be read next Quarterly Meeting & balloted for.

A Petition from Francis Stebbins Esq'r, praying to become a Member was received and read, ordered ! to be read again next Quarterly Meeting and ballotted for, if a Sufficient Number of Members shall then be present.

Mr Lewden informed the Society that Elizabeth Hays, had been put to School with Mrs Myers on the fourth of February last, agreeable to the orders of this Society, of the 7th of January last.

(Quarterly Meeting, April 1, 1793, held at the Filature; 18 present.)

2

Resolved; That the Governor and his Suite, the Clergy and the Mayor & Aldermen, and the Judges, be invited to dine with the Society, at the next Anniversary. And that the Stewards, do provide on that Day a Dinner, at the Filature for Thirty five Persons.

Resolved : That the Members of the Society be advertized to meet precisely at Nine o'Clock in the forenoon on that day at the Filature. And the usual Advertizement be published in the Gazette.

The Petitions of Joseph Clay jun'r and Francis Stebbins Esquire to become Members, were again read. ballotted for and admitted.

In the Box 5s. 3d.

_____

(43d *Anniversary, April* 23, 1793, *held at the City Hall in the Filature*, 32 *present.*)

Joseph Clay junior, Esquire, having been admitted a Member of the Union Society at the last Quarterly Meeting, now attended, Signed the Rules and took his Seat.

*   *   *   *   *   *   *   *   *   *

RESOLVED! That Country Members, whose Actual Residence is exceeding One Mile from Savannah, be Subject only to the Annual Contribution, any thing in the Eighth Rule to the contrary; notwithstanding, And that all former Fines for Non-Attendance, demanded of such Members, be remitted ;

RESOLVED! That the Monthly Contributions be augmented to One Shilling and two pence per Month, instead of One Shilling, as heretofore.

RESOLVED! That the President employ an Attorney to recover all Arrears due this Society, or to take such other Steps as will compel a Settlement ; and that the President pay out of the Funds, as much as will pay Fees of Officers, necessary to sue out Such Processes.

Mr. President laid before the Society his Account for the last Year :

Ordered ! That Mr. McCredie, and Mr. William Gibbons Senior, be appointed to examine the same ; who Reported that they find the President had received Fifty two Pounds thirteen Shillings and Nine pence half penny and had expended Thirty Seven Pounds three Shillings and two pence half penny, and there is in Cash the Sum of Fifteen Pounds ten Shillings and Eight pence half penny. which Report was agreed to.

Mr. Stephens adjusted the Sum due on his Bond to this Society and gave his Note for Twenty Six Pounds and two pence being the Balance due this day, on which his Bond was cancelled.

Mr. Scheuber adjusted the Sum due on his Bond to this Society and gave his Note for the Balance, being Seven Pounds three Shillings and Seven pence, on which his Bond was cancelled.

Mr. James Milledge Settled his Arrears, with the Society, took up his former Note, and gave another for Five Pounds two Shillings and three pence.

Mr President, who appears to have been fined five Shillings, for one Evenings Absence;—Doctor Jones, who stands charged with five Shillings fine, from the Year before last, and which had been remitted last Anniversary, but no Notice on the Minutes taken thereof—And Mr Mordecai Sheftall who stands fined Seven Shillings and two pence, for not attending the last Anniversary and the funeral of John Ruppert deceased; moved the Society that those Fines be remitted them, and they giving Satisfactory Excuses Ordered accordingly.

The Petitions of the following Gentlemen, to become Members of this Society, viz't from

Mr. Peter Samuel Laffitte	Major John Berrien
Richard Wayne, Esquire	Mr. John Tebeau
Robert Bolton Esqr	Captain George Throop and
Mr. Daniel Course	John Y: Noel Esquire

were received and read, and Separately ballotted for, and Severally duly elected Members of this Society.

John Y: Noel Esquire one of the Members elected, attended the Society, and agreeably to the Rules of this Society paying part of his Admission Money to the President, and having given his Note for the Balance of Two Pounds eleven Shillings and two pence half penny, took his Seat accordingly.

The Society then proceeded to the Election of Officers for the ensuing Year, when the following were elected viz't.

The Hon'ble JOSEPH HABERSHAM Esquire *President*

The Honble WILLIAM STEPHENS Esquire *Vice President*

JUSTUS HARTMAN SCHEUBER, *Secretary*

Messrs PORT and JOSEPH CLAY junior *Stewards*

Mr Clay having declined to accept of the Stewardship and paid the Fine. Mr Isaac Fell was chosen Steward in his room.

Mr Courvoisie, Mr. Lewden and Mr. Edward Lloyd, were then appointed a Committee, to superintend the schooling of such Children, as shall be admitted, and are now Schooled, on the Bounty of this Society.

Account of Monies received this Day from the Members

from Noble W: Jones in full for Contribution & Fines			£ 0 14 7
" William Gibbons Sen'r in full for do	do		0 18 8
" William Gibbons jun'r in full for do	do		0 19 11½
" James Port in full for do	do		0 12 10
" Peter Deveaux in full—in full for do	do		2 3 2
from Levi Sheftall in part of Interest			2 6 8
from William Stephens in full of Contribution and Fines			1 6 4
from The Church Wardens, in full of Interest			4 8 0
from James Milledge, in part of Account			3 14 9

from Isaac Fell, in full of Account.	12	9	9
from Frederic Fahm, in full of Contribution and Fines	0	16	4
from William Bryan, in full of Account	2	3	2
from William H. Spencer in full of Contribution & Fines	0	17	0
from John G. Williamson, in full of Account	5	6	4
from John Herb, in full for Contribution and Fines	0	15	10
from Joseph Habersham, in full of Contribution & Fines	1	14	0
from Francis Courvoisie, in part of Account	1	17	4
from George Millen, in full of Contribution & Fines	0	19	8
from Mordecai Sheftall in part of the same	2	6	8
from James B. Young, in full of Account	1	17	0
from Andrew McCredie, in full of Ditto	4	17	0
from John Y. Noel, in part of his Admission	2	17	6½
from James Habersham, in part of Account	3	10	0
from William Lewden, in full for Contribution & fines	0	15	0
from Thomas Cumming in full for his Contribution	3	0	0
from Joseph Clay Sen'r in full for his Contribution & Fines	1	2	0
from Edward Lloyd in part of Account	1	6	9
from Joseph Clay jun'r in full for his Admission ..£2 12 6			
from Same , a Fine for not acting as a Steward ... 10	3	2	6
from John Habersham, in part of Account	2	11	4

TOTAL Cash Recived, the 43d Anniversary from Members...£61 8 6
Say Sixty one Pounds Eight Shillings and Six pence.

(Monthly Meeting, May 6, 1793, at Filature; present, Justus H. Scheuber Secretary; Frederic Fahm and Peter S. Laffite.)

(Monthly Meeting, June 3, 1793, at Filature; 15 present.)

Sir George Houstoun made an Excuse, for his not attending the last Anniversary, which was admitted.

Mr. Daniel Course and Major Berrien, two Members elected on the last Anniversary, attended the Society, and agreeable to the Alteration of the Second Rule, each paid the Sum of Two Pounds Sixteen Shillings in Cash for part of their Admission Money into the hands of the President, and for the Balance being Two pounds Nine Shillings, each gave his Note, payable with Interest on the 23d day of April next, Signed the Rules and took their Seats

JOS: HABERSHAM.

(Quarterly Meeting, July 1, 1793, at Filature; 12 members present.)

Mr. John Tebeau a Member elected, attended the Society and having paid the Sum of Two Pounds Sixteen Shillings, and given his Note for Two Pounds Nine Shillings, took his Seat in the Society.

Ordered, That Martha Jones, Daughter of ———— Jones deceased also Mary & Sarah, the Daughters of Peter Stoner, deceased, be Schooled on the Bounty of this Society, with Mrs. Meyers School Mistress.

Messrs. Johnstons the Printers presented their Accounts for printing Avertisements in the Gazette from the 30th of Decr 1790, to the 27th of June 1793, amounting to Two Pounds three Shillings

Ordered that the President do pay the same.

Mr. Richard Wayne paid the Sum of Two Pounds Sixteen Shillings Specie, and gave his Note for two Pounds Nine Shillings, being the Balance for his Admission Money as a Member of this Society.

(Monthly Meeting, August 5, 1793, at the Filature; present, President, Vice President, Joseph Clay, Sir George Houstoun, Frederic Fahm, William Lewden, William H. Spencer, John Eppinger, Justus H. Scheuber.)

Mr. John Krieger of Savannah, Tailor applied for a Loan of Money not exceeding Fifty Pounds.

RESOLVED! That agreeable to the XX Rule of this Society, the President be authorized to loan to Mr. John Krieger the Sum of Forty Pounds Sterling, on Condition of his giving Bond with Mr. John and Frederic Herb as Securities, payable next Anniversary with Interest from the date.

Mr. Daniel Course was elected Stewart in the Room of Isaac Fell, absent from the State.

JOS. HABERSHAM.

(Monthly Meeting September 2d, 1793, at the Filature; present, Joseph Habersham President, William Stephens V. P., Justus H. Scheuber Secretary, William Lewden, Joseph Clay jun'r, Benjamin Lloyd, John Berrien, Peter Deveaux.)

(Quarterly Meeting, October 7, 1793, at Filature; present, the Secretary and John Herb.)

(Monthly Meeting, November 4, 1793, at Filature; present, Joseph Habersham President, Justus H. Scheuber Secretary, John Berrien, William Lewden, William H. Spencer, Benjamin Loyd.)

No other Members attending, those present, agreeable to the Rules could not proceed to Business.

(Monthly Meeting, Dec'm 2, 1793, at the Filature; present, Justus H. Scheuber Secretary, Joseph Clay, Sir George Houstoun, John Berrien, James B: Young, Joseph Clay junior, John Habersham.)

The Honb'le Joseph Clay was appointed Chairman.

Two Daughters of a poor Widow Woman, named Henry, were recommended to be schooled on the Bounty of the Society, in the room of the two Daughters of Mrs. Stoner, who do not choose to accept of that Bounty Referred to the next Quarterly Meeting.

(Quarterly Meeting, January 6, 1794, at Filature; 9 members present.)

Ordered ! That Patsey Henry, Daughter of Mrs. Henry a poor Widow woman, be schooled on the Bounty of this Society with Mrs. Myers, Schoolmistress from this date.

RESOLVED! That this Society will in future meet at the House of Mr. John Carsan's in this City.

(Monthly Meeting, February 3, 1794, at Mr. John Carsans; 10 members present.)

Resolved!

That William Gibbons, Sir George Houstoun, Joseph Clay, James B: Young and the Secretary be a Committee, to report by next Anniversary a Statement of all Monies due this Society and to give their opinion what Debts, are by them considered to be good, and may be obtained; And those due by persons, or their Estates, that shall be considered as lost, from the Circumstances of the persons, or Insolvency of their Estates

(Monthly Meeting, March 3rd, 1794, at Mr. John Carsans; 11 members present.)

(Quarterly Meeting, April 7, 1794 at Mr. John Carsans; 17 Members present.)

Mrs. Wilson (formerly Widow Prior) begs that her Sons Marlow & John Prior, be transferred from the Womans School, to Mr. Ports, to enable them to be taught writing & Arithmetic. Referred to the Committee, for superintending the Schooling of Children

On Motion made and seconded, Notice was given, to alter the 8th Rule of the Society, so, that it may be the Interest of Members, to attend the Meetings of the Society, more punctually than heretofore, and to read thus :

The Members of this Society, shall contribute and pay annually the Sum of Three Dollars, as a Contribution, towards, the Funds of the Society.

Any Members resident, within the City of Savannah or within One Mile thereof, neglecting to attend the Monthly Meetings of the Society, shall be charged with a Fine of ———— and for neglecting to attend the Quarterly Meetings ———— for each Neglect ———— A reasonable Excuse shall always be admissible

Mr. Robert Bolton, a Member admitted, last Anniversary, attended the Society, paid his Admission Money of Five Pounds five Shillings to the President, Signed the Rules, and took his Seat.

Mr. Mordecai Sheftall, paid into the Hands of the President the Sum of Two Pounds and four pence half penny, being the Balance of his Account, due last Anniversary.

Mr. Noel, paid four Dollars in part of his Account.

Mr. George Throop, who had been admitted a Member, last Anniversary attended, and paid Ten Dollars in part of his Admisson Money to the President, gave his Note, for Two Pounds eighteen Shillings and four pence, for the Balance, payable on Demand, with Interest from the 23d April 1793. Signed the Rules and took his Seat.

Resolved! That Mr. Spencer and Mr. Laffitte are to assist the Stewards on the Anniversary, And that they Do provide a Dinner for Thirty five Persons.

RESOLVED, that the Governor and his Suite, the Judges of the Federal and State Courts, the Clergy, and the Attorney General of the State be invited to dine, on that day, with the Society, and that the President and Vice president, are requested, to invite, any such Strangers as they may think proper, and who may be then in Savannah, not exceeding four Persons, to dine with the Society.

RESOLVED! that the usual Notice be given for the Celebration of the Anniversary &c and that the Society meet at the Filature, precisely at 9 o'Clock in the forenoon, on that day, for the dispatch of Business.

Proposed and Seconded, that it be an Alteration of the fifth Rule of the Constitution of this Society, that when the real expence of the Anniversary Dinner, shall be more than two Dollars each Man, the Surplus shall be paid in proportion by the Members present at such Anniversary & not taken from the Funds of the Society.

JOS: HABERSHAM President.

44th Anniversary, April 23d, 1794, at Filature; 37 members present.

John Herb, attended and paid his Arrears, but did not dine with the Society, nor paid towards the Expence of the Anniversary.

Absent Members to be charged with one Dollar for their part of the Anniversary Expence.

1, Levy Sheftall
2, Joseph Gibbons
3, James Habersham
4, Peter H. Morel
5, Frederic Rester
6, Benjamin Lloyd
7, David Rees
8, Jame Bulloch
9, Thomas Cumming
10, John Milledge
11, Isaac Fell
12, William Bryan
13, Charles Oddingsells
14, Richard Leake
15, Edward Lloyd
16, Francis Stebbins
17, John Herb
    Remark as before
18, James Moore
19, James Port and
20, Daniel Course,
N B: The Secretary paid their Arrears for them, they having previously paid them to him.

The President having made proper Excuses, for his Absence at five different Meetings of this Society.

ORDERED! that the Sum of Twenty five Shillings, be remitted him.

RESOLVED! That from the Age and Infirmity of David Montaigut his Fines amounting to fourteen Shillings and six pence, for not attending the Monthly and Quarterly Meetings, be remitted him.

James Port having offered an Excuse, to the Society, that he was prevented by his ill state of Health, from attending the Monthly and Quarterly Meetings, as a Steward

RESOLVED! that Twenty five Shillings being his fines therefore, be remitted.

Oliver Bowen having stated to the Society, that he has been mostly absent from the State, and therefore it was out of his Power, to attend the Anniversaries and other Meetings regularly.

RESOLVED! That on settling for the annual Contributions, while absent from the State, the remainder of his Account be remitted.

Agreeable to this Resolve he paid the Sum of Forty four Shillings (See List of Monies paid) and gave his Note for Four Pounds ten Shillings being the Balance of Contributions by him due.

It appearing that Justus H. Scheuber the Secretary of the Society is indebted to the Society by Note which with the Interest due thereon and one Years Contribution, makes in the whole Eight Pounds Nine Shillings and one penny, and as the Annual Salary of Ten Pounds to the Secretary is now due.

RESOLVED, That the Note be delivered up to him, and the Balance of One Pound ten Shillings and eleven pence be paid the Secretary.

Sir George Houstoun, Oliver Bowen and Richard Wayne, were then appointed a Committee, to examine the Presidents Account, who reported as follows:

"We have examined the Presidents Account and find that he received from the last to the Present Anniversary the Sum of Ninety eight Pounds thirteen Shillings and ten pence, and paid the Sum of Sixty Nine Pounds Seven Shillings and ten pence, for which Expenditures, satisfactory Vouchers have been produced to us, and that there remains in his hands a Balance of Twenty Nine Pounds Six Shillings, which Sum the Committee find in the Box in Cash.

GEO: HOUSTOUN, O, BOWEN, R WAYNE;

The Petition of George Jones, John Cunningham, Joseph Miller, Thomas Rice, Robert Montford, Mathew McAllister George Woodruff and Sheftall Sheftall, praying to be admitted Members of this Society, were received and read, Separately ballotted for and duly elected.

George Jones and Sheftall Sheftall, attended, paid their Admission Money as Sons of Members, Signed the Rules and took their Seats.

Mathew McAllister and George Woodruff also appeared, paid part of their Admission Money, and gave each his Note for Two Pounds Nine Shillings the Balance due yet, Signed the Rules and took their Seats, also Joseph Miller appeared, who signed the Rules and took his Seat, having paid his admission Money

RESOLVED!

That a Sum not exceeding Forty Pounds, be appropriated for Schooling Children on the Bounty of this Society, and that Mordecai Sheftall, John Berrien and George Jones be a Committee to superintend the schooling of such Children

Resolved!

That Mary Lavender, Daughter of Benjamin Lavender deceased and Betsey and Lotty —— the Daughters of Major Talmage Hall, deceased, be schooled on the Bounty of the Society, in addition to those already at School.

The alteration of the 8th Rule, as proposed the last Quarterly Meeting, was taken up and, considered, when on the Question being put, the same was negatived.

The Alteration of the 5th Rule, as then proposed, was then considered, and the following Resolved!

That when any deficiency shall happen, in adjusting the Anniversary Expence, not exceeding two Dollars each Member attending, such deficiency shall be paid out of the fund of the Dollar t. be charged each absent Member, for their part of such Anniversary Expence, any Rule to the contrary notwithstanding.

Monies received by the Society this day, from the following Persons.

Ordered! to be credited them respectively.

James Moore, in full of Contribution & Anniversary fine 4s 8	£2.	7.	4
James Port, in part of his Account	0.	15.	9
Daniel Course, in full of Contrib: fines and Interest	1.	17.	4
John Berrien, in full of Note, Interest, Contrib: and Fines	3.	8.	10
John Krieger & al: in full of Interest	2.	1.	10
Robert Bolton, in full of Contribution, Fines and Interest	1.	9.	5
Mordecai Sheftall, in full of Contribution and Fines	1.	0.	10½
Francis Courvoisie, in part of his Account	4.	4.	0
Noble Wimberly Jones, in full of Contribution and Fines	0.	18.	11½
Venables Bond, in part of Account	3.	10.	0
John Tebeau, in full of his Note, Interest and Contribution	3.	6.	11
William H. Spencer, in full of Contributions and Fines	0.	18.	0
William Gibbons, sen'r, in full of Contribution	0.	14.	0
Frederic Fahm, in full of Contribution and Fines	0.	18.	0
Peter Deveaux, in full of Contribution	0.	14.	0
Richard Wayne, in full of Contribution, fines and Interest	1.	5.	11
Sir George Houstoun, in full of Contribution and Fines	1.	15.	5
William Lewden, in part of ditto	0.	9.	4
William Gibbons jun'r, in full of Contribution	0.	14.	0
John Eppinger, in part of Account	2.	6.	8
John G: Williamson, in full of Contribution	0.	14.	0
James B: Young, in full of Contribution and Fines	1.	0.	0
Josiah Tatnall, in full of his Note, Interest, Contrib: & Anniv: Expence	4.	13.	0
Oliver Bowen, in part of his Contribution	2.	4.	0
John Herb, in full of Contribution and Fines	0.	18.	0
Andrew McCredie, in full of Do. and do.	1.	1.	6
Joseph Clay Senior, in full of do. do.	0.	18.	0
George Millen, in full of Contribution	0.	14.	0
Joseph Habersham, in full of Contribution and Fines	1.	5.	9
William Stephens, in full of Contribution, Fines and Interest	3.	6.	1
John T: Noel, in part of Account	1.	3.	4
Samuel Beecroft, in part of Account	4.	13.	4
John Morel, in full of Contribution, fines and Interest	2.	0.	4

3

Nathaniel Pendleton, in part of his Account............................ 1. 3. 4
George Jones, in full of his Admission Money this day................ 2. 12. 6
Mathew McAllister, in part of ditto.................................. 2. 16. 0
Christ. Church, in full of one Years Interest....................... 4. 8. 0
John Habersham, in part of his Account.............................. 0. 18. 8
Joseph Clay Junior, in full of Contribution & fines................. 1. 0. 0
George Woodruff, in part of his Admission, this day................. 2. 16. 0
Seth John Cuthbert's Estate in part of Account...................... 1. 3. 4
Sheftall Sheftall, in full of Admission this day.................... 2. 12. 6
Joseph Miller, in full of ditto..................................... 5. 5. 0

                                                                   84. 3. 2

Total of Monies received from the different Persons aforementioned, amounts to Eighty four Pounds three Shillings & two pence.

The Committee appointed on the third of February last, for the purpose of reporting at this Anniversary a statement of all Monies due the Society, and to give their opinion of what Debts are good ; reported that they had made some progress in the Business, and wished to be allowed a further time to complete the same.

It was ordered accordingly.

The Society then proceeded to the Election of Officers for the ensuing Year, when the President, Vice President and Secretary were re-elected, and Peter S. Laffitte and George Throop were elected Stewards.   JOS: HABERSHAM.

(Monthly Meeting, May 5th, 1794, at the Filature; 9 members present.)

Mr. John Cunningham, a Member elected last Anniversary, paid by the hands of the Secretary, to the President, the Sum of Five Pounds five Shillings for his Admission money.

        *   *   *   *   *   *   *   *   *   *

Messrs Spencer and Laffitte, who were on the 7th of April last appointed to assist the Stewards, in providing the Anniversary, rendered an Account of their Receipts and Expenditures for the same, by which it appears that the Balance of one Pound four Shillings and four pence half penny, has been saved for the benefit of the Society, and which Balance, was by them paid into the hands of the President.

Mr. Thomas Rice, a Member elected last Anniversary, attended, and paid the Sum of Two Pounds Six Shillings and eight pence, in part of his Admission Money, and gave his Note for the Balance say for Two Pounds eighteen Shillings & four pence, to the President &c, signed the Rules and took his Seat.

Mr. John Cunningham, made Application for a Loan of money of about £100 and offered James Mossman as his Security. Also Messrs Hopkins & Parker, apply for a Loan of Money of from £47 to £50. and offer Capt. Howell and Colonel Tatnall for their Securities.

Mr. Francis Stebbins gave his Note for Seven Pounds four Shillings & Nine pence payable with Interest from the 24th April last, in full of his account to that day per the Secretary.

JOS: HABERSHAM President.

(Monthly Meeting June 2d, 1794, at the City Hall; 12 Members present.)

RESOLVED

That the Sum of Fifty Pounds be loaned to Mr. John Cunningham, Mr. James Mossman with another person to be approoved of by the President becoming his Securities, in a Bond to the Society.

RESOLVED

That the Sum of Twenty five Pounds be loaned to Messrs Hopkins, Meers & Parker, on Captain Howell and Colonel Tatnall, becoming their Securities

RESOLVED

That Maria Cameron the Step-daughter of Absolom Bull deceased, be schooled on the Bounty of this Society with Mrs Myers—

JOS: HABERSHAM.

President.

(Quarterly Meeting July 7, 1794, at the City Hall in the Filature; 19 members present.)

Mr President reported

That he had loaned John Cunningham on the 7th June last the Sum of Fifty Pounds, and took his Bond of that date with James Mossman and Andrew McCredie as Securities, payable to the President of this Society or his Successors in office, on or before the 23d April 1795, with Interest from the date of said Bond.

Also that he had loaned the Sum of Twenty five Pounds on the 16th June last, to Elisha B: Hopkins, Samuel Meers and John Parker, and took their Bond with Josiah Tatnall and John Howell as Securities, payable with Interest from the date of the Bond, to the President of the Society or to his Successors in Office, on or before the 23d April 1795.

That he had paid Lydia Myers per Account and Receipt the Sum of One Pound nineteen Shillings and eight pence, for schooling Marlow & John Pryor and Betsy Hays on the Bounty of this Society, to the 23d of April last.

further that he had paid James Carey the Printers Account, for Advertisements the Sum of Thirteen Shillings

Also the Sum of Six Pounds two Shillings and eleven pence to James

Port in full, for schooling of Children on the Bounty of this Society, to the 15th of June last.

And that he had received the Sum of Eight Pounds eighteen Shillings and four pence, from Charles Oddingsells, in full for his Admission Money and all Arrears due the Society on the last Anniversary.

Mr James Moore, paid to the President One Dollar, being his part of the Expence of the last Anniversary and in full of his Account

ORDERED ! That the Committee appointed for superintending the schooling of Children, be authorized to put Murray Washington, the Son of Mrs Washington, to school with the Rev. Mr. McCaule for one Year, on the Bounty of this Society.

RESOLVED, That the Claims of this Society against the Estate of John Morel, Joseph Wright and Mathew Roche, Samuel Stirk and Raymond Demere' and George Walton for Oate's Estate, be put in Suit, as the Interests of the Society requires the Measure.

RESOLVED ! That the Committee appointed on the 3d of February last, to report on the other Debts due this Society, be requested to proceed on the Business without delay.

JOS: HABERSHAM
President.

(Monthly Meeting, August 4th, 1794, at the Filature; 12 Members present.)

The Committee appointed to report " a Statement of all Monies " due this Society, and to give their Opinion, what Debts are by them " considered to be good, and may be obtained, and those due by Per- " sons or their Estates, that shall be considered as lost, from the Cir- " cumstances of the Persons, or Insolvency of their Estates ;" having taken the same into their Consideration, agreeably to an Extract from the Books of the Society furnished them by the Secretary

REPORT, as their Opinion as follows :

That the several Debts, due by the following Estates, to this Society are not recoverable, as from the best Information, they can obtain, they are all insolvent, and if sued for, the Society would probably, loose the Expences attending the same; viz't

Estate			£	s.	d.	Estate			£	s.	d.
John Martin	dec'd		2.	0.	0	Leonard Cecil	dec'd		2.	5.	2
"	Mathew Roche	"	2.	1.	2	"	William Leconte	"	2.	16.	0
"	Jonathan Bryan	"	3.	10.	2	"	Benjamin Andrews	"	6.	6.	8
"	John Wandin	"	13.	5.	0	"	William Pierce	"	13.	15.	11
"	John Brown	"	11.	0.	0	"	George Handley	"	16.	11.	4
"	Anderson & Knowles	"	25.	0.	0	"	James Field	"	7.	3.	4
"	John Holmes	"	10.	5.	1	"	David Rees	"	14.	1.	4½
							Total		130	5	2½

That the following Persons or their Representatives, ought to be called on for immediate Payment, or Security for Payment of Principal & Interest due by them, within a reasonable time and in Case of their refusing or neglecting so to do, that their several Debts, ought to be put in Suit as soon as conveniently may be. viz't

Levy Sheftall, his Bond &c	£50.	17.	4	George Walton's Acct incl: order....	15.	6. 4
Peter H. Morel, his Note &c	16.	12.		Same for his Assumption in favour of John Oates Est:...	80.	3. 6
Raymond Demeres Est: Acct	6.	19.	5			
Josiah Powells Estate Do	4.	3.	4	James Bulloch—Account	7.	9. 4
Samuel Stirks Est; Note &c	13	19.	2	John Milledge— Do	7.	12. 8
Frederic Rester Acct	6.	17.	4	Peter S. Laffitte— Do	6.	12. 5
James Milledges Est: Note &c	5.	18.		Joseph Gibbons, Note &c	11.	17. 2
Benjamin Lloyd, Note &c	16.	8.	9	Math'w Roche & Joseph Wrights Bd.	66.	10.

That about Emanuel Peter Delaplaigne deceased inquiry ought to be made whether he had not Specie Certificates or other Papers for Monies due him, from this or the United States and where they now are, or if disposed of, whether any Person is responsible to his Estate for their Amount; this being ascertained the Society will be enabled, to judge what farther Steps to take for the Recovery of this Debt, the amount of which as per Statement rendered by the Secretary is £15. 3 2d.

Your Committee, taking the whole State of the Society's Funds into View, as stated by the Secretary, to the 23'd April last, find them as follows :

Debts due the Society of every Description	£748,18,—
of which they are of opinion, their are Debts entirely bad, to the Amount of	£130, 5,2½
And of such as may be reckoned doubtfull about	200,00,
And of good Debts	418,12,9½— £748,18,—

The Committee further observe, that the Debt said to be due to the Society by the Estate of John Morel Esquire deceased, is not included in the above Statement, as they were not acquainted with the Amount. which Report, the Society proceeded to take into Consideration, and thereupon Resolved !

That the first part of the Report, which alludes to Debts due by insolvent Persons or their Estates, be postponed

That the Second part of the Report, which alludes to Persons, or their Estates, to be called upon for Security, or pay up their Debts be agreed to. And that the Report in Regard to such Persons, be acted upon as therein directed ; and the President be and is empowered, to direct the Secretery to inform the Persons indebted, that unless their Debts are settled as the Report directs, by the first Monday in September next. their Demands. will be put in Suit by the next Return day of the Inferior Court, in conformity to former Resolutions of the Society in such Cases.

Mr Port informed the Society that Mary Lavender and John Warnock who were schooled on the Bounty of this Society, had been
withdrawn by their Friends
RESOLVED!

That Benjamin Alter, Son of Ulrich Alter deceased, and
David—Nestler, Son—of Adam Nestler, be schooled with Mr Port
on the Bounty of this Society.

Mr Vice President gave Notice, that he should on the next Quarterly Meeting move the Society that the Sum of £   be appropriated for building a House, on the Lot in this City, appropriated for
the Use of this Society.

W STEPHENS
Vice President.

(Monthly Meeting, Sept. 1st, 1794, at the Filature; 11 members
present.)

The Secretary reported that agreably to the Resolutions of this Society and by the direction of the President, he had wrote, to all the
Debtors mentioned in the Second part of the Report, and acquainted
them with the Determination of the Society.—

That James Gunn the Representative of Joseph Wright deceased,
had acquainted him verbally, that his Attorney at Law, was directed
to receive a Process.

That Philip Milledge the Representative of James Milledge deceased, had promised to pay the Debt next fall.

That Mr. Levy Sheftall, had promised, to give the Security required

That he had received a Letter from Joseph Gibbons Esqr, complain-
ing that the Society meant to distress old Members, that had always
paid punctuall that his Situation was such, that he could not ask any
Man to be his Security.

Also from John Milledge Esqr, who promises to call, correct some
Errors in the Account and settle the same.

which Letters were read, and the whole referred to the President,
agreably to the Resolutions passed, on that Subject
RESOLVED!

That Mordecai Sheftall Esqr (the oldest Member of this
Society) be and is now requested to make his Affidavit, stating facts, in
respect to his Knowledge of a Bond and Mortgage, given by the late
John Morel Esquire deceased, for a Debt due this Society, and when
such Affidavit is compleated, to lodge the same with the Secretary; and
that Mr Secretary, Mr Laffitte & Mr Lewden, be a Committee to attend to the Business.

W. STEPHENS V: P..

(Quarterly Meeting, Oct. 6th, 1794; 11 members present.)

The Secretary reported that agreeable to the orders of the Society Messrs Clay and Woodruff, had been employed by the President, to commence Suits against the following Persons and Estates viz't. 1 against the Estate of Raym'd Demere, 2 the Estate of Samuel Stirk 3 the Estate of Joseph Wright 4 against Levy Sheftall on his Bond and 5 the same on Account of Arrears 6 Benjamin Lloyd 7 Frederic Rester 8 Peter H: Morel 9 James Bulloch 10 John Milledge 11 Peter S: Laffitte 12 Joseph Gibbons 13 George Walton and 14 against the same on Account of his order in favour of the Society to Mess: Edward and William Telfair

The Secretary presented an Account of Seven Pounds fourteen Shillings being Clerks and Sheriffs fees, on Account of Eleven Suits commenced in the County of Chatham;—Also an Account of Two Pounds two Shillings Clerks and Sheriffs fees, for Suits to be commenced against George Walton in Richmond County and against Frederic Rester in Effingham County.

ORDERED, that the President pay the same, in Advance.

The Committee appointed, to obtain the Affidavit of Mordecai Sheftall Esqr reported, that they had effected the Business of their Mission, and produced an Affidavit respecting the Loss of a Bond and Mortgage of the deceased John Morel, to this Society.

ORDERED that the Affidavit be placed in the Hands of Mr. Clay junior to be proceeded in, as the Law directs in Cases of lost Papers.

A Confirmation of the Title to Lot No 2. in Perceival Ward, Holland Tything having been made to this Society, by the Board of Wardens, on the Sixth of November 1787. for Public purposes, yielding to the Corporation 5 Shillings per annum, and it appearing that the said ground Rent has never been paid.

ORDERED that the President pay the same to Mess: Lewden, Herb & Course who are appointed a Committee, to pay the same to the City Council and take a Receipt therefor :

Mr Vice President moved, and it was agreed to, that the Motion, for voting a Sum of Money, for erecting a Building on the Lot belonging to the Society, should be postponed.— And a Committee was appointed, to propose a Plan, and bring in an Estimate of the Expence of the proposed Building; The Committee have it in Charge, to make Inquiry after the Claim of this Society to the Lot adjoining the said Lot No 2. in Holland tything Perceival ward, and to report as early as may be.

Committee appointed Mr Vice President Stephens, Mr Lewden, Mr Scheuber, Mr Bolton and Mr Eppinger.

W STEPHENS V: P..

(Assembled October 25th, 1794, at the Filature, 28 members present, to attend the funeral of deceased member Dr. William Bryan.)

(Monthly Meeting, Nov. 3d, 1794, at the Filature; 9 members present.)

The President proposed that the Son of Mary Bueley a Poor Woman be schooled on the Bounty of this Society.

ORDERED to lie over for the next Quarterly Meeting.

The President reported, that he had delivered to Messrs Clay & Woodruff the following Specialities, to be sued for, as directed by the Society.

1) Mathew Roche and Joseph Wrights Bond for £33,,5,,0 dated April 23d 1769.

2) John Oates Bond for £40,,1,,9, dated the 23d August 1772.

3) Levy Sheftalls Bond for £31,,8,, dated the 1st June 1789.

4) George Waltons Order on William & Edward Telfair for £66,,16,, 11d dated the 31st December 1777.

5) Samuel Stirks Note for £5,,5,,0d. dated 23d. April 1783.

6) Peter H. Morels Note for 5. Guineas dated 1st December 1784.

7) Benjamin Lloyds Note for £5,,5,,0d. dated 1st August 1785.

8) Joseph Gibbons's Note for £8,,14,,0d. dated 23d. April 1792.

9) George Waltons Order on Joseph Day for two Barrells of Rice, dated 23d. April 1786.

And that he had paid two Dollars to the Rev'd Mr McCaule as Entrance money for David Murray Washington.

that he had paid Mr Ports Account for Schooling down to the 15th of September last the Sum of Six Pounds Nineteen Shillings & Six pence.

that he had paid Sheriffs and Clerks fees on Eleven Suits as per order amounting to Seven Pounds and fourteen Shillings

that he paid Mr Clay Two Pounds two Shillings for three Suits to be brought against George Walton and frederic Rester in Richmond and Effingham Counties.

that he paid one Pound fifteen Shillings being Seven years Ground Rent for the City for Lot No 2. Holland tything Perceival Ward due the 6th instant.

also that he paid Mrs Lydia Mayers for schooling Children from 23d April to 23d October 1794. the amount of Three Pounds Seven Shillings and eleven pence half penny.

JOS: HABERSHAM

Monday the first of December 1794.

This day being a stated Monthly Meeting of the Union Society, but the St Andrews Society having Possession of the Filature and no other Place appointed where the Society could meet—Notice was given to the members residing in Savannah, that no Meeting would be held this day.

(Quarterly Meeting, January 5th, 1795, at the Filature; 12 members present.)

ORDERED! That James Bucley—the Son of Mary Bucley a Poor woman, be schooled on the Bounty of this Society, to commence from the third day of November last, as was then proposed.

The Committee to whom it was referred to report a Plan of a Building to be put on the Lot belonging to this Society having presented a Plan accordingly They are requested to inform the Society at the next Meeting of the expence necessary to compleat the same. And it is requested they will also report what Kind of Buildings could be placed on the said Lot, to produce the greatest Quarter yearly Rent, for a Sum of Four Hundred Pounds.

Mr Pendleton gives Notice that he will propose a Bye Law—by way of ordinance, to regulate the Terms and Conditions on which Children who have Parents or Guardians, shall be educated by this Society. The Principle of which shall be, to authorize the Society to bind out such Children, independent of the Consent of such Parents or Guardians to usefull Professions and occupations.

(Monthly Meeting, February 2d, 1795; 10 members present.)

In the Absence of bothe the Presidents, Mr. Mordecai Sheftall was appointed Chairman.

The Committee appointed to report the probable Expence, for building on the Lot belonging to the Society, at this Meeting, request further indulgence, which was granted.

Mr William Lewden recommends, a Daughter of John Gilbert deceased, to be schooled on the Bounty of this Society.

(Monthly Meeting, March 2d, 1795; present, Stephens V. P., Scheuber Sec., Fahm, Eppinger and Sheftall Sheftall.)

No other Members attending, those present recommend that a Child of William Gilbert deceased, be schooled on the Bounty of the Society.

(Quarterly Meeting, April 6th, 1795; "the following members (15) met at the Filature by public advertisement.")

The President reported that he had received the following Sums of Moneys viz't

from James Powell Four Pounds three Shillings & four pence in full
 of Josiah Powell deceased for his Arrears

from Peter S: Laffitte Seven Pounds Six Shillings and five pence in

4

full of Arrears due by him on the 23d. of April last, and also including fourteen Shillings for Sheriff & Clerks fees.

from John Eppinger Ten Shillings and Six pence in full of his Arrears due last anniversary.

And that he had paid the following Sums, viz't to

James Port Seventeen Pounds Seven Shillings and Nine pence for schooling to the 22d. March last, as per two Receipts.

To the Rev'd Thomas H. McCaul Three Pounds Nineteen Shillings and four pence for 5. Months Tuition for D. M. Washington ending 19th December last

To Mrs Lydia Myers Two Pounds Sixteen Shillings and Nine pence half penny for Schooling to the 23d. of January last.

The following Petitions were then read, viz't from John Reutz—Joseph Roberts, Slaughter Cowling, William Norment and Frederic Herb, praying to be admitted Members of this Society

ORDERED! that their Petitions do lie over, until the next Anniversary

ORDERED! That John Gilbert, Son of John Gilbert deceased, be schooled on the Bounty of this Society with Mrs Myers.

The Committee to whom were referred, the propriety of building on the Lot of the Society, agreeably to the the Spirit of the Resolution are of Opinion, that the Measure proposed in the Motion, on which the Resolution is founded, and the whole Business ought for the present to be postponed, and lay over, to such Period, as the Society may chuse to revive it.

RESOLVED, That the President or Vice President be authorized to invite the Clergy, and any Number of Strangers who may be in the City not exceeding Six, to dine with the Society on the day of its Anniversary; And that the present Stewards provide a Dinner for Forty Persons.

ORDERED! That the usual Notice for the Celebration of the Anniversary be published in the Georgia Gazette.

JOS: HABERSHAM Presid't

Forty-Fifth Anniversary April 23d, 1795, at the Filature; 36 Members present.

Edward Lloyd, stating that ever since the Month of Ssptember 1793. he had been Sick and indisposed, which prevented his attending the Society, wherefore ordered, that his Fines from that period amounting to Nineteen Shillings & Six pence be remitted him.

The President, on behalf of Sir George Houstoun, Stated that

Since August last, he had been Sick, and unable to attend the Society, wherefore his fines amounting to eight Shillings were remitted.

George Woodruff and Andrew McCredie, Stating that from June to October last, they had been absent from the State, wherefore Five Shillings and Six pence of their Fines respecticely, ought to be remitted them; Granted!

The President made Excuse for being twice absent at the Meetings of the Society when unavoidably detained in the Country, the excuse was admitted and Ten Shillings of his Fines remitted him.

The Vice President also made Excuse for being twice in default, which was thought sufficient, and Seven Shillings of his Fines ordered to be remitted him.

William H. Spencer, made Excuse, that he was out of Town at the Funeral of Doctor Bryan, deceased—Ordered that Two Shillings and Six pence be remitted.

John Herb, alledging that he was indisposed during the last Anniversary, wherefore he could not stay with the Society, which being admitted, the Fine or Expence of One Dollar was ordered to be remitted.

Mr Peter S: Laffitte, being fined 5s—for being absent two Meetings as Steward, made Excuse, on Account of Self & family being indisposed—the Society ordered the said fine of Five Shillings, to be remitted.

Noble W: Jones, William Gibbons and Jonn Berrien were then appointed a Committee, to examine the Presidents Accounts, who having done so, Reported ! that they find He has received from the last to the Present Anniversary the Sum of *One hundred forty,, Seven Pounds Nineteen Shillings and eleven pence*, that he has loaned out by order of the Society on two Seperate Bonds the Sum of *Seventy,, five Pounds*, And that he has expended for the Use of the Society the Sum of *Fifty Seven Pounds thirteen Shillings and eleven pence*, making in the whole the Sum of *One hundred and thirty two Pounds thirteen Shillings and eleven pence*; The Bonds and Vouchers for the Loans Receipts and Expenditures have been produced.—And that there remains in the Box the Balance of *Fifteen Pounds Sixteen Shillings and Nine pence*.

The Society notice with pleasure, the Appropriation of the personal Fines of the late Mayor & Aldermen. (agreably to their Rules) to charitable purposes, when collected, by the City Clerk, who has already paid the Sum of Six Pounds Six Shillings, and informed the President he would pay the Balance of Fines, when received by him.

The Printers having produced their Account for advertizing Socie-

ty Meetings &c from 3d October 1793, to this day, amounting to One
Pound eighteen Shillings and ten pence half penny.

Ordered that the same be paid.

The Secretary presented his Account for One Years Salary & Stationary amounting, after deducting Seventeen Shillings his Contribution & fine, to Nine Pounds three Shillings.

Ordered, that the President do pay the same

In Consequence of the Notice given in January last, Mr. Pendleton proposed an Ordinance, to regulate the Terms, on which Children are to be schooled, on the Bounty of this Society, which being three times read, considered and amended, is agreed to.

Ordered, to be engrossed, Sealed with the Seal of this Corporation and Signed by the President. which is as follows :

AN ORDINANCE

To regulate the Terms on which Children are to be schooled on the
Funds of the Union Society

Whereas it may happen, that Children who have been schooled by the Funds of this Society, may afterwards be taken away by their Parents, Guardians or Friends, and instead of being put to some usefull Trade, or occupation, may be permitted to pursue vicious Courses, whereby both they and the Community, may be deprived of those advantages, which it was the design of this institution to procure, for remedy whereof : Be it ordained, that from and after the—First Monday in July next, no Child or Children shall be received, to be schooled on the Funds of this Society, nor shall any Child or Children, that are now at School on its funds, be continued beyond that time, unless the Parents, Guardians, or Friends of such Child or Children, shall before their admission in future, or before that day in respect to those already admitted, execute and deliver to the Secretary for the time being, under their hands and seals an Article or Deed, in the following form, to wit : "Know all Men by these Presents that "——————— (father, Mother, Guardian or) ——————— of "——————— an Infant of the Age of —— Years, do hereby put "and bind the said ——————— unto the President and Vice Pres- "ident of the Union Society of Savannah, for the time being, to be by "them, at such time, as they shall think proper put and bound by an "Indenture of Apprenticeship, to whomsoever they shall think "proper, to learn such usefull and honest trade, occupation, profession "or calling, and for such length of time and on such Conditions, as "the said Society by their rules or orders may direct, and the said "Society are hereby authorized, to assign this Article, at the time of

"binding the said —————— unto the person or persons to whom
"—— may be bound. In Witness &c
which said Deed the Secretary shall take & keep, untill the next Quarterly Meeting of the Society, and then deliver to the President or
Vice President.

RESOLVED! That the Secretary be and he is hereby directed to
form an Alphabetical List of the Members of this Society, marking
in Columns, the time of their Admission, resignation or Death.

Whereas the Duties of the Secretary are greatly augmented and as
the expenditure of Stationary of Course increases:

RESOLVED! that from and after this day the Salary of the Secretary be Sixty Dollars per Annum.

The Petitions of John Rentz, Joseph Roberts, Slaughter Cowling,
William Norment and Frederic Herb, praying to become Members of
this Society, were again read, Separately ballotted for, and Severally
duly admitted

Also the Petitions from John Howell, John Armour, John D: Dickinson, Hampton Lillibridge and James Jones, were this day received
and read, Separately ballotted for and each of them duly elected.

RESOLVED! That a Sum not exceeding Three hundred Dollars is
hereby appropriated for the schooling of Children, and instructing
them in psalmody and also for the purchase of necessary Books &
Stationary and that James B: Young, Richard Wayne and George
Woodruff be a Committee, to superintend, the education of such
Children as may be schooled on the Bounty of this Society.

* * * * * * * * * * *

On Motion made and seconded, RESOLVED, that from and after this
day inclusive, all Accounts of Money, and Bonds hereafter to be
made, shall be kept in Dollars and Cents, and that all sums relative
to the Society, that are now expressed in Pounds Shillings and pence,
be estimated received and entered, at the rate of One Dollar for four
Shillings and eight pence.

George Throop gave his Note for Six Pounds three Shillings and
two pence half penny, being in full for principal, Interest. Contribution & fines, whereupon his former Note was cancelled.

Mr. Vice President paid the amount of Emanuel Delaplains Note
dated 2d. June 1783, for Five Pounds five Shillings, with 11 Years
and 11 Months Interest thereon; whereupon the said Note, was given
up to him.

John Y. Noel, George Woodruff and Thomas Rice, having each
paid off their respective Notes, they were therefore cancelled.

John Armour, a Member this day elected appeared, paid his Admission Money, Signed the Rules and took his Seat.

Hampton Lillibridge, a Member also this day admitted, appeared and gave his Note for his Admission Money, payable on the first Monday in May next, whereupon he was permitted to sign the Rules and take his Seat

The Society then proceeded to the election of Officers for the ensuing Year,

when WILLIAM STEPHENS Esqr was elected President

MORDECAI SHEFTALL, Esqr, Vice President

JUSTUS H. SCHEUBER, Secretary and

GEORGE WOODRUFF and SHEFTALL SHEFTALL, Stewards

George Woodruff declining to serve, and having paid his fine, Mathew McAllister was elected in his room, Sheftall Sheftall also declining to serve & paying the fine, John Y. Yoel was elected in his room, he also declining & paying the Fine, Richard Wayne was next chosen in his room, but he declining and paying the Fine, John Berrien was chosen Steward in his place.

Account of Cash received at the Society this day,

Mordecai Sheftall, in full of Contribution and Fines	£1. —. 6
Levy Sheftall, in part of Account	1. 14. 4
Noble W. Jones, in full of Contributions & Fines.	. 17. 6
William Gibbons, in full of Contribution	—. 14. —
Joseph Clay, in full of Contribution & Fines	—. 18. 6
Mathew McAllister, Interest, Contribution & Fines.	1. 7. 5
Peter Deveaux, in full of Contribution	—. 14. —
Joseph Habersham, in full of Contribution and Fines	1. 14. —
John Habersham, in part of Account	3. —. 8
Mr. Stephens, for Emanuel de la Plaign's Estate in full of Note & Interest	10. 5. 3½
Samuel Beacroft, in part of Account	2. 6. 8
William H. Spencer, in full of Contribution & Fines	—. 18. —
John Herb, in full of Contribution & Fines	—. 18. —
William Lewden, in full of Contribution & Fines	1. 3. 8
Frederic Fahm, in full of Contribution & Fines	—. 19. 6
George Millen, in full of Contribution.	—. 14. —
John Milledge, in full of Contrib: & Fines (but no Costs of Suit)	5. 6. 8
Andrew McCredie, in full of Contribution & Fines	—. 18. 6
Nathan Pendleton, in full of Contribution & Fines.	1. 17. 4
Venables Bond, in full of Int: Contrib: & 4s. 8. anniv: expences.	1. 2. 5½
James Port, in full of Contribution & Fines.	1. 6. 6
Charles Oddingsells, in full of Contribution	—. 14. —
John G. Williamson, in full of Contribution & Fines.	1. 3. 4
James B. Young, in full of Contribution & Fines.	1. 1. —
Christ Church, in full of Interest	4. 5. —
William Stephens, in full of Interest, Contribution & Fines	3. 2. 7
John Y. Noel, in full of Note, Interest, Contrib'n & Fines	3. 12. 2½
John Berrien, in full of Contribution & Fines	—. 19. —
Richard Wayne, in full of Interest, Contribution & Fines.	1. 15. 4
John Kreeger &c in full of Interest.	3. 4. —
Robert Bolton pr Scheuber, in full of Contribution & fines	1. 4. —
George Woodruff, in full of Note, Interest, Contrib: & Fines	3. 19. 10

Sheftall Sheftall, in full of Contribution & Fines................................. . . 1. 5. —
John Cunningham, in full of Interest, Contribution & Fines.................... 4. 14. 8
Thomas Rice, in full of Note, Interest, Contrib: & Fines......................... 4. —. 6
From Peter S: Laffitte, Surplus from Quarterly & Monthly Meetings............. —. 5. 8
John Armour, in full of Admission Money..................................... 5. 5. —

Say Eighty three Pounds, eleven Shillings, and two pence half penny............£83. 11. 2½

List of Absent Members, who are to be charged with One Dollar each,
towards the Expences of the Anniversary.

1 Venables Bond   15. Sir George Houstoun
2. Andrew McCredie and   16. James Moore
3. Edward Lloyd, who attended   17. Thomas Cumming
   but did not dine, nor paid   18. Richard Leake
   towards Same   19. Francis Courvoisie
4. David Montaigut   20. Isaac Fell
5. Oliver Bowen   21. John Eppinger
6. James Habersham   22. Josiah Tatnall
7. Joseph Gibbons. excused sick.   23. Joseph Clay junior
8. Frederic Rester   24. Francis Stebbins
9. John Morel   25. Robert Bolton
10. William Gibbons junior   26. John Tebeau
11. Benjamin Lloyd   27. Daniel Course
12. David Rees   28. George Jones
13. George Walton   29. Peter H. Morel
14. James Bulloch

JOS: HABERSHAM,
President.

The President, having withdrawn, after an affectionate Leave of the
Society, previous to his departure to Philadelphia, to take upon him
the Duties of his Appointment, as Postmaster General of the United
States.

Whereupon the late Vice—President took the Chair, and on Motion
it was resolved unanimously

That this Society by their President and Vice President elect present to Joseph Habersham late President, their hearty. Approbation
of his good Conduct—They feel the importance of the appointment of
Joseph Habersham as Postmaster General, and although they regret
the want of his Personal services—Yet as part of the Nation, they
rejoice, that so early an Asserter of the Liberties of America is appointed to fill so honorable an Office.

W STEPHENS V: P..

(Monthly Meeting, May 4th, 1795 ; 11 members present.)

The President informed the Society, that he had received from the
late President the Sum of Fifteen Pounds Sixteen Shillings and Nine

pence, being Surplus Money that remained in the Box, and also the Sum of Eighty three Pounds, eleven Shillings and two pence half penny, being the Sum of Money collected at the last Anniversary.

Mr. Joseph Roberts and John Rentz lately elected Members of this Society appeared, and paid each twenty two and one half a Dollar for their Admission, Signed the Rules and took their Seats in the Society

Mr Frederick Herb and John D. Dickinson, also appeared, and each paid Eleven and one quarter of Dollar into the hands of the President for their Admission, and gave their Notes for the Balance, Signed the Rules and took their Seats.

Applications were made by Mr. Berrien, Mr. Krieger and Mr. Tetard for the Loan of Money, but on the question being put, it was resolved in the negative, and the Business postponed, because it appeared that £100. is appropriated, and lays dormant, until the Committee appointed to report the Estimate of a Building on the Lot of this Society.

The President and Vice president informed the Society, that agreably to their order, they inclosed Joseph Habersham Esquire late President, a certified Copy of the Resolution passed at the last Anniversary in respect to him; and laid before the Society a Letter from Mr. Habersham in answer thereto, which being read is as follows, viz't.

"GENTLEMEN!

"The Approbation of my public Conduct by the Union Society as "expressed in their Resolution on the last Anniversary, which you "enclosed me, has made a gratefull impression on my Mind, as I have "always endeavoured to support such measures, as, I conceived, would "have a tendency to promote the real welfare of my country.

"I sincerely wish that your benevolent Institution may continue to "prosper, and that under its protection, many otherwise friendless, may "become usefull members of the Community, an object highly inter-"esting to every friend of Humanity.

"I thank you Gentlemen, for your friendly wishes, while I am dis-"charging the Duties of my Appointment under the Federal Govern-"ment and you will please to accept of mine for your Prosperity and "Happiness as well as for that of every Member of the Society. I am "with much Esteem Gentl'n

Your Mo Obdt. Servt.
JOS: HABERSHAM.

"SAVANNAH 4th May 1795.

"The Honorable William Stephens Esqr President and Mordecai "Sheftall Esqr Vice President of the Union Society."

W STEPHENS
Pret.,

(Monthly Meeting, June 1st, 1795, at the Filature; 12 members present.)

The President reported, that he had paid Mrs Lydia Myers the Sum of Ten Dollars and twenty seven and one half Cent for schooling, from 23d January to the 23d April last.

* * * * * * * * * * *

ORDERED! that Malsy Kitchin, a poor Orphan, now in the Care of Mrs. Jenkins, be schooled on the Bounty of this Society.

W STEPHENS
Pre't..

(June 10th, 1795, by order, assembled (37) at the house of Mr. Carsans, to attend the funeral of George Houstoun, deceased.)

and the following Town Members (14) did not attend, tho' Summoned.

(Quarterly Meeting July 6th, 1795, at the Filature; 19 members present.)

The President, laid before the Society the Receipt of James Port for Forty one Dollars and one half of a Dollar for schooling Children on the Bounty of this Society, and for Paper up to the 15th of June last, agreable to the Certificate of the School Committee

RESOLVED UNANIMOUSLY, that from hence forth, for Not attending the Society Meeting, the Fines shall be for

the President.................... One Dollar
the Vice President ....Seventy five Cents
the Secretary.............. .....Sixty two and one half Cents
the Stewards ....fifty Cents
the other Members for not attending
   a Monthly Meeting ....Twelve and one half Cents
   a Quarterly Meeting ....Twenty five Cents
and for not attending the Funeral of a deceased Member, when Summoned..... } Fifty Cents.

* * * * * * * * * * *

Mr. William Gibbons junior, made excuse, that he was Sick during the last Anniversary so that he could not attend the same, wherefore RESOLVED that the Fine be remitted him.

Mr. Peter Samuel Laffitte, stated to the Society, that from some documents he had discovered, through the medium of Mr. Stephen Britton, that the late James Papot, had borrowed a Sum of Money from the Union Society and that Papot had given said Britton as Security for the payment of Twenty Pounds Some time in May Seventeen hundred and Seventy four and that Papot had secured Britton by a Counter-bond.

It appeared also by a Letter of David Zubly junr. who had formerly presided in the Society, to Britton that on the 24th of April 1775. James Papot had paid the Interest and Ten Pounds of the Principal of the said Bond to the Society. To lift James Papots' bond to Britton, Mr. Laffitte who married the Heir of Papots, proposed to the Society, to give his Bond, for the Balance being £10, and including the Interest, for the Sum of Twenty Pounds Dollars at four shillings and eight pence in full discharge of James Papots's bond to the Society with a proviso, that if it should appear, the Sum had been originally paid, the Bond should be cancelled, or if the Money paid, refunded.

As the Period to which this transaction alludes, involves in it, the Loss sustained by the Society, in the destruction of their Bonds and documents, during the War, whereby no Vouchers appear, the Society receive the Information in good part; Whereupon the Society

RESOLVE, That they will accept the Bond of the said Peter Samuel Laffitte for the Sum of Eighty Six Dollars equal to twenty Pounds, payable on the 23d day of April next, with Interest from this date, with a defeazence, to refund in case of proof of former Payment by James Papot, or any other person for him to the Society. And that in Case the original bond of James Papot & Stephen Britton, Should ever hereafter be found, the said Stephen Britton, his Heirs, Executors and Administrators are fully discharged thereof

W STEPHENS
Pres't,,

(Monthly Meeting, August 3d, 1795, at the Filature; 11 members present.)

Mr. Peter Samuel Laffitte gave his Bond to the Society for Eighty Six Dollars, in Conformity to the resolution of the 6th of July last, which being read, and approoved, was deposited with the President.

W: STEPHENS
Pres't..

(Monthly Meeting, September 7th, 1795, at the Filature; 11 members present.)

No Business before the Society.

MORDECAI SHEFTALL V. P

SAVANNAH Thursday the 10th Septbr 1795.

John Rentz late a Member of this Society, being deceased, and to be interred at Captain Nicholas Millers plantation near Thunderbolt the Members of the Society were notified thereof, and requested if convenient, to attend the Funeral, but being out of Town, the Rules do not impose a Fine for Non-attendance. the following Members (6) attended the Funeral

MORDECAI SHEFTALL V. P

(Quarterly Meeting, October 5th, 1795, at the Filature; 12 members present.) *

*   *   *   *   *   *   *   *   *   *   *

The President reported, that on the 10th of August last he paid Mrs Lydia Myers Twelve Dollars and fifty Cents, and to James Port on the 23d of September last Thirty six Dollars for schooling and one dollar and thirty Seven Cents and one half of a Cent for books.

Mr. John Tebeau, made excuse, that he was Sick during the last Anniversary, wherefore he could not attend,

RESOLVED that the fine of one Dollar, be remitted him.

Mr. Tebeau paid into the hands of the President Three Dollars being the Amount of his Contribution, due the 23d. of April last.

RESOLVED !

That One hundred Dollars, be and are hereby appropriated, to promote the building of a Poor house and Hospital in this City; and that the President apply the same to the Purchase of Lottery Tickets, as Shall be most conducive, to aid so charitable an institution.

W: STEPHENS

(Monthly Meeting, November 2d, 1795; 8 members present.)

*   *   *   *   *   *   *   *   *   *   *

MORDECAI SHEFTALL V P

(Monthly Meeting, December 7th, 1795, at the Filature; 5 present, Justus H Scheuber Sec., Joseph Miller, John Berrien, Steward, Sheftall Sheftall, James Port.)

No other Members attending, no Business could be done.

JUSTUS H SCHEUBER Secry

(Quarterly Meeting, January 4th, 1796, at the Filature ; 12 members present.)

Capt'n John Howell a Member, elected last Anniversary, attended the Society paid his Admission Money with Twenty two and one half of a dollar also One dollar twelve and one half cent Interest on the same, to this day, whereupon he was admitted to take his Seat.

*   *   *   *   *   *   *   *   *   *   *

The President reported that on the 7th October last he paid Justus H. Scheuber a Commissioner of the Seamans Hospital & Poorhouse Lottery One hundred Dollars, for fifty Lottery Tickets & produced his Receipt.

He also reported that on the 18th December last he paid James Port Schoolmaster Thirty two Dollars Six½ Cents for schooling Children on the bounty of this Society.

It appearing that the adventure of the fifty Tickets in the Hospital and Poorhouse Lottery for which the hundred Dollars as aforesaid were appropriated, lost to the Society forty five dollars and drew prizes to the amount of Fifty five dollars.

ORDERED ! therefore that these fifty five Dollars be continued and are appropriated to purchase Tickets, to that amount in the Second Class.

The Members present, having by a Collection made up ⸺ Dollars more, this, with the former Sum, enabled the Society to take Twenty Tickets in the said Second Class.

RESOLVED !

That the Committee appointed at the Anniversary to superintend the Education of the Children at School on the Bounty of this Society, report, at the next Meeting what progress the Children have made in their education, and that the Copy of this Resolution be sent to them or either of them.

W STEPHENS Pre't.

(Monthly Meeting February 1st, 1796, at the Filature ; 10 members present.)

None of the Presidents attending, Mr. Clay was chosen Chairman.

ORDERED, That Mary Brown, Daughter of John Brown deceased be schooled with Mrs Myers on the Bounty of this Society

RESOLVED ! That Mr. Stephens, Mr. Sheftall & Mr. Bolton be a Committee, to inquire into the Estates of John Brown, James Milledge and Robert Montford deceased, whether there is any Assets left, from which the Society may obtain, their Demands on them, and that they do report at the next Meeting.

(Monthly Meeting, March 7th, 1796, at the Filature; present— William Stephens Esqr. Pres., Justus H. Scheuber Sec., John Howell, James Port.)

there not being a constitutional Number no Business could be done.

SAVANNAH Monday, the 14th of March 1796

Mr. Daniel Course a Member of this Society, having deceased, the President ordered the Members at present in Savannah to attend his Funeral, when the following (24) Members attended.

(Quarterly Meeting, April 4th, 1796, at the Filature ; 15 members present.)

The President reported that he had paid Peter S. Laffitte Twenty

Six Dollars, agreably to two orders of the 23d. April and 6th of July last . Also to James Port Thirty Nine Dollars and Sixty two and one half Cent for tuition of Children, as per receipt of 21st March last and to the Reverend Mr. McCaule Six Dollars and Seventy Cents for the tuition of Murray Washington.——And that he had received Three Dollars from Peter S. Laffitte, for his Contribution due the 23d of April last.

RESOLVED ! that the Stewards provide a Dinner at the next Anniversary sufficient for Forty Persons.

RESOLVED ! That the President and Vice President be authorized to invite the Clergy and any number of Strangers, who may be in the City not exceeding Nine, to dine with the Society on the day of its Anniversary

ORDERED ! That the usual Notice be published in the Georgia Gazette the Members to meet at 9 o'Clock in the forenoon precisely.

ORDERED ! That Joseph Roberts, John Armour and Peter S: Laffitte be appointed a Committee to superintend the Anniversary Dinner.

Doctor Edmund Dillon Sent in a Petition to become a Member of this Society.

ORDERED ? to lie over

W STEPHENS
P't.

Forty-Sixth Anniversary, April 23d, 1796, *at the Filature;* 35 *members present.*

Mr. John Krieger paid up One hundred and eighty five Dollars and fourteen one half Cents in full of his Bond with Interest, whereon the Bond was delivered up to him.

The President made excuse that he was out of the City and Sick when one hundred and fifty Cents Fines were remitted him.

Joseph Clay said he was Sick, at George Houstouns funeral fifty Cents fines where therefore remitted him

Thomas Rice Stating that he had been from the City during the whole year, all his fines were therefore remitted

Mr. McAllister saying he had been absent from the State for five months, therefore two Dollars & fifty Cents fines were remitted him & he paying up the Balance his Note was delivered up to him.

John Morel making excuse, that he was not liable to fines, considering himself a Country Member, wherefore one hundred Sixty & three quarter Cents were remitted him,

Mr. Vice President Sent in an excuse, also Mr. Norment, which were read & ordered to lie over till the next Quarterly Meeting.

David Montaigut, Sent in an excuse, Stating on account of Sickness he could not attend the Society, which was admitted and on account of his age & infirmity all former & future fines are to be remitted him.

John Berrien, sent in a Letter, that he had incurred Several fines as a Stewart by being absent, whereupon the Society resolved, that all fines incurred Since the first Monday in January last, be remitted him, amounting to two Dollars.

James Jones, having paid Sixteen Dollars in full of his Contribution and Interest & in part of Admission Money, gave his Note to the President for Eleven Dollars & thirty Cents being the Balance yet due.

*   *   *   *   *   *   *   *   *   *   *

The President reported, that he had taken twenty Tickets in the Second Class of the Savannah Hospital and Poorhouse Lottery, agreably to a Resolution of the Society of the 4th day of January last, which twenty tickets have only drawn thirty eight dollars

– RESOLVED

That these thirty eight Dollars, together with two Dollars more to be taken by the President out of the Funds, be again adventured, by purchasing ten Tickets in the 3d Class of the said Lottery

*   *   *   *   *   *   *   *   *   *

Noble W: Jones, Charles Oddingsells, Oliver Bowen and George Jones, were then appointed a Committee to examine the Presidents Account.

This Committee having examined the Presidents Account of Receipts and expenditures, find that the Sum of Five hundred and Sixty Six Dollars and fifty Cents were received by him from the twenty third of April 1795. to the 4th instant, that the sum of three hundred and Seventy three dollars and fifty three cents has been paid by him for which he has produced Satisfactory Vouchers and that the Sum of one hundred and Ninety two dollars and Ninety Seven Cents is the Balance in his hands as per Account rendered to the fourth instant.

RESOLVED, that the President be and he is hereby authorized to loan the Monies of the Society in his hands on Interest, taking good and Sufficient Security agreable to Rule, reserving three hundred Dollars for the contingent expences of the Society.

ORDERED! that the former School Committee, be continued the ensuing Year.

The Comittee appointed to superintend the education of the Children schooled by the Society

REPORT, that they have examined the said Children. and find that they have made as great progress, as they could possibly; and that much Credit is due to their teachers Mr. Port and Mrs Myers. at Mrs Myers there is a Girl, Mary Curtis, who has made such Progress in reading that a removal to Mr. Ports School for other necessary branches of education is strongly recommended.

They are also induced to recommend that the Salary of Mr. Port be raised to four Dollars and fifty cents for each Scholar per Quarter for his particular attention to them : which was agreed to.

RESOLVED ! That in future the Accounts of the President and Members of the Society shall be settled and paid up on the Quarterly Meeting previous to the Anniversary, and that the Society shall meet on the forenoon of that day at 10 o'Clock for that purpose, instead of the evening.

RESOLVED, that no Person, wishing to become a Member shall be ballotted for on the Anniversary unless Application is made at least one Meeting previous to the same

The Society then proceeded to the election of Officers for the ensuing Year, when

WILLIAM STEPHENS was re-elected President

GEORGE JONES elected Vice President

Justus H. Scheuber, stating that on Account of the Post Office he could not regularly attend the stated Meetings of the Society begd Leave to decline standing as a Candidate, when

PETER SAMUEL LAFFITTE, was elected Secretary, and

JOHN D. DICKINSON and FREDERIC HERB were elected Stewards.

The Society then proceeded to ballot for those whose Petitions lying before them, applying to become Members of this Society When the Petition of Edmund Dillon was read, ballotted for but not admitted.

The Petitions of

1 Isaac Benedix
2. John Gibbons
3. William Hunter
4. Ebenezer Jackson
5. Philip Milledge
6. Thomas M. Woodbridge
7. Robert Mitchell
8. William Belcher
9. Robert Watts

14. Nicholas Ancieaux
15. David Gugel
16. John Grommet
17. John McCall
18. John N. Brailsford
19. James Shaw
20. George J. Hull
21. Solomon Shad
22. John Glass

10. Rev'd Thos H: McCaule   23. John McKinnon
11. William Wallace   24. James McIntosh
12. John Moore   25. Thomas Netherclift and
13. Thomas Young   26: David Brydie Mitchell

were severally read and ballotted & duly admitted.

The Petition of Frederic Shick, to become a member, was also read ballotted for but not admitted.

Monies received at the Society from the following Members &c viz't.

	Doll	Cents
from William Gibbons, in full of Contribution	3.	
John Krieger in full of Bond and Interest	185.	14½
Mordecai Sheftall, in full of Contribution and Anniv, Expences	4.	
Sheftall Sheftall, in full of ditto, ditto & fines	4.	62½
Richard Wayne, in full of Contrib: fines and Interest	6.	34
James Port in full	3.	87½
John Y: Noel, in full	5.	50
James Jones in part	16.	
Hampton Lillibridge in full of Contrib: fines & Interest	6.	55
John Tebeau, in full	3.	
John Armour, in full	3.	87½
William Lewden, in full	3.	62½
Oliver Bowen, in full of Contrib: fines & Interest	8.	71½
Noble W: Jones, in full	4.	75
John Howell, in part	3.	
Peter Deveaux, in full	3.	
Charles Oddingsells, in full	3.	
John Herb in full	4.	
Frederic Horb in full	16.	27½
William H. Spencer, in full	4.	87½
Andrew McCrodie, in full	6.	50
James B. Young, in full	4.	62½
Thomas Rice in full	3.	
John G. Williamson in full	3.	8½
Joseph Clay in full	4.	62½
George Jones, in full	9.	96½
William Stephens, Interest, Contrib'n & fines	14.	91
George Woodruff, in full	5.	50
John Morel, in full	10.	25
Mathew McAllister, in full	18.	34
Nathaniel Pendleton, in full	6.	
Justus H Scheuber in full	3.	
David B: Mitchell, in part of Admission	15.	

Say Three hundred Ninety Seven Dollars and forty Cents....................Ds 397.   40

The following new admitted Members attended the Society and for want of time could not comply with the Rule in their Case made and provided, which Business was therefore postponed to the next Meeting, they were permitted to partake of the Celebration of the Anniversary, viz't.

1. George J. Hull   5. David Gugel   9. Ebenezer Jackson
2. Solomon Shad   6. Thomas Netherclift   10. Robert Mitchell
3. David B. Mitchell   7. Philip Milledge   11. William Hunter
4. John Grommet   8. Thos M. Woodbridge   12. John Gibbons

The following Members (30) were Defaulters at the Anniversary.

31 Andrew McCredie & 32, George Millen, attended the Society & paid up their Arrears, but they not dining with the Society, nor paying their Share of Expences, are therefore Severally, to be charged with one Dollar each, for the Expences incurred at the Anniversary, agreably to the Rules.

Mr. Oliver Elsworth, Chief Justice of the United States dined with the Society.

W STEPHENS P't.

SAVANNAH 30th. April 1796.

By order of the President the Stewards were required to Summon the members in Town to meet at his House, for the purpose of attending the funeral of Mr. Frederick Fahm deceased (late a member of this Society) when the following members (26) attended the funeral, the deceased was aged 67 years & 7 months.

W. STEPHENS, Pre't..

(Monthly Meeting, May 2d, 1796; 13 Members present.)
No business before the Society.

W STEPHENS
P't.

SAVANNAH 3d June 1796.

The Vice President in the absence of the President directed the Stewards to Summon the members to attend the funeral of David Montaigut Esq'r a member of this Society, this day at 9 o'clock and to meet at the House of the deceased, when the following members attended the remains of the deceased who was aged Eighty years.

(39 attended—names on Minutes.)

GEO: JONES Vice Presid.

(Monthly Meeting, June 6th, 1796; 15 members present.)
The President reported

*   *   *   *   *   *   *   *   *

That he had paid Mrs. Lidia Myers Twelve dollars & fifty Cents for Schooling Children 21 May.

That he had loaned to Justus H. Scheuber and Balthaser Shafer on Bond Two Hundred and Fifty Dollars, (13th May.)

That he had received from

John Gromet Twenty-two dollars & fifty Cents for his admission in full

Isaac Benedix Twenty two dollars & fifty Cents for his do. in full

Thomas Young Twenty two dollars & fifty Cents for his do in full

6

Thomas M. Woodbridge Twenty two dollars & fifty Cents for his admission money infull

David Gugel Fifteen dollars inpart of his Admission also David Gugels Note for Seven dollars & fifty Cents payable 23d, April next, for the Balance of his admission

Nicholas Anciaux, Twenty-two dollars & fifty Cents for his Admission money infull,

William Wallace Twenty-two dollars & fifty Cents for his admission money infull.

Robert Mitchell Twenty-two dollars and fifty Cents infull for his admission money, and from

George Woodruff Esq'r. recovered from the Estate of Samuel Stirk, Sixty-four dollars and Twenty Cents

ditto, recovered from the Estate of Joseph Wright Two Hundred and Seventy-five dollars and fifteen Cents,

Doctor Noble Wimberly Jones, informed the Society, that the Reverend Adam Boyd had instructed him to present to the Society, Six dollars and fifty Cents, together with certain Subscription papers, that had been circulated to promote the printing certain Religious, discourses for the Benefit of Youth, of which Doctor Boyd was the Author, that as there was still money due on such Subscription papers, Doctor Boyd wished the Society to collect, what may be due and apply the same in aid of the funds

WHEREUPON RESOLVED, That the Society accept the offering of Doctor Boyd, and for which they return him thanks, and that the same be communicated to him by the Secretary inclosing a Copy of the minutes. The papers are directed to be left with the Secretary for Collection, who is to report occasionally.

RESOLVED, That Mr. Vice President, Mr. Scheuber, and Doctor Jones, be a Committee to report the existing Rules and bye Laws of this Society—and where amendments may in their opinion be requisite that such Amendments, be suggested, that the whole may form a digest, and printed if such report, should meet the opinion of the Society at the next quarterly meeting.

ORDERED, That, the Secretary attend the Committee with the Rules and minutes for the above purpose

Mr. Vice President laid before the Society a Pamphlet written by Doctor Boyd called "A Christmas Gift" the circulation of which he wished the Society to promote, the Consideration thereof was postponed to next quarterly meeting.

W STEPHENS
pres't.

(Quarterly Meeting, July 4, 1796, at the Filature; 23 members present.)

* * * * * * * * * * *

On Motion of Mr. Sheftall Sheftall, that the Ordinance entitled "An Ordinance to regulate the Terms on which Children are to be Schooled on the funds of the Union Society" be published in one of the Gazettes in this City,

ORDERED, that, the Consideration thereof be postponed untill the next Meeting.

Mr. Laffitte one of the Executors to the Estate of Frederick Fahm deceased, informed the Society that Mr. Fahm was very ill at the last Anniversary, and moved that the fine incured for his non attendance on that day be remitted which was agreed to;

Mr. Belcher, produced a Certificate that his father William Belcher deceased was admitted a member of this Society on the 23d. day of April 1768.

WHEREUPON RESOLVED, that he be admitted to take his Seat agreeable to the seventh Rule

Mr. Solomon Shad attended, paid Twenty-two dollars and fifty Cents, the amount of his Admission money Signed the Rules and took his seat.

* * * * * * * * *

A Petition was received from John Carroway Smith, praying to be admitted a member of this Society, which was read and ordered to lay over untill the next meeting.

GEO. JONES Vice Pres't

(Monthly Meeting, August 1st. 1796, at the Filature; 10 Members present.)

The President and Vice President being absent Doctor Noble Wimberly Jones was appointed Chairman.

One of the Stewards having informed the Society (that this being one of the stated meetings) he had applied to Mr. Simpson the City Marshall for the Key of the Room that the City Council had permitted the Society to meet in—and was Refused the same.

ON MOTION of Mr. William Gibbons

RESOLVED, That the City Council be informed of the said refusal made by their Officer.

ORDERED, that Mr. Sheftall's motion, at the last quarterly meeting, be postponed to the next meeting.

Mr. John C. Smith's petition was read a second time.

(Monthly Meeting. Sept. 5th. 1796, at the Filature; 11 members present.)

The President and Vice President both being absent, Mr. Oliver Bowen was appointed Chairman.

Mr. Sheftall Sheftall's motion, made on the 4th July last was taken up, and being debated passed in the Negative.

The Secretary reported, that, he had presented a Copy of the report of the Steward, and the subsequent resolution thereon (passed at the last monthly meeting) to the Mayor and Aldermen, but had received no answer thereto. And Mr. Alderman Young being present informed the Society, that, in consequence of the said resolution the City Council had repremanded their officer for his refusing the Key. and had directed that in future the Key of the Filature should at all times be delivered to the Society. whenever called for.

RESOLVED, that, the Secretary do call on the late Secretary and inquire if he has taken an Indenture from the Parents or Gardians of such Children as were Schooled on the Bounty of this Socie y on the first Monday in July 1795, and provided that the same has been neglected, that the present Secretary have the same done before the next quarterly meeting, and make report thereof.

ON MOTION of Doctor Young. that in future the fine for non attendance of the members at the monthly meetings of the Society be raised from 12½ Cents to 25 Cents. ORDERED, that, the Consideration thereof lay over untill the next quarterly meeting

Mr. John C. Smith's petition was again read.

SAVANNAH 14th September 1796

The Vice President in the absence of the President directed the stewards to summon the members to attend the funeral of the Rev'd. Thomas Harris McCaule a member of this Society this afternoon at 3 o'Clock and to meet at the Filature, when the following (25) attended.

The Vice President being indisposed and not attending. Doctor Noble W. Jones was appointed Chairman.

(Quarterly Meeting, October 3d, 1796, held at the House of Mr. Steward, John D. Dickinson the key of the long room of the Filature being withheld from them ; 11 members present)

The President having given sufficient Reasons, for his not attending at the Meetings of the 7 of August and 5th & 14th of September.

RESOLVED, That he be excused from any fine for non attendance.

Mr. Armour being absent from the State for three meetings past.

RESOLVED. That he be also excused.

(Mr. Peter Deveaux and Mr. Oliver Brown also made excuses for defaults, which were accepted)

The President Reported, That since he last met the Society he had paid the following sum of Money viz : on the 26th June 1796, James

Port for educating Children Forty three dollars and Twenty five Cents. Lydia Myers for ditto the 3d. August last Eight dollars

That he had loaned to, George Woodruff, Joseph Stiles, and Joseph Clay Junior, Two Hundred and fifty dollars, to Joseph Clay Junior, George Woodruff, and Joseph Stiles, Two Hundred and fifty dollars, to John Young Noel, William Wallace, and Richard Dennis, Two Hundred and fifty dollars, and to John H. Roberts, Ebenezer Hills, and Samuel Sargant One Hundred and fifty dollars.

That, he had received from James Shaw Twenty-two dollars and fifty Cents, from Solomon Shad Twenty-two dollars and fifty Cents from Robert Watts Twenty-two dollars and fifty Cents from William Belcher Eleven dollars and Twenty five Cents and from John Glass Twenty-two dollars and fifty Cents, being the amount of their Admission money

That, he had recovered from Levi Sheftall Two Hundred and fifty dollars and from Peter Henry Morel Eighty-seven dollars and Thirty-nine Cents.

A Sufficient Number of Members not attending to ballot for Mr. John Carroway Smith, his petition was postponed, as also the Motion of Doctor Young, respecting the Augmentation of the fines.

The Society frequently being embarrassed to gain admittance into the long room of the Filature.

RESOLVED, That, the Stewards have a seperate Key made that will open the lock of the room, of which the Secretary will inform, the Mayor and Aldermen. and to request them, to take order thereon.

W STEPHENS
P't..

(Monthly Meeting. November 7th, 1796, at the Filature; 7 members present.)

No business before the Society. adjourned.

(There are no regular Minutes in the possession of the Society from the last date above to May 4th 1815, and none of any kind save rough memorandums in a somewhat mutilated book. from August 1st 1796, to October 1st, 1798, and from which, it is thought, the Secretary had been in the habit of writing out the Minutes fully into another book, and which has been lost. What follows, to October. 1798, is from the book here alluded to.)

(Quarterly Meeting, 2d January. 1797, at the House of Mr. John Hamilton; 11 members present.)

(Monthly Meeting, February 6th. 1797, at the House of Mr. John Hamilton; 14 present.)

The President reported, that he had paid Mrs. Lydia Myers Six dollars this day for one quarters schooling of Lotty Hall and John Gilbert—due the 23d ultimo—and that he had paid James Port, Forty dollars &   on the   ultimo for Schooling. Children to

(Monthly Meeting, March 6th, 1797, at Mr. John Hamilton ; 14 present.)

(Quarterly Meeting,   at the new Theatre in Warren Ward at 10 o'Clock in the forenoon ; 30 present.)

1 The Report of the Committee respecting the Presidents Acco't.

Mr. George Jones made excuse that he was sick & absent from the State at the meetings of, October, February, Aug't, Sept'r & Nov'r, and at the funeral of Mr Fahm, & Mr. McCaule. Resolved that he be excused from any fine for non attendance 475—

Mr. Rice made Excuse that he was absent from the City the greatest part of the last year—

Ordered, that 2 dollars of his fine be remitted—

Mr. Hunter made excuse that he was absent from the State from 1st July to 26t nov'r fines remitted 100C

Mr. Williamson remitted 212½

Mr. Millidges note—30:54½

Joseph Roberts remitted 75—

Peter Deveaux—   37½

3 petitions—read—

W. Stephens—fines remitted 450

E. Jackson remitted 50—note 29,30

P. S. Laffitte—remitted 125

Anniversary Motion—2—

Mr. Hamilton's bill—600 Cents

Mathew McAllister.. 5. 62½
Noble W. Jones... 4. 12½
James Port......(accounted for)....................................... 3. 12½
John McCall............do.. 25. 00
John Moore. .....do.. 11. 25
Philip Milledge interest &.. 29. 17½
William Belcher 4. 25
Justus H. Scheuber Inst. 1777 &c...................................... 22. 15
John Gromet... 1. 62½
Oliver Bowen.. 8. 00
John Eppinger... 17. 41
James Shaw.. 5. 25
George Jones.. 4. 50
William Gibbons Sen'r... 3. —

Thomas Rice	3.	87½
Frederick Herb	4.	00
John Habersham	10.	12½
Isaac Benedix	5.	37½
Thomas Young	5.	12½

At a Regular Meeting of the Union Society held at the Filature on monday the 24th April 1797. being the 47th Anniversary of the Society—

Present—(36.)

(A statement of excuses of the Hon'ble Mr. Clay, Mr. Woodbridge, Mr. Anciaux, Mr. J. D. Dickenson, Mr. Sheftall Sheftall and Mr John Moore is here given and which are omitted.)

Resolution No. 1. new Rule

Mr. Thos. Cumming's fines of 7 dollars remitted, for non attendance on the diff'l Anniversarys under the Spirit of the New Rule of this day.

The president Informed the Society. that since the 3d. Instant he had Loaned Wm Moore, John Glass & J· G, White 200 dollars—and also

p'd   J. Port. 42:25   for Educating children 3d. April for the use of his room.

and had now in hand 122—72½—Mr. Vice pres't. and Mr. Wm Gibbons Sen'r examined the Vouchers & reported accordingly.

Rule No. 2. Loan of Money

An Account of monies Received at the Society this day.

John Moore, on acco't	12:	25
William H. Spencer in full	4:	00
Robert Watts—in full	5:	62½
Nicholas Anciaux in full	4:	62½
Thomas Woodbridge in full	4:	00
Joseph Clay Senr	4:	50
Mr. Noel	20:	00
Mr. S. Sheftall Con: & Ann: Exp:	5:	
Mr. John Moore in full	4:	12½
James Jones in full	15:	90½
James B. Young in full	4:	37½
John Tebeau	3:	00
John Morel	4:	15
Robert Bolton Con: fines & An: Exp:	13:	37½
Thomas Cummings in full	12:	00
John Berrien in full	7:	50
J. McKinnon	6:	00
J. Gibbons	30.	00
W. Lewden	1.	00
Joseph Miller	15:	87½
	171:	97½

Moved, That the Rule Restricting Country members, from being off'rs
of this Society be rescinded, to be brought forward next quarterly
meeting: 171. 97¾
                                                               4. 62½
                                                          ─────────
                                                          176. 60¼

Corporation acco: passed.   2: 14
                                                          ─────────
Acco: Sec'y   do.   40—
                                      15. 87½
                                     ─────────
                                      55. 87
                                      20—
                                     ─────────
Ordered to be paid   75. 87½

The Petition of Mr. J. C. Smith, was again read and ballotted for
& admitted—

William H. Lange ditto—admitted

Thomas Pitt—ditto—admitted

John Roberts—do. admitted—

G. J. H.ull's fines remitted since 10th June—

The Society proceeded to the choice of Officers—elected—

GEO: JONES—Esqr. President.

J. B. YOUNG—Vice President

P. S. LAEFITTE Sec'r.

ROBERT MITCHELL ⎱ Stewards.
ROB'T WATTS— ⎰

(Monthly Meeting, May 1st, 1796, at the Filature.)

Present George Jones President

James B—Young Vice President

John Glass Sctr— P— T—

the Filature Being Occupied By the Artilery Company it was tho
opinion of the President and Vice President that there would be no
Meeting of the Society for that Evening therefor adjourned at eight
O'clock.

At a Monthly Meeting of the Union Society held at the Filature
on Monday the 5th. June 1797

Present. J. B. Young Vice P.

P. S. Laffitte Secy.

R. Mitchell ⎱ Stewards
R. Watts ⎰

5 W: H. Spencer   6 Sheftall Sheftall

7 John Glass   8 John Armour—

No business before the Society

Adjourned

(Quarterly Meeting. July 3d, 1797, at the City Hall; 14 members present.)

SAVANNAH 7th July 1797.

The President & Vice President; directed the Stewards to Summon the members to attend the funeral of Mordecai Sheftall Esq'r the oldest member of this Society, this day at 3 o'clock and to meet at the House of Justus H. Scheuber Esq'r it being near the Habitation of the deceased. who has been a member of this Society upwards of 40 Years, and died in the 62nd years of his age, in consequence of the rain none of the members attended but the following (30.)

(Monthly Meeting, August 7th. 1797, at the Filature.)

Present

Peter S. Laffitte Sec'y.

W. H. Lange

The Weather being very bad, and there being no prospect of more members attending. Adjourned

(Monthly Meeting, September 4th. 1797, at the Filature; 17 members present.)

The President, (agreeable to an order of the 3d July last) reprimanded the Stewards for Neglect of duty on that evening—

SAVANNAH 26th September 1797

The President Directed the Stewards to Summon the members of the Society to meet at the Filature this afternoon at four oclock, for the purpose of attending the funeral of John Moore Esq'r late a member of this Society, when the following members attended. viz: (31.)

(Quarterly Meeting, October 2d. 1797, at the Filature; 17 members present.)

On motion: RESOLVED, That the Secretary do remind the Gentlemen appointed a Committee to collect from the minutes of the Society all amendments & alterations of the rules; & of the Necessity of making their report and that they be requested to prepare the same by the next quarterly meeting—The Secretary at the same time is ordered to furnish them with the original Rules, Minutes and other papers they may think necessary—

(Monthly Meeting. November 6th. 1797, at the City Hall.)

Present John Glass. Sec'y. P: T.

(Monthly Meeting, December 4th, 1797, at the Filature; present, Peter S. Laffitte Sec'y—J. B. Young V P. Jas. Shaw, John Eppinger.)

(Quarterly Meeting, January 1st, 1798, at the Filature; present.

7

J. B. Young Vice President, P. S. Laffitte Sec'y, John Howell. Wm. Lewden, John Eppinger, W. Hunter, James Shaw.)

(Monthly Meeting February 5th, 1798, at the Filature ; 11 members present.)

The Vice President, informed the Society that from his indisposition he could not attend to the duties of his office this evening, whereupon Mr. O: Bowen was appointed chairman—

(Monthly Meeting, March 5th, 1798, at the Filature; present— Peter S. Laffitte Sec'y, Thomas Rice, Robert Mitchell, Thomas Rice.)

(Quarterly Meeting, April 2d, 1798, at the Filature ; present—O Jones Pres't, Peter S. Laffitte Sec'y, John Gromet, William Norment, Frederick Herb, N. W. Jones, Joseph Clay.)

Mr. Stephens, made Excuse—being absent 75 Cents remitted—

Mr. John Herb, informed the Society that he was not summoned to attend the funerals of Mr. Moore & Mr. Roberts excused, one dollar rem :

Mr. McAllister made absence an excuse at 4 meeting July. Aug't Sept'r. & Oct'r. 75 cents remitted—

The President made excuse he was absent Jan'y. & February and sick in October & November, and had attended at Mr. Sheftalls funeral, but too late 5 dollars remitted—

Mr. J. Gibbons—Same at Mr. Sheftalls funeral 50—re—

Mr. Clay same Excuse at Mr. Sheftalls- funeral—remitted—Same at Mr. Roberts's- 1 dollar remitted—

The President paid

James Port. (4th July. $40.) 29th. Sept'r. $35:25c)

Dec'r. 21st. $35)—   40

Lydia Myers—(21st May. $6,) (Nov'r. 9th. $12: 00)   35. 25

P. S. Laffitte—67: 62½   35

                                                                                 ————

                                                                                 110. 25

                                                                                 18—

                                                                                 67. 62½

                                                                                 195: 87½

_____

(*Forty Eighth Anniversary April 23d, 1798, at the City Hall ; number and names of members present not stated.*)

Mr. Woodbridge made excuse that he was one of Mr. Moores pall bearers, ORDERED : that the fine be remitted...................... ⌠ 50

Also Mr. Sheftall & Mr. Roberts's.............................. ⎨ 100

                                                                            ⎩ ———

                                                                              150

Mr. Rice made excuse that he was sick, at Mr. Sheftalls & Mr. Moores funerals. Ord: his fines be remitted—100 Cents—

Mr. Ancieaux, made Excuse that that he attend at Mr. Sheftalls fu neral & at Mr. Roberts's he was not summoned 100 remitted

Messrs. James & Nicholas Johnston & N. Johnston & Co Account

Mr. Glass, made Excuse that he attended at Mr. Roberts's funeral but could not stay, and at the last quarterly meeting he was obliged to attend a meeting of the Corporation—75 remitted

Mr. Glass also made excuse that at the last anniversary he was, Sick, and moved to have his fine for non attendance at that time be remit- ted, and on the question being put it passed in the negative—

Officers Elected.

GEORGE JONES President
J. B. YOUNG Vice President
P. S. LAFFITTE, Secretary
DAVID GUGEL } Stewards
ISAAC BENEDIX }
MR. WOODBRIDGE }
MR. MILLEDGE   } School Committee
MR. MCALLISTER }

Mr. Wayne made Excuse that he attended but could not Stay. 50 cents remitted.

Dr. Young made excuse that he was in Bryan County at the time Mr. Moore was buried—50 Cents remitted.

(Mr. Hunter, Mr. Jackson, Mr. Williamson and Mr. Mitchell also made excuses, and had different amounts remitted.)

At a Monthly Meeting of the Union Society held at the City Hall on Monday evening the 7th May 1798.

Present.

Mr. J. Benedix *Steward*.   Mr. John Gibbons
Peter S. Laffitte. Sec'y.   John Eppinger
David Gugel *Steward*   James Shaw
John Armour—

There being no business before the Society
            adjourned

At a Monthly meeting of the Union Society held at the City Hall on Monday the 4th June 1798.

Present
P. S. Laffitte Sec'y.
David Gugel, Steward
William Gibbons, James Shaw

(Quarterly Meeting July 2d, 1798, at the City Hall; 22 members present.)

(Mr. Benedix made excuse and had fine remitted.)

Dr. Young the Vice President of this Society, and a member of the Corporation of the City of Savannah, and Mr. Glass a member also of each Body, stated to the Society, that they were directed by the Corporation, to give notice that it would be moved in that Body to-morrow to declare void their Grant to this Society of the Lotts in Holland Tything Percival ward

Whereupon—ORDERED, That Mr. Clay, Mr. Gibbons and Mr. Stephens, be a Committee to attend the Corporation, hear the grounds of Complaint, and State the impropriety of such an interference.

RESOLVED, that the President be authorized to pay the arrears of ground rent of the Lotts in Holland tything Percival Ward, to the Corporation of the City of Savannah, due in terms of the Grant of the said Corporation and that he do continue to pay the said ground rent as the same shall become due.

A petition was received and read from Thomas Savage Esq'r praying to be admitted a member of this Society.

ORDERED that the same do lay over untill the next meeting

Adjourned—

(Monthly Meeting, August 6th, 1798, at the City Hall. Present. George Jones Esq'r President, James B. Young Esq'r V. president, Peter S Laffitte Sec'y, David Gugel Steward, James Shaw, W. Norment, John Eppinger, Dr. Noble W. Jones.)

A letter was received from Mr. Anciaux notifying his resignation as a member of this Society dated 24th April 1798

The Vice Presented an Extract from the minutes of the City Council &c—

(Monthly Meeting. Sept. 3d, 1798, at the Filature ; 11 members present.)

Mr. Lewden was appointed Chairman

(Quarterly Meeting, October 1st, 1798, at the Filature : present, George Jones Esq'r President, Peter S. Laffitte Sec'y, David Gugel Steward, John Eppinger, James Shaw, William H. Spencer, John Armour, Robert Mitchell.)

Mr. Mitchell Reported his Acco: &C as Steward—

(In a 4 qr. demy book of old style, rough, cream laid, unruled, English paper, in half sheep binding, labeled on the side "Rules Union Society Savannah." are transcribed the following Rules, signed as below—the signatures about an inch and a half apart—the whole occupying 10 leaves of the book, the balance of which is entirely blank.)

GEORGIA.

RULES

OF THE

UNION SOCIETY

OF THE

CITY OF SAVANNAH

ADOPTED 23d MAY 1808

RULES OF THE UNION SOCIETY OF THE CITY OF SAVANNAH, established in the year 1750, and incorporated in the year 1786; which said Rules have been collected, arranged, digested, revised, and amended, from the Ancient Rules of the Society, by a Committee appointed for that Purpose, and now finally adopted and established by the said Society, at a Special Meeting of the same, this 23d May 1808.

RULE the first.

This Society shall be known by the name of the UNION SOCIETY.

RULE the second

That any person, not under the age of twenty-one years,—desirous of becoming a Member of this Society, shall signify his intention thereof by petition, addressed to the President and Members; which petition shall be read on the first regular Meeting, and again on the next regular Meeting, and then ballotted for, and if a majority of the votes shall be found in favor of the person so ballotted for, he shall be declared duly elected; provided, nevertheless, that no person shall be ballotted for as a Member of this Society unless twenty-one Members are present.

RULE the third.

The Meetings of this Society shall be quarterly, on the evenings of the first* Mondays in July, October, January; and in the morning of the first Monday in April, at which times each Member residing within the limits of the City shall attend, by summons or otherwise, the duties of the Society, and in default thereof, and on failure to make a sufficient excuse, to be approved by the Society, shall pay the following sums, viz. the President, three dollars; the Vice President, two dollars and twenty-five cents, the Secretary, one dollar and eighty-seven and an half cents; the Stewards, each, one dollar and fifty cents; and each private Member, fifty cents; and on failure to attend on the

*Altered to the Second Mondays &C. Res. of Jan. 6, 1814.

first Monday in April, for the payment of arrears, and for the transac-
of the business of the Society, until the adjournment of the same,
all and every Member, residing within the limits of the City, or within twenty-five miles thereof, so absent or absenting himself without
leave, shall be fined one dollar, unless excused by the Society.

RULE the fourth.

When the Society is on business no person, except the Members
thereof, shall be admitted in the room.

RULE the fifth.

The accounts of the Members of the Society shall be settled and
paid up on the anniversary, or on the quarterly meeting previous
thereto

RULE the sixth.

The Accounts of the President shall be settled on the anniversary.

RULE the seventh.

The anniversary of the Society shall be held and celebrated on the
23d day of April annually, except when that day happens on Sunday,
then the anniversary shall be celebrated on the Monday following, the
expence of which shall not exceed three dollars to each Member present ; but no part of such expence shall be taken out of the funds of
the Society, but shall be borne by the Members thereof residing within the City of Savannah, or within twenty-five miles ; and such Members who shall be absent on that day shall pay a fine of one dollar and
fifty cents, unless excused by the Society; and if the Members present are not sufficient to defray the expences of the dinner, the deficiency shall be made up from the above fine of one dollar and fifty
cents from the defaulting Members; and every Member who shall
invite at his house any gentleman on that day, so as to interfere with
the invitations of the Society, shall be fined ten dollars

RULE the eighth.

On every anniversary of the Society the President shall request
some one of the Ministers of the Gospel of the City of Savannah to
deliver an appropriate sermon† to the Society, and the Members
thereof are solicited to attend the same.

RULE the ninth

Every person admitted a Member of the Society shall pay, on his
admission, twenty-two dollars and fifty cents to the Society, and seventy-five cents to the Secretary, for reading his petition and granting

† Or some member of the Soc'y to deliver an appropriate Oration. See resolution 1514.

a Certificate, except the son of a person who has been seven years a Member of the Society; and such applicant shall be entitled to admission on payment to the Society of one half of the usual admission money, and full fees to the Secretary; but this privilege is confined to the son of of such Member who shall first apply for admission: That no person elected shall be considered a Member unless he has paid the above sum of money, and subscribed the rules; but should any Member elect prefer to pay one half at the time, and give his note for the balance, payable one year from the date of his admission, he shall then be considered a Member on subscribing the rules.

RULE the tenth

That all persons elected, who have not paid the amount of their admission, or given their notes for the same, be notified, that unless they do comply with the ninth rule before the anniversary their names will be erased from the books of the Society; and every person petitioning to be admitted a member of this Society, whose petition shall be signed by a Member, as the friend of the petitioner, such Member signing the same shall, on the admission of such new Member, be chargable with the admittance money, unless the same be paid by the admitted Member.

RULE the eleventh.

The Members of the Society shall contribute and pay annually the sum of four dollars, as a Contribution towards the funds of the Society.

RULE the twelfth.

Any Member neglecting to pay his arrears due the Society, on the anniversary thereof, or the quarterly meeting previous thereto, if in the State, shall, on notice given him by the Secretary of the Society, be required so to do by the next quarterly meeting, which if he neglects, then, the name of such Member shall be erased from the rules of the Society, and he be no longer considered a Member thereof, unless excused by the Society.

RULE the thirteenth.

There shall be elected, by majority of ballots, on the anniversary of the Society, a President, Vice President, Secretary, and two Stewards, out of the Members resident in the City of Savannah, who shall be Officers for the ensuing year. The President shall preside at all meetings, unless prevented by absence out of the State, sickness, or other good excuse, in which case the Vice President shall preside, and in case of his absence also, then the Members present shall appoint a Chairman for the meeting. Any person elected to the foregoing offices, and declining to accept the same, shall pay the following fines, to be appropriated towards the funds of the Society, viz : the President, five dollars ; Vice President, four dollars ; Secretary, three dollars ; Stewards, three dollars each ; the Society shall then proceed to ballot for other Officers in the room of such as decline accepting.

RULE the fourteenth.

The Secretary shall be allowed a sum not less than one hundred and fifty dollars per annum, whose duty it will be to keep the minutes and accounts fair, and provide books and paper for the Society, and give notice to the Members of their meeting.

RULE the fifteenth.

The President shall keep good order, and cause it to be observed by the Members, and if any Member shall so far forget himself as to make use of any profane or indecent language, during the sitting of the Society, he shall for the first offence pay two dollars, the second offence four dollars, and for the third, and continuing obstinate, shall be ordered to withdraw from the Society for that meeting, and shall not be considered as a Member until he shall pay such fines, and make such concessions as the President, and a majority of the Members present, shall think fit, at the next meeting of the Society, and the attendance of such unruly Member thereon.

RULE the sixteenth.

The Stewards shall provide necessaries for the Society, attend all regular meetings, and provide for the anniversary, summon the Members of the Society to attend the funeral of any Member that dies, and also observe the orders given by the President for the time being, taking special care that the expence of each night does not exceed twelve and an half cents to each Member present, any extra expence must be at the charge of the Stewards.

RULE the seventeenth.

There shall be a Box provided for the Society, which shall be kept by the President and Vice President ; in which box shall be deposited the monies, bonds, notes, and specialities, with the archives, belonging to the Society.

RULE the eighteenth.

Any person having been a Member of the Society for seven years and upwards, and having paid his arrears, who shall through misfortune be reduced, and stand in need of assistance from the Society, shall be allowed out of the stock and funds of the same, a sum not exceeding four dollars per week, and shall be provided with a Doctor in case of sickness at the expence of the Society; and in case such old Member shall die in distress, the Society shall bear the charge of such funeral, so that it does not exceed thirty dollars.

RULE the nineteenth.

The widow of such deceased Member as may require the assistance of the Society shall be allowed fifty dollars, and his children educated at the expence of the Society, as soon as the funds thereof will admit; and all children who are educated on the bounty of the Society, shall be bound to the same by an indenture.

RULE the twentieth.

Every Member of the Society shall attend the funeral of a deceased Member, on being summoned, or forfeit one dollar unless a reasonable excuse is made.

RULE the twentyfirst.

The Society having heretofore put their money at interest, shall continue so to do, always reserving a sufficient sum in order to answer the immediate demands of the Society. All monies lent on interest shall be in sums not exceeding three hundred dollars to any one person, and the bonds securing the payment of such money shall be made payable to the "President and Vice President of the Union Society in Savannah" and their assigns, and that such loan be made by the President, and he is hereby required to take, as a security for monies loaned, bond and personal security, (but the principal and his security must not be both Members of the Society) with a Mortgage on personal property, or a bond without personal security, with a Mortgage on real estate, the same to be for double the amount of the money so loaned, and the property to be within the County of Chatham taking care that a certificate from the proper officers be produced shewing that there are no prior encumbrances on the property Mortgaged; such bond and Mortgage to be drawn and recorded in the Clerks office, at the expence of the person borrowing the money; and that the interest on all monies loaned (in case the principal is not required) shall be paid annually on the anniversary of the Society, or a note, with personal security, payable in thirty days, with interest from the date, given therefor; and, on failure so to do, the President is hereby required to put the bond and Mortgage of the person so failing in immediate suit.

RULE the twentysecond.

That, in case of the death or resignation of the President, or Vice

S

President, the Society, at their next regular meeting thereafter, shall fill up such vacany agreeably to the Rule for the election of Officers.

RULE the twentythird.

No monies of the Society shall be voted away but at their regular or extra meetings called for that purpose, when at least thirty-one Members shall be present.

RULE the twentyfourth.

The President, Vice President, and, in case of their absence any five Members, may call an extra meeting, and the Members shall be bound to attend the same, or be subject to a fine of fifty cents.

RULE the twentyfifth.

The Society shall have a common Seal emblematical of their Institution.

RULE the twentysixth,

The Society shall continue so long as three Members are living, and will meet together, and in case no more than three Members be living they shall have power to dispose of the stock of the Society to public charitable uses, and not otherwise.

Done in Society, this twenty third day of May, in the year of our Lord one thousand eight hundred and eight, and in the thirty-second year of the Independence of the United States of America.

1	Levi Sheftall	1772	139	Thomas Telfair	1809
2	Jos Habersham	1790	140	I. Minis	"
3			141	Joseph P. McKinne	"
4	Peter Deveaux	"	142	Joseph Maxwell	"
5	W: Stephens	"	143	Rich'd W Habersham	"
6			144	F.. T., Flyming	"
7			145	Oliver Sturges	1810
8	Wm H'y Spencer	"	146	Philip D: Woolhopter	"
9	Wm Lewden	"	147	Thomas W Rodman	"
10			148	Wm Gaston	"
11	Geo. Millen	1791	149	Henry Hall	"
12	Francis Courvoisie	"	150	J. P. Henry	"
13			151	John Ralston	"
14			152	Benj'n Jacobs	"
15			153	Lewis Cooper	"
16	John Eppinger	1810	154	Steele White	"
17	John G. Williamson	1791	155	A Cuthbert	"
18			156	Tho's Young (in pencil)	"
19	James Port	1790	157	Wm Mein (in pencil)	"
20			158	Jno Eppinger J'r	"

21			159	Norman McLeod	"
22	R Wayne	1793	160	D. M. McConky	"
23			161	Joseph J. Davis	"
24	John Y Noel	"	162	Henry W. Williams	"
25	Geo. Jones	1794	163	James Boyle (in pencil)	"
26	Joseph Miller	"	164	Edmund Roberts	"
27	Thomas Rice	"	165	E Nichols (in pencil)	"
28	Matt. McAllister	"	166	Geo: Glen	"
29	G Woodruff	"	167	Walter Roe	"
30	Sheftall Sheftall	"	168	Charles E. Futot	"
31	Slt'r Cowling.	1795	169	Jno: J: Evans	1811
32			170	George Myers J'r	"
33	Frederick Herb	1790	171	John C. Gugel	"
34			172	Sam'l Griggs	"
35			173	T. V. Gray	1812
36	John Gibbons	1796	174	Cha's Howard	1811
37	P Milledge	"	175	F. S. Fell.	"
38			176	David Polock	1812
39	Rob't Mitchell	"	177	Jos W Pinder	"
40			178	James E Morris	"
41			179	John Gindrat	"
42	Tho Young—U: Sto'y	"	180	J Dufoure	"
43			181	Geo: Low	"
44	John N. Brailsford	"	182	Abm Nichols	"
45			183	Murdoch McLeod	"
46	John McKinnon	"	184	Jno Kerr	1811
47			185	Robert Small	"
48	D: B: Mitchell	"	186	S. G. Bunch	1812
49			187	Jno Hunter	1813
50	Tho: Savage	1802	188	John Wallace	"
51	Ed. White		189	John Bolton	"
52	Rich. Wall	"	190	Jas Hunter	"
53	Peter Miller	"	191	Wm C Yonge	"
54	Ben: Wall	"	192	J. E. Hartridge	"
55	Charles Harris	"	193	Fred'k Densler	"
56	J Cuyler	"	194	Raymond P. Demeré	1814
57			195	Jos. Habersham	"
58	Edward Stebbins	1803	196	J Fahm	"
59	J: Lawson	1802	197	Jas Eppinger	1816
60	Joseph Bryan	"	198	James Morrison	"
61	W. B. Bulloch	"	199	Tho's N. Morel	"
62	Jno. H Morel	1803	200	Jno., Morel	1818
63	John P. Williamson	"	201	Jno: J. Bulloch	"
64			202	S. C. Schenk	"
65	J. P. Oates	"	203	John Carr	"
66	Thomas Dechenaux	"	204	Lowell Mason.	"
67	J W Shaffer	"	205	Henry Kollock	"
68	Moses Sheftall	"	206	Wm. Smith	"
69	Willi'm Davies	1805	207	James M. Wayne	1818
70	F. D. Petit de Villers.	"	208	Josiah Penfield	"
71	Morris Miller	"	209	Norman Wallace	1818

72	G W Davidson	..
73	Jas Powell	..
74	Frederick Shaffer	1806
75		
76	Adam Cope	..
77	Charles Cope	..
78	James Johnston Jun'r	..
79	A M Allen (in pencil)	..
80	James Alger	..
81	Joseph Grant	..
82	George Enoe	..
83	Wm J Spencer	..
84	Edward Harden	1803
85	James McGee	1806
86	William A. Moore	..
87	Jn: Macpherson Berrien	..
88	Jos'h Ad's Scott.	..
89	Peter Ward (in pencil)	..
90	James Bond Read	..
91	Fred'k Ball	..
91	Rich'd M. Stites.	..
93	Tho. Schley	..
94	Tho:s U: P: Charlton	..
95	francis Roma	..
96	Robert Habersham	..
97	Tho's Bourke	..
98	N,, Greene Rutherford	1807
99	E Mounger (in pencil)	..
100	C,, Gugel	..
101	John Waters	..
102	John Dillon	..
103	Alex'r S. Roe	..
104	Joseph Hill Clark	..
105	Wm Woodbridge	..
106	Alex'r. Habersham	..
107	Griffin L, Lamkin	..
108	Robert J Houstoun	1808
109	John Brickell	1806
110	Richard Leake	1790
111	Will: F: Port	1805
112	Moses Cleland	1808
113	Geo. Harral.	..
114	P. Hebera	1806
115	James Bilbo	..
116	Gardner Tufts	1808
117	Samuel Williams	..
118	John Miller.	..
119	Benj'n Ansley	..
120	Joseph Stutz	..
121	And'w Low	..
122	Robert Isaac	..

210	Asahel Howe	..
211	Silas Hollis	..
212	James S. Bulloch	..
213	Th: Edward Lloyd	..
214	Eben: S: Rees	..
215	M Herbert	..
216	John Tanner	..
217	Jno Speakman	..
218	Jno J Roberts.	..
219	L M Furth	..
220	Isaac Cohen	..
221	Wm H: Joyner	..
222	Jno Bogue	1819
223	Arch'd Smith	1818
224	P. Guerard	1819
225	John Lewis	..
226	James Cutter	..
227	Jno C Nicoll	..
228	Tho's Clark	..
229	Geo. G. Faries	..
230	Jacob Miller	..
231	Jacob Shaffer	..
232	Michael Brown	..
233	Jno: F: Lloyd.	1821
234	J. George	1819
235	Step'n S Williams	1818
236	W: C. Daniell	1819
237	Ben Sheftall	..
238	F. M. Stone	..
239	Alex'dr Telfair	..
240	Hugh Rose	1822
241	Jno M Jarvis	1823
242	John Davidson	1822
243	Jos. Auze	..
244	Jno Shick	..
245	Geo., W.. Anderson.	..
246	Isaac D'Lyon	..
247	Wm Belcher	1823
248	J. T. Rowland	1822
249	Wm Cooper (in pencil)	..
	J P Henry (in pencil)	1810
250	Geo. M Waldburg	1825
251	H. O. Wyer	1828
252	Francis Sorrel	1825
253	W. W. Wash	1828
254	John B. Gaudry	1832
	Jno,, W,, Anderson	1828
	Geo White	..
	Henry McAlpin	1832
	John Gardner	..
	Jno, C, Starr	1830

123	Tho: Mendenhall	"	Henry Roser.	1832
124	William Parker	"	S L W Harris.	
125	A. S. Bulloch	"	Charles S Henry	1826
126	W. B. Barnes	1809	A. A. Suares (admitted a	
127	D D Williams.	"	member for life in) 1833	
128	Jno. f. Everitt	"	Anth: Barclay	1832
129	John Grimes	"	John Millen	1828
130	Jno Cumming	1806	David Bell	1833
131	Jno: W: Mendenhall	1809	Wm K Gaston	"
132	William Maxwell	"	Robert Birch	1831
133	George Herb	"	Fredk. A. Tupper	1833
134	Daniel Gugel	"	William Roche	1834
135	John Shick	"	John Williamson Jr	1835
136	Jno Habersham	"	Tho's Purse	1833
137	James Armstrong	"	Wm Herb	1837
138	Alex,, Hunter	"	John M Cooper	"

(The Minutes in possession of the Society next in order, date from May 4th, 1815; the book in which they are contained, like the two others from which the preceding minutes have been taken, is a quire book of *unruled*, very rough surface English laid paper, white, or perhaps cream colored originally, but very dingy from age; it is a Minute Book of the *Board of Managers*, and begins with the date and heading below, and contains the minutes of the Board to May 2d, 1820. This was the first Board of Managers formed, and the meeting of May 4th, 1815, their first meeting.

The minutes are also missing from May 2d, 1820, to April 1st, 1828.)

MINUTES

OF THE BOARD OE MANAGERS TO THE UNION SOCIETY.

THURSDAY 4th May 1815

Members of the Board.

MOSES SHEFTALL, P U. S.	E HARDEN. V. P. U. S.
JOHN BOLTON	JAMES HUNTER
JAMES M. WAYNE	GEORGE GLEN
GEORGE MYERS—	
	J: WALLACE Sect'y—

At a meeting of the Board of Managers to the Union Society formed in pursuance of a resolution of the general Society, on the 24th day of April last, the following Members attended—

Moses Sheftall,	Edward Harden,
John Bolton,	Jas, M Wayne
James Hunter.	

The Board proceeded to the adoption of such measures as they deemed immediately necessary to the promotion of the Interest of the Society over which they preside

Upon Motion of Mr. John Bolton,

RESOLVED, that the Secretary of this Board be required forthwith to make a list of all the claims of the Society and hand the same to the Board on the eighteenth of the present month.

RESOLVED, that as soon as the Board be furnished with the list of Claims, the same shall be handed to Mr Wayne as the Attorney of the Board, whose duty it shall be to proceed to the collection without delay, (calling first on the debtors,) and to institute suits against all who fail to pay by the next return day of the Inferior Court, and that he be allowed for his services the usual compensation, to wit. fees and Commission—

Upon MOTION of Mr. Harden

RESOLVED, that ——————————— be a Committee to enquire into the affairs of the Union Society and to make as soon as possible a general exposé of its situation to this Board & that the aforesaid Committee report at the next Meeting, Bye rules and regulations for the government of the Board—

Messrs Harden & Wayne were appointed that Committee

RESOLVED that the Secretary furnish himself with a Book for the purpose of transcribing the minutes of the proceedings of this Board—

The Board adjourned till Thursday 18th—

THURSDAY 18th May 1815

Meeting of the Board postponed by *order of the* PRESIDENT until Thursday : 1 June—

JUNE 1. 1815.

(Met, James Hunter, James M Wayne, & George Glen.)

There not being a sufficient number present to transact business, the meeting was adjourned indefinitely—

(Meeting June 20 ; present : Sheftall, Edward Harden, Wayne Hunter and Glen.)

A letter from Mr. John Bolton (Signifying his wish to withdraw from the Board) was read and agreed to—The President nominated Mr. Fredk Herb to fill the vacancy occasioned by Mr Boltons resignation—

The following Petition of Mary Lewden was read and acted upon—

THE UNION SOCIETY } Judgment in Ch. S. Court
       vs
EX'IX JOHN GLASS }

Amount of the Condition of the Bond............ ....250—
Int from 21st June 1800 to 2d May 1815....................297,, 21
Costs... 14., 50
Fi Fa 50

                                                    ─────────
                                                    562,, 21

The foregoing is a correct Statement of the Debt due to the Union Society from Est John Glass

                    Signed   W B BULLOCH

                                      SAVANNAH 20 June 1815.

To the Honorable the President, Vice President and Members of the Union Society.

                                      The Petition of

Mary Lewden, late Mary Glass humbly Sheweth.

That Your Petitioner is unable to pay the Whole Amount of the Judgment above mentioned at present, and therefore prays, that your honorable body will upon her paying the Amount of Interest now due and the Costs of suit, indulge her for one year from this date for the payment of the Principal, she securing the payment of the Principal in such manner as your honorable Body shall think proper—

And as in duty bound she will ever pray &c

Sav'n 20 June 1815

                    Signed, MARY LEWDEN.

The above Petition was granted, provided Mrs Lewden give bond and mortgage on real property to the Amount.

RESOLVED that an additional compensation of One Hundred Dollars be allowed the Secretary for the extraordinary duty imposed upon him by the Board of Managers, to be paid Quarterly.

                    WEDNESDAY EVENING 10th Jan'y 1816

At a meeting of the Board at the Exchange in pursuance of notice from the President

(Present; Sheftall, Harden, Herb Wayne and Glen.)

RESOLVED that Mr. George Glen do call upon the Secretary Mr. Wallace for all the Books & papers appertaining to the Union Society & that Mr. Glen act as Secretary to this Board.

                    MONDAY EVENING 29 April 1816

At a Meeting of the Board of Managers to the Union Society at the Exchange in pursuance of notice from the President.

Present   Moses Sheftall President
Edward Harden V. P.
Moses Cleland
John Hunter
Frederick Herb
James B Read*

The following Rules were adopted for the Government of this Board.

RULE 1st

That the Board of Managers shall meet the first Monday in every month, or oftener if required by the President.

RULE 2nd

That every member absent fifteen Minutes after the President has taken his seat (who shall take his seat at six o'Clock from the month of November untill the month of April & from thence untill October at Eight o'Clock) shall be fined two Cents per minute, & if absent during the whole evening Fifty Cents, reasonable excuse to be admitted; and if the President or Vice be absent at the time pointed out, then a Chairman protem be appointed.

RULE 3rd

That two Members of the Board be appointed by the President a School Committee, to serve Two months, whose duty it shall be to visit the School where the Boys are placed once a week, and at the Expiration of their time to report in writing to the Board, what number of Boys there are on the bounty of this institution & their opinion of their Improvement.

RESOLVED that the Boys under the Care of this Institution be compelled to attend Divine Service every Sunday in a Body to move from their School room to such Church as may be directed by the Master or by the School Committee, they shall visit different Churches on the different Sabbaths.

RESOLVED that in future no Boy shall be received on the Bounty of this Institution, untill he shall have been regularly bound (by his Parent or Guardian) untill he arrives at the Age of Twenty One Years.

RESOLVED That each of the Boys be furnished with a suit of cloths to be by them Worn only on Sundays, for the purpose of giving them an Uniform and decent appearance, to attend Divine Worship.

RESOLVED that notice be given to such persons who have not settled up their Accounts, that the Same are placed in the Hands of the

President. & that unless immediately paid, they will be placed in the Hands of an Attorney for Collection ; (to be Published.)

The following Members were appointed the School Committee, to serve two months in rotation. MOSES CLELAND, MOSES SHEFTALL & JOHN HUNTER, First Committee—

EDWARD HARDEN and F DENSLER Second Committee

Doct'r J B READ and F HERB Third Committee

RESOLVED that Doct'r Read and Mr Hunter be a Committee to obtain Lumber Sufficient to make the Doors & Windows for the Union Society part of the Academy & to have the same immediately put up in such manner as to prevent the Building from sustaining further Injury from the Weather.

MONDAY 3d June 1816

At a meeting of the Board of Managers at the Exchange, pursuant to notice.

Present   M Sheftall Presd't

J B Read

M Cleland

E Harden

F Densler

J Hunter

F Herb

The President reported he had placed at Mr. D D Williams's a Boy by name of Wm Shearer, agreeable to a proposition made by Mr W to board a Boy at the same rates that Mrs Christie does those in her charge. Which was assented to by the Board.

The President laid the following letter from R Watts before the Board.

To the President & Board of Managers
    of the Union Society

GENTLEMEN,

    An account was presented me on the 1 Inst exibiting a Balance due the Union Society of 69.50$. In removeing from this State to South Carolina in the Year 1800 I conceived it as disqualifying me from being a member of the Institution. In the Year 1811 (when I again returned to Town) I was however presented with an account & Informed that it was necessary in withdrawing to send in a formal resignation I then spoke to Mr Davies who I believe was President for that Year on the subject, and he advised me to submit in writing the Views I had taken of it to the members at their next meeting, this was accordingly done, and not

9

having heard anything further on the subject, concluded they did not
Consider me as belonging to the Society, having in no one Instance
been summoned on any occasion whatever— Under these circumstances I conceive it peculiarly hard that the sum of 69,, 50S should
be exacted from me, particularly at a time when I can so illy afford to
pay it,— I certainly did consider my Communication in 1811 as a
resignation.— I admire the Institution & should not have had an
Idea of withdrawing from it were it not from the circumstance of removing from the State.

I am &c
R WATTS

Sav'h 3d June 1816

On Motion of Mr Harden, Resolved that in Consideration of the
misunderstanding of Mr Robt, Watts as express'd in the within
Note, that the President be and is hereby authorised to remit five
Years of the last charges in his account for Contributions & fines but
that he will according to the rules of the Society be considered as a
Member thereof untill all arrearages are paid and a formal resignation
made.

RESOLVED that Public Notice be given, requiring all Gentlemen
of the Law, to make an immediate return of the Bonds & Notes in
their possession belonging to this Institution.

RESOLVED that the Committee of repairs be authorised to purchase
a sufficiency of Lumber to lay the lower floor of the building & to Contract with a Carpenter for doing the Work upon the best possible
terms.

RESOLVED that Mr John Hunter be authorized to rent to Mr
Johnson the lower room of that part of the academy belonging to
this Institution, upon the best terms he can for Twelve months.

The following letter was received from Mr R J Houstoun,

MONDAY EVENING.

To the Board of Managers of the Union Society

GENTLEMEN,

An excellent School is now Established at White
Bluff, and it occurr'd to me the other day as an object worthy the
consideration of Your Board, Whether this School does not hold out
superior advantages to the Boys under your charge. I have never
suggested this to the School Committee at W B, nor have I mature-
ly Consider'd it myself, it was an Idea that occur'd to me only a day
or two since & I immediately suggested it to the President of the
Union Society whom I accidentally met I therefore do not know
whether it is practicable, but should it appear important & You think

proper to enter Upon this Subject, I will readily give you every information you could desire & for this purpose, if proper Will attend your meeting this Evening (at your request.

Yrs &c

R J HOUSTOUN

The Society are of opinion that at present it is unnecessary to change the Situation of the Boys

T. V. GRAY Sect'y

At a meeting of the Board of Managers Monday evening 1st July,

Present   M Sheftall Pres'dt

John Hunter

. F Herb

T V Gray Sect'y

there not being a sufficient number present the meeting was adjourned.

At a meeting of the Board of Managers Monday evening 5th August 1816

Present   M Sheftall President

F Herb

J B Read

F Densler

M Cleland

The President laid before the Board a Communication from the Trustees of the Chatham Academy relative to a tract of land lying in Glynn County, the Joint property of this Institution the Academy & Hospital & Poor House. in the following words.

At a meeting of the Trustees of the Chatham Academy.

Present

Wm Stephens Esqr Presd't

Messrs Bulloch

Bolton

Lawson

H Kollock

L Kollock

RESOLVED that the Tract of land, situate in Glynn County, owned Jointly by this Institution, the Poor House & Hospital and the Union Society, in the Opinion of this Board, ought to be sold for the benefit of said Institutions, and that the Secretary be a Committee to confer with Committees from the said Institutions to that effect—

. Extract from the minutes

RICHD W HABERSHAM

Set'y C A

RESOLVED that the President, be authorised to meet any Committee's appointed by the other institutions to make arrangements for the
sale of said Tract of Land to the best advantage for said Institutions,
and that the Secretary furnish the Trustees of the Academy & the
Managers of the Hospital with Copies of this resolution as speedily as
possible.

ON MOTION of Mr. Cleland it was RESOLVED that the meetings of
this Board in future be on the first Tuesday in Every month.

T. V. GRAY
Sect'y

At a meeting of the Board of Managers Tuesday evening 3d September 1816

Present   M Sheftall Presd't
               Read
               Herb
               Cleland

Minutes of last meeting being read ; The President reported that
he had met the Committees on the part of the Chatham Academy &
the Poor House & Hospital on the Subject of the resolution relative
to a tract of land lying in Glynn, and that they had advertised said
Land for Sale on the first Tuesday in January 1817—

RESOLVED that the President be a Committee from this Board to
unite with such Committee's as may be appointed by the Poor House
& Hospital and Chatham academy for the purpose of making a demand of all Titles for lands or other papers that may be in the Hands
of any Individual, the Joint property of these Institutions & to de-
posit them for safe Keeping in such place as the Committee's may
deem proper. The Secretary will notify the Secty's of each Board.

T. V. GRAY
Sect'y

At a meeting of the Board of Managers to Union Society held
Tuesday Evening 5th Nov'r 1816

Present   M Sheftall Presd't

     M Cleland   F Deusler
     F Herb   J B Read

The President stated that since the last meeting of the board, that
Mr D D Williams had departed this life, that in consequence of which
the lad named Shearer who was living with him at the time on the
bounty of this Institution had been thrown out of a Home & that in
consequence of his situation he had directed him to be placed with
Mrs Christie which had been done,

The Board approved what had been done & directed him to be continued there.

The President informed the Board that he had advertised for proposals to finish that portion of the Academy belonging to this Institution and that he had received only one proposal, which he laid before the Board. & from the amount thereof the Board declined acting on it for the present.

RESOLVED, that the School Committee be authorised to Call on Mr John Carr to ascertain from him on what terms he will undertake the Instruction of the Children on the bounty of this Institution & if they can come to terms with him then, they be authorized to place them under his care for Instruction.

T. V. GRAY Sect.

At a meeting of the Board of Managers to Union Society held Tuesday Evening 3d Dec'r 1816

Present M Cleland,
F Herb
Jno Hunter,
M Sheftall Presd't

RESOLVED that Mr John Hunter be empowered to have all the Floors in the building belonging to this Institution, laid and to have two rooms finished immediately in a plain and neat manner and to have the windows finished.

The School Committee report, that in Consequence of a resolution made by this Board to place the Children on the Bounty of this Institution w't Mr John Carr, they have done so at Eight Dollars per Quarter Commencing 25th Nov'r 1816

T. V. GRAY
Sect'y

At a meeting of the Board of Managers to Union Society held Tuesday Evening 7th Jan'y 1817

Present   M Sheftall Presd't
M Cleland
F Herb
Jno Hunter
J B Read

The President stated to the Board that on Saturday last he had a conversation w't R Richardson Esqr. relative to Estate of Joseph Hills, and that he informed him that the Executors had paid the Estate of R Stites Esqr Three Thousand Dollars on account of its Demand against Hills Estate, that he believed there now remained a balance of somewhat more than Two thousand Dollars due Est'e Stites, that he believed the other Debts could & would be extinguished by property either already sold or that would be sold, that he advised this Institution and the female asylum to take up money at Bank to pay off that demand & to lease out the Bridge to the best advantage, it being a property that wou'd not at present fetch its Value. & that a good Tenant could be got for it, at he believes Fifteen Hundred Dollars per annum. In Consequence of the above communication. Resolved that the President be authorised to pay out of any money he shall have by him, or receive, whatever may be due Estate of Stites, on acc't of Es'te Hills so far as this Society is liable, & if he has not sufficient, that he be authorised to borrow the same from either Banks in this City and to act in such manner as he may deem to be most advantageous to this Institution.   Which was agreed to.

The undersigned begs leave to report that the repairs now going on at the Academy having interrupted the religious Society that had rented one of the rooms, they have given the same up, & have paid the rent for the Six months which they have occupied it. Say Fifty Dollars.

(Signed)   JNO HUNTER
7 Jany 1817
T. V. GRAY Sec'y

At a Meeting of the Board of Managers to Union Society held Thursday Evening 3 April 1817

Present M Sheftall Presd't
M Cleland
J Hunter
F Densler
Fred'k Herb

RESOLVED that the President be authorised to allow Mrs Ann Christie Ten Dollars pr month for Board of the Boys under her care, in consequence of the great rise in the Markets.

RESOLVED that the President be authorized to place with Mrs Christie Two more Boys in place of Anthony Suares & William Durasseau, who were to be bound to F S Fell to learn the Printing Business.

The Board were of opinion that the Printing Business, was not of Sufficient Importance to bind any of the Boys of this Institution to, therefore RESOLVED that the President be directed to withhold the binding of said Boys to that Business and that Mr. John Hunter be requested to apply to some Respectable Carpenter, Bricklayer or some other mechanic to place such of our Boys who may be educated sufficiently to be bound out.

T. V. GRAY Sect'y.

At a meeting of the Board of Managers on Tuesday evening 6th May 1817

President   M Sheftall Pred't
                 Jno Hunter V. P.
                 M Cleland
                 S White
                 J Morrison
                 F Herb

The Resolution made in Society 23d Ult'o respecting Sale of the Interest of this Institution, in & to the Estate of Joseph Hill dec'd was read, Whereupon

RESOLVED that the same be acted on, & that the Interest of the Union Society in & to the Est'e of Jos Hills dec'd, as devised to that Institution be advertised for Sale for the space of 30 Days.

James Tracy the son of Mrs Pearce, being represented to this Board as a fit object for the Charity of this Institution & his Mother totally incompetent from her decrepid & destitute situation to give him support & maintenance.

RESOLVED that the President be & is hereby authorised to place with Mrs Christie, the said James Tracy on the same conditions as the other Boys under its protection, in Conformity with the regulations of the Society.

RESOLVED that Messrs. Hunter & White be a subcommittee to Confer with a Committee on the part of the Free School for the purpose of adopting measures to secure a permanent teacher jointly for that institution and the Union Society—and to report their proceedings to the next meeting of this Board.

The following were appointed School Committees for May & June F HERB M CLELAND July & Aug't JNO. HUNTER & JAS EPPINGER, Sept'r & October MORRISON & WHITE.

Building Committee JOHN HUNTER.

                               T. V. GRAY
                                  Sect   -

At a meeting of the Board of Managers to the Union Society on Tuesday Evening   June 1817

Present   Moses Sheftall Presd't
                 Jas Morrison
                 M Cleland
                 F Herb

The President informed the Board, that in pursuance of their resolution of 6th May relative to James Tracy, he had his Indentures sign'd by his Mother & that he is now placed with Mrs Christie, that since binding him his Mother, had Departed this life, he further Reports that he has placed William Duressor as apprentice to Mr J R King, Taylor, & that his Indentures have been signed, he also reports that he has advertised the Interest of this Institution in & to the Estate of Joseph Hill, for the time pointed out by their resolution of 6th May and that no offer has been made to purchase! he laid before the Board a general account of Mr. Jeremiah Cuylers transactions with Estate J Hill; he has not been able to obtain from Mr R Richardson any statement of the Business relating to same Estate, altho he has repeatedly promised to furnish it.

T. V. GRAY, Sect'y

At a meeting of the Board of Managers on Tuesday 5th August
Present   M Sheftall Presd't
               Jno Hunter V P
               Steele White
               Fred'k Herb
               M Cleland

The President Inform'd the Board that since their last meeting, Mr R Richardson informed him that he had leased out the Ogechee Bridge at Twelve Hundred Dollars pr Year; the leaseor to put it into & Keep it in repair, subject to be delivered up whenever called for and that Mr Richardson has since left the City, that for these and other reasons, he had not complied with the resolution of the general meeting of calling the Society together, if no offer was made to purchase out their right to the Estate of Hill, among the reasons for not convening them was the absence of a number of Members at this season of the Year. he regrets extremely the Society did not borrow the money to pay off the Debts & Legacies as the Bridge would have Yielded to each Institution a nett Income of Four hundred Dollars pr Year, which at this time would be all important. Since the last regular meeting of this Board Mrs Christie who had charge of Several of the Boys has departed this Life & the Boys remain at present with her son Mr Robert Christie, it will now be the duty of the Board therefore to pass some resolution for their future disposal.

RESOLVED that Steele White & John Hunter be a committee to contract w't Mr. Carr for boarding, Washing mending & Tuition of the Boys now on the bounty of the Union Society, And also to contract w't him for the use of that part of the Academy belonging to this Institution.

RESOLVED further that the above named Committee be & they are hereby appointed & empowered to rent out per annum such parts of the aforesaid Tenement that may not be taken by Mr Carr, on such terms as they may be able to contract for.

RESOLVED that the Secretary to the Union Society be and he is hereby required to ascertain what number of Debts due to the Society have been sued, the Date of the Suits against whom the amount & progress of such suits, together with any other particular connected therewith, and to report the Statement to the next meeting of this board.

T V GRAY Sect'y

At a meeting of the Board of Managers on Tuesday evening 9th September 1817

Present   M Sheftall Presd't
        Jno Hunter V?P
        Steele White
        Fred'k Herb
        James Eppinger
        Moses Cleland

The President laid before the Board a letter from Mr Jeremiah Cuyler as follows

Dr Sir, I have an offer of 10,000 D'ls for Hills Bridge, I have not Mr Bolton to advise with & only Mr Hall the Young Gentleman in Mr Richardsons place, We have upon the best consideration we can give this case determined

If the Union Society & the female Assylum are of opinion with me, to sell, if with Mr Hall, who thinks more can be got, not to sell—

I will thank you to procure for me by monday next 10 oClock the determination of the Institution over which you preside. the Applicant is to get an answer Monday 12 oClock

Yours w't Friendship & Respect

J: CUYLER

Aug't 28th 1817

also a proposition from Mr Abbott for the purchase of the Ogechee Bridge—

ORDERD that the Letter & Proposition be laid over untill the next quarterly meeting of the Society.

The Committee appointed to Contract with Mr Carr report.

That they have Concluded a Contract with Mr Carr on the first proposition viz, that he Mr Carr will take the Boys to the number of Twelve, more or Less at the rate of One Hundred & Sixty seven Dolrs (167$) per annum each, for Tuition, boarding, Washing, lodging, mending and such other attention as they may require or be entitled to; as boys in their situation ought to receive, both as well as to

10

these particulars as to their morals; And on the second proposition, That they have agreed to give Mr Carr the whole of that part of the Academy belonging to the Society (reserving one room for the use of the Members, for the sum of Six Hundred Dollars ($600) per annum, to be reducted from the amount payable by the Society under the contract Contained in the first proposition.

Signed   JNO HUNTER
S WHITE

RESOLVED that the report of the Committee relative to the propositions of Mr Carr be received & that the Same be laid before the next quarterly meeting of the Society.

T. V. GRAY Sec't

At a meeting held Tuesday Evening 7th October at the Exchange

Present   M Sheftall Presd't
             J Hunter V P
             Jas Eppinger
             F Herb
             M Cleland

In Conformity of Resolution passed 5 Aug't the Secretary reports That he called on Mr J Cuyler who stated he had nothing in his possession belonging to this Institution, Mr Habersham is not in Town; that he has frequently requested Mr Wayne to give him a statement of the Papers in his Hands & has waited at his office this afternoon but cou'd not see him, Mr Morrison is at at the N–rthward and therefore a return cannot be made by him, Will endeavour to procure statements by the next meeting of this Board.

The President handed a Letter rec'd from Mr John Carr as follows

SEPT'R 15th 1817

Doct'r M Sheftall

Sir, A boy named Wm Bollinger was brought last Saturday eveuing to my House who says that he was formerly on the bounty of the Union Society and apprenticed to them, that he went to see his mother, who carried him to Milledgeville & there married, but left that place & he apprehended Came here. He came here accordingly in pursuit of her but could learn nothing of her, he is now he says desirous of returning & Committing himself to the Care of the Society! But as your approbation is requisite first, I cannot Continue him without it. I therefore, take this method of enquiry what is your will respecting him? Is he to be continued, or cast upon the world.

I am &c &c
J CARR

RESOLVED that the Boy named Bollinger mentioned by the President be continued w't Mr Carr as by him directed

T. V. GRAY Sect'y

Meeting 4 Nov'r 1817
Present J Hunter V P.   F Herb
      Jas Eppinger,   M Cleland
      Steele White.

The President being absent Mr Hunter took the Chair; who handed a Petition to be presented the Legislature of this State, for the purpose of obtaining Lands adjacent to Ogechee Bridge; which was directed by the Board to be forwarded to our Representatives in the Legislature:

RESOLVED, that the Vice President of this Society & Mr Cleland, be a Committtee to request the Ministers of the Gospel in this City to preach Charity Sermons in their respective Churches for the purpose of aiding the funds of this Institution, Commencing on the last sunday in the present month.

T V GRAY
Sect'y

Meeting of the Board of Managers 2nd Dec'r 1817.
Present   M Sheftall Presd't
        J Hunter V P.
        F. Herb
        Jas Eppinger
        Jas Morrison
        M Cleland

The President laid before the Board, the following Communication from J H Ash.

D'r Sir, Being quite buisy on this day it entirely slipt my memory that I was to call upon You, relative to the Estate of Burnside—but now hasten to address you these few words— Mrs Burnside will take a fair and reasonable valuation for the House, concerning which I spoke to you, my opinion relative to the best mode of settling the price should the Union Society conclude to purchase, wou'd be to leave the Valuation of the same to the Discretion of Arbitrators appointed for that purpose

Yrs &c
J H ASH

M Sheftall Pres't
     U. S

On the Communication of Mr Ash in behalf of Mrs Burnside, relative to some property belonging to the Society & Mrs Burnside.

RESOLVED that the President Mr Hunter and Mr Herb be a committee to meet Mrs Burnside & when met, that they be authorised to take such Steps with regard to arbitrators & the purchase of said property as they may think proper & report the same at the next meeting of this Board.

T V GRAY Sec't

At a Meeeing of the Board 3d Feb'y 1818

Present M Sheftall Presd't

        M Cleland.   J Morrison

        James Eppinger.

The Acc'ts of J Cuyler & R Richardson agent for Jno Bolton Ex'or Est'e J Hills were laid before the Board; and orderd to be presented at the next quarterly meeting of the Society.

RESOLVED the President be a Committee to meet a Committee of the Hospital & of the Chatham Academy for the purpose of advertising for sale a Tract of Land lying in the County of Glyn belonging to these Institutions, on such terms as they may agree upon.

T V GRAY Sect'y

Extra meeting of Board Managers 26th March 1818.

Present M Sheftall Presd't

        J Hunter V P.

        F Herb

        M Cleland

The Committe appointed to meet Mrs Burnside, for the purchase of her House report that they had called on Mrs B & could not agree on terms.

T V GRAY Sec't.

At a meeting of the Board of Managers of the Union Society May 5. 1818.

Present John Hunter President

        Moses Cleland

        Frederick Herb

        Joseph A Scott

        James Bilbo—V. P.—

The President having represented to the Board that Hills Bridge is now advertised for sale under executions obtained against the estate of Hills

Whereupon RESOLVED That the President & Vice President be a committee to meet the Female Asylum to devise means to protect the property & preserve it for the Institutions—

RESOLVED that the Secretary be directed to publish in the Savannah Gazettes the resolution changing the mode of the admission of applicants for membership from the Society to the Board of Managers—

The following gentlemen having been proposed for admission at the last meeting were unanimously admitted—viz Donald McLeod—John Speakman—Moses Herbert—John Tanner & John J. Roberts

ORDERED that the Sec'y notify them of their admission & receive their admission money—

RESOLVED that the President be requested & directed to procure a marble slab to be placed on the outside of the building immediately over the entrance door, with a suitable inscription upon it, pointing out the time when the Society was founded and its object—

Adjourned   JAMES MORRISON
                                                    Sec'y—

At a meeting of the Board of Managers of the Union Society June 1. 1818. Present

John Hunter President.—
James Bilbo—V. President—
James Eppinger—
Frederick Herb.—

Mr Hunter the President, reported that he, in conjunction with Mr Bilbo V. P. had called on the managers of the Female Assylum, & that they had come to a determination not to let Hills Bridge be sold for a less sum than ten thousand Dollars—and that should it not bring that sum, the two Societies, would purchase it jointly, and jointly defray the expence of the same—

RESOLVED that the President be a Committee to attend the Sheriffs sale at the Court House tomorrow and that he be directed to purchase in Hills Bridge for the use of this Society & the Female Assylum unless the same should exceed ten thousand Dollars—

RESOLVED that Mr Bilbo Vice President, be requested to attend the Shffs sale to aid the President in discharging the above duties—

The President reported that he had procured a marble slab, with a suitable inscription on the same agreeable to the resolution of the last meeting of the Board & that the expence of the same was forty Dollars, which was ordered to be paid—

The Petition of William H. Joyner praying to become a member of this Society was read, and ordered to lay over untill the next meeting—

RESOLVED that the President be directed to bind out as an apprentice James S., Hoffman, to such, persons & upon such terms, as he may think proper,—

RESOLVED that Daniel Philips be received & admitted as one entitled to the bounty of this institution—

RESOLVED That not more than two of the boys under the Patronage of this institution be permitted to sleep in one bed—that they have a mattrass for two, & a Pillow or bolster for each—that they be provided with a pair of clean coarse sheets weekly, and coverlid in the Summer, and a pair of Blankets & coverlid in the Winter—

RESOLVED that Mr Cleland & Dr Sheftall be a Committee to see that the above resolution is carried into effect for the months of June & July—Mr Herb & Mr Eppinger for the months of August & September & Mr Bilbo & Mr Scott for the months of October & November

Adjourned

J. MORRISON
Sec'y

At a Meeting of the Board of Managers of the Union Society July 7. 1818.

Present John Hunter President
Moses Sheftall
Frederick Herb.
James Eppinger—

The President reported that he had purchased in Hills Bridge for the joint benefit, and at the joint expence of this Institution & the Female Asylum for the sum of Five thousand Five hundred Dollars—And that agreeable to a former resolution he had got a note discounted at the Bank of the State of Georgia for two thousand Dollars—That the Female Assylum had paid also two thousand Dollars—That twenty five hundred Dollars has been paid to the Sheriff for the purpose of extinguishing Judgments, and that the Ballance of the four thousand Dollars is now in the hands of the President for the purpose of meeting legacies or other Judgments—

RESOLVED That the President be authorised to make such repairs on the said Bridge as may be necessary to keep it in a proper state—

RESOLVED, That the President be directed to have the lands adjacent to Hills Bridge belonging to the same surveyed by the County Surveyor as soon as practicable—

RESOLVED That the President be directed to make an application to the Justices of the Inferior Court to have the sum of five hundred Dollars due by the estate of Hills to said County remitted for the benefit of this Society—

William H Joyner having at the last meeting petitioned for admis-

sion to this Society, was at this meeting ballotted for and unanimously admitted—

RESOLVED That the President be directed to bind out to John F.
Herb to learn the art of a Blacksmith Stephen Walsh, upon such
terms as he may think proper—

There being no other business before the Society the same was adjourned.—The Petition of Archibald Smith for admission to this Society was read and ordered to lay over to the next meeting—

Adjourned

J. MORRISON
Sec'y. U. S.

At a meeting of the Board of Managers of the Union Society held
at the Societys Rooms in the west end of the Academy August 5.
1818 Present, John Hunter Pres.

Joseph A Scott—
Frederick Herb.
Moses Sheftall

The President reported that he had leased the Bridge to William
Hanna for one year at twelve hundred Dollars per annum payable
monthly, he, W. Hanna to keep the face of the Bridge in repair—

The President further reported that he had received from said William Hanna two months rent of the said Bridge whereupon it was ordered that he do pay over to the Female Assylum the one half of the
amount he has already received, and that he do also pay the one half of
every future sum which he may receive to the same Institution—

The Petition of Archibald Smith to become a member of this Society was read a second time, and he was unanimously admitted—

RESOLVED That the President be authorised to bind out such of
the boys on the bounty of this Institution as he may think
sufficiently advanced in education, to such persons and to
learn such trades as may be deemed most advisable—

Adjourned

JAMES MORRISON
Sec'y U. S.

At a meeting of the Board of Managers of the Union Society at
the Societys Room in the west end of the Academy September 1.
1818.

Present John Hunter Pres.
Joseph A Scott
Moses Sheftall
Frederick Herb.
Moses Cleland
James Eppinger

The minutes of the last meeting were read & confirmed

The Petition of Samuel M. Bond for admission to this Society were read the first time and laid over to the next meeting—

RESOLVED That the President do make known thro' the medium of the Public papers, That the Board of Managers will receive upon the bounty of this Institution one additional orphan boy and that he request applicants for admission, to present their Petition to the Secretary within the month of September.

Adjourned

JAMES MORRISON
Sec'y—

At a meeting of the Board of Managers of the Union Society in the Societys room in the West end of the Academy October 6. 1818

Present—John Hunter President

> Dr Moses Sheftall
> Joseph A Scott
> James Eppinger

The Petition of Samuel M Bond to become a member of this Society was read a second time, and he was admitted a member of the same—

(Petitions for membership read the first time omitted here.)

*   *   *   *   *   *   *   *   *   *   *

The Petition of Samuel M Bond, Guardian of Richard Strop to have his Ward placed upon the bounty of this Society was read— Whereupon, Resolved That the Board will receive the said Strop upon the bounty of this Society, upon condition that his Guardian will continue to superintend the management of his property, and pay annualy to the President, the amount of his annual income—

Adjourned

JAMES MORRISON
Sec'y—

At a meeting of the board of managers of the Union Society at the Societys room at the west end of the Academy Tuesday November 3d 1818.

Present John Hunter President

> Moses Cleland
> Frederick Herb—
> James Eppinger—

The Petitions of S. S. Williams, Worthington Gale & Joseph King were read a second time, and were unanimously admitted members of the Society—

*   *   *   *   *   *   *   (Petition read first time.)

Mr Bilbo & Mr Scott, the visiting & School Committee for the months of October & November were requested to report at the next meeting the State of the boys clothing and their progress in education—

Adjourned

JAMES MORRISON
Sec'y—

At a meeting of the Board of Managers of the Union Society, at the Societys Room in the West end of the Academy Tuesday Evening December 1. 1818—

Present John Hunter President
Moses Cleland
Frederick Herb.
James Eppinger

The Petition of William M Kelly to become a member of the Society was read a second time and upon balloting for him, he was unanimously admitted—

The President reported that he had bound out to S. C. & J Schenk, James Johnston to learn the trade of a Book-binder untill he shall have arrived at the age of twenty one years—

RESOLVED That the President of this Society be authorised to confer the Female Assylum on the subject of a sale of the Bridge at Ogeechee & that he do report at the next meeting—

RESOLVED that Mr Scott & Mr Bilbo be continued the visiting and school Committee for the month of December, and that they be requested to report at the next meeting the situation of the boys, particularly their progress in education & their domestic situation—

Adjourned—

JAMES MORRISON
Sec'y—

At a meeting of the Board of Managers of the Union Society, at the Societys Room in the west end of the Academy on Tuesday evening January 5. 1819.—

Present John Hunter President
Moses Cleland
Frederick Herb
James Eppinger

The President reported that he had had a conference with the female assylum on the subject of a sale of Hills Bridge, and that they had agreed to dispose of it as soon as convenient— That he had advertised for persons who felt disposed to purchase it to make their proposals on or before the fifteenth of January instant, at which time

11

should no proposals have been received a public sale was contemplated—

* * * * * * * * * * *

RESOLVED that the President & Mr Cleland be a committee to
wait upon and request the ministers of the Gospel in this City to
preach Charity sermons in their respective Churches for the purpose
of aiding the funds of this Institution commencing as soon as practicable

RESOLVED that the debts due to this Society from the following
persons be cancelled & their accounts ballanced viz: George H Davidson $79.70.—Estate of Joseph Davis $29.30—James E. Houstoun
$56.50—Benjamin Jacobs $21.50 Estate of William Lewden $20.50.
George Millen $87.50—Nathaniel Pendleton $49.12. William Stephens $161.50.

RESOLVED that the President be authorised to employ a suitable
person to collect the debts due to the Society, & that he be authorised to allow a proper compensation for the same—

RESOLVED that William Middleton & ——— Dent aged 12 years
be admitted to the bounty of this Institution—the former recommended by John Bryan, & the latter by Mrs Frances Dent, both of whom
were required to give such indentures as have been heretofore required

RESOLVED that Mr Cleland & Dr Sheftall be the visiting Committee for the months of January & February—

Adjourn'd

JAMES MORRISON
Sec'y—

At a meeting of the Board of Managers of the Union Society held
at the Societys Room in the West end of the Academy on Tuesday
evening Feb'y 2d 1819 Present

John Hunter President

Doctor Moses Sheftall

Frederick Herb

Moses Cleland—

The Petition of Thomas Wright & Charles Manul to become members of this Society was read a second time and they were unanimously admitted—

* * * * * * * * * *

The resignation of Membership of John P. Henry & James Hunter was received & accepted they having paid their accounts in full—

* * * * * * * * * *

The President Reported that he with Mr Cleland had applied to

Mr Kolloch to preach a Charity sermon & was by him informed that the members of the free school had made an application previous to theirs, Whereupon

RESOLVED that another application be made as soon as convenient for the same purpose—

RESOLVED, That Richard W. Habersham & James Morrison be a committee to Examine the claims of this Society to the estate of the late Justus H Scheuber

Adjourn'd

JAMES MORRISON
Se'y

At a meeting of the Board of Managers of the Union Society held at the Societys room in the West end of the Academy on Tuesday evening March 2d 1819.

Present   John Hunter President
           James Eppinger
           Moses Cleland
           Frederick Herb

The Petition of Edward F. Tattnall, Francis H. Welman Joseph Clay. Habersham, Benjamin Howard, William Neff & William C. Wayne, was read a second time & they were unanimously admitted members of this Society—

*   *   *   *   ●   *   *   *   *   ●   ●

The President reported that he in conjunction with the female asylum had sold Hills Bridge to Stephen Williams, & David F. Bourquine, for the sum of eight thousand Dollars—one half cash, and the balance at one and two years, with mortgage on the premises—

Mr Cleland & Dr Sheftall the visiting committee for the months of January & February reported that they had repeatedly examined the situation of the boys & the advancement they had made in their studies—and that they were pleased with their improvement in learning & satisfied with the accommodation afforded them by Mr Carr—

Upon the representation of J Morrison that a Mr Couper had taken possession of the College tract in Glynn County owned by this Institution, The Chatham Academy & The Poor House & Hospital, Resolved That Mr Morrison be a committee, in conjunction with a committee, to be appointed by the other institutions to enquire into the situation of the said Tract of land, and report as early as possible—

RESOLVED That this Society will receive upon its bounty McLagan, an orphan boy now at the Hospital—

RESOLVED That the use of this room be given to the Sunday

84

School, and that a committee be appointed to wait on Mr Carr, to renew his contract with the Society

RESOLVED That the President & Mr Cleland be that Committee—

RESOLVED that the President & Mr Cleland be the School Committee for the months of March and April

Adjourned

JAMES MORRISON Sec'y

At a meeting of the board of managers of the Union Society held at the Societys room in the West end of the Academy on Monday morning April 5 1819—

Present   John Hunter President

James Bilbo, Vice President

Frederick Herb

Moses Cleland

Moses Sheftall

James Morrison Sec'y—

The Petitions of William T. Williams. Durham T. Hall Benjamin Sheftall, John Shelman, Josiah Lawrence, Rich'd. Wayne, Francis H. Welman, Edward F. Tattnall, Charles H. Hayden, Charles Kelsey, William C. Daniel, John Carnochan Dimas Ponce, John Lewis, William H. Thompson, John McNish, Benjamin W Leach, Jonas Cutter, Alexander Irwin, George F Palmes, George G Faries Jacob Miller, John C Nicol Joseph George, John Morrall, Peter Guerard, Thomas Polhill, Francis M Stone, Andrew G Semmes, Peter Mitchell, John Crane, James McHenry, & Fleming Akin were read a second time and they were unanimously admitted

Adjourned

JAMES MORRISON

Sec'y

At a meeting of the Board of Managers of the Union Society held at the Societys Room in the West end of the Academy on Tuesday evening May 4 1819.

Present.

James Morrison Sec'y

Moses Cleland

Frederick Herb..

John Lewis

There not being a quorum present the members adjourned untill Thursday evening next—

Adjourned

J. MORRISON

Sec'y—

At a meeting of the Board of Managers of the Union Society held at the Societys rooms in the West End of the Academy on Thursday evening May 6. 1819—

Present   John Hunter President
          Frederick Herb
          Moses Cleland
          Moses Sheftall
          John Lewis
          James Morrison Sec'y—

  ●   *   *   *   *   *   *   *   (Petitions read.)

A letter was read from Joseph Bacon desiring the Society to take charge of Henry Hatfield an Orphan child of the late Mr & Mrs Hatfield—

WHEREUPON RESOLVED—That Henry Hatfield be received upon the Bounty of this Institution; and that he be bound to the Society together with the other boys on the bounty of this Institution who have no guardians, as soon as they can be appointed by the Court of Ordinary

The Resignation of John Dillon a member of this Society was read and received—

A letter was received and read from Mr John Carr praying that the rent of the building may be reduced from six, to four hundred Dollars—which was rejected by the board

RESOLVED that the Sec'y notify the Public that there is vacancy in the Society for one boy to be received upon its bounty—

RESOLVED, That arrangements be made to receive the President of the United States who is about to visit this City for the purpose of showing him in the Academy the different charitable institutions, & the number of pupils who attend the respective private Schools in this City—

RESOLVED That Mr Herb. & Mr Lewis be a Committee to examine the situation of the boys on the bounty of this Institution for the ensuing month—

                    Adjourned

                         J. MORRISON
                             Sec'y.

At a meeting of the Board of Managers of the Union Society held at the Societys room in the West end of the academy on Tuesday evening June 1. 1819.

Present John Hunter President
        James Bilbo V. P—
        Ebenezer S. Rees
        John Lewis
        Frederick Herb—

The minutes of the last meeting were read and confirmed—

The Petition of Joseph Bacon, J H Bruen, Elias Reed, Alexander Telfair, Thomas Clark, & Jacob Shaffer to become members of this board was read a second time and they were unanimously admitted— Whereupon RESOLVED that the Secretary do notify them of their admission—

Agreeable to arrangements previously made the President of the United States visited the Institution was received in an appropriate style, on Wednesday the twelfth day of May eighteen hundred & nineteen, at which time the President of the Board of Managers & of the Society delivered the following address—to his Excellency

Sir,

The high honour of receiving the Chief Majistrate of our Country has seldom fallen to our lot, and it is with no common feelings of gratitude and joy, that we welome you among us—

The sweetest recollections of many now before you, are those which were produced, when he, who was justly styled *"The Father of his Country"* visited his people, and, you Sir, moving in the footsteps of that *Great Man* are securing the affections of a community, of which the children we this day present to you, form a most interesting part—

Religion, Peace and Learning flourish under your auspices;—may they long continue the bright characteristics of that Government, so wisely administered by your Excelency"—

To which the President of the United States made an appropriate reply—.

The President reported that he had bound to John M Hanny, Alexexander Marlome to learn the art or trade of a Printer—

RESOLVED that the boys bound by this Society to John R. King, viz John F. W. Duresseau & Philip J. Chaly be discharged from their apprenticeship if the Justices of the Inferior Court should approve of the same, and that they be bound, Duresseau to Cannon & Fowler, & J. Chealy to Rolf & Newman

RESOLVED That the President be requested to reinstate Benjamin Philips (now with Mrs Fitzgerald), upon the bounty of this Society.

Mr. Rees, and Mr Cleland were appointed a committee to examine the situation of the boys for the ensuing month

Adjourned

J. MORRISON.

At a meeting of the board of Managers held at the Societys room in the West end of the Academy on Tuesday evening July 6. 1819

Present

James Morrison Sec'y—
Moses Cleland
John Lewis—

There not being a sufficient number to constitute a board the meeting was adjourned to the next meeting in Course—

JAMES MORRISON
Sec'y

At a meeting of the Board of Managers of the Union Society held at the Societys room at the West end of the Academy Tuesday evening August 3. 1819
Present John Hunter President
      Dr Moses Sheftall
      Frederick Herb.
      James Morrison Sec'y
There not being a sufficient number present to constitute a board the same was adjourned—

JAMES MORRISON
Sec'y

At a meeting of the Board of Managers to Union Society held at the Societys room in the west end of the Academy, Tuesday evening September 8th 1819.
      Present John Hunter President
      James Morrison Sec'y—
There not being a sufficient number present to constitute a board, the meeting was adjourned

JAMES MORRISON
Sec'y

At a meeting of the Board of Managers of the Union Society held at the Societys room in the West end of the Academy Tuesday evening October 5 1819.
      Present John Hunter Pres't
      Dr Moses Sheftall
      Frederick Herb
      John Lewis
      Moses Cleland
      James Morrison Sec'y
The minutes of the last meeting were read and confirmed—
Mr. Morrison having to attend a meeting of Council was excused for the evening—
  *   *   *   *   *   *   •   *   *   *   *
Edmund Walsh who was formerly on the bounty of this institution, having returned to this place and wishing to serve the remainder of his time to the painting business, the President is hereby authorised to engage him with a suitable person for that purpose

The Visiting Committee having reported that the boys appear to stroll more in the streets than seems proper it is therefore

RESOLVED,

That in future they be confined in the Academy, except those who may be required to attend market in the morning before breakfast, and a reasonable time for relaxation in the afternoon after School hours—

Visiting Committee—John Lewis Fre'dk Herb—

Adjourned—

At a meeting of the Board of Managers to the Union Society held at the Societys Room in the West end of the Academy on Tuesday evening Nov: 2d. 1819.

Present Moses Cleland
Frederick Herb—
John Lewis—

There not being a sufficient number present to constitute a board the meeting was adjourned to the next regular meeting in course—

At a meeting of the Board of Managers of the Union Society held at the Societys room in the West end of the Academy on Tuesday evening December 7th 1819.

Present John Hunter President
James Bilbo Vice President:
John Lewis
Frederick Herb
Moses Cleland
James Morrison Sec'ty—

The minutes of the two last meetings were read and confirmed—

The Petition of Michael Brown to become a member of this Society was read a second time, and he was unanimously admitted a member of the Society

RESOLVED that the President be requested to call on the several Clergymen in this city, and request them to preach charity sermons in their respective churches for the benefit of the Society—

The President appointed Josiah Penfield one of the Board of Managers to supply the vacancy occasioned by the removal of Ebenezer S. Rees—

The visiting committee reported that they had not observed much improvement in the boys on the bounty of the Institution since the last meeting

RESOLVED That Moses Cleland & Josiah Penfield be the visiting committee for the months of December & January—

Adjourned

JAMES MORRISON
Sec'y

At a meeting of the Board of Managers of the Union Society
Jan'y 4. 1820—
 Present, Frederick Herb Pres Pro Tem—
    Moses Cleland
    John Lewis—
    Josiah Penfield—
    James Morrison Sec'y—
The minutes of the last meeting were read and confirmed—
There being no business before the Board the same was adjourned—
      JAMES MORRISON,
          Sec'y
At a meeting of the Board of Managers of the Union Society, held
at the Societys room in the West end of the Academy on Tuesday eve-
ning February 1 1820.
 Present John Hunter President
    John Lewis
    James Morrison Sec'y
There not being a sufficient number present the board adjourned to
the next regular meeting—
      Adjourned
      J. MORRISON
          Sec'y
At a meeting of the Board of Managers of the Union Society, held
at the Societys room in the West end of the Academy Tuesday eve-
ning March 7 1820
 Present John Hunter President
    James Bilbo Vice President.
    Frederick Herb.
    John Lewis
   Dr. Moses Sheftall
    Moses Cleland
    James Morrison Sec'y—
The minutes of the last meeting were read and confirmed—
The President reported that the collections in the several churches
had been made and that he had received from the
Presbyterian Church $423-12½
Christs Church.................... .... 97 62½
Methodist Church.. 68,,56

Amounting in all to..$589,,31
 RESOLVED, That, Messrs Cleland & Lewis be a committee to consult with Mr Carr on the subject of a reduction of the annual amount
12

to be paid for the support of the Boys on the bounty of this institu
tion, and that they be requested to report at the next quarterly meeting

*   *   *   *   *   *   *   *   *   *   *

There being no other business before the Board, the same was adjourned untill the next regular meeting—

Adjourned

JAMES MORRISON

Sec'y—

At a meeting of the Board of Managers of the Union Society held
at the Society's Hall on Tuesday evening April 4th 1820

Present   John Hunter President

Moses Cleland

Frederick Herb

John Lewis

Josiah Penfield

James Morrison Sec'y

The minutes of the last meeting were read and confirmed

The Committee appointed to confer with Mr Carr on the subject of
a reduction of the amount paid him for the support of the boys, *report*,
That they had agreed with Mr Carr to support & instruct the boys on
the bounty of this Institution for one hundred and fifty Dollars per
annum each, to commence at the expiration of this quarter

The following accounts having been open on the Ledger for many
years, the Board directed to be ballanced, believing that some of them
had been paid, and that the remainder never could be collected, or
that the persons from whom they might be collected were themselves
objects of Charity—

Estate Noble W. Jones...	9.62	Est. R Leake...............	1.00
Estate of W. Gibbous.....	1.50	Est. A McCradie...........	74.88
Estate of John Morell.....	54.66	Est. J. B. Young...........	186.09
Estate of Samuel Beecroft	69.91	Est. R. Bolton.............	4.25
Est of George Houstoun..	4.85	Est. Jno Tebeau...........	6.50
Estate of F. Fahm.........	4.25	Est. Jno Rentz............	1.25
Estate of John Armour...	3.50	Est. Edward Harden.......	1.12
Estate of Jno D. Dickinson	32.00	Estate of James Alger....	10.50
Estate of John Grommet.	10.75	Estate of Levi Sheftall....	143.72
Estate of John Glass......	439.72	Peter H Morel.............	14.50
Estate of James Robertson	44.60	William H Spencer........	29.00
Estate of Z Horskins......	26.00	Charles Odingsell..........	2.66
Edward Lloyd..............	129.27	Joseph Clay...............	12.00
Slaughter Cowling.........	12.00	John N. Brailsford........	122.92
John Howel................	68.60	James McIntosh...........	140.67
Richard Wall..............	49.00	Benjamin Wall.............	37.50
John P. Oates.............	94.50	Morris Miller.............	50.65

James Magee	38.00	Estate Peter Ward	27.40
Thomas Schley	4.00	Christian Gugel	1.00
Alexander S. Roe	2.50	Griffin L. Lamkin	10.00
Richard Leake	13.50	Samuel Williams	8.00
D. D. Williams	62.50	John Grimes	62.80
John F Everett	49.00	William Maxwell	46.60
F. T. Flyming	7.50	P. D. Woolhopter	8.50
Lewis Cooper	20.00	James Boyle	37.85
Enoch M*****	42.15	Walter Roe	26.85
Charles Fritot	4.50	John J Evans	29.50
W. B. Barnes	48.50	William Lloyd	31.50
J. Dufaure	40.00	Murdoch McLeod	43.00
John E. Hartridge	50	John Wallace	6.00
Jacob Hersman	22.00	Edward Stebbins	25.50
John Gibbons	3.50	George V. Proctor	22.50

The petition of Lazarus Petty to become a member of this Society was read the first time, and laid over to the next meeting—

Adjourned

J. MORRISON
Sec'y

At a meeting of the Board of Managers of the Union Society, held at the Societys Hall on Tuesday evening May 2. 1820—

Present John Hunter President.

Dr. Sheftall
Moses Cleland
Joseph George
John Lewis
James Morrison Sec'y Pro Tem

* * * * * * * * * * *

The Board proceeded to the election of Lazarus Petty when upon counting the votes he was elected, his petition having been read at the last meeting—

The first annual payment to this Society, & the Female Assylum from Mr Bourquin, for Hills Bridge, having become due on the 17th April, and no part of it having been paid—RESOLVED That the President be required to apply to Mr. Bourquin for the money, and that the amount when received be vested in stock for the benefit of the Society—

The following persons were appointed the visiting committee for the months of May & June—viz Dr M Sheftall & Joseph George—

* * * * * * * * * * *

Adjourned

J. MORRISON
Sec'y. P. T.

(Here ends the Minute Book of the Board of Managers—and from this time to April 1st, 1828, there are no minutes whatever in the possession of the Society.)

(The books now in our possession besides the Minute Books are—

Ledger and Journal No. 3 (6 qr Cap)		1802 to 1810.
Ledger No. 4	(12 qr Cap)	1810 to 1824.
Ledger No. 5	(6 qr Cap)	1823 to 1832.

Registry Book of Beneficiaries (2 qr Med. ½ bound)
Book of Rules and Signatures of Members. (2 qr Demy ½ bd) 1808 to 1837.
Cash Book, (4 qr. Royal 4to,) kept by President Fay and now continued by Treasurer Courvoisie.)
Minute Book (Demy 6 qr.) new, opened in 1858.
Registry Book of Boys,   "   "   "   ".
Registry Book of Members, ··   "   " 1859.
Ledger (12½ crown)   "   "   "   "

Book of Rules and signatures of members 8vo opened in 1859 with printed lists of members and officers as far as could be ascertained.

(Ledgers 1 and 2 are missing, also a "Blotter" referred to in Journal No. 3.)

(The Society has also in its possession the Copperplate of Certificates of Membership referred to in the earlier minutes; also some 56 copies of the Certificates. Five of these are signed by W. B. Bulloch, Pres., Willi'm Davies, V. P., John N. Brailsford, Sec.; and filled up each with a member's name, and one not filled up signed by Davies P., Jn: Macpherson Berrien V.P. and Brailsford Sec.

(There is no seal now in possession of the Society.)

(We have also, out of the numerous sermons and orations that have been delivered and asked for to be deposited in the archives of the Institution, but one in MS., that of Judge R. M. Charlton.)

(*From Journal to Ledger No. 3, for the years* 1802 *to* 1810.)

SAVANNAH, April 23rd, 1802.

1. Cash new Account Dr to Cash old Account. For balance of said account paid by Matthew McAllister, late President, to Joseph Habersham elected President this day 135.44
For amount received from sundry members this day, and for which they have, severally, been credited in Ledger No. 2............................166.35   301.79

Sundry Accounts   Drs.

1. To Cash—viz:

9. Disbursements for Children for this sum paid Lydia Myers for tuition of Abraham & Henry Gilbert and Mary Lacie, each one quarter................... ..   9.—

4 Contingent Expenses: for this sum paid Peter S. Laffitte for his Salary as Secretary to the Union Society for one year ending this day.............. 60.—   69.—

26.

4. Contingent expenses..Dr.

1. To Cash: for this sum paid Edward White, Steward, being the amount of expenses on the Anniversary, exclusive of the sum paid in by members on that day.... 82.50

93

27.

7 Subscription for Building an Exchange in Savannah...Dr
1 To Cash: for this sum paid Thomas Pitt Secretary, for
Instalment on two shares No 133 & 134.................   40.—

May 18.

9 Disbursements for Children   Dr.
1 To Cash: for the sum paid John G. Williamson the
amount of E. Yarnell's account of sundry articles of
clothing........ ....   12.—

SAVANNAH, June 21st 1802.

9 Disbursements for Children   Dr.
1. To Cash. For this sum paid William F. Port for tuition
of John Gilbert, Thomas McLain, Daniel Baas, Thomas
Steel, William Patterson, Thomas Patterson, William &
John Randolph, one quarter due on the 15th in-
stant... 36.—
Abraham Gilbert ½ quarter due at the same
time.. 2.25
Paper, Ink & Quills................................. 2.—   40.25

September 15.

9 Disbursements for Children   Dr.
1 To Cash. For this sum paid William F. Port, for one
Quarters Tuition, due this day, of John Gilbert, Thomas
McLain, Daniel Baas, Thomas Steel, William Parker,
Thomas Patterson, Abraham Gilbert, William Ran-
dolph, & John Randolph, at $4 50/100 each............40.50
Paper, Ink & Quills .... 2.—   42.50

October 29.

9 Disbursements for Children   Dr.
1 To Cash. For six months Tuition of Henry Gilbert &
Mary Mannon due on the 23d instant to Mrs. Lydia
Myers ....   12.—

SAVANNAH, March 22nd 1803.

Sundry Accounts   Drs.

1. To Cash ....viz :—

7 Subscription for Building an Exchange in Savannah.
For this sum paid Thomas Pitt, Secretary; for an instalment on two shares, No. 133 & 134..... ....   40.—
9. Disbursements for Children. For this sum paid William
F. Port for tuition ....   26.—

66.—

SAVANNAH in GEORGIA 17th January 1805

7 Subscription for Building an Exchange Dr to Cash
135
    paid Thomas Pitt for an instalment on 2 shares......... 12.00

SAVANNAH in GEORGIA 1 April 1805

6 Sundry Accounts Dr To Stock for leaving the Society
this day without permission

138	William Davies for amo't his fine....................			1.00
38	Charles Odingsells " "			1.00
114	Zachariah Horskins " "			1.00
82	Thomas M. Woodbridge, "			1.00
116	James E. Houston " "			1.00

                                                                     5.00

135 Cash Dr To Donation Account   for
139
    this sum received from Barack Gibbons Executor of
William Gibbons Jun'r in full for a Legacy left the
Society by the said W. Gibbons....................... 100.00

SAVANNAH IN GEORGIA 23 April 1806

    Sundry Accounts Dr to Cash

4 Contingent Expenses for
    paid P. S. Laffitte 1 years salary................ 60:00
9 Disbursements for Children for
    paid D & C Gugel for Clothing &C............. 20:06¼
    paid W. F. Port for Schooling 166.87½
    paid J. Lawson for Clothing &C................. 32.37¼ 219.31¼
139 Donation Account.
    rec'd from Thomas Dechenaux........... .... 20.00

SAVANNAH in GEORGIA 23d April 1807

135 Sundry Accounts Dr To Cash as per the Presidents
Account Current laid before the Society this day viz:

4 Contingent Expenses for
    paid Everett J McLean for printing.......... ... 3:00
    paid Mr Petit a balance due him on the Anni-
versary dinner...................................... 65:00
    paid Seymour & Woolhopter for printing......... 6:00
    paid J Heley for printing.......................... 9:75
    paid S. P. Laffitte 1 years salary................. 60:00
    paid W. B. Bulloch for having blank Certifi-
cates struck in New York....................15:37½ 159 12½
9 Disbursements for Children for
    paid Mr. Port for Schooling....................203:75

paid Mrs Myers for do............................ 10: 50
paid Mr Lawson for Clothing &C furnished the
  Children... 35: 00   249. 25

SAVANNAH IN GEORGIA 23d April 1808

9 Disbursements for Children Dr to Cash
  paid W. F. Port for Schooling.................238: 12¼
  paid Mrs McGavar for ditto..................... 20: 00
  paid J. Lawson for Clothing.....................148: 85 406. 97¼

May—23d 1808.

Sundry Accounts Dr to Stock
173 for amount of fines this day ⅌ Blotter* which have been
  debited to their respective Accounts in Ledger..... 18. —

SAVANNAH GEORGIA 24th April 1809—

4 Contingent Expenses Dr to Cash paid P. S. Laffitte 2 yrs
  salary .... 120,,—
8 Disbursements for Children Dr to Cash   paid
Wm. F. Port for Schooling....................299,,37½
Mrs McGavar... .... 34,,—
E Stebbins & others for Clothing &C for Child-
  ren..281,,13 614,,50

SAVANNAH GEORGIA 23d April 1810.

Sundry Accounts Dr to Cash as ⅌ Presidents Acc't curr't
  of this date viz't
Stock—paid the Stewards balance of their Acc'ts last An-
  niversary Dinner....................................... 50,,
Contingent Expenses paid J N Brailsford† 5 qrs salary... 187,,50
  paid Everett and Evans Bill...................... 14. 75
    "   Mrs Shaw.............................. 39. 14
    "   Job T. Bolles Recording Deeds.......... 21,,25
    "   Seymour and Woolhopters bill.......... 21. 87½ 97,,01½
Disbursements for Children
  paid Taylor & Scribners bills.................... 40,,50
    "   Jno Lawsons bill......................... 2,,25
    "   J. Cuylers bill........................ 18,,27
    "   Edw'd Stebbin's bills....................442,,05
    "   W'm F. Port...........................382,,25
    "   Mrs McGavar............................. 18,,—
    "   Mrs Christie............................277,,—
    "   Mr Jenneys bill......................... 33,,25 1213,,57

                            1548,,08

*Blotter not now in possession of the Society.
†Mr. B. was Secretary in 1809 and 1810, as appears by the six Certificates of Membership above referred to, five of them filled up and signed by Bulloch, Pres., Davies, V. P., and Brailsford, Sec., as also appears by the hand writing in Journal; and by which it appears also that he was Secretary a part of the year 1808—Mr. B. died July 21 or 20, 1811.

(Ledger No. 4, folio 241,

T. V. Gray, Sec., is credited April 23, 1818, By 1 yrs salary...$250,00

Also, on folio 270 James Morrison Sec'y credited

May 20, 1819 By 1 yrs salary.................................... 250,00
April 3, 1820 By 1 yrs salary.................................... 150,00

Also, on folio 352 Lowell Mason Sec'y is credited by salary
  in 1821, '22, and '23, each.................................. 150,00

On folio 335 is the following account)

	Exchange Shares	Dr.	Cr.
1819			
Jan'y 1.	To Interest on 2 Shares for 2 years ⅌ Certificates No 87 & 88........................$48 —		
June 8	By Cash from City Treasurer........................		$48 —
1820			
Jan. 1	To interest on 2 shares for one year ⅌ Certificates No 87 & 88...................$24 —		
April 22	By Cash from City Treasurer........................		$24 —
1821			
Jan'y 1	To interest on 2 shares for one year ⅌ Certificates Nos 8 & 88....................$24 —		
" 9	By Cash from City Trea'r............................		$24 —

(ITEMS FROM JOURNAL 3 CONTINUED FURTHER ON.)

RULES*
AND
REGULATIONS
OF THE
UNION SOCIETY.
Instituted 1750, Incorporated 1786.

Savannah
PRINTED BY HENRY P. RUSSELL
1822

At a Quarterly Meeting of the **Union Society,** *at the Society's Hall, on Monday Evening, July 10, 1820.*

On motion of STEELE WHITE, Esq. seconded by JAMES MORRISON, Esq. "*Resolved,* That the Secretary be and he is hereby authorized under the direction of the Board of Managers, to have digested, the Rules of the Society, as they now are—and to submit the same to the Society, at the next Quarterly Meeting."

*From a very small pamphlet of twelve pages, of which there are some thirty in our possession.

At a Meeting of the Board of Managers of the Union Society, on Tuesday Evening, Sept. 5, 1820.

The Secretary presented to the Board, a Digest of the Rules of the Society, in conformity with the *Resolution* of July 10th. Whereupon Resolved, that the Arrangement of the Rules this evening presented by the Secretary, be approved; and that the same be recommended to the Society at its next regular Meeting, as its permanent Rules and Regulations.

At a Meeting of the Union Society, on the 23d April, 1821—the same being the SEVENTY-FIRST ANNIVERSARY :—

A Digest of the Rules was presented to the Society, in conformity with the Resolution of July 10, 1820, which was accepted, adopted as the Constitution of the Society, and ordered to be published, with the names of the members belonging to the Institution. And it was requested that each Member should furnish himself with a Copy.

Extract from the Minutes.

LOWELL MASON,
Secretary Union Society.

RULES, &c.

Name and Object of the Society.

RULE 1...This Society shall be known by the name of the UNION SOCIETY. Its object shall be to support and educate Orphan Boys.

Boys to be Bound to the Society by Indenture.

RULE 2...All Boys received upon the bounty of the Society, shall be legally bound to the same by indenture.

Meetings of the Society.

RULE 3...The Meetings of the Society shall be Quarterly, viz. :— on the evenings of the second Monday in July, October, and January; and on the morning of the first Monday in April. Each Member, residing within the limits of the city, shall attend the quarterly meetings; and in default thereof, and on failure to make a satisfactory excuse to the Society, shall be fined in one of the following sums, as the case may be. The President, Three Dollars; the Vice President, Two Dollars and Twenty-five Cents; the Secretary, Two Dollars; the Stewards, One Dollar and Fifty Cents each; and the private Members, Fifty Cents, each, except on the first Monday in April, when the fine of a private Member shall be One Dollar.

Anniversary.

RULE 4... The Anniversary of the Society, shall be celebrated on the twenty-third day of April. annually, except when that day shall come on Sunday, it shall then take place on the Monday following. Previous to every Anniversary, the President shall request some one of the Ministers of the Gospel in the city of Savannah, to deliver an appropriate Sermon, or some Member of the Society to pronounce a suitable Oration on that occasion—after which, the Members of the Society shall dine together. The expense of the Dinner shall be defrayed by the Members who dine ; but shall not exceed Three Dollars each. Any extra expense shall be made up by absent Members; who shall pay a fine of One Dollar and Fifty Cents each, unless excused by the Society ; and if any Member shall invite company to his house, or accept an invitation to dine out on that day, so as to interfere with the arrangements of the Society, he shall pay a fine of Ten Dollars.

Election of Officers.

RULE 5... There shall be annually elected, by ballot, on the Anniversary, from the Members resident in the city. a President, Vice-President, Secretary, and two Stewards. Any person, who upon an election to either of the foregoing offices, declines serving, shall pay one of the following fines, as the case may be :—the President, five dollars; Vice-President, four dollars ; Secretary or Stewards, three dollars each.

Appointment and Duties of a Board of Managers.

RULE 6... The President, elect, shall annually, on the Anniversary, appoint a Board of Managers, to consist of five members of the Society. The President and Vice President shall be members of the board ex-officio, and the Secretary of the Society shall also act as Secretary to the Board. The Board of Managers thus formed shall have full power to transact any business of the Society, for which purpose they shall meet on the first Tuesday of every month.

Duties of the President.

RULE 7... The President shall preside at all meetings of the Society and of the Board of Managers ; he shall preserve order, and in case of an equal division, have the casting vote. He shall also act as Treasurer, and to his keeping shall be committed all monies, bonds, notes and specialties belonging to the Society. He shall annually, on the Anniversary, report to the Society, its progress and the state of its funds. He shall also exhibit his accounts as Treasurer, certified to be correct by a committee of two members of the Society appointed for that purpose at the Quarterly meeting on the first Monday in April.

Duties of the Vice President.

RULE 8...The Vice-President shall perform the duties of the President in case of his absence from the meetings of the Society, or Board of Managers.

A Chairman to be appointed in case of the absence of the President or Vice-President.

RULE 9...In case of the absence of both President, and Vice-President from the meetings of the Society, or Board, a Chairman shall be appointed who shall perform the duties of President for the meeting

Duties of the Secretary.

RULE 10...The Secretary shall notify and attend all meetings of the Society, and of the Board of Managers—keep the minutes and accounts, and perform such other duties as may be required. As a compensation for his services, he shall be allowed the sum of one hundred and fifty dollars, per annum.

Duties of the Stewards.

RULE 11...The Stewards shall attend the anniversary and other meetings of the Society, and provide all necessaries for the same. They shall also perform other duties as the President may require.

Annual Contribution.

RULE 12...Each member of the Society shall annually contribute towards its funds, six dollars,(*) which sum, together with all other amounts due to the Society, shall be paid on the anniversary, or on the quarterly meeting previous thereto.

Admission of Members.

RULE 13....Any person desirous of becoming a member of the Society, shall signify the same by petition addressed to the board of managers, who may admit or reject such applicant as they think proper. Each member on his admission, shall subscribe the rules of the Society, and pay into its funds twenty-two dollars and fifty cents; and also pay to the Secretary seventy-five cents for reading his petition and granting a certificate of membership. But in case the son of a person who has been seven years a member, shall apply, he shall be admitted, on paying one half of the usual sum, with full fees to the Secretary.

*The annual contribution was changed from three to four dollars May 23d, 1808. See Journal 8, folio 131, and previously; also minutes adopted May 23d, 1808.

Resignation of Members.

RULE 14....Any person wishing to resign his membership, **shall** signify the same, in writing, addressed to the board of managers;—but such resignation shall not be accepted, until all demands against the said person have been paid.

Extra Meetings.

RULE 15...Extra meetings of the Society may be called by the President, or in his absence, by the Vice-President;—or in the absence of both, by any five members:—And the fine for non attendance at meetings thus called, shall be the same as at the quarterly meetings.

Common Seal.

RULE 16...The Society shall have a common seal emblematical of the institution.

Funerals of Deceased Members.

RULE 17...The Boys supported on the bounty of the Society, shall attend the funeral of a deceased member of the Society, accompanied by their teacher upon being notified by the Secretary.

Continuation of the Society.

RULE 18...The Society shall continue as long as there shall be three members living;—but in case there shall be but three, they shall have power to dissolve the Society, and to dispose of its funds, to public charitable uses only.

Alteration of these Rules.

RULE 19...These rules shall not be altered but at a regular meeting of the Society, three months notice of such intended alteration having been previously given.

Members of the Union Society.
April 1st, 1822.

Akin, Fleming
Armstrong, James
Bacon, Joseph
Berrien, John M.
Bilbo, James
Bond, Samuel M.
Bolton, John
Brown, Michael
Bruen, John H.
Bulloch, William B.
Bulloch, James S.
Bulloch, John I.
Carnochan, John
Charlton, T. U. P.
Clark, Thomas
Clark, Joseph Hill
Cleland, Moses
Cope, Adam

Habersham, Robt.
Habersham, Joseph
Habersham, Jos. C.
Harden, Edward
Harris, Charles
Hall, Durham T.
Herb, Fred.
Herb, George
Herbert, Moses
Howe, Asahel
Hollis, Silas
Hunter, John
Jones, George
Joyner, Wm. H
Isaac, Robert
Kell, John
Kelsey, Charles
Lawrence, Josiah

Nicoll, John C.
Neff, William
Parker, Wm.
Palmes, George F.
Penfield, Josiah
Petty, L.
Pinder, Jos. W.
Polhill, Thos.
Polock, David
Read, Jas. B.
Reed, Elias
Rees, E. S.
Roma, F.
Roberts, John J.
Rutherford, N. G.
Scott, Jos. A.
Schenk, S. C.
Semmes, Andrew G.

Cope, Geo. L.
Cohen, Isaac
Courvoise, Francis
Crane, John
Cumming, John
Cuthbert, Alfred
Daniel, Wm. C.
Davies, William
De Villers, P.
Densler, Fred.
Eppinger, James
Faries, Geo. G.
Fahm, Jacob
Fell, Fred. S.
Fuerth, L.
Gale, W.
Gaston, Wm.
George, Jos.
Glenn, George
Grant, Joseph
Gray, T. V.
Griggs, Samuel
Gugel, David
Gugel, Daniel
Guerard, Peter
Hayden, C. H.
Habersham, Richd. W

Lewis, John
Leach, B. W.
Lloyd, John F.
Low, Andrew
Low, George
Maurel, Charles
Maxwell, Jos.
Mason, Lowell
M'Henry, James
M'Call, Hugh
M'Allister, Matthew
M'Leod, Donald
M'Leod, Murdoch
M'Nish, John
M'Konkey, D. M.
M'Kinnon, John
Mitchell, Peter
Mitchell, David H.
Miller, Jacob
Miller, John
Miller, Joseph
Morrall, John
Morel, John H.
Morel, Thomas N.
Morel, John
Morrison, James
Nichols, Abraham

Sheftall, Sheftall
Sheftall, Moses
Sheftall, Benjamin
Shellman, Jno.
Shaffer, Jacob
Shick, John
Shad, Solomon
Smith, Archibald
Smith, Wm.
Spencer, Wm. J.
Stone, F. M.
Tattnall, Edward F.
Telfair, Alexander
Thompson, Wm. II.
Tufts, Gardner
Watts, Robert
Wallace, Norman
Wayne, Richard
Wayne, Jas. M.
Wayne, Wm. C.
Welman, F. II.
White, Steele
Williams, S. S.
Williamson, John P.
Wright, Thomas
Young, Thomas

UNION SOCIETY.

INSTITUTED A. D. 1750.

Its Object..............................The Support of Orphan Boys.

QUARTERLY MEETINGS.

On the second Monday in July, at 8 o'clock, P. M.—Fine for non-attendance 50 Cts.
On the second Monday in Oct., at 7 o'clock, P. M.—Fine for non-attendance 50 Cts.
On the second Monday in Jan., at 7 o'clock, P. M.—Fine for non-attendance 50 Cts.
On the first Monday in April, at 10 o'clock, A. M.—Fine for non-attendance 1 Dol.

ANNIVERSARY.

On the 23d. of April, fine for non-attendance 50 Cts. Fine for non-attendance at the Anniversary Dinner, $1.50.

"If any member shall invite company to his house, or accept an invitation to dine out on that day, (the Anniversary) so as to interfere with the arrangements of the Society, he shall pay a fine of $10.—*Extract from Rule 4th.*

Contribution, Six Dollars annually, payable on the first Monday in April.

Boys Supported by the Society, April 24th, 1826.

John Mc'Laggen, aged 14 years, born in Scotland.
Abner Townsend, " " " Georgia.
Lewis Trevoyer, 12 " " "
Samuel R. Buffalo, " " " "
Joseph Wilson, 9 " " New York.
Edwin Wilson, 7 " " "
Robert Trout, 4 " " Georgia.

Members of the Society, April 3, 1826

Anderson, George W
Auze, Joseph
Bulloch, W. B.
Bulloch, James S.
Butler, Thomas.
Charlton, T. U. P.
Clark, Thomas.
Cleland, Moses.
Cope, Adam.
Cope, George L.
Coe, George W.
Cohen, Isaac.
Cooper, Wm.
Cumming, George B.
Cuyler, Wm. H.
Davies, Wm.
Daniel, Wm. C.
Davidson, John.
De Villiers, P.
D'Lyon, Isaac
D'Lyon, Levi S.
D'Lyon, Abraham I.
De Lamotta, J.
Eppinger, James.
Fahm, Jacob
Farles, George G.
Fell, F. S.
Foster, Andrew, Jr.
Fort, Elias.
Gaston, Wm.
Gale, W.
Gray, T. V.
George, Joseph.
Glen, George.
Griggs, Samuel.
Girodon, L.
Gugel, Daniel.
Greene, H. D.

Gordon W. W.
Harris, Charles.
Habersham, E. W.
Habersham, Robert.
Habersham, Joseph.
Habersham, Joseph C
Henry, J. P.
Hartridge, Charles.
Harden, Edward.
Hayden, C. H.
Herb, Frederick,
Higgins, C. A.
Hoyt, C. H.
Helnemann, F. W.
How, S. B.
Jones, George.
Jenner, Wm.
Johnston, George H.
Johnston, James.
Lawrence, Josiah.
Long, John W.
Lamar, G. B.
M'Nish, John.
Mason, Lowell.
Miller, Jacob.
Morel, Thomas N.
Morel, John.
Morel, John H.
Morrison, James.
Myers, M.
Marshall, Wm. P.
M'Intire, Charles.
Nicoll, John C.
Nichols, Abraham.
Parker, Wm.
Palmes, G. I.
Penfield, Josiah.

Petty, L.
Parkman, S. B.
Porter, A.
Read, James B.
Re d, Elias.
Rose, Hugh.
Rutherford, N. G.
Rockwell, C. W.
Shaffer, Jacob.
Sheftall, Moses.
Sheftall, Sheftall.
Sheftall, Benjamin.
Schenk, S. C.
Shellman, John.
Shick, John.
Smith, Archibald.
Scudder, John.
Scudder, Amos.
Sorrel, F.
Stites, E. W.
Stiles, B. E.
Screven, James P.
Tattnall, Ed. F.
Telfair, Alexander.
Thompson, Wm. H.
Waters, John.
Wayne, James M.
Wayne, W. C.
Wallace, Norman.
Welman, F. H.
Williams, S. S.
Williamson, John P.
Williams, Wm. T.
Waldburg, G. M.
Waldburg, Jacob.
Willcox, Jacob.
Young, Thomas.—Total 117

(From Minute Book, 6 qr Medium, opened April 1st, 1828, and continued in use uninterruptedly until the last Anniversary, 1858.)

(From President Nicoll's Report, April 23d, 1828.)

No change in the number of the objects of the bounty of the Society or of their situation has taken place since the last Anniversary—Their number is as was then, six. Their tuition is still received at the Free School, and they continue under the immediate charge of Mrs. Cooper who devotes her attention to them with the same kindness and acceptableness as heretofore.

(The *ordinary* receipts and expenditures per annum at this time appear to have been about $900. Total Receipts this year, with $198:35 balance from last, $2,273:12¼ Total Expenditure, $1,725:93. —balance carried forward to next year $547:19¼.)

(From President 'Nicoll's Report, April 23d, 1829.)

It may however be considered certain, that unless the sources of expenditures be increased, a sum exceeding $1000 will remain on hand at the expiration of the year—It therefore becomes a matter of interesting inquiry whether it be advisable to husband these resources or a portion of them by some profitable investment, or to employ them

108

in the maintenance and education of a further number of objects worthy of charity. Should our funds be applied exclusively to the latter purpose, although the amount of our charity may be immediately increased, it will be so but temporarily, and must from the exhaustion of its means become speedily restricted. The present accumulation of funds, is by no means an indication of continuing prosperity, but is the result of the sale of lands whose proceeds ought perhaps, from the object of their donation, to be converted into a permanent fund for the support of the Society, and the accomplishment of its benevolent designs, which, should those funds be immediately exhausted, will be left to depend entirely upon the contributions of the members, and the contingent and uncertain bounty of future donors. Yet at the same time, in as much as objects whose claims upon the benevolence of the institution may be as strong as those of such as shall at a future period appeal for aid, may present themselves, it might not comport with an enlightened and just charity that those should be entirely postponed for the benefit of others, and the society deny itself the performance of a certain for a future and contingent good. It is desirable therefore, that the Society should indicate its wishes upon the Subject, and what, should it determine upon an investment, shall be its amount and mode.

Sav 23d April 1829   Signed   JNO. C. NICOLL.

(At the 81st Anniversary, April 23d, 1831, after election of officers, Geo. W. Anderson, President, and F. Sorrel, Vice President, the following resolution was unanimously passed.)

RESOLVED That so much of the Constitution as relates to dinner be abolished

(The boys (12) were this year sent to Springfield, Effingham county. See President's Report in 1832.)

(April 23d, 1832; the above resolution, offered by Rev. Mr. White at the last Anniversary, and as amended by Mr. Sorrel, April 2d, 1832, was taken up and passed, as follows :)

RESOLVED that the Constitution of this Society be so amended as to abolish fines for non attendance at the Anniversary dinner and also all fines for Quarterly meetings with the exception of the meeting on the first Monday in April Annually and the anniversary meeting—

The following resolution was offered by Doctor Sheftall as an Amendment to the latter clause of Mr. Sorrel's resolution and was adopted viz

RESOLVED that, the fine for non attendance at the meeting on the first monday in April Annually be one dollar, and for the Anniversary meeting one dollar and fifty cents.

(From Report of President Socrel, April 23d, 1833.)

Our late fellow Citizen, Thomas Young, Esquire, a regretted member of this Society, who died in August last, has by his last will and testament bequeathed to the President and Vice President of the Union Society the sum of 5000$, in Trust, to be invested in Bank Stock, or other securities, at Interest, for the benefit of said Society. The interest accruing thereon only to be used in promoting the benevolent designs of the Institution. The Principal to be kept for ever entire and untouched; It is uncertain when this legacy shall be made available; I have been informed that it may not be before two or three years. The four shares of Exchange Stock owned by the Society having been called in by the City Council for redemption, they were accordingly surrendered and the sum of 7028 received for Principal and Interest.

(At the Anniversary dinner, April 23d, 1833,)

The Following Sentiment was offered by Samuel B. Parkman, Esquire, and adopted as one of the Regular Toasts of the Society, viz:

The Memory of Mordecai Sheftall, Josiah Powell, John Martin & John Stirk, who preserved the existence of this Society with all its rights and privileges, by holding regular meetings and keeping the Anniversaries of the Society, for three years, while detained prisoners of War at Sunbury.

(At an extra meeting of the Board of Managers, July 29th, 1833.)

The President informed the Board that he had summoned them to attend this meeting for the purpose of aiding him by their advice, in properly noticing a donation of 500 Dollars, received from Mr. A. A. Suares, a former pupil of the Society, & who has also requested to be admitted a member of the Institution. Whereupon

The following Resolution was offered by A. Barclay. Esqr., and Seconded by N. Wallace, Esqr.

RESOLVED. That a Committee of Two be appointed of whom the President shall be one, with power to appoint a colleague, to acknowledge the receipt of Mr. Suares' Letter & donation, and forward to him a diploma of Membership for life, neatly framed, and that a time be appointed by said Committee for Mr Suares to sign the Rules & Regulations of the Society.

The President then appointed Anthony Barclay, Esqr., to act with him.

(The following letter was addressed to Mr. Suares.)

SAVANNAH, July 30th 1833

A. A. Suares Esq—

Sir,

The President of the Union Society in this City, having laid before the Board of Managers your letter of the 27th Inst. addressed to him, covering a Donation of Five Hundred Dollars to the Society, requesting to be admitted a member of the same, and desiring to be informed when & where you could subscribe your name; we, the undersigned, were thereupon appointed a Committee, to express to you the sincere thanks of the Society, for your munificent remembrance, and the gratification they will experience in receiving you as a member. For the purpose of enrolling your name, we beg to trouble you, to call at the office of the President, where the Books of the Society are deposited, any morning which may be convenient to you, between the hours of 8 and 9.

The Society feel the greater gratification in accepting and recording this token of your liberality, because they are persuaded the exercise of the emotions of a generous and grateful heart confers the highest happiness on the individual from whom they spring.

In compliance with our instructions, we have the further satisfaction of presenting you a Diploma of membership for life, which will accompany this letter—

We have the honour to subscribe ourselves
Sir, Very Sincerely
Your much obliged &
Most Ob Servants
FRANCIS SORREL
Pres. U. Society.
ANTH'. BARCLAY.

(*From the President's Report, April 23d, 1834.*)

Gentlemen of the Union Society, the past year has been remarkable for some of the most interesting incidents which have ever occurred in the history of the Institution. Mr A. A. Suares now of Louisiana but formerly a pupil of this Society, on a visit to this City last year, presented a donation of $500 in aid of your funds—no circumstance could be more creditable to the Institution, or more honourable to the beneficiary. In his prosperity he has not forgotten the Institution from which he received the education which was the basis of his fortune. At the time of making this liberal donation, Mr Suares requested to be admitted a member of the Society—The Board of Managers wishing to notice in a distinguishing manner this first act of remembrance from a prosperous beneficiary, admitted him, without requiring the payment of the admission money and left him at liberty to pay the annual contribution or not as he might think fit— This being contrary to the Rules & Regulations I respectfully solicit that you will by a special resolution approve & confirm the

14

act of the managers that it may not be availed of as a precedent. The next occurrence is the recollection of this Society by one who, when a resident of this his native city, was foremost in promoting the benevolent designs of this association. John Bolton Esquire of New York, remitted me last fall the sum of 20 $ for the use of the Society— The last incident I shall bring to your notice, and by far the most gratifying, is what you have this day seen and heard— Gentlemen, you have been addressed on the present Anniversary occasion by one who has shared in your benefaction! I shall not enlarge or detain you on this very interesting occurrence—if you feel as I do, & I have no doubt you do, we shall make new resolutions to be more active in promoting the advantages of education to those unfortunate Orphans who are thrown upon our charity, and draw fresh encouragement from the renewed proofs of the blessings, which the Union Society under Providence, has conferred upon the fatherless.

On MOTION of Dr Read, seconded by W B. Bulloch

It was unanimously RESOLVED that for the high gratification which the Society have derived from the celebration of this Anniversary, they are principally indebted to the orator of the day, who, with so much Candour, Simplicity, and eloquence, both by example & by precept illustrated the advantages of the Institution. Whereupon it is moved that the cordial thanks of the Society be presented, with a copy of this resolution, to Colonel Howell Cobb, for the kind feelings which induced him to meet the Society on this day & for his appropriate & Eloquent Oration ; with a request that he will confer a further favour on the Society, by furnishing a copy thereof to be preserved in the Archives of the Society.

On MOTION of Jno C. Nicoll Esqr, seconded by George Jones. It was unanimously resolved That, Colonel Howell Cobb be admitted an Honorary member of the Society.

RESOLVED, that the Report of the President be accepted & the thanks of the Society be presented to him & the Board of Managers for the management of the affairs of the Union Society

RESOLVED that the Act of the Board of Managers, admitting A. A. Suares Esqr a member of this Society for life, as stated by the President in his report this day, in consequence of the very liberal donation made by said Suares to the Society, is highly approved & the same is hereby confirmed.

(The following letter was addressed to Colonel Howell Cobb :)

SAVANNAH, April 23d, 1834.

Col. Howell Cobb—

Dr Sir,

It is my distinguished privilege not less than a deep felt satisfaction to be the organ of the Union Society in transmitting you, herein enclosed copies of resolutions unanimously adopted at a large meeting of the members of that Institution— I beg leave also to hand you a certificate of your Admission as an Honorary member of the Society. Permit me to avail myself of this opportunity to tender you my individual thanks for the gratification I have enjoyed in our short intercourse—The recollection of your visit to this City will frequently recur to my mind with renewed pleasure. Recommending you to the Choicest blessings of a kind Providence, & wishing you a safe Journey back to the bosom of your family—

I remain very respectfully, your obd ser

Signed FRANCIS SORREL, President Union Society.

At the 85th Anniversary, April 23d, 1835.

The following Resolutions were offered by the Rev'd Geo White, seconded by Geo Jones, Esq.

Whereas the Union Society duly values the services of those members who have supported and sustained it when its usefulness has been limited, from lukewarmness or other circumstances, to which all Institutions are liable— And whereas it conceives it a duty which it owes to record its sympathy for the loss of any member who has been active and zealous in its support. Be it therefore unanimously Resolved, that this Society highly appreciates the services rendered by Doct. Moses Sheftall in his life time, and deeply deplores his death— That it entertains for his memory that respect & regard which his zeal & usefulness in acts of charity so fully merit.

Be it further Resolved that his family be furnished with these Resolutions, as evincing the high esteem felt for his memory by the Union Society, of which he was one of the oldest members, and most active supporters.

His Excellency Baron Behr, the Rev Mr Bullinch, Captain Joseph Jones, Mr John Charlton & Doctor James were guests on the occasion & as well as Edward Wilson, a former beneficiary of the Society—

To Sheftall Sheftall Esq—   SAVANNAH May 1. 1835.

Sir, As the organ of the Union Society, it has been made my duty to convey to you, the nearest surviving relative of the late Doct. Moses Sheftall, the annexed Resolutions, unanimously adopted on the last anniversary meeting of the Union Society—In the performance of this act, you will permit me to express my individual sympathy in your bereavement, and the assurance of the high regard I entertain for the memory of the deceased member of our benevolent Institution. That you & his other relatives may long live to enjoy the pleasing reflection that his life was not so long spared in vain, is the wish of your most ob. servant

FRANCIS SORREL
President Union Society.

SAVANNAH Feby 19 1836

To Mr F. Sorrel Treasurer Union Society—
  Dear Sir,

In Accordance with the last request of Mr Robert Cooper deceased I herewith enclose you a Check of this date, on the Bank of the State of Georgia, for Fifty Dollars, as a donation from him to the Savannah Union Society—may I ask an acknowledgement of the receipt of the same

I am respectfully your obdt sevt

Signed   W. E. LONG

SAVANNAH 20th February 1836

Dear Sir,

I have pleasure in acknowledging the receipt of your note of yesterday, enclosing a check on the State Bank for Fifty Dollars for the use of the Union Society, being a donation in accordance with the last request of Mr Robert Cooper deceased

I am Respectfully your obdt sevt

Signed   FRANCIS SORREL
President Union Society

Mr W. E. Long—Savannah

(In December, 1837, the boys were brought from Springfield to the city and placed on board with Mr. John Haupt, whose offer to board, wash and mend for the boys for one year at $125 each was accepted by the Board on the 8th of the same month. They were instructed in the elementary branches of Education at the Savannah Academy under the direction of the Rev. Geo White.)

(*From President Purse's Report, April 23d, 1839.*)

On the 6th November last I received Script for four Shares of the Stock of the Planters' Bank upon which Eighty dollars per share had been paid, from the Widow of the late William M. Evans, of West Chester New York, bequeathed by the deceased to the Society. Mr. Evans was a worthy resident of Savannah some years past and it is grateful to us to know that our institutions are remembered in their after years by those who have made our City their early home—

(At the 90th Anniversary, April 23d, 1840.)
On motion of F Sorrel Esq'r, Seconded by Geo Glen Esq'r

RESOLVED,

That the Secretary be and he is hereby authorized under the direction of the Board of Managers to have digested, the Rules of the Society, as they now are, and to submit the same to the Society at the next annual meeting:—

(*From President Arnold's Report, April 23d, 1841.*)

The boys are still boarded by Mr. Haupt, and I cannot speak too highly of the manner in which they are treated & the excellent discipline they are under— Nor ought I to omit an acknowledgement to Dr. Posey for his kind & gratuitous attention to such of them as have been sick during the past year. They are still under the tuition of the Rev'd Geo White, whose reputation as a Teacher is a sufficient guarantee for their faithful instruction—

(The Secretary in conformity to a resolution passed at the last anniversary, submitted the digested Rules of the Society. It was agreed that the rules submitted should be submitted for action thereon to the next regular quarterly meeting, or to any subsequent quarterly meeting held prior to the next Anniversary.)

(Receipts this year, $1.883.81; Expenditures. $2.095.43; Balance from last year, $260.17; Balance carried to next year, $48.55.)

(The following resolution was passed by the Board May, 1842.)

RESOLVED, that the Secretary make out the accounts against the members, and place all those over twelve dollars, in the hands of Joseph Felt, Esquire, J. P., for collection, by suit *or otherwise.*

(*From President Arnold's Report, April 24th, 1843.*)

The Secretary informs me that owing to deaths resignations & inability to pay, the paying Subscribers of the Society are reduced to between ninety & one hundred— The present salary of the Secretary is one hundred & fifty dollars— It would be well before proceeding to the election of officers, to take into consideration the propriety of reducing this salary.

Previous to the Election of Secretary, it was on motion Resolved That the Secretary's Salary be Seventy-five Dollars per annum

(*From President Cohen's Report, 94th Anniversary, April 23d, 1844.*)

I would recommend a change in our rules so as to admit members without charging an admission fee, & reducing the annual contributions to Five Dollars, which would perhaps induce some of our citizens to add something in aid of a charity so honorable to the giver, so inestimable to the recipient. I would also advise the propriety of taking away the salary from the secretary, & to allow him a per centage on his collections—

The subject of the reduction of the subscription of the members from Six Dollars to Five Dollars was on motion lost.

The subject of the Secretary's salary being now before the meeting— The Secretary stated that he would serve as such Secretary without compensation, provided he had nothing to do with the Collections. & that a Collector be appointed.

On motion, the subject was referred to the Board of Managers with power to act.

From President Cohen's Report, 96th Anniversary, April 23d, 1846.)

Our Society is manifestly on the decline, and unless something is done to resuscitate it, the period cannot be far distant when it will only be reckoned among the things that have passed.

I beg leave to renew my recommendation that the rule requiring a fee of twelve dollars for admission be abrogated. It is an anomaly in charitable societies, and is a great bar to any increase of members.

I would also recommend that the annual subscription be reduced to five dollars, and that a Committee be appointed to endeavour to enlarge our numbers by making personal applications to our fellow citizens—

The finances of the Society are rather in an improving condition By a rigid system of economy in the minor details, and by reducing the annual sum paid for the board and lodging of each boy, from one hundred and twenty-five dollars to one hundred (a saving of twenty five per cent) I have been enabled not only to expend a large sum in the two past years in repairs, painting and papering our houses, but have also been enabled to make an investment of seven hundred dollars in a Bond of the Central Rail Road & Banking Company of Georgia, bearing seven per cent interest.

On motion

RESOLVED.

That Rule 13th of the Bye-Laws be amended by striking out the words "and pay into its funds twelve dollars, and also pay to the Secretary seventy five cents for reading his petition and granting a Certificate of Membership— But in case the son of a person who has been seven years a member shall apply, he shall be admitted on paying one half the usual sum, with full fees to the Secretary" so that the same shall be read *"nothing be paid for admission*

RESOLVED.

That Rule 12th of the Bye Laws be amended by striking out the word "Six" and inserting "five"—

The above resolutions were severally put and adopted.

On motion

RESOLVED, That the President appoint a Committee of Six to endeavour to obtain Subscribers on the new terms.

The President appointed as that Committee the following members, to wit.

Laomi Baldwin
Benjamin Snider
M. Prendergast
Joseph Felt
Jn Murchison
Matthew Hopkins—

(*From President Cohen's Report, 97th Anniversary, April 23d, 1847.*)

So far as the pecuniary affairs of the Society are concerned, I have the pleasure to report, that they are in a healthy and flourishing condition, and refer you for particulars to my account current, a copy of which is hereunto annexed—

＊　　＊　　＊　　＊　　　　　　　＊　　＊　＊

This *lessening* of our members is the more to be regretted from the fact that their places are *not supplied* by new members. This is a melancholy fact, and I fear, too surely foretells the dissolution of our venerable institution—

ON MOTION of Richard D. Arnold, M D, Seconded by John W Anderson Esq

RESOLVED,

That the thanks of the Society be tendered to John F Posey, M D, for his gratuitous medical attendance on the beneficiaries of the Society for the past and several previous years, and for his uniform kindness exhibited towards them.

ALTERATION OF THE BYE-LAWS.

The amendment offered to Rule 13th of the Bye-Laws, proposed at the last meeting, came up for action, and was unanimously adopted.

(*From President Cohen's Report, 99th Anniversary, April 23d, 1849.*)

We have ten beneficiaries on the Society, and I have applications for several more, but do not deem it prudent to increase the number for the present.

This year several new members have been added to our list but, not in sufficient numbers to make up the losses of past years.

100th *Anniversary, April 23d, 1850.*

The Minutes of the last meeting were read and confirmed

A beautiful Box, manufactured from the Live Oak, under which the Charter of the Society was preserved during the occupancy of the City by the British, in the Revolutionary War, was exhibited to the meeting, as a present to the Society from Mrs. Perla Sheftall Solomons, a daughter of (Dr. Moses Sheftall, Pres. Union Society in 1815.)

The President read the Letter making the present.

On motion of Hon John C. Nicoll, seconded by Benjamin Snider Esq'r, the following Resolutions were read and unanimously adopted viz—

RESOLVED That the Union Society accept with great gratification the Valuable present of which they are made the recipients through the kindness of Mr L. Solomons, & will preserve it as a precious memorial of the patriotism & benevolence of the small but noble band whose devotion to this Society was only strengthened & brought into more active exercise by their glorious struggle for their liberties & honors, & by the calamities of captivity.

RESOLVED, That the Secretary communicate to the esteemed donor a copy of the above resolution, together with the cordial thanks of the Society for the cherished relic of which she has made it the depository & guardian—

The President then submitted his Annual Report— viz

REPORT of the President of the Union Society on the Centennial Anniversary

Fellow Members—

One Hundred Years have passed away since the founders of this Society laid the corner stone of the noble charity now committed to your charge. How sacred the trust—how imperative the duty to transmit it to your posterity unimpaired in usefulness—and strengthened by increased means in the power to relieve the distressed—to wipe the tear from the orphan's cheek—to clothe the naked, to feed the hungry, and to instil into the minds of the youthful poor that education & moral culture which may fit them for time & eternity. This day is full of interest to us and may be to the unborn poor and needy through unnumbered years.

Who can calculate the good that has sprung from the dispensation of our charity during the Century that has just closed upon us? Who can tell of the amount of misery and want that has been relieved, of crime prevented?

The past gives food for reflection, but the future is the field for labor. Our ancestors have done well; their charitable deeds have ascended to heaven, a sweet incense to a God of mercy, and it is now left to us to profit by their example, and labor as they labored. The dispensation of charity is one of the most sacred and important duties that devolves on man and the neglect of this duty is treason against Heaven—

Let us then make this the commencement of a new Era—let each of us determine to do more, than merely pay our annual Subscription— Let us determine to double our numbers—this may easily be done with proper exertions, and no one can doubt the propriety of effecting an object so dear to every charitable heart.

This day, so interesting to us as Members of this Society, has been marked by a most agreeable event. Mrs. Perla Sheftall Solomons, a descendant of one of the Founders of this noble Charity, has, through me, presented to the Society a beautiful box made from the Oak under which, in 1779, Mordecai Sheftall, John Martin, John Stirk and Josiah Powell, though Prisoners of War, assembled to celebrate the anniversary of the Society. These were "good men and true"—True to their Country, and amidst the horrors of war, and the pains of imprisonment, still true to those principles of love and charity, which taught them "to love their neighbors as themselves".

*　*　*　*　*　*　*　*　*　*　●

The affairs of the Society may be regarded as in a comparatively prosperous condition, though I am not prepared to say that we can yet extend the sphere of our usefulness—and we surely should so husband our resources, as to meet the increased wants of an increasing population—

The amount of money received from all sources during the past year has been $2488,40, and the amount expended $1841,98—leaving a balance in hand of $646,42, of which I recommend that $500 be invested in a City Bond.

Resolutions read and Adopted
By Joseph S Fay Esq.

RESOLVED, that the report of the President and the accompanying papers, with a statement of the property of the Society, be printed

RESOLVED, that the President & Board of Managers digest & have printed with the President's Report, the Rules of the Society as they now exist, and lay before the Society at a regular or special meeting to be called by the President through the Secretary when prepared to report—

RESOLVED—that the President be requested to add to the pamphlet a synopsis of the History & objects of the Society.

(*From President Cohen's Report*, 101st *Anniversary, April* 23d, 1851.)

With the consent of the Board of Managers I have caused to be built an addition to our building, at an expense of about Twenty Six hundred Dollars, and the present occupant Mr Clarke will, from November next, pay a rent of One thousand Dollars—

At your last annual meeting you directed that the report of the President & accompanying documents, with a statement of the property of the Society should be published, that the rules of the Society should be digested, & prepared for publication, and also a Synopsis of the History and objects of the Society, and the same reported to the Society— All of which I have carefully prepared, and now report the same for your inspection and amendment or approval—

Resolved that the Secretary have printed in Pamphlet form the report of the President, and the accompanying documents, the rules of the Society, and a synopsis of the history & objects of the Society, as reported by the President— (See Rules, &c., below.)

By A. Minis Esq, Seconded by Edward Padelford—

WHEREAS IT HAS BEEN the Will of Providence to remove from us since our last Anniversary the REV'D EDWARD NEUFVILLE, an old and highly esteemed member of this Society, the privilege is claimed to express our sorrow of his loss—

Resolved, that we deeply deplore the demise of the REV'D EDWARD NEUFVILLE, as one who has left a void in almost every sphere of this Community, but particularly in this Society, where his active benevolence was ever found in cheerful co-operation for the cause of the humble & needful orphan—

Resolved, that our sympathy be expressed to the Widow & family of the deceased on this heavy affliction—

Resolved that our appreciation of this late and most excellent member be recorded on the minutes, and a copy of the above be communicated to the relict of the deceased by the Secretary of this Society—

By A. Minis, seconded by A. A. Smets Esq

Resolved that the President & Stewards be authorized to furnish a dinner for the members of this Society, at 4 o'clock, P. M, on the next Anniversary, and that the President & Stewards have authority to invite twenty five Strangers as Guests (no inhabitant save Clergyman), and the same be paid for by Subscription.

RULES AND REGULATIONS.

RULE I.

Name and Object of the Society.

This Society shall be known by the name of the UNION SOCIETY. Its object shall be to support and educate Orphan Boys.

RULE II.

Boys to be Bound to the Society by Indenture.

All Boys received upon the bounty of the Society shall be legally bound to the same by Indenture.

RULE III.

Meetings of the Society.

The Meetings of the Society shall be Quarterly, viz. :—On the second Monday in July, and October, at eight o'clock in the evening; on the second Monday in January, at seven o'clock in the evening; and on the first Monday in April, at ten o'clock in the morning. Each Member, residing within the limits of the city, shall attend the quarterly meetings; and in default thereof, on failure to make a satisfactory excuse to the Society, shall be fined in one of the following sums, as the case may be, to wit—one dollar for default on the first Monday in April, and one dollar and fifty cents for default at the anniversary meeting.

RULE IV.

Anniversary.

The Anniversary of the Society, shall be celebrated on the twenty-third day of April, annually, except when that day shall come on Sunday, it shall then take place on the Monday following. Previous to every Anniversary, the President shall request some one of the Ministers of the Gospel in the city of Savannah, to deliver an appropriate Sermon, or some member of the Society to pronounce a suitable Oration on that occasion.

RULE V.

Election of Officers.

There shall be annually elected, by ballot, on the anniversary, from the members resident in the city, a President, Vice-President, Secretary, and two Stewards. Any person, who upon an election to either of the foregoing offices, declines serving, shall pay one of the following fines, as the case may be: the President, five dollars; Vice-President, four dollars; Secretary or Stewards, three dollars each. That in all elections, a majority of the members present shall be required.

RULE VI.

Appointment and Duties of a Board of Managers.

The President, elect, shall annually, on the Anniversary, appoint a Board of Managers, to consist of five members of the Society. The President and Vice President shall be members of the Board ex-officio, and the Secretary of the Society shall also act as Secretary to the Board. The Board of Managers thus formed shall have full power to transact any business of the Society, for which purpose they shall meet on the first Tuesday of every month.

RULE VII.

Duties of the President.

The President shall preside at all meetings of the Society and of the Board of Managers; he shall preserve order, and in case of an equal division, have the casting vote. He shall also act as Treasurer, and to his keeping shall be committed all monies, bonds, notes and specialties belonging to the Society. He shall annually, on the anniversary, report to the Society, its progress and the state of its funds. He shall also exhibit his accounts as Treasurer, certified to be correct by a committee of two members of the Society appointed for that purpose at the quarterly meeting on the first Monday in April

RULE VIII.

Duties of the Vice President.

The Vice-President shall perform the duties of the President in case of his absence from the meetings of the Society, or Board of Managers.

RULE IX.

A Chairman to be appointed in case of the absence of the President and Vice-President.

In case of the absence of both President, and Vice-President from the meetings of the Society, or Board of Managers, a Chairman shall be appointed, who shall perform the duties of President for the meeting.

RULE X.

Duties of the Secretary.

The Secretary shall notify and attend all meetings of the Society, and of the Board of Managers, keep the minutes and accounts, and perform such other duties as may be required. As a compensation for his services, he shall be allowed the sum of one hundred and fifty dollars, per annum.

RULE XI.

Duties of the Stewards.

The Stewards shall attend the anniversary and other meetings of the Society, and provide all necessaries for the same. They shall also perform other duties as the President may require.

RULE XII.

Annual Contribution.

Each member of the Society shall annually contribute towards its funds, five dollars, which sum, together with all other amounts due to the Society, shall be paid on the anniversary, or on the quarterly meeting previous thereto. Any member resisting the claim of the Society for contributions due, and also does not plead inability to liquidate the same, shall after a copy of this rule has been served upon him, be stricken off the role of the Society as a member.

RULE XIII.

Admission of Members.

Any person desirous of becoming a member of the Society, shall signify the same by petition addressed to the Board of Managers, who may admit or reject such applicant as they think proper. Each member on his admission, shall subscribe the rules of the Society.

RULE XIV.

Resignation of Members.

Any person wishing to resign his membership, shall signify the same, in writing, addressed to the board of managers; but such resignation shall not be accepted, until all demands against the said person have been paid.

RULE XV

Extra Meetings.

Extra meetings of the Society may be called by the President, or in his absence, by the Vice-President, or in the absence of both by any five members.

RULE XVI.

Common Seal.

The Society shall have a common seal emblematical of the institution.

RULE XVII.

Funerals of Deceased Members.

The Boys supported on the bounty of the Society, shall attend the funeral of a deceased member of the Society, accompanied by their teacher, upon being notified by the Secretary.

RULE XVIII.

Continuation of the Society.

The Society shall continue as long as there shall be three members living; but in case there should be but three, they shall have power to dissolve the Society, and to dispose of its funds to public charitable uses only.

RULE XIX.

Alteration of these Rules.

These rules shall not be altered but at a regular meeting of the Society, three months notice of such intended alteration having been previously given.

List of Members on the 23d April, 1851.

Anderson, Geo. W.
Anderson, John W.
Arnold, R. D.
Allen, Robert A.
Bell, David
Battersby, Wm.
Cumming, Geo. B
Cohen, Isaac
Cohen, Solomon
Cohen, Moses S.
Charlton, R. M.
Cuyler, W. H.
Cooper, J. M.
Clark, W. P.
Cumming, M.
Cope, John L.
Davis, W. H.
Dunning, Ralph
Falligant, L. S.
Felt, Joseph
Fay, Joseph S.
Green, Charles
Griffin, R. H.
Habersham, Robert
Hutchinson, Robert
Hartridge, Charles

Hardee, N. A.
Holcombe, Thos.
Knapp, N. B.
King, Wm.
Ladd, J. H.
Low, Andrew
Lawton, A. R.
Locke, J. L.
Lloyd, Thos. E.
Murchison, John
Mercer, Hugh
Mallery, John
Minis, Abram
Myers, Levi J.
Moore, A. K.
Marsh, Mulford
Nicoll, John C.
Norris, Jas. A.
Nevitt, J. W.
Neyle, G. N.
Olmstead, Jas.
Potter, James
Potter, Thos. F.
Padelford, Edward
Purse, Thomas
Palmes, Geo. F.

Reynolds, L. O.
Russel, W. S.
Sorrel, Francis
Smets, A. A.
Solder, Benjamin
Solomons, A. A.
Shaffer, Geo. W.
Stewart, Danl. H.
Turner, Thos. M.
Turner, Jos. M.
Van Horn, Charles
Wallace, Norman
Willink, H. F.
Waldburg, Geo. M.
Waldburg, Jacob
Williamson, John
Washburn, Joseph
Wilson, Edward G
Wadley, W. M.
Walker, Robt. D.
Williams, S. B.
Williams, Wm.
Wayne, Richard
Wright, Allen E.
Yonge, W. P.

(In published proceedings the President stated.)

Being directed by resolution to add to the pamphlet, "A synopsis of the History and Objects of the Society," I have deemed it best to republish the following from an Oration delivered before the Union Society in April, 1833, by the Rev. WILLARD PRESTON.

(Instead of the extract only, the whole address is here given.)

AN ORATION

DELIVERED BY THE REV. WILLARD PRESTON

Before the Union Society in Savannah, 23d April, 1833, being its Eighty-Third Anniversary.

Within the last fourteen months we have been convened on two centennial occaisons: one to commemorate the nativity of him who, under God, was the Father of his Country; the other to celebrate the landing of the Founder of this State—epochs in the history of both, of proud and inspiring recollection to the citizen and the soldier; and the events and incidents associated with each occasion, were recounted with an ability and celebrated with a splendour, which will long perpetuate a vivid recollection of them. Far different is the occasion which convenes us to-day; while even the hope is not entertained of awakening equal interest, much less of affording equal gratification. The present anniversary occasion admits, indeed, of an extended retrospect. The next epoch, (for it merits that designation,) in fair and hopeful prospect, on the list of centennial distinction in this place, is the origin of that society which celebrates to-day its eighty-third anniversary. But that retrospect embraces few or no incidents to gratify the fancy, to excite curiosity or command the applause of the world. It awakens no thrilling recollections of daring deeds or splendid achievements; points to no battle fields, where, on the issue of contending armies, was suspended the reign of despotism or the triumphs of freedom: such as were the attractions which the revolving years of a century had been gathering around the hallowed spot where was presaged a nation's birth, in that of her WASHINGTON; or the charms which, for a like period, had been clustering about the first footsteps, on the banks of your Savannah, of the first warrior-patriot, the venerated OGLETHORPE.

We can summon no such attractions, no such charms, about us to-day.

This Society, too, has its monuments; but not those monuments which patriotism rears to the valor of the Hero, or the wisdom of the

Statesman, which are seen & felt in the freeest and happiest form of human governments : nor yet such as are witnessed in the transforming power of civilization, turning the wilderness into a fruitful field ; erecting habitations of social order and happiness, where once stood the Indian wigwam, and temples of worship and justice, and science on spots where burned the council fires of savage warriors ; and the bustle and thrift of a commercial city, where lately roamed the wild beasts of the forest.

These, truly, are noble monuments ; monuments of liberty, of patriotism, of enterprize, of civilization over barbarism, of freedom over oppression. But the institution in whose behalf I address you, has none of these ; yet it has claims—noiseless, but powerful, as that benevolence on which it is founded—unostentatious, but urgent as that charity which it administers.

Its achievements consist in rescuing the *mind* from the worst of despotisms—the cruel, degrading, *withering* grasp of *ignorance* ; in training it to effort and to useful enterprise ; in rescuing the child of misfortune from the deep and overwhelming, and but too often demoralising and ruinous depressions of poverty, and consequently, relieving the widow from those burdens which often sink her to an untimely grave. In a word, in training to habits of industry & virtue, and furnishing the means of useful and respectable employment, and even of eminent standing in society, to those, many of whom might otherwise become the inmates of your poor-house, your hospital, or your prison. Such are the efforts which this Society has put forth for more than three-quarters of a century. Such the monuments which have been rising and annually multiplying during three generations. Such the achievments which its munificence has, in unnumbered instances, effected. Monuments of mind, the achievements of knowledge over ignorance, of industry over idleness, of liberal charity over squalid poverty, of active, systematic benevolence over the lowest depths of human misery. Let the marble and the brass record the deeds of others, be these trophies the mementos rather of my life ; these shall live when those shall have crumbled into dust ; shall be told, when the last historian shall have laid aside his pen, and the chisel shall have forever fallen from the grasp of the sculptor. But the best commentary on those institutions which have their origin in an enlightened and liberal charity, is their permanency ; and the best eulogium which can be pronounced upon them is the good which they have been the means of effecting. These are both the tests and the proofs of their excellence, and they furnish the best and strongest claims to public patronage. Associations of a benevolent character have often suddenly risen into being, and almost as suddenly expired. The chief incident in their history was the simple record of their birth, having been left to expire without even an obituary notice. Much of the benevolence of the world is of that fantastic character which can pity and shed tears and recommend relief, but adopts no measures to alleviate distress. This may be denominated the benevolence of poetry—mere fancy, mere fiction. There is another department of it which confines its sensibilities, and of course, limits its charities to present objects of wretchedness. Its views do not reach to coming generations; nor does it consult the permanent good of its objects, pursues no plan of systematic effort; bestows without wise and prudent discrimination, and is satisfied with administering momentary relief. This may be denominated a secular benevolence. This is characteristic of those who either have no leisure or inclination to seek out the objects of their charities, or devise measures for their permanent good. But true benevolence does not consist in a mere paroxism of feeling, however violent or tender, which expends itself in the heaving of a sigh or the shedding of a few tears, or in sudden bursts of pity; nor in a single effort, however well applied or successful. It looks to future results. It contemplates its objects in relation to their future benefit and their eternal destination, and aims at the greatest amount of attainable good; and to secure this there must be systematic action, combined effort and untiring perseverance. And when an institution possesses these characteristics, believe me, there is a spirit of liberality which lies deep, but beats strong in the bosom of an enlightened community, on which the claims of a generous patronage are never urged in vain—and in the confidence that these positions will be amply sustained by the history of the Union Society, I am myself sustained in addressing you on this occasion.

Unfortunately, the records of this Society have not been preserved entire. Large portions of them have been destroyed, particularly such as were made previously to the summer of 1782; when the British army evacuated this city, the records of this Society shared the fate of every thing else which possessed value, in the wanton destruction which that army caused; nor from that period till 1791, are there either printed or written documents, of which the speaker is aware, to show the operations or state of this Society. A chasm, therefore, of forty-one years, remained to be supplied from traditionary information, and occasional references to transactions during that period, found in the records of a subsequent date. This information, however, it is believed, is entitled to the credit of historical facts, from the consideration that it comes from some of the oldest and most active members of the Society, the immediate descendents of no less active members, whom a kind Providence has yet spared from the infirmities and ravages of numerous years : and to whom, for the information they have communicated, I take pleasure in thus publicly expressing my grateful acknowledgements. If these facts shall possess interest, the labor of no little research will be amply repaid.

The Society which celebrates to-day its eighty-third Anniversary, was, of course, founded in the year *one thousand seven hundred and fifty;* thus possessing a veneration for the antiqity of its origin, which no other institution in this State can boast, or of a similar character, which few, if any, in much older settled portions of our country can claim. This alone constitutes a bright feature in an institution of enlightened and liberal charity ; the more worthy of admiration from the fact, that its origin was nearly contemporaneous with the existence of Georgia as a colony, being but seventeen years subsequent to the first visit of Oglethorpe, and at a period of peculiar embarrassments. With most men thus circumstanced, the common maxim of the world, in its most restricted sense, would have possessed a sovereign and an omnipotent force, that *Charity begins at home.* Though in the very infancy of their settlement, when personal protection from savage foes, and the supply of present and pressing wants, might reasonably have been presumed to have excluded from their calculations and their thoughts, objects of charity, which future and far distant generations might furnish ; yet *with these men*, charity was not a mere *domestic.* It was too diffusive and too strong to be the fondly cherished nursling of their own bosoms. It could do more than pity the misfortunes and weep at the woes of others. While it had a voice to speak and say to the naked and the hungry, *Be ye clothed and be ye fed*, it had a hand to act and furnish the garments and spread the board. Theirs was a charity, which sought for its objects, and when found, took them in charge ; a charity which, while it relieved the wants of the body, made provision for the cultivation of the mind ; and which extended its views to future generations, and adopted a system of benevolence for the benefit of unborn orphans, doomed to indigence. But who were these men? These acts have reared monuments to their enlightened patriotism and their active benevolence. But on these monuments should be inscribed their *names.* They should be enrolled on the fairest page of the records of this Society —be deposited in its archives. Every beneficiary should be taught to pronounce them with respect and affection. They should find a place in every anniversary address. We have carefully searched those records, but found them not there. We have minutely surveyed those monuments, but found no inscription, save the deep bright lines of their charity, without a signature to tell the hand which first engraved them. Tradition, however, has happily rescued some of them from oblivion; they were, originally, five in number. We deeply regret we can give the names of only three of them—BENJAMIN SHEFTALL, PETER TONDEE and RICHARD MILLEDGE.

With an institution bearing so high an origin, and without official records of its commencement and early operations, it might be expected that much of fiction would be connected. But so far as pretended tradition has associated with its origin incidents which detract from its character as a charitable and most laudable institution, careful inquiry has produced a full conviction that they have no foundation in truth. The character of its early members as given in the history of this State, (and the character of many of them is given in terms of the highest commendation,) would, indeed, be sufficient to disprove their claim to credit. None have stood higher, in this, or any other community, than many who have been members and warm patrons of this Society. Many of them have received the highest honors of their State and country, and occupied places of no less distinction in the church.

But we do not rely wholly on the evidence which these facts afford: this evidence is confirmed by direct and positive assurances, in relation to the circumstances of its commencement.

In the year 1750, there was a society in this place, composed of Scotch emigrants, the particular objects of which are not known to the speaker; but probably combining entertainment and charity. It was, however, too exclusive and national in its character, to admit as members, those not of the same extraction. This circumstance first gave rise to what was termed a club; a term, by the way, which according to the popular vocabulary of our day, has somewhat depreciated in its meaning, from its ancient usage. This club was composed of the five gentlemen to whom allusion has been made. They proposed, for its leading object, the education of orphan children, in indigent circumstances. For the purpose of raising the means, each member was required to contribute two pence, weekly. This was, indeed, a small beginning. But a very few years showed that they had no occasion to *despise the day of small things*. And it is here worthy of remark, that it is agreeable to the history of most charitable institutions, that those have grown to the greatest importance, and been the most permanent and useful, whose beginnings were small. It seems to be a general law, as applicable to societies as to the productions of nature herself, that what is rapid in its increase, soon reaches its growth, and of course is soon on the decline. Large subscriptions and donations, in the outset, (unless to secure some specific object,) have generally proved injurious and often fatal, especially to those charitable institutions which were intended to benefit future generations : their permanence and success depend on the constant application of means, while rich endowments often serve only to relax and paralyze effort. Gradual success alone keeps up vigilance and exertion. Apprehension of failure and hope of success, when properly balanced, constitute the mainspring to benevolent enterprises. Mankind require the stimulus of a constant and a pressing necessity. The terms of membership, however, were gradually increased, when in 1793, they were £5. 5s. and the following year the sum of $3 was levied as an annual tax upon each member towards the funds of the Society. In 1795 the tuition of about thirty scholars was paid by this Society, which then consisted of sixty-six members.

It has been an object of careful examination to ascertain the full amount of the receipts and expenditures of this Society, from its origin to the present anniversary. Accuracy could not be reached. But from annual reports since 1791, and other data, it cannot have fallen short of $70,000 ; about $40,000 of which have been expended for the education of orphan children. About $10,000 is vested in real estate, in the condition of productive funds.

But it is proper here to remark, that the bounties of this Society have not been exclusively appropriated to educational purposes. Donations have been made to a large amount to other benevolent objects ; the Poor House, the Hospital, and the Female Asylum have shared largely in its munificence, as well as individuals, particularly widows in necessitous circumstances. Many losses have been sustained, but in most instances they were in consequence of that benevolence which prompted this Society to make loans in aiding mechanics at the commencement of business, but who were unable to reimburse them. The full amount, therefore, of the receipts of this Society, has been expended for charitable purposes. Its riches have consisted, emphatically, of good deeds, liberal charities and bountiful alms. Little has been appropriated to defray incidental expenses ; these have been paid by a contribution of its members. It has had no salaried officers. For the first forty-five years, its Secretary, notwithstanding the duties of that office were far from light, and attended with no inconsiderable expense, received no compensation ; and from that time but $60 per annum, till 1816, when it was increased to $150, the present salary. We are thus minute to show that the internal operations of this Society have been in perfect character with the noble objects for which it was instituted. It originated in charity, and it has been conducted on the same disinterested principle. It has also been an object of no less strict inquiry to ascertain the number of the beneficiaries of this Society: but exactness here could not be attained. There are, however, data from which an estimate may be formed of considerable accuracy, agreeably to which the number cannot fall short, it is believed, of nine hundred. In some years, committees appointed to ascertain proper objects for receiving the charities of this Society, reported that not an individual was found who was not then receiving them. Such a report was made as late as 1807, notwithstanding the increased population of this city. In 1811, the number of boys was twenty-five. It is proper also to remark, that formerly, no distinction was made between male and female orphans: both received assistance as necessity required. This continued till the institution of the Female Asylum in the year 1801; when, after making a liberal donation to that institution, its bounties were exclusively applied to the education and entire support of boys. These, as they completed their course of instruction, have, since the year 1795, been bound, to express it in the words of the ordinance which required it, to some "useful trade, occupation, profession or calling." The course of instruction has been unusually liberal under such circumstances. It has not been restricted to those branches which are indispensable to the ordinary pursuits of life, but in many instances it has embraced the classics, and laid the foundation for the liberal professions, upon which some have entered. With the character of not a few of them, as they have risen to manhood and discharged the duties of citizens and of social life, many of you are acquainted.

At what time this club, as it was at first called, was regularly organized into a Society, it does not appear; but it was not long after its origin. Its first President has not been ascertained. Its first Secretary was PETER GANDY, a teacher of youth. The title it assumed, when organized, was the ST. GEORGE'S SOCIETY. Hence its anniversaries have always been held on the twenty-third of April, the kalendar day of the canonization of the tutelar Saint of England. In 1786, it was incorporated by an act of the Legislature of this State, by the title of "THE UNION SOCIETY," the President of which at that time, was WM. STEPHENS, Esq. The relinquishment of its old name, it is believed, was a matter of patriotic feeling; the assumption of its new one, was an expression and a proof of a liberality of sentiment and feeling most honorable to its early associates; the Society embracing gentlemen of *five distinct religious denominations.* Distinctions of faith were here laid aside, when so noble an object for combined effort was presented, which would at once test the sincerity, at least, of their respective abettors. Such differences, instead of preventing, should provoke to holy emulation, and invite to cordial co-operation in enterprises of benevolence.

There is one provision in the Constitution of this Society which, as connected particularly with a portion of its history, deserves special notice, viz: that the existence of this Society, with all its rights and privileges, should be continued, on condition that any three of its members should hold regular meetings and observe its anniversary occasion. Twenty-eight years after its formation, this provision saved the Society from extinction. On the defeat of the American army in this city, in December of 1778, and Sunbury, a town on the seaboard, forty miles south of this city, had fallen into the possession of the British troops, several members of this Society, with others, were put on board of a prison-ship. But those who were officers in the American army, were subsequently sent, on their parole, to Sunbury. Among these were four members of this Society, viz: MORDECAI SHEFTALL, JOHN MARTIN, JOHN STIRK, and JOSIAH POWELL. They were there detained more than three years, during which time they observed the meetings and kept the anniversaries of this Society; at the first of which, MORDECAI SHEFTALL was chosen President. On that occasion, several of the officers of the British army joined in the celebration and furnished the entertainment. The sentiments which were given on that occasion, equally express the noble and honorable feeling of both parties. The first by a member of this Society was, "*The Union Society;*" the second by a British officer, "*General George Washington,*" which was responded to with equal magnanimity by an American officer, "*The King of Great Britain.*" These gentlemen thus preserved its existence, in consequence of which it afterwards secured much of the property which had been leased or loaned to individuals. To these gentlemen, therefore, under the circumstances in which they were placed, not less than to the original founders of the institution, many hundreds and probably thousands of destitute orphan children, have been and will be indebted to an immense amount of gratitude. Had this Society at that time become extinct, in all probability under the increased embarrassments of that period, it had never been revived. The happy results of its continuance, both to individuals and to the community, on the one hand, and the sad consequences which would have followed its extinction, on the other, who can estimate or conceive? An institution, that, as it were, creates and multiplies and extends benefits and blessings which but for its existence had never been known is a noble institution. But when without such an institution, the necessary alternative had been positive detriment to a whole community, and personal wretchedness to hundreds of individuals, it possesses an importance beyond all estimation and praise; and just such is "*The Union Society.*"

In the examination which it became necessary to make of the records of this Society, I may be permitted to express the very high satisfaction derived from a knowledge of many of its regulations. They attach to it a moral and religious character, which claims for it the unqualified approbation and cordial support, of the religious part of the community, as well as of society in general—regulations adopted at an early period of its existence, and probably at its commencement. Of this nature are such as require those who are under the care of this Society to attend public worship, as it is expressed, both parts of the Sabbath, (under the special charge of their teacher) and when Sabbath-schools were established, to become members of those important institutions. The morals of those youths were guarded with parental and christian care, and books, specially designed and calculated to promote their moral and religious improvement, were recommended and procured by this Society. And all the rules adopted by the Society for the regulation of its own members, show a high regard to moral and religious obligations.

Such are some of the interesting facts connected with the history of the Union Society, and such the claims which it presents to the unqualified approbation and liberal patronage of an enlightened and religious community. The highest commendation which can be bestowed upon it, and the strongest motive to public patronage which can be urged, is the simple statement of its object and its operations. And this must be my apology for having indulged in so many minutiæ in addressing you on this occasion. But although you have already indulged me with your attention beyond the ordinary length of an address on such occasions, yet, at the hazard of a trespass on your patience I shall venture to say more. This is no ordinary occasion; it is the anniversary of a Society of no ordinary character : an association for no ordinary purposes; it embodies principles and motives, and involves objects and results of incalculable importance. What is there that is dearer to the citizen, the neighbor, the friend, the patriot, the philanthropist, the christian, which forbids fellowship of feeling, which does not demand co-operation of effort in promoting the objects of this Society. Had one doubt existed in the mind of the speaker on this subject, another's voice had been heard to-day, or this anniversary had passed in silence. Or, were the object of this So-

ciety merely secular in its character, he would have used his little
influence against unfolding the doors of this sanctuary for this occasion. But it is one for which all the churches in this city have been
repeatedly opened, and the charities of the respective worshippers in
them been solicited by the ministers at their altars. Religion herself is not exclusively confined, either in her motives or principles of
action, to the interests of another world. She draws, indeed, from thence
her highest sanctions, but those sanctions are designed and calculated to
influence and promote the temporal welfare of mankind. She is fitted
to preside over all her interests. In her obligations the binding force
of all other obligations is to be sought, and is alone to be found. One
grand principle, supreme love to God! should prompt to every enterprise and every action. It overlooks no duty which results from all
that variety of relations which men sustain to each other here; but
the actions to which it prompts are often limited in their immediate
results to this life. All those objects, therefore, whose promotion
conduces to the best temporal good of individuals or Society, fall
within the legitimate province of the Christian religion, and all the
solemn weight of her holy sanctions bears directly upon them. What
a field then, is thrown open before us, from which to gather arguments
in support of the objects of this Society. What a variety and an array of motives which press the obligations of a warm and liberal patronage. Temporal and eternal interests are here combined; not, indeed, inseparably, for men can form no such bond, but hopefully and
intimately. Let us take a closer inspection.

This Society, in the prosecution of its benevolent purposes, pro-
motes the respectability, the usefulness, and the happiness of those
who are the objects of its benefactions. On this point we could give
you the united testimony of its nine hundred beneficiaries, with the
corroborating declarations of the community in which they have lived,
abating those only who in despite of all that human benevolence could
do for them, perverted its bounties and became moral suicides. A few
such there may have been. It is true that the opposites of these
traits of character or conditions of life are not the necessary results
of poverty. On the contrary, some of the greatest benefactors of the
human race, and the very salt of the earth, have had their origin and
spent their lives in the lowest depths of poverty. But it is not on
this broad ground we now place this subject. What is the testimony
of the general community? What the voice of strong probability in
relation to those children who are orphans in indigence. And such
are the sons, by adoption, of this Society, without whose parental
supervision and support they must necessarily grow up in igno-

rance and, without an interposing miracle of grace, in vice. Why should they not? Even honest ignorance is unfavorable to virtue. It leads to idleness, idleness to vice, and vice abandons to ruin; and this ruin finds its consummation, but too often, in the future destination of the lost soul. Against such a result, this Society, to say the least, rears a strong barrier. It snatches the child of misfortune from the precincts of vice; rescues it from the overpowering influence of a thousand temptations; instructs it, places it within the direct influence of motives to virtue, trains it to habits of industry, of social order, and of enterprise; and entrusts it to the immediate guardianship of those who are bound, by the force of their own moral and religious principles, as well as the obligations imposed by this Society, to give it an education which an enlightened and religious community shall approve. What is the hopeful if not certain result of all this? You at least save the individual from the degradation of ignorance and almost inevitable vice, relieve a widowed mother from an insupportable burden, prevent a pest or a nuisance to society, and hopefully save an immortal being from future and endless ruin. Were this negative good all that this Society achieved, who would not commend and patronise it? But this negative good is necessarily connected with positive benefits. If you rescue from ignorance, you enlighten; if you save from vice, you render virtuous; if you relieve the widow of a burden you afford her a support; if you prevent a pest or a nuisance to society, you bless society with a useful and active member; and if an immortal being be saved from endless ruin, that being secures immortal glory. Within this short compass, there are embodied all those motives which can be conceived to exert an influence on those who feel themselves responsible, as citizens, as neighbors, as friends, as patriots, as philanthropists and christians; and which of them has not a direct bearing on the objects of this society? The feelings of true benevolence are kindred and social in their nature, and the circle of their influence is limited only by the objects which can be promoted by the efforts of those who possess them. In their nature they grasp a world, while in their operation they are necessarily limited to objects within their reach. Here then is another principle on which this Society founds a claim to the patronage of those who are able to yield it. For it is the same feeling, so far as it is a benevolent one, which prompts to the proper education of an orphan child, that would send the Gospel to a distant heathen. The objects of this Society are benevolent, and we appeal to benevolence for their support; and the same benevolence, too, which, were it within its influence, would bless a world with

moral and spiritual light, and restore its inhabitants to social order
and to happiness. But in whatever point of view we contemplate this
Society, even though it were exclusive of that distinguishing benevolence which characterizes the christian, if we look at it as citizens, as
philanthropists, or as patriots, it is one of the noblest monuments of
an enlightened and liberal charity, which this or any other State can
boast. You have, indeed, a proud monument erected to deeds of
valor and heroism, in the heart of your city. But the fruits of the
munificence dispensed by this Society, constitute a far nobler one,
set up in many a grateful human hearts—a monument which, instead
of being impaired by the revolutions of years, is constantly increasing
in splendor, and to which every beneficiary who fulfils the just expectations of his benefactors and the public, will be an additional ornament. This should stimulate those youths who are now enjoying
the liberal bounties of this Society—and whom I have the pleasure
to see before me, to prosecute their studies with the utmost diligence;
to form and establish habits of industry; to imbibe and cherish the
sacred principles of rigid morality and pure religion. Do not forget
it my young friends; your prosperity, respectability, usefulness and
happiness depend on your possession of these qualities. While your
possession of them is all the remuneration which this Society asks
or can desire for its care and solicitude and liberality in your
behalf. But however rich an ornament this Society is to this city
and county in which it is established, it is not as citizens within
these limits merely, that its importance is to be estimated by you; it
is intimately associated with the noblest institutions of the State.
What legitimate object of patriotism is there to which it does not
contribute? It increases her wealth; the wealth of a virtuous population, of enterprizing citizens, of industrious members of Society, of
firm supporters of her civil and her religious institutions—a wealth,
compared with which her mines of gold are tinsel and are dross. It
may furnish (why not?) ornaments in the learned professions, heroes
in the field, and champions of her rights in her halls of legislation.
Such things have been, such things now are, and why may they not
be again? We could read to you a long catalogue of names, high
on the list of distinction, in every State in the Union, and on both
sides of the Atlantic, of men born in indigence and educated by
charity. Talents are not confined to the rich. Distinction is not the
necessary consequence of high or noble birth. Rather, oft times, to
these different conditions of men, the God of nature seems to have
assigned endowments and defects to equalise their states. But to
whom belongs the high honor of rescuing them from their obscurity?

of bringing them forth to light, to usefulness and distinction? under God, to their benefactors—to the patrons and to the members of the Union Society. These are deeds which claim for you, gentlemen of this Society, the affectionate regard of your adopted sons: which bespeak for you the gratitude of many an unborn orphan, which ensures to you and yours, the prayers and blessings of many a widowed mother—deeds which demand the grateful acknowledgments of your State, and the high commendation of your country; and which entitle you to distinction among patriots, philanthropists and the benefactors of mankind. But while these are your honors, most solemn are your responsibilities; you have immortal as well as temporal interests confided to you—you are guardians of orphans. To train up children for God, to render them good citizens, is but half your work, and should be far less than half your aim. Let it be your high and holy purpose to secure the reward of another life; then receive the approbation of your final Judge, and in that last of days, when these and all your deeds shall be reviewed, and your eternal state shall be adjudged, may it be your unspeakable privilege to say—"here Lord are we, and the children Thou gavest us," and receive for yourselves the richest of all gratuities—the gift of God, which is eternal life—through Jesus Christ, Our Lord.

(*From President Cohen's Report*, 102d *Anniversary, April 23*, 1852.)

The addition to that wing of the Academy belonging to you is now completed, and the rent is increased to One Thousand Dollars per annum, from the first of November last. The cost of the addition was three thousand two hundred & eighty 35-100 dollars, which has been paid in full, though the Society is indebted for the sum of one thousand dollars, balance of money borrowed to pay the builder. The whole, however, I think will be paid in the ensuing year.

*　　　*　　　　*　　*　　*　　*　　*　　*　　*

Resolutions read and unanimously adopted.

By Joseph S. Fay Esq.,

Seconded by Edward Padelford Esq.

RESOLVED, That in the death of Benjamin Snider Esqr., this Society has experienced the loss of one of its most zealous and interested members, which is deeply to be deplored.

RESOLVED, That while we would express our sincere regret for the vacancy thus created in our number, we would offer our sympathy to his widow & family, to whom the Secretary is requested to communicate these resolutions.

*　　*　　*

By Thomas Purse Esqr, seconded by David Bell Esq.

RESOLVED, that the President, Vice President and Board of Managers, be authorized to improve Lot No 2 and East half of Lot No 3, Percival Ward, with brick buildings, if in their judgment the interests of the Society would be thereby promoted, and that they be authorized to apply the money at interest, and sell such stocks as may be needed for the purpose.

By A. Minis Esq., seconded by Jos S. Fay Esq.

RESOLVED, that the President and Board of Managers should unite in an application to our member of Congress representing this District, to procure the appointment of a Cadet at West Point or a Warrant as midshipman in the Navy, should at any time one of our beneficiaries incline to either of these professions.

(*From President Cohen's Report*, 103d *Anniversary, April 23*, 1853.)

You have at present on your bounty only eleven boys, but as you are now free from debt, and will have a greatly increased revenue you may extend the sphere of your usefulness.

The receipts from all sources during the past year, including a balance of $28.45, amount to......................................$3015. 63
of which there has been expended for ordinary

    expenses $1909. 02
Extraordinary　"　.............................. 1065. 03
leaving a balance of................................. 71. 58 3045. 63

The extraordinary expenses consist exclusively of the sums paid for the addition to the Academy, the rent of which, I presume, will be increased at the expiration of the present lease.

I think your means may be greatly increased by looking after the vacant lands in this County. I have conferred with Mr. William Hughes on this subject, and herewith submit his offer.

In conclusion, I will add, that it is impossible for me to continue longer as the President of this Society. I have had the office for ten years—more than double the term of service of any of my predecessors,—during which time, by rigid economy and minute attention to details, I have freed the Society from debt, and have added to your capital (including the sum invested in the addition to this building) Five thousand Dollars.

I do not mention this in a boastful spirit, but simply to render a final account of my stewardship.

Respectfully submitted,

SOLOMON COHEN,

President

Savannah 22 April 1853.

LIST OF ASSETS

belonging to the Union Society and delivered by Solomon Cohen, President, to his successor.

Note of Henry Dittmers, secured by mortgage, for		$3000
" " Judge Fleming ditto		1000
Scrip No. 3014 for 6 shares Planters Bank $100		600
" " 237 " 4 " " " 80		320
" 2000 " 18 " " " "		1140
2080 " 2 " "		160
2078 " 20 "		1600
173 " 30 Central Rail Road		3000
" 1807 " 6 "		600
" 12 " 7 " Preferred Stock		700
No. 61 Bond of the City of Savannah		500
		$12,920

Lease of the Academy to W. P. Clark, at $1,000 per annum. Lease expires 1st Nov., 1853.

The three small tenements on York street, west of the 2d Baptist Church, are rented as follows:

To Stephen Cubbedge, at $100; on the 1st May he will owe one quarter, viz.	$25 00
To C. A. Magill, at $175; on the 1st May he will owe two quarters	87 50
To John Sherlock, at $175 per annum; on the 1st April he owed three quarters	131 25
On the 1st May Mr. Clark will owe one quarter	250 00

Mr. Starr leases the Lot on which he lives at $50 per annum, payable 4th December, March, June and September. He has paid in full to March.

SAVANNAH, May 11, 1852.

Solomon Cohen, Esq

Dear Sir,

I am willing to ferret out, survey and make plots of the vacant lands to which Chatham Academy and the Union Society are entitled, for twenty-five dollars on every hundred acres. I would be unwilling to undertake for less, as I know the many difficulties I shall have to encounter, and obstacles to surmount. I am willing to sell these lands, as fast as located, at 2½ per cent commissions, the agents of the above named institutions executing titles. In undertaking as proposed, I must be allowed the liberty of employing one or more deputies.

Yours, with respect,

WM. HUGHES

Resolutions read and adopted unanimously.

*   *   *   *   *   *

By Joseph S. Fay, Esq.,

Seconded by Col. Noah B. Knapp.

RESOLVED

That the Report of the President has been heard with pleasure and accepted.

RESOLVED

That the thanks of this Society are due to the late President for the zealous and skilful attention he has bestowed upon the affairs of the Society—creditable to him and a good example to his successors.

(Mr. Edward Padelford was elected President—resigned May 11, and Joseph S. Fay, Esq., elected President.)

(104*th Anniversary, 23d April*, 1854.

*   *   *   *   *   *   *   *   *

The President stated that it was the intention of the Stewards to meet this day at 9 o'clock, and adjourn for recreation at the 45 mile station, C. R. R., but Mr. Fillmore's arrival had prevented the arrangements from being completed.

(*From the President's Report.*)

The Children have enjoyed good health, and are well attended to and cared for by Mr. Haupt, but it seems to me that their education does not progress much, and the general system so far kept up by the Society is not such as I approve, as calculated to do much effectual or practical good. The Children are well maintained, and suffer in no way, but they do not make that progress in intellectual or moral attainments that it should be our aim to have them do. It has seemed to me that some plan could be devised by which they could partially support themselves, and receive a closer supervision and more thorough teaching.

I would recommend the purchase of a place, not too remote or inaccessible, where the President, the Board of Managers, and even the members could and would often visit them, and overlook their condition; where they could practice gardening and various other employments conducive to their comfort, health and support, and where they could have a teacher devoted to them exclusively, who would not only instruct them in school hours, but supervise them at other periods. It seems to me that this would cost no more, or if it did, a larger benefit could be derived to the boys—and certainly if a greater outlay were required, a greater number of children could be educated and prepared for the active business of life, without a corresponding increase of expense.

We now expend $2,200 (about) per annum, for fifteen boys; for double the number, in the way suggested, probably not over one half as much more expense would be incurred. It seems to me that our income could be enlarged to meet any increased expense, by additional subscriptions, if we could show an enlarged and more thorough usefulness.

* * * * * * * * * *

I would suggest a change in the Rule about the appointment of an Orator by the President, to enable him to select some other suitable person besides a Minister of the Gospel, or a member of the Society, if he should find it desirable.

I subjoin a statement of the property of the Society and its income.

* * * * * * *

There has been added to its property, besides the cost of building addition referred to, ten shares of the Augusta and Waynesboro Rail Road stock.

I submit an abstract of the Act of the Legislature ceding to the Chatham Academy, the Union Society and the Free School, the ungranted lands of Chatham County.

It will be seen that all action on our part is dependent upon that of the Trustees of the Academy, and as one might as well try to move a *dead* body, all effort expended upon them having proved vain, the Act is valueless, without further legislation on the subject. I believe, with proper energy on the part of the Trustees of the Chatham Academy, something very valuable might be realized for the Society, at least a handsome domain, on which to settle and maintain all the Orphan Boys that might be offered to us. (See the Act in full below.)

LIST OF UNION SOCIETY'S PROPERTY AND INCOME.

			Value		Income
10	shares Augusta & Waynesboro Rail Road, par value		$1,000	income ..$	70
6	shares Planters' Bank, par value		600	"	60
44	" " " " "		3,520	"	352
43	" Central Rail Road & Banking Co...		4,300	"	344
1	Bond City of Savannah, par value		500	"	35
2	Bonds, Flemming, $1,000; Dittmers, $3,000		4,000	"	280
			$13,920		$1,141
1½	Lots west of Baptist Church, with three houses on same		8,000	"	150
¼	Lot west of above, occupied by W. Starr..		2,000	"	50
	Academy Building, west end, per lease..$1,200 Cost of additions $1,800 @ 12½.. 225		1,125	"	1,425
			$38,170	"	$3,066

And we have full 80 paying members at $5 per annum.......... 100
The Society owes Mr. Haupt a bill of.......$373,63
and a balance to Mr. Clark, on addition to Pavilion...................... 550,00

$923,63

AN ACT, *to ascertain, dispose of and appropriate the ungranted lands in the County of Chatham, and to vest the proceeds of the same in certain charitable societies.*

Be it enacted by the Senate and House of Representatives of the State of Georgia, in General Assembly met, That all the ungranted and unappropriated lands in the County of Chatham shall be disposed of and appropriated, after the passing of this Act, in the manner hereinafter pointed out.

SEC. 2. *Be it enacted by the authority aforesaid,* That William B. Bulloch, Isaac Minis, William T. Williams, Robert W. Pooler, and Alexander Telfair, be appointed Commissioners, whose duty it shall be to employ a fit and competent Surveyor to designate the metes and boundaries, and landmarks of all the ungranted lands in said County, designating each grant

SEC. 3. *Be it enacted by the authority aforesaid,* That within six months after said survey and map are completed, and notice thereof to the trustees, it shall be obligatory on the trustees of the Chatham Academy to select 5,000 acres of said land for the sole use, benefit and behoof of said Academy, and for which they the said trustees shall be entitled to and obtain a grant or grants of the same upon the payment of the usual fees.

SEC. 4. *Be it further enacted by the authority aforesaid,* That the surplus of land vacant and ungranted in said County, over and above the said 5,000 acres aforesaid, shall be sold by the said Commissioners aforesaid, and on such terms, and at such times, as may in the opinion of a majority of them seem fit and proper, and the interest arising from the purchase money of said land shall be annually paid over to the Treasurer of the County, whose duty it shall be to pay over the same in equal proportions to the Treasurer of the Free School Society in the city of Savannah, and the President of the Union Society, for the use of said corporations. *Provided,* no sale of said lands shall be made upon credit, unless good and sufficient security of personal and real estate shall be given to said Commissioners, to secure the payment of the principal and interest of the debt arising from said sale; *and provided also,* that if the said lands be sold for cash or money, the said cash or money shall be invested in the stock of one of the chartered banks of the State, in the name and for the use of the said trustees of the Free

School in sai l city aforesai.l, and the President of the Union Society; and the Treasurer of said County is hereby directed and required to draw from said bank or banks, the dividend arising from said stock, annually or semi-annually, and pay the same in equal proportions, to the said trustees of the said Free School and the President of the Union Society, for the purpose of educating any poor orphans within the County aforesaid, whose parents have died residents thereof.

Sec. 5. *Be it enacted*, That the said Commissioners with the Trustees of the Chatham Academy shall pay the surveyor employed, in equal proportion, the compensation which the said Commissioners may agree and covenant with the said surveyor to pay for his services in making the survey aforesaid, from the money arising from the first sale of said lands or in any other manner they may deem just and equitable,

Sec. 6. *Be it further enacted*, That where any person shall be in actual occupation of said vacant lands or purchased the same and improved them, it shall and may be lawful for the Commissioners to appoint one disinterested freeholder, and the persons in possession another, who, if they do not agree, shall call in a third freeholder, and place a value on the said lands, exclusive of the improvements so made on them, and their judgment or decision shall be final and conclusive; and the persons in possession shall have the right of purchasing the same at such valuation and on such terms as the Commissioners and the purchasers may agree upon.

WARREN JOURDAN,
Speaker of House of Representatives.
THOMAS STOCKS,
President of Senate.

Assented to Dec. 21, 1829.

GEORGE R. GILMER, Governor.

AN ACT, *To alter and enlarge "An Act, entitled an Act to ascertain, dispose of and appropriate the ungranted lands in the county of Chatham, and to vest the same in certain charitable societies," and for other purposes.*

Section 1st. Be it enacted by the Senate and House of Representatives of the State of Georgia, in General Assembly met, and it is hereby enacted by the authority of the same, That from and after the passage of this Act, George Paul Harrison, Thomas Holcombe and Joseph F. Waring be appointed commissioners to fill the vacancies caused by the death of William B. Bulloch, Robert W. Pooler and Alexander Telfair, and that any vacancies hereafter occurring by death, resignation or otherwise, may be filled by the majority of the remaining commissioners.

Sec. 2d. *And be it further enacted by the authority aforesaid*, That the Act of a majority of the commissioners shall be legal and valid, and that they be authorized to act by a majority.

Sec. 3d. *And be it further enacted by the authority aforesaid*, That the Surveyor appointed under the authority of the said Act, shall be empowered for the purpose of making his survey and map, and fulfilling all duties connected therewith, to cross existing lines, without being subject to the pains and penalties in such cases made and provided, nor be held civilly liable for trespasses.

Sec. 4th. *And be it further enacted by the authority aforesaid*, That if any dispute shall arise between the said Surveyor and other parties, as to the existence of lines previously run, it shall and may be lawful for the said Surveyor to require the production of original grants and surveys, or either, in the possession, custody, or control of the party so claiming the existence of a previous line.

Sec. 5th. *And be it further enacted by the authority aforesaid*, That if the Trustees of the Chatham Academy fail to select the land in said Act reserved to their use for six months after the said survey and map have been completed, that then it shall and may be lawful for the said commissioners or a majority of them, to appropriate the said lands according to the provisions of the Fourth Section of the Act aforesaid.

Sec. 6th. *And be it further enacted by the authority aforesaid*, That all titles heretofore executed by the Trustees of the Chatham Academy to any person or persons of any part of said ungranted lands, be and the same are hereby declared valid, subsisting, perfect and legal, and further that the number of acres so aliened, or sold by the said Trustees, shall be deducted from the said five thousand acres, in said Act, reserved to them.

Sec. 7th, *That the said Commissioners or a majority of them*, shall be authorized to require from the said Trustees a statement of the quantity and location of the lands aforesaid, for which they may have executed titles to any person or persons, and the number of acres, that they may be deducted as aforesaid.

Sec. 8th. *And be it further enacted by the authority aforesaid*, That after the said survey

18

and map shall have been completed, the titles to the said ungranted lands shall vest in the said commissioners, so as to enable them or a majority of them to bring suit in he name of the whole against any person or persons occupying or trespassing upon any part of the same.

SEC. 9th. *Provided nevertheless*, that any actual occupant shall be entitled to the benefit of the provisions contained in the Sixth Section of the said Act, if he shall appoint a Freeholder to represent him within twenty days after it shall have been notified in writing, of a similar appointment on the part of the commissioners or a majority of them.

SEC. 10th. *And be it further enacted by the authority aforesaid*, That all necessary expenses incurred by the commissioners in carrying out the provisions of this Act, shall be chargeable and defrayed in the same manner as the cost of the survey and map: *Provided however*, that if the extent of the lands ungranted should prove but five thousand acres then all the charges of survey and maps and all other expenses borne or incurred, shall be entirely chargeable upon such lands as may be surveyed and mapped, and thus accruing chiefly to the Trustees of Chatham Academy aforesaid, and in any event pro rata according to the number of acres received by each,

SEC. 11. *And be it further enacted* that all laws and parts of laws militating against this Act be and the same are hereby repealed

WILLIAM H. STILES,
Speaker of House of Representatives.
DAVID J. BAILEY,
President of the Senate.

Approved March 1st, 1856.

HERSCHEL V. JOHNSON,
Governor.

Office of the Secretary of State,
MILLEDGEVILLE, GA., March 5th, 1856.

I hereby certify that the foregoing is a true and correct copy of the Original Enrolled Act, of file in this office.

GIVEN under my hand and seal of office, the day and year above written.
E. P. WATKINS,
Secretary of State.

[SEAL]

Resolutions read and adopted.

By Gilbert Butler,

Seconded by Robert D. Walker.

RESOLVED, That this body approves of the suggestion of the President, to an establishment for the Beneficiaries of the Union Society, and that he, with the advice and co-operation of the Board of Managers, consummate the arrangement, if they in their judgment find it practicable so to do.

Alteration of the Rules, read 1st time.

RULE 4TH.

Proposition to alter Rule 4th, by adding the words "or some other suitable person" after the word "Gospel," was read the first time.

ELECTION OF OFFICERS.

The Society then went into the election of Officers, for the ensuing year, and upon counting out the ballots, the following gentlemen were declared duly elected, viz:

JOSEPH S. FAY, President.

JOHN W. ANDERSON, Vice President.

EDWRD G. WILSON, Secretary.

Stewards.

JOHN L. COPE,   JAMES H. JOHNSTON.

John W. Anderson, Vice President elect, declined said election. Whereupon ABRAHAM MINIS was duly elected Vice President of the Union Society.

The President then appointed the following

BOARD OF MANAGERS.

Solomon Cohen.
Robert D. Walker.
John R. Johnson.
Allen R. Wright,
Alexander A. Smets.

SAVANNAH, 24th June, 1854.

Board of Managers met.
Present—
    Joseph S. Fay, President.

DIRECTORS.

Solomon Cohen,   Robert D. Walker,
John R. Johnson,   Allen R. Wright,
    Alexander A. Smets.

Resolutions read and adopted.

It is ORDERED, that a purchase of the Place called Bethesda, or the Orphan House Tract, be perfected, at a price not exceeding twenty-five hundred dollars, on such terms of payment as may be agreed upon with the proprietor.

*   *   *   *   *   *   *   *   *   *

RESOLVED FURTHER, and it is hereby ordered that a Committee of three be appointed to aid the President in carrying out the preceding order, and to contract for three buildings, (18x30) eighteen by thirty feet, suitable for School, Eating Room and Dormitory, and carry out their erection, to be completed by the first day of October.

*   *   *   *   *   *   *   *   *   *

RESOLVED FURTHER, and it is hereby ordered, That Robert D. Walker, Allen R. Wright and John R. Johnson be the Committee, and the same are hereby appointed as the Committee, to aid the President in carrying out the first resolution, and to contract for the three buildings, and to have the same completed.

BETHESDA, Chatham County, Georgia, }
23d April, 1855. }

105th Anniversary.

The minutes of the last meeting were read and confirmed.

The President submitted the following annual report, viz:

To the Members of the Union Society,

GENTLEMEN— It is my duty under the 7th Rule of the Society to report to you its progress, and the state of its funds. Its affairs are just now in a transitive state, yet, I trust, not without progress in the right direction. At the last annual meeting the suggestion was adopted, that a location in the country should be obtained, where the boys could be placed away from city influences, and where they could learn habits of industry, as well as receive a more thorough education by a teacher specially devoted to them. The Board of Managers availed themselves of an opportunity to purchase this place, the original locality of Whitfield's Orphan House, and in the course of the summer and autumn erected here some cheap but suitable buildings.

In January last the boys were removed hither. The place cost $2,500, the buildings $2,700, and the outfit about $2,000, including two negroes and a pair of horses. To render the place suitable to its objects and purposes, however, new fences and new farm buildings were requisite, and the expenditure is not yet at an end. The Board of Managers are, however, proceeding as economically as possible to place everything on a comfortable, convenient and serviceable footing. The expense of supporting the establishment has so far been heavy, owing to the fact that there was nothing to start with. All the provisions, fodder for horses, and all kinds of supplies, have to be hauled from town, which is expensive, added to the fact that everything this season is particularly dear. We have to expend much labor in preparing for a useful and sufficient crop, which is now in the ground, and, with God's blessing, will make our expenses next year comparatively light.

At my last report there were fifteen boys in the care of the Society. During the summer and fall, George Gwyn, Thaddeus E. Fisher, Richard H. Manning and Henry H. Manning, were withdrawn by their friends, and help was afforded the parents of the two last, to go back to Columbus from which place they originally came. On the 22d January, preparations having been completed, the remaining eleven boys were brought to Bethesda. A few days afterwards Owen Brittle ran away, and returned to his mother, and under the circumstances it was deemed undesirable and injudicious to attempt to reclaim him. Since then, all have lived here contentedly, and eight boys having been added, from time to time, the number is now eighteen. I am glad to say that as a whole they are orderly, well disposed, obedient and industrious boys. I subjoin a list of their names.

It is very creditable to Mr. and Mrs. Haupt, under whose care the children of the Society have been, that the boys received from them are all well mannered and well behaved, and will compare favorably, in a moral point of view, with the same number anywhere.

They exercise a good influence upon new comers, and the whole now present the spectacle of a united, diligent and happy family, creditable to the past and hopeful as to the future. During the past summer, all the boys, but one, had the yellow fever in Savannah, and recovered, owing, under God, to the good nursing of Mrs. Haupt, and the judicious treatment of Dr. Posey.

This gentleman having, for seventeen years, attended gratuitously and faithfully the children under the charge of the Society, the Board of Managers have thought proper to make some suitable testimonial of their appreciation of his kindness. They have procured a handsome silver pitcher to present to him, which you will doubtless approve. It is to be regretted that circumstances prevent his being present to receive it, and accept personally our tribute of thanks for his benevolent labors. During the period referred to, there have been sixty-one boys in the care of the Society, and boarding with Mr. Haupt, of whom but four have died, and of them two were sick when received.

During the past year we have lost three members by death, Messrs. John L. Cope, Charles Hartridge, and Jonathan Olmstead; and, including those elected to-day, sixty-six members have been added. The large accession during this year is an indication of increased interest in the Society and its objects, and an earnest that it will take no steps backward.

The property of the Society, as it now stands, is as follows:

Bethesda, containing about 125 acres of land, and improvements and outfits, costing about	$6,400
Two negroes	800
Seven Shares Central Rail Road Stock	700
Ten Shares Planters' Bank Stock	800
Ten Shares Augusta & Waynesboro' R. R. Stock	800
One Bond City of Savannah	590
Note of Wm. B. Fleming	1,600
Note of Trustee of H. Dittmers	3,000
Two Lots and improvements on South Broad Street, west end of Academy, known as the "Pavilion"	20,000
Two lots and improvements adjoining Second Baptist Church in York street	8,000
	$42,000

The Annual Income of the Society from all sources is as follows :

From	Seven Shares Central Rail Road Stock			56
"	Ten " Planter's Bank "			56
"	Interest on Notes			280
"	Rents from Estate in York street			500
"	" " Pavilion			1,530
"	St. Andrew's Society towards E. Mortimer's support...			100
"	W. E. Long, Guardian of Jos. Clark's Orphans.........			180
"	Interest on City Bonds			35
"	Augusta & Waynesboro' Railroad Stock..................			
"	Members Annual Subscription.............................			715
	Total			$2,782

To pay for Bethesda, and for the buildings fitting up there, and improvement of the same, it was necessary to sell a large part of our Planters' Bank and Rail Road Stocks ; and to meet the out-standing accounts, and to finish the improvements at Bethesda, it will be necessary to apply a part of the money to be received for the notes of Wm. B Fleming and H. Dittimers, which fall due next month. The Society receives from the St. Andrew's Society $100 annually towards the support of Ewen Mortimer, and from Mr. Wm. E. Long, Guardian of Josiah Clark's orphans, $15 per month towards their support, as appears in my statement of annual income. It seems safe to calculate that when the establishment at Bethesda is complete and fully paid for, the income of the Society from its other property and from the contributions of members will be at least $3,000. Something too may yet be derived from the ungranted lands in Chatham County. It seems probable too that the produce of the farm will contribute materially to its support, and it is fair to expect that there will be some surplus annually that can be allowed to accumulate, or be used immediately for the enlargement of operations.

It may be that the plan adopted at the last anniversary, and commenced by the Board of Managers, may not prove a pecuniary saving, yet that the money expended will be productive of better results, and provide for the support of more children at a not proportionably increased expense, can hardly be doubtful. At any rate the new system appears, so far, to commend itself to the approval of the Society.

In choosing Bethesda, though at a higher price than that at which some other place might have been obtained, and perhaps above its market value, the Board of Managers were influenced by the fact that upwards of a century ago, it had been consecrated to the same noble purpose, that it has an unblemished reputation for health, and that the desirable services of the occupants, Mr. and Mrs. Murphy, could be secured for the management of the children. So far they have, by the interest they have manifested in the success of the experiment, and by the contented industry, and the comfortable condition of the boys, realized the expectations formed of them.

A good and competent teacher, Mr. R. C. Tasker, has been temporarily engaged, and the boys have manifested a fair degree of interest in learning and as rapid improvement as could be expected from the short period of their present instruction, after an interval of five months in which they were not at School before leaving town. Mr. Tasker may be induced to remain until another year. His compensation in the mean time, is indefinite, as he came out from the North more as a matter of health than employment.

Mr. and Mrs. Murphy receive $2.75 per day, and find their own supplies.

The Society is indebted to the Central Rail Road Company for an old locomotive bell, which will serve to call the family to its several employments, and to several friends for plants. So much had to be done in arranging for crops of the more needful character, that not much progress has been made in the higher branches of horticulture, to which it is designed to bestow considerable attention hereafter.

The children received into the care of the Society this year have not been indentured to it according to its rules. It is rare that any one has the power to do it, and it seems a vain expenditure of money to take out letters of Guardianship for this purpose only. If there was a law by which children voluntarily placed and left in charge of the Society by their nearest relatives or friends, or by the public authorities, were by that fact and act indentured to it, it would be a simple matter. As it is, a heavy labor is imposed on your officers if the rule is carried out. Joseph E. Campos indentured last year to Mr. Dugald Ferguson, and who is here to-day, seems to be doing well, and so far is a credit to the Society. Jerry Manning was taken to Columbus by his parents.

Were not this report already a long one, it would be pleasant to note some coincidence between the position of affairs at Bethesda now and one hundred years ago. Mr. Robert Habersham who is on this spot for the first time for upwards of sixty years, has kindly submitted to my inspection copies of some of the letters of his Grand Father, Mr. James Habersham, written from the year 1741 to 1751. This gentleman, abandoning a career more promising in worldly matters, came to Georgia as the friend and companion of Whitfield, to share his labors. He nobly aided in carrying out this work, and was President of Bethesda College, and manager of the Orphan House for many years.

They had many difficulties to contend with, which we are spared, and the adverse circumstances which conspired to impede their efforts and finally to break up the establishment, do not exist now. We should not be deterred, therefore, by the interruption of their good work, from endeavoring, from this small beginning, to build up an institution that will be a blessing not only to the children it may protect and educate, but to those who foster and maintain it—an institution, too, which may go on enlarging its usefulness to an extent that will fulfil the utmost wishes and heartfelt fervent prayers of the pious and devoted Whitfield. May his spirit animate us, and may God bless us in this and all other good works.

I would gladly be relieved of my responsibilities as your President, but if it is desired by you that I should continue to carry out your wishes until everything is more complete and more thoroughly systematised, I will not decline the honor. I must ask in all things your favor, kind interest and co-operation, to enable me to fill properly a place of so much importance, and in which I have had so many able and distinguished predecessors.

While agreeable and inspiring associations surround us and crowd in upon us, let us congratulate each other upon the awakened interest that is manifested in our Society, and upon the cheering prospects which open before us.

I submit herewith my annual account and vouchers, which I hope will be found correct.

Your obedient servant,

JOS. S. FAY,
President.

LIST OF BOYS.

Alexander K. Wilson, 13 years old, has a mother.
Ewen Mortimer, 10 years, orphan.
William Henry Sagurs, 13 years, has a father.
Charles A. Sagurs, 12 years, has a father.
Robert A. Beasley, 12 years, has a mother.
George Washington Cole, 14 years, has a father.
Jacob Rohr, 8 years, orphan.
Frederick Rohr, 4 years, orphan.
James E. Beasley, 8 years old, has a mother.
Joseph James Singer, 14 years old, orphan.
William S. Clark, 9 years old, orphan.
Josiah T. Clark, 5 years old, orphan.
Samuel Miller, 5 years old, has a mother.

John O'Keefe, 4 years old, orphan.

Cornelius A. Long, 10 years old, has a mother.

Charles H. R. Thorpe, 11 years old, has a mother.

Matthew Dotson, 13 years old, orphan.

Daniel Towles, 5 years old, has a father.

CORRESPONDENCE WITH DR. JOHN F. POSEY.

The pitcher prepared for Dr. Posey has the following inscription:

"To Dr. John F. Posey, from the Union Society, in remembrance of his long efficient and gratuitous medical services to the boys under its charge while in Savannah."

BETHESDA, April 23, 1855.

Dr. Posey not being present to receive this testimonial, the President sent it to him with the following letter, which is accompanied by the Dr.'s reply:

SAVANNAH, April 23, 1855.

My Dear Sir:

The inscription on the accompanying pitcher will explain why it is sent to you. It gives me much pleasure that it is my province, on behalf of the Union Society to present this mark of their gratitude and esteem. It was exhibited to day at a large meeting of the members at Bethesda, on the occasion of their anniversary, the first one celebrated there. Much regret was felt that you were not present to receive their kind assurances personally. You do not, however, require this gift or these assurances as compensation for a long, gratuitous, and faithful medical services to those boys under charge of the Society, and indeed they would be quite inadequate. You have what is far more precious to you, the testimony of a good conscience. It may nevertheless be a satisfaction in the decline of a well spent life to know that a part of your labors have been appreciated, and to have before you this simple testimonial of it.

With my best wishes for your welfare and happiness, I am,

Yours, very respectfully,

JOS. S. FAY,

President Union Society.

To Dr. John F. Posey.

Reply.

SAVANNAH, April 24, 1855.

Dear Sir:

I read the letter which accompanied your beautiful memorial with deep feeling, and I wish I could convey to you in words the sense I I have of your very flattering notice of my services to the boys under

the charge of our Society. Aside from the reward received while performing such services, I can conceive of no gratification equal to the
consciousness of the estimation you have placed upon them.

Be pleased to accept for yourself and your Society my most hearty
thanks for the memorial and for the expressions of regard and esteem
conveyed in your letter.

I wish the boys under the charge of the Union Society may have
the good fortune to have your services spared to them long enough to
stamp your impress indelibly on their characters.

I am with great respect yours,
JOHN F. POSEY.

To Jos. S. Fay, Esq.,
    Pres't. Union Society.

ADDRESS,

BY ROBERT H. GRIFFIN.

It is now more than one hundred and fifteen years, since on this
spot a company was first assembled for a purpose nearly akin to that
which has brought you, Gentlemen of the Union Society, here to-
day. Foremost among them, was a man of noble presence and com-
manding action, young in years, but grey in spirit; poor in the riches
of the world, but with a right royal income of love and gratitude;
self-exiled from the land of his birth, where thousands and tens of
thousands had beset his pathway with homage amounting almost to
idolatry, and where the faintest whisper that fell from his silvery
tongue, was more potent in the ravished ears of his listeners, than the
labored eloquence of any other living man. On the extreme frontier
of civilization, and surrounded by primeval forests, he had that day
gathered around him—that new apostle—a few friends who dearly
loved him, and who were of kindred spirit, and with an earnest confidence that the cause in which he was about to labor would bring success to the work of his hands, he commenced what afterwards came to
be called *Bethesda*,—a House of Mercy. No formal corner stone,
filled with memorials of the fleeting day, was laid; he left his heart
for a corner stone, and there that heart remained throughout the
storms and trials, the glories and triumphs of his after life.

There is no name of man which Georgia should teach her children
to pronounce with greater reverence than that of GEORGE WHIT-
FIELD. Sprung from an humble parentage; in his boyhood, even a
menial in his mother's inn; suddenly inspired with a dim presentiment

of his destiny, and entering Pembroke College by charitable aid, in the
lowly position of Servitor; following at a distance, with self-abasing
reverence, the rising lights of Methodism; discovered accidentally by
the WESLEYS to be one of their disciples, and caught at once their
hearts; advancing, step by step, until at a premature age, the good
Bishop of Gloucester gave him ordination; approaching with bitter
dread of failure the delivery of his first sermon; descending from the
pulpit, and passing over the prostrate hearts of a congregation, of
whom fifteen are said to have gone mad; borne on a rising gale of
popularity with such tremendous force, that those who came to hear
him sometimes numbered more than twenty thousand, and many who
were forced to stand outside prayed only for a sight of "his blessed
face;" the gates of church preferment thrown wide open before him,
and the mitre and the crosier glittering in the prospect—he turned
his back on fame and fortune, and sought what were then the wilds
of Georgia, because he believed that God was calling him to undertake the mission. Even after his embarkation, the voice of JOHN
WESLEY, to whom he looked up with filial affection and respect, was
raised in vain to call him back, but fortified with a serene and pious
self-reliance, he went on his way.

Almost contemporaneously with his arrival, the idea of establishing
an Orphan House, suggested to him originally by the younger WES-
LEY, became indelibly impressed upon his mind; and, as he himself
wrote back to England, he determined, "by the Divine assistance, to
get about it in earnest." The mismanagement of the Colony had reduced the people to such poverty that he said that such an institution
was imperatively demanded. He labored long and diligently, assisted
always by one who came out in the same ship with him, whom he
called his "beloved fellow traveller," and whose name has since become one of our household words, JAMES HABERSHAM. He returned to England to further his object, and found the Trustees of the
Colony in a generous mood. They gave to the Charity, for a location,
five hundred acres of any vacant land which he should select. The
people, to whom he preached, appealing for assistance out of their
over abundance, gave with liberal hands. The ground was selected
by Mr. HABERSHAM—this ground formed part of it—and on the
25th day of March, 1740, WHITFIELD stood not far from where we
now are, "and with his own hands," in the language of one of his
historians, "laid the first brick of this great house, which he called
Bethesda."

He had not waited for that event, but had already commenced his
work. Even then he had collected forty children, who depended

upon him for daily food and raiment. From that time forth, until he rested from his labors, his Orphan House was never out of WHIT- FIELD'S thoughts. With a parent's ardor and abiding love, he clung to it and labored for it. Even when calumny and detraction assailed him and blackened his name, and when the gorgeous robe of popular- ity which he had won, was trampled in the dust, he had spirit enough left to think of its *Bethesda*. And afterwards, when he again stood up before the world the "Prince of Preachers," the "Apostle of the English Empire," he knew no moment of elation in which he forgot his orphans. For thirty years this labor lasted, and in the very year of his death, when his strength had yielded and his life was fast eb- bing away, he projected the plan of a College to be added to the House of Mercy, and preached *here* in the Chapel before the Gover- nor, Council and Assembly, whom he had invited hither to secure their co-operation. He spoke with all the fire of his by-gone time. The hearts of his auditors were touched, as he alone could touch men's hearts. His object seemed to be within his grasp, and any one would have carried away from that assembly the conviction that the calm confidence which had selected the text from which he preached, "The hands of Zerubbabel have laid the foundation of this house, his hands shall also finish it," was the out-speaking of a prophet's spirit. Alas! there was no prophet there. A few months gone, and he who then spoke with so much zeal, and hope, and earnestness, lay beneath the sod, far, very far, from his beloved *Bethesda*.

The love and veneration which had waited on his living presence could not be torn away from his soulless body. Men came from many churches to beg that his ashes might be sent to rest with them. The Legislature of Georgia, being then in session, unanimously appropria- ted a sufficient sum of money to bring his body here, that it might repose in the shadow of his Orphan House. Fortunately, considering the fate which soon befel *Bethesda*, even this request was denied, and he sleeps in Newburyport, before the pulpit once occupied by the friend under whose roof he died. But now, that the retributive jus- tice of time has restored his *Bethesda*,—shorn of its fair proportions, it is true, but still *Bethesda*—to the destiny for which he intended it, what act can be more becoming than for us, into whose hands his work has fallen, to revive the dormant prayer of the State, and to ask, once more, that Massachusetts shall give up our dead? In our own time, the world has almost stood still to see the ashes of a fallen conqueror brought back, in the full glare of imperial pomp, from the island prison where he died, to repose among the people whom he said he loved so well; and, yet again, the son from whom he was torn, on whose features coldly expressed in marble, his dying eyes were fixed, that son, too, like himself, a prince dethroned, is to be given back to his side in death. If to the memory of carnage and usurpation such tributes be paid, how much more are they due to one who was a Prince of Peace? If to tyranny such honors belong, how much more to charity? Let then the bloodless conqueror be brought home; let his revived *Bethesda* receive into her bosom his sacred ashes; let monumental marble rise above his newer grave, and let it bear this truthful record of his life:

"Assailed by scandal, and the tongue of strife,
His only answer was a blameless life,
And he that forged and he that threw the dart,
Had each a brother's interest in his heart.
Paul's love of Christ and steadiness unbribed,
Were copied close by him and well transcribed.
He followed Paul—his zeal a kindred flame,
His Apostolic charity the same.
Like him crossed cheerfully tempestuous seas,
Forsaking country, kindred, friends and ease—
Like him he labored, and like him content
To bear it, suffered shame where'er he went.

Blush calumny, and write upon his tomb,
If honest eulogy can spare thee room,
Thy deep repentance of thy thousand lies,
Which, aim'd at him, have pierced th' offended skies,
And say, 'blot out my sin, confessed, deplor'd,
Against thine image in thy Saint, O Lord.'"

It seemed to me, Gentlemen of the Union Society, when your President did me the honor to invite me to address you on this anniversary, that it would be well to dedicate this, our first meeting since the purchase of *Bethesda*, to the memory of the great man at whose life and labors we have just thrown back a hasty glance. I trust, that in this, you, gentlemen, agree with me; but having named the name of Whitfield, I cannot expect pardon from the ladies, who have graced the occasion with their presence, unless I pay a passing tribute to his constant friend, his generous benefactress, the heiress of *Bethesda*, Selina, Countess of Huntingdon. Born amid the splendor of high rank, young, beautiful, eminently gifted, rarely accomplished, daughter and wife of belted Earls, worshipped by all who knew her, and ruler of her set, which included Sarah, the proud

Duchess of Marlborough, MARY WORTLEY MONTAGU, MARGARET MONTAGU, PHILIP DORMER STANHOPE, Earl of Chesterfield, HENRY ST. JOHN, LORD BOLLINGBROKE,—a lordly and illustrious array of genius and irreligion—so born, so bred, and so surrounded, what had this proud woman to do with chapels and conventicles, and the strange men who promulgated the doctrines of Methodism? Earnest, serious, and almost sad, from her early childhood, her mind was exactly fitted to receive the impressions which the rising sect of Methodists sought to make. But she and they were separated by a wide interval. Social barriers prevented her from hearing anything more than the distant echoes of their preaching. Her soul was yearning for the spiritual food which they were scattering with lavish hands, and whenever some thrice distilled reports of their meetings reached her ear, she unwittingly cherished them in her memory. Stricken with illness, she suddenly saw the light which she had needed but not sought, and rose a follower of the WESLEYS. She was not the woman to fear conventionalities or dread the loss of social influence. She gave herself, at once, with all her native enthusiasm, to the work, and until death, remained unwaveringly the same. The names of other women equally exalted in rank, her cotemporaries and her friends, have passed into oblivion, or come down to us with no claims to extraordinary respect, but above the grave of SELINA, Countess of Huntingdon, sweet flowers perpetually bloom, and grateful hands, unceasingly, cast votive chaplets.

The house of the Earl and Countess of Huntingdon became the favorite resort of the leading Methodists. The Earl himself had neither lot nor part with them, save as their ever courteous host. First came the WESLEYS, and after them, by degrees, as they raised themselves above the level of the crowd, came other great names in Methodism. WHITFIELD, was, of course, at some time or another, one. When it was, however, that the Countess and himself first met, is not known with certainty, though it must have been after his first voyage to Georgia, and it may have been after his second, or even his third. Be that as it may, the Orphan House soon became a favorite object with the Countess. She gave her money, her counsel and her countenance to WHITFIELD. It became almost as much her work as his, and, when he died, his will was found to contain a clause devising *Bethesda* to her. She did not falter when the intelligence was communicated to her. The Orphan House was incumbered with many debts. It had always been a great labor to keep it up. But she assumed the burden and submitted herself cheerfully to the responsibility. All things were done that could be done; but the star of

Bethesda had descended into WHITFIELD's grave. Lightning smote the buildings, and they were consumed. After their restoration, disaster followed disaster, sometimes with lingering footsteps and sometimes with rapid march, until just twelve years after the death of its founder, and in the closing year of the Revolution, *Bethesda* was reclaimed by the Government of the State, after the Royal troops had destroyed almost everything that was valuable. From that time until this Society became its proprietor, *Bethesda* was perverted from its destiny. In the lapse of time, nearly all vestiges of the "great house of brick" and its attendant buildings have passed away; but although there remains nothing that is material, except the consecrated ground, to connect us with WHITFIELD, yet we have constituted ourselves his heirs, and by reviving the object of his life, have reclaimed our inheritance. Spirit of the illustrious dead! if, in this moment of our rejoicing, thou hoverest near us, impart, if thou canst, to us, the fervor which possessed thee living, so that, in our day and generation we may prove ourselves worthy to have succeeded thee, and may transmit to those who shall come after us thy *Bethesda*, thy *Bethel*, thy *Peniel*, arrayed in all the loveliness and light for which thou didst pray and labor.

For you, children of *Bethesda*, there is a solemn but a splendid moral to be drawn from the story of the life of WHITFIELD. Remember what he was and what he became. Remember that he was once a servant of servants; and that when he was older, yes, much older than nearly all of you, the future frowned upon him like one, great, black cloud. Remember, too, that when that cloud turned on his enraptured gaze its silver lining, he did not carelessly bask in the sunshine, but gave himself at once, soul and body, to labor. Remember also, that he raised himself, until while yet alive, legions of men spoke of him as you have heard me speak to-day; and when he died, the world took up the chorus. Remember yet again, that you live in happier times than he lived in. When he stood here, the Indian and the wild beast were his nearest neighbors. Since then, this great State has been born, and growing with a glorious growth, has given you a name which vails its crest before no other name—the name of Georgians. She beckons you to her honors. There are no such obstacles in your way as WHITFIELD fought and conquered. The cold shade of no aristocratic form of government interposes difficulties which only genius of the highest order can overcome. The one talent which will achieve for you success, is patient labor. Engrave that word upon your hearts. Fix, like the eaglets, your eyes upon the sun, and perchance, on the rushing current of time, some one of you, my children, may be borne to the highest honors which our country can bestow, and then, oh! WHITFIELD! thy *Bethesda* will be illustrious indeed.

"Lives of great men all remind us,
We can make our lives sublime,
And, departing, leave behind us,
Footsteps on the sands of time.

Footprints, that perhaps another,
Sailing o'er life's solemn main,
A forlorn and shipwrecked brother,
Seeing, may take heart again..

Let us, then, be up and doing,
With a heart for any fate.
Still achieving, still pursuing,
Learn to labor and to wait."

ODE,

BY REV. JOHN PIERPONT, JR.

Within old Salem's walls,
In sight of gorgeous halls,
    A crystal spring
In olden time once rolled,
Whose sparkling drops of gold,
Beamed with a love untold ;—
    Its praise we sing!

Around its waters bright,
At early morning light,
    Multitudes lay :—
Impotent folk, and blind,
Withered, diseased in mind,
The halt, here came to find
    Healing for aye.

O'er the sweet gushing springs,
With healing in her wings,
    An angel form
Troubling the waters there,

Answered the earnest prayer
That floated on the air,
　　Fervent and warm.

Though many hoping came—
The blind, the deaf, the lame,—
　　Around the pool,
Who first the waters pressed,
Who there surpassed the rest,
E'en him the angel blest,
　　And made him whole.

Around the market place,
Face answering to face.
　　Eye to eye,
Those crowds are seen no more,
Impatient as of yore ;
Nor near Bethesda's door
　　Is heard their cry.'

Angels have left those springs,
Folding their golden wings.
　　Obedient bow—
Bethesda's gate is still,
No cries its porches fill,
And e'en the murmuring rill
　　Is silent now.

But here, where now we meet,
Within this cool retreat,
　　Angels have trod :—
Angels of Joy and Light,
Angels of Love and Might,
Angels of Truth and Right,
　　Angels of God !

A new Bethesda here,
To human hearts most dear,
　　Healing imparts ;
Here orphan tears are stayed,
Here orphan prayers are prayed,
Here nameless blessings craved
　　For orphan hearts.

Bless those, O God, who bless
The poor and fatherless,
With loving care :
Though here no angel wings,
Wave o'er Bethesda's springs,
Receive thou, King of kings,
The orphan's prayer.

*   *   *   *   *   *   *   *   *   *   *

The Rules of the Society were read, and the following amendment
adopted, viz :

RULE 4TH.

The proposition to alter Rule 4th, by adding the words "or some
other suitable person" after the word Gospel, read the first time at
the last anniversary, was again read and unanimously adopted.

ELECTION OF OFFICERS.

The Society then went into an election of Officers for the ensuing
year, and upon counting out the ballots, the following gentlemen were
declared duly elected, viz :

President.	Vice President.
JOSEPH S. FAY.	ABRAHAM MINIS.
Secretary.	Stewards.
EDWARD G. WILSON.	DANIEL H. BALDWIN,
	JAMES M. PRENTISS.

The President then appointed the following

BOARD OF MANAGERS, viz :

John R. Johnson,	Allen R. Wright,
Robert D. Walker,	Francis G. Dana,
William Battersby.	

(106th *Anniversary, April 23d,* 1856.)

The minutes of the last meeting were read and confirmed.

Joseph Story Fay, Esq., the President of the Union Society, then
submitted the following annual report, viz :

BETHESDA, April 26th, 1856

GENTLEMEN : Members of the Union Society—

In accordance with your Rules I am again called upon to make a
report to you, "of the progress of the Society and state of its funds."

The first year of our experience here has rolled round, and I think
with a high degree of encouragement. At my last report we had in
our charge 18 boys. Of these George Washington Cole has been
placed with Mr. John S. Sturtevant, to learn the trade of a carpen-

ter, and promises well.   Charles H. R. Thorpe was sent to his mother in Charleston, by her urgent request, with the prospect of being properly maintained and brought up.   Owen Brittles, under the influence of some of his nomadic friends, ranaway and has not been reclaimed

We have added the following named boys, making the total of 25

Francis J. Hunt, 13 years old, taken June 23, 1855.

Julius A. C. Heidt, 7 years old, taken June 23, 1855

Albert J, Carolan, 9 years old, taken August 13, 1855.

Jacob B. Trump, 7 years old, taken August 23, 1855

George E. Trumpler, 7 years old, taken Nov. 7, 1855.

Sylvester Syntis, 11 years old, taken Dec. 10, 1855

Thomas Smith, 10 years old, taken Feb. 22, 1856.

Patrick O'Brien, 12 years old, taken March 15, 1856

Edward Wall, 8 years old, taken April 7, 1856.

These make as many as our present buildings can accommodate, and perhaps as many as our means warrant us in taking at present.

I cannot give you a reliable opinion as to the extent to which we can carry our plans of benevolence, as circumstances prevent any thing like an accurate estimate of the cost of sustaining those we have begun.   There has been, as you will perceive, a great deal done in the way of farm improvements, and in adding to the convenience and comforts of our large family.   This has required, beyond the cost of materials, a considerable expenditure in the support and wages of mechanics, transportation, &c., which cannot well be separated from the current expenses of the establishment.   Our crop last year relieved us of some outlay, but was not sufficient for our wants, much labor having been diverted to buildings, fencings, &c.

We begin this year out of debt, with our expenditure for improvements at an end for the present, with the prospect of a good crop, and the hope of showing more clearly, if needed, that a great amount of good can be done at a moderate comparative cost.   Our buildings, as you perceive are but temporary in their character, as was proper in the outset of our experiment, but as its success developes itself we must look forward to improvements of a more permanent kind.

In hours of leisure, hereafter, it should be our policy to collect from neighboring deposits a sufficiency of shells, to commence, before long, the construction of larger and more substantial edifices of tabby.   Much of the labor can be performed by the boys, who are very apt and useful in all employments of the kind—and they in turn promote the views which led us to adopt the change in our mode of maintaining the children in our charge.   So far these views have been fully realized, and need only to be persevered in.   The children take part in all the labor going on, learn habits of industry and usefulness, become familiar with the use of tools, and with farming and mechanical operations, and at the same time, from their limited number, receive strict attention in their schooling, so that without drudgery or over confinement, they have advanced rapidly in their education. In all these points we have been highly favored in such faithful, kind and zealous supervisors as Mr. and Mrs. Murphy, and so good, thorough and judicious a teacher as Mr. Tasker. The children are very orderly and intelligent, and well behaved, and cannot be surpassed by the same number any where.

To complete our improvements and pay for them, has required a further reduction of our funded means.

The property of the Society stands now as follows:

Bethesda, containing about 125 acres of upland, and improvements, stock, outfit, and farming tools, flat, &c., costing about $10,000
3 negroes 1,500
7 shares Central Rail Road Stock, par...................... 700
10 " Augusta & Waynesboro Rail Road Stock, cost........ 800
1 Bond City of Savannah, par................................. 500
2 Lots and improvements on 1½ in York street.............. 8,000
2 Lots and improvements, the Pavilion, on South Broad street 20,000
                                                        _____
                                                        $11,500

One half of one of the Lots in York street is under ground rent to William Starr, Esq., without any lease, as has been mentioned by my predecessors in their reports. He may be considered as a tenant at will or an annual lessor, a tenure which can at any time be changed by an equitable arrangement between him and the Society, should such change be deemed desirable.

The legacy of $5,000 left to the Society by the late Thomas Young, was doubtless intended to be an endowment of which the income only should be applied to the use of the Society. This has been rather lost sight of, and as a matter of good faith and good policy, we should look to replacing and setting this amount sacredly apart, in the future accumulation of this Society, as a special fund, the income of which should be used.

The income of the Society is as follows:

From 7 Shares Central Rail Road Stock...................... $56
  " Rent of Estate in York street.......................... 500
  " " " Pavilion... 1,580
  " St. Andrews' Society, towards E. Mortimer's support.... 100

" Wm. E. Long, Guardian, towards support of Josiah
    Clark's Orphans.................................. 180
" Interest on City Bond................ 35
" 269 annual Members 1,815
                                                          ——————
                                                          $3,746

I truly hope that this income will maintain 24 boys, and provide
something towards the special fund alluded to, or towards the renewal or increase of our buildings. I also cannot but hope that something will accrue to the Society from its long slumbering interests in
"the ungranted lands in Chatham County." A law passed in 1829
provided for a survey of these, and on its completion 5,000 acres
were to be set apart or chosen by the Trustees of the Chatham Academy, and the balance sold and the proceeds invested equally for the
benefit of the Free School and the Union Society. The total is estimated at the least at 20,000 acres. Of the five Commissioners appointed to carry out the law, three died, from which and other causes
no action was ever perfected, and there was no provision for filling the
vacancies in the commission. The Society is indebted to Messrs.
Lloyd & Owens for gratuitously furnishing a most lucid opinion on
this law, upon which they based an Act filling the vacancies in the
commission, and reviving the old law and remedying its defects.
This Act was passed by the last Legislature: Col. Lawton, a member
of this Society, interesting himself in its behalf; and I have sanguine
hopes that some advantages from it will accrue to this Society. The
new Commissioners Messrs. Harrison, Holcombe and Waring, are
men of action, and I am sure will not allow the statute to become a dead
letter. Many of these lands, comprising marsh, swamp and wood land,
are now of considerable value, and it would be very satisfactory if we
should receive from this source a very handsome addition to our means
of usefulness. But let us not depend upon it, but rather upon ourselves. Let us try to gather means to place our new orphans' home
upon permanent foundations—let us rally our affections round it, and
I doubt not that the remembrance of our labors in alleviating the sorrow and in elevating the lot of the poor homeless and schoolless orphan
will be more than an adequate reward.

Another law was also passed by the last Legislature to legalize the
binding of children to the Society by their natural guardians or nearest friends, or by the public authorities, which is so easy a proceeding
that the rule of the Society requiring children to be bound to it can
readily be complied with and is now enforced.

During the epidemic of 1854, a considerable sum was contributed to the relief of the poor and suffering in the city, and each charitable Society received a portion of it except ours, which, nevertheless, took charge of its full proportion of bereaved children. I received, however, from his Honor, the Mayor, this year the sum of $75, which appears in my account herewith submitted.

Situated as we are it is impossible to comply with the rule requiring the children to attend the funerals of deceased members without great expense and trouble. This and the rule exacting fines for non-atten dance of members at meetings I think should be repealed.

The Society has to lament the death of three of its members during the past year. Robert H. Griffin, Esq., who so eloquently addressed you on the last anniversary, and Mulford Marsh, and Charles S. Ar nold, Esqrs. W. Z. Florance, Esq., has resigned and removed from the city. There have been added to it 101 members, making the total of 207. This is a higher number, I believe, than was ever en rolled at any one time upon the lists of the Society, and is a gratifying evidence of increased interest in its object and plans. It has been in times past considered an honor to belong to the oldest charitable Society in the State of Georgia, but beyond this there should be a pleasure in promoting its welfare, that should make membership a privilege to be asked for, as was formerly the practice, the privilege of bestowing charity.

> "The quality of mercy is not strained,
> It droppeth like the gentle dew from Heaven
> Upon the place beneath. It is twice blessed,
> It blesses him that gives and him that takes."

For a report of what has been accomplished in the way of farming, I refer you to an extract from a note from Mr. Murphy on the subject and in reference to the stock belonging to the place, from which it appears that we have 364 acres planted in corn, melons, ground nuts, sugar cane, &c., and that we have 52 head of neat cattle, and 56 head of swine, with poultry innumerable.

I have procured of Mr. Hughes a survey and plat of the place, as a matter of reference.

The Society is indebted to Mr. Battersby, the Rev. Mr. Pierpont, Mr. E. J. Purse, and others, for useful and entertaining reading books, which will form the nucleus of a library—a good and suggestive example.

Congratulating the Society on its present promising condition, and praying that its affairs may prosper and its usefulness increase, a result depending, under God's blessing, upon the interest and attention of all its members,

I subscribe myself, respectfully,

JOS. S. FAY,

President.

On motion of Charles Green, Esq.,

Seconded by Charles Van Horn, Esq.

The report and account of the President and Treasurer were received, adopted and ordered to be entered on the minutes.

Resolution read and adopted.

By Robert D. Walker,

Seconded by W. T. Thompson.

RESOLVED, That the report of the President be furnished to the city press for publication free of charge.

AMENDMENTS TO RULES.

By Alderman Walker,

RESOLVED, That Rule 17th, rendering it obligatory to attend funerals of deceased members, be repealed.

RESOLVED, That the fines levied for non-attendance at meetings by Rule 3d be repealed.

In compliance with the By-Laws the above stated amendments to the Rules were read the first time, and laid over for action at the next anniversary.

ELECTION OF OFFICERS.

The Society then went into an election for Officers, for the ensuing year, which resulted in the unanimous election of the following named gentlemen, viz:

JOSEPH S. FAY, President.

ABRAHAM MINIS, Vice President.

EDWARD G. WILSON, Secretary.

JAMES H. DEMUND, } Stewards.
JAMES W. McALPIN, }

The President appointed the following officers for the ensuing year, viz:

BOARD OF MANAGERS.

Charles Green,   John M. Cooper,

Francis S. Bartow,   Charles Van Horn,

Charles F. Mills.

160

James M. Prentiss,   Daniel H. Baldwin,
John R. Johnson,   William F. Holland.

The Society then adjourned for dinner. After partaking thereof, in company with the ladies and other invited guests, the whole assemblage retired to the grove, at 3 o'clock, for the purpose of hearing the address from the Hon. Francis S. Bartow, the orator of the day.

By invitation of the President the exercises were opened by a brief and appropriate prayer by the Rev. A. J. Karn, of the Lutheran Church.

After which the following song was sung with fine effect by the boys, who occupied a place near the speaker's stand, viz :

SONG.

Oh, come, come away, from labor now reposing,
Let busy care awhile forbear,
    Oh, come, come away ;
Come, come, our social joys renew,
And there, where love and friendship grew,
Let true hearts welcome you :
    Oh, come, come away.

From toil and the care, on which the day is closing,
The hour of eve' brings sweet reprieve,
    Oh, come, come away ;
Oh, come where love will smile on thee,
And round its hearth will gladness be,
And time flies merrily ;
    Oh come, come away.

While sweet Philomel, the weary traveller cheering,
With evening songs, her note prolongs,
    Oh, come, come away ;
In answering songs of sympathy,
We'll join in tuneful melody,
With hope, joy, liberty ;
    Oh come, come away.

The bright day has gone, the moon and stars appearing,
With silver light illume the night,
    Oh come, come away ;

161

We'll join in grateful songs of praise,
To him who crowns our peaceful lays,
With health, hope, happiness;
    Oh come, come away.

The Hon. Francis S. Bartow, the orator of the day, then gave an eloquent, practical and forcible address, which was listened to by all present with deep interest and profound attention, particularly that portion addressed to the boys.

At the close of the address the following song was sung by Wm. Francis Holland, Esq., assisted by several ladies and gentlemen.' (See Ode, by Rev. J. Pierpont, sung at last anniversary.)

The benediction was pronounced by the Rev. Mr. Clark, of the Episcopal Church, after which the boys sang another song, and the company retired from the grove.

The members of the Society then convened in the School Room. Resolutions read and adopted.

By Charles Green, seconded by James W. McAlpin.

RESOLVED, That the thanks of the Society be presented to the orator of the day, for his eloquent address, and to the poet, our worthy President, for his beautiful ode, and that each be requested to furnish a copy of the same to be spread on the records of the Society.

By Charles Green, seconded by Robert D. Walker.

RESOLVED, that the approbation of the Society be accorded to the Stewards for their efficient and acceptable services on the present anniversary.

(At a meeting of the Board of Managers, in the summer of this year, date not on minutes, the following was read and adopted :)

RESOLVED, That the Society will unite with the Chatham Academy and Savannah Free School in sustaining the Commissioners on ungranted lands of Chatham County, in the expense of surveys and plats, and that Messrs. Minis and Mills be a committee to consult those parties and arrange it. If they decline then this Society will take the responsibility.

(107th Anniversary, at Bethesda, 23d April, 1857.)

*   *   *   *   *   *   *   *   *   *   *

Just after 11 o'clock, A. M., many of the members, and visitors, including a large number of ladies, having arrived, a fine American Flag, with the words "Union Society" in large letters across it, was presented by the President, in behalf of the Stewards, to the Beneficiaries of the Society.

21

162

*　*　*　*　*　*　*　*　*　*　*

The Boys being assembled around the Flag Staff, Joseph S. Fay. Esq., the President, in the presence of members of the Society, surrounded by the ladies and other invited guests, delivered the following address :

My dear Boys :

I am requested, by the Gentlemen who act to day as Stewards, and their Assistants, to place this beautiful flag, which they give to Bethesda,.in your charge. You know it is the emblem of the country to which you belong, than which none is more beautiful or glorious. It was devised and designed by the patriots and great men who first founded this government, and made ours a free and happy nation. It floats in every town and village of our land ; it is carried at the mast head of a thousand ships to every shore, and tells the world that they belong to America, the land of Washington. You must remember that he, and those who labored with him, were once little boys, with no more to boast of than you. What they became, they, with God's help and blessing, achieved for themselves. Whenever then you look upon this flag, or any other like it, remember that you must never disgrace it; that you must try to imitate the virtues of those who originated it, and who have left to you and millions of others, the glorious inheritance of their good works. In remembering this you will reward fully the care and kindness of those who have given your early days a happy home, and make them look upon their good work with joy. And as additions are made to your numbers, and other boys join and succeed you, they must learn from *your* example, and must be influenced by *you*, to follow in the path of goodness, which alone leads to happiness in this world, and beyond the grave.

At the conclusion of the address, Master Cornelius Long, made the following reply :

We have heard your remarks with pleasure. We receive this flag, and will try to be grateful for this kind remembrance of the Stewards of the Union Society. Whenever, hereafter, we shall see the American flag streaming to the wind we will endeavor to remember that we have lived under the shadow of one which bears upon it the name of the Union Society ; that under its protection, as do the happy people of this mighty country, we have lived in peace and quiet happiness. I hope we may appreciate the many blessings we enjoy here, and that we may never disgrace it by our conduct, but rather, that we may live to do honor and credit to those who have sustained us, and who have so anxiously watched over and cared for us.

May God bless the efforts of the Union Society, and guide aright us and the successors who are the objects of its protection, and who have been placed in charge of that beautiful flag of our beloved country.

To this the boys responded Amen! and while the flag was being raised, the boys gave three cheers for the flag, three for the Stewards, and three for the worthy President of the Society, in which they were joined by the members and guests. After which the party separated and partook of lunch, prior to the Society's being organized for business.

About 1 o'clock the members assembled in the school room and proceeded to the business of the Society.

The minutes of the last meeting were read and confirmed.

Joseph Story Fay, President of the Union Society submitted the following annual report:

GENTLEMEN—Members of the Union Society:

It is again my pleasant duty to make to you an annual report of the progress of the Society and the state of its funds. I am happy to say that the former has come fully up to any expectations that may have been formed, and is such as should gratify your best wishes, while our motto should still be "*onward*." Much *has* been done, but there is still more to be accomplished.

At my last years report there were 24 boys in the charge of the Society. Of this number 5 (Alexander K. Wilson, William H. Sagurs, Charles A. Sagurs, Joseph J. Singer, and Patrick O'Brien,) being of suitable age have been placed at proper trades and employments, and 3 others (Robert A. Beasley, James E. Beasley and Samuel Miller,) have been withdrawn and provided for by their friends. On the other hand, there have been added 10.

June 25, 1856, Randolph Williamson, aged 10 years.

"	"	"	Henry Ennis,	" 5 "
Feb.	18, 1857	Louis Andres,	" 12 "
March	1,	"	John Crawford,	" 10 "
"	"	"	Rufus E. Thompson,	" 8 "
"	"	"	Charles V. Biecker,	" 7 "
"	"	"	Albert Hunt,	" 10 "
"	18,	"	William J. Friend,	" 8 "
April	10,	"	Joseph Lopez,	" 4 "
"	23,	"	Thomas W. Robbins,	" 8 "

Making our present number 26. There are six more applicants, a part of whom being cases of great need will probably be admitted, though our accommodations are hardly adequate to any increase.

I am glad to state that the children maintain a high character for their general deportment, and in every way show themselves worthy of the care bestowed upon them. Their progress in education is as great as can be expected, they have been industrious, useful and orderly, and are as happy and healthy as the same number of children anywhere. I believe there has been no case of sickness requiring the attention of a physician since they have been at Bethesda.

The property of the Society stands the same as at the last report, viz:

Bethesda with its improvements, costing about	$10,000
3 Negroes	1,500
7 Shares Central Rail Road Stock, par	700
10 " Augusta & Savannah Rail Road Stock, cost	800
1 Bond City of Savannah, par	500
2 Lots and Improvements on 1½ in York street, Savannah	8,000
2 " " " the Pavilion on South Broad street	20,000
	$41,500

Of this the city property and stocks only are productive of revenue, and the total income of the Society will vary but little from last years, which was set down at $3,746 namely,

From Rents	$2,010	17
" Interest and dividends	91	00
" Contributions to support of orphans	295	00
" Donations	85	00
" Members	1,260	00
	$3,741	17

I remarked in my last report that we began the year with our improvements completed, and out of debt, and that we could now see the actual expense of maintaining our establishment. I had lost sight of the Teacher's salary, which was in arrears, and a further amount of investment which has been required in iron bedsteads, and in a pair of mules to replace a valuable horse which died during the summer. These and some other extra items, however, can be separated, and our current expenses appear to have been not far from $3,600.

Our total disbursement has been as follows:

Anniversary expenses by Stewards	$153	69
Wages for carpenters, &c., and servants clothes	133	25

Materials for building, hardware, &c.	198	89
Seeds, trees, manure, &c.	171	91
Groceries and salt provisions	643	50
Dry goods, clothing, hats and shoes	388	97
Medicines and seeds	51	12
Corn	105	27
Beds and bedding	33	25
26 new iron bedsteads	130	00
Insurance at Bethesda	78	50
Insurance of property in Savannah 2 years in part	159	25
Repairs, Pavilion Hotel and improvements, &c.	64	50
Advertising, (old bills)	26	20
Commissions, Collecting Subscriptions	16	37
Commissioners ungranted lands advertising	8	12
Disbursed by S. Z. Murphy for fresh provisions, making clothes, corn of the boys &c., &c.	620	22
Teachers salary to 23d April, 1855	105	00
" " " " " 1856, balance	225	00
" " " " " 1857, 1 year	400	00
School Books	18	73
S. Z. Murphy and wife, salary to 1st May 13 mo	1,083	33
1 pair of prime mules	369	35
	$5,184	42

This will show a balance against the Society (after deducting the balance over from last year of $233 76) and in favor of the President and Treasurer of $1,209 49.

In this am't of disbursement there is included nothing for negro hire to work the place, which has not been paid and will go to swell the cost of maintaining our family. Counting this as $600, it would appear that the legitimate expense of our 24 boys for the year has been about $175 each or $4,200. This is as cheap as the expense of maintenance was in town, with this difference against the funds of the Society, that the number of beneficiaries is more than doubled. But suppose the cost of maintenance were twice as great as under the old system, should we curtail our operations? Should we not rather enlarge them and meet the responsibilities like men? Have we not made an advance and shall we not maintain it? There is not a member of the Society, I trust, who does not recognize this and feel proud of it. Formerly we had to seek out beneficiaries, now they seek us.

There is one advantage in our change of system which has been demonstrated, and which recommends our institution as a great moral conservator. We have had several instances of boys who were unmanageable by their mother or father, and who were truants and vagabonds in Savannah, who have become obedient, useful and steady boys. This reforming influence could not have been exerted in the city, where the boys would daily have been brought into contact with their old associations. This, among other considerations, will satisfy you, gentlemen, that it is not a mere matter of dollars and cents. You are doing a great public good, and you must take no steps backward.

It is a little curious that during last summer, taking occasion to enquire into the organization of the Farm School in Boston, where a large number of boys are maintained, I found its history and system to be very similar to our own. It was an orphan asylum in the city, which convinced of the advantages of country life and education for boys, the managers converted it to a Farm School. They located it on a beautiful island in Boston Harbor, nearer but, less accessible, than Bethesda is to Savannah. The orphan house in Charleston is a glorious example to us of solid comfort, yet they lack the invigorating influences of country life. They have no scope for the cultivation of industrious habits. Our own experience and that of others must satisfy us, that we are on the right course, and have only to pursue it. If we find defects let us correct them, but let us steadily enlarge the sphere of our operations as occasion offers.

The Commissioners for the ungranted lands of Chatham County have not been idle; quite the contrary, but having no funds at their command they have been able to accomplish nothing towards procuring a full survey of the county, which the law requires and which will be rather expensive. Further legislation may be needed and called for. I am sure the matter is in good hands, and I hope that good progress will be made before another year comes round. It will be a happy thing if the Society can realize enough from this source to put up permanent and substantial buildings and enlarge its resources and usefulness. If not, we must rely upon private liberality and individual beneficence.

I would recommend the creation of a new officer, namely: that of Treasurer, as distinct from the President, who should collect all monies and disburse them on the order of the President or acting President. It will relieve this officer from a heavy labor, which added to his other duties is rather onerous.

I would also recommend the appointment of visiting and examining Committees. If every member of the Society would pledge himself upon the call of the President to pay Bethesda *one* visit a year there would be here every week no less than five members. This would be light upon all, and a great help to your President and to the Society.

The rules require quarterly meetings. It would be well if it is not considered desirable to hold them, to modify the rules, and it might be well to make an entire revision to suit our altered position and plans.

The number of members reported at the last anniversary was 257. Of these there have died 5, namely: Messrs. Wm. H. Kelly, Jacob De La Motta, John H. Ladd, Isaac Minis and James Sullivan. 7 have removed from the city, and 1 has resigned—leaving 244. To these there have been added 16 new members, bringing our present number up to 260.

I regret to say that our teacher, Mr. R. C. Tasker, contemplates leaving us as soon as we can supply his place. He has been faithful and efficient, exerting a good influence upon all those under his care.

Everything has gone on satisfactorily on the place, and Mr. and Mrs. Murphy assisted by Mrs. Chitty, have well carried out the objects of the Society. There is much yet to be done, but with the means at command, and taking all things into view, I cannot but feel that we have reason to be encouraged by the past and hopeful for the future. A fair crop was made on the place last year, and we shall not have much corn to buy. With God's blessing, I hope we shall do better and better from year to year in this particular.

The Society is indebted to Mr. William Battersby for a handsome donation of books, and also for the same to Mr. John Stoddard, and to Mr. W. R. Symons, and others, for a neat book case and numerous other kindnesses. You are also indebted to Mr. Andrew Low for a land warrant for 160 acres land. It has been located in Alamakee County, State of Iowa, and it may prove very valuable. To the Stewards of this year, and their Assistants, the boys are under obligations for being placed in charge of the beautiful American flag that to-day waves over us for the first time. It is a handsome gift.

I submit my account with the vouchers. There appears as is shewn by the summary already given a balance against the Society of $1,209 49. As it appears that the current income is nearly adequate to meet the annual expenses, it is very desirable without further reducing our capital to meet this balance and to start the year fairly and above board. I recommend this to your consideration.

As your representative and agent I have had much at heart the welfare and success of your venerable Society, and have done what I could to carry out your views. If I had not full faith in the enthusiastic interest you take in it, and were not confident that you will not fail to let any future anniversary show the *"progress* of the Society," I should regret to say that I cannot be a candidate for re-election. Circumstances may necessitate my being much absent during the year, and it is not proper or consistent with my notions for me to *hold* a place I cannot *fill.* I am heavily indebted to you for your encouragement and approbation in the past, and I shall feel it the highest compliment if you show that approbation by a zealous promotion and increase, under God's blessing, of the usefulness of the Society.

The renascent Bethesda will always have my warmest prayers, my fondest good wishes, and my untiring labor, whenever and wherever it is in my power to make that labor useful.

My friend Mr. Abraham Minis, your Vice President, whose unflagging zeal and interest in behalf of the Society are worthy of the highest praise, is necessarily absent. He has requested me to say that he is also desirous of retiring from office, though, as in my case, it will not lessen his devotion to the interests in which we have been so long and so happily united.

Respectfully submitted,

JOS. S. FAY,

President.

On motion the report and account of the President and Treasurer were received, adopted and ordered to be entered on the minutes.

ELECTION OF OFFICERS.

The Society then went into an election for Officers, for the ensuing year, and upon counting out the ballots the following result appeared, viz :

JOSEPH S. FAY, President.

ROBT. D. WALKER, Vice President.

EDWARD G. WILSON, Secretary.

WILLIAM HONE, } Stewards.
JAMES B. FOLEY, }

The President having declared the result of the elections made the following appointments, viz :

ASSISTANT STEWARDS.

James Wallace McAlpin,	James H. Demund,
James M. Prentiss,	William Francis Holland.

On motion the said appointments of Assistant Stewards was unanimously confirmed by the Society.

RESOLUTION READ AND ADOPTED

By John R. Johnson,

RESOLVED, That the Bye-Laws be referred to the Board of Managers, to report such alterations as they may deem necessary.

AMENDMENTS TO RULES, *Read 2d time.*

The following amendments to the Rules or Resolutions offered at the last anniversary and laid over, were again read, put to vote and declared carried, viz :

RESOLVED, That Rule 17th, rendering it obligatory to attend funerals of deceased members, be repealed.

RESOLVED, That the fines levied for non-attendance at meetings by Rule 3d be repealed.

The Rules were then declared amended accordingly.

The meeting then adjourned and proceeded to the Grove, the place prepared for the annual address. The exercises were opened with prayer by the Rev. Joseph S. Key, of Trinity Methodist Church, after which the Rev. George H. Clarke, of St. John's Episcopal Church, delivered a brief and well written address, which was listened to with deep attention by the Society and the visitors.

The President then announced that as most of the boys were small they felt themselves unable to sing for the gratification of the audience, and therefore some of their friends would be heard in their place.

The following Ode, written by Rev. John Pierpont, Jr., of the Unitarian Church, was sung with much spirit and effect, by Mrs. Scholl, Wm. F. Holland, and others.

THE ORPHANS' WELCOME.

AIR.—"What fairy like music."

Kind friends, we are orphans, all sad and alone,
No father to greet us, no mother to bless;
On the wings of the night-wind we utter our moan,
No eye to beam kindly, no hand to caress.
'Neath the sod in the graveyard, our parents' forms lie ;
Their spirits look on us in love from the sky.

Oh ! could they surround us, as once, even now,
With visible blessings, their love and their care,
Ere death pressed in silence its hand on the brow,
And angels above caught their last pleading prayer,
We should not be left to this heart-anguished moan,
Nor fatherless, motherless, feel all alone.

22

And yet to the will of our Father in heaven
  We bow in submission, as orphan hearts should ;
He bereft us of parents, but still He has given
  True faith in His kind, ess : true faith in the good,
Whose hearts and whose hands here in mercy provide
Kind parents to those whose own parents have died.

Perhaps 'tis but little we give in return,
  For the love that has blessed every day of our youth ;
We may not *say* much, but our grateful hearts burn
  To repay all your kindness by love and by truth;
We feel that dear friends are near us to bless ;
"We ask not, we pray not, for one sorrow less."

Then welcome, kind friends, to the orphans' "sweet home,"
  For the smile of our Heavenly Father is here ;
These blue skies may greet ye where ever ye roam,
  But they smile not more sweetly, they shine not more clear,
Than over the home for the fatherless reared,
  Bethesda, the sweet spot to orphans endeared.

The exercises were closed with a benediction by Rev. A. J. Karn, of the Lutheran Church.

The members of the Society then returned to the school room, when the following resolutions were offered and unanimously adopted, viz :

By Mr. Joseph B. Ripley, seconded by Enos O. Withington.

RESOLVED, That the thanks of the Society be tendered to the Orator for his eloquent address, and to the Rev. Mr. Pierpont for his Ode, so beautifully sung by the amateur choir, and that a copy of each be requested to be placed in the archives of the Society.

By Thomas Purse, Esq., seconded by Wm. Hone, Esq.

RESOLVED, That the thanks of the Society be presented to the Stewards for the manner in which they have provided for our wants to-day.

By Mr. Frederick W. Sims,
                              as ameded by Hon. John C. Nicoll.

RESOLVED, That the thanks of this Society are due to Mr. William Battersby and Mr. John Stoddard for books, and Mr. John M. Cooper, and others, for a bookcase, and also to Mr. Andrew Low, for the gift of a land warrant of 160 acres of land, which has been located in Iowa.

In order to pay the amount advanced by the President, for certain expenses necessary in starting the improvements, &c., at Bethesda, as mentioned in his report, John Schley, Esq., moved that the subscription fee of members be ten dollars per year annually. After some discussion, the following resolution was read and adopted, viz:

By Thomas Purse, Esq.

RESOLVED, That the members of the Union Society pledge themselves to pay five dollars or procure a new member, to meet the present deficiency of the Treasury, within the next 3 months.

* * * * * * * * * *

The President then appointed the following Board of Managers for the ensuing year, viz:

John M. Cooper, John R. Johnson,
William Battersby. William M. Wadley,
George W. Wylly.

The Society (in company with the male visitors) adjourned to the dinner table, (where the ladies had previously been,) and did full justice to the ample provision made for their refreshment by Mr. Chick, under the direction of the Stewards and their assistants.

The boys enjoyed the table spread before them, and were very kindly waited upon by Messrs. James W. McAlpin and James H. Demund, the Stewards, and their Assistants.

The Society then adjourned, and the company separated for their respective homes, after having spent a delightful anniversary.

(108th Anniversary, at Bethesda, 23d April, 1858.)

The minutes of the last meeting were read and confirmed.

Joseph S. Fay, Esq., the President of the Society submitted the following annual report, viz:

ANNUAL REPORT.

To the Members of the Union Society:

It is again my duty, as your President, under the 7th Rule of the Society, to report to you "its progress and the state of its funds."

The property of the Society is the same as heretofore reported, with slight variation, say about $41.000. This includes the cost of Bethesda, its outfit and servants, which, of course, produce no income. The productive property is as follows:

The Pavilion Hotel in South Broad street.

Two Lots and Improvements on York street.

7 Shares of Central Rail Road Stock.

10 Shares of Savannah & Augusta Rail Road Stock.

1 Bond of the City of Savannah for $500.

6 Shares of South Western Railroad Stock.

Besides this there is a quarter section of land located in Iowa.

The late Mr. Wm. Starr occupied a house on the western half of one of the Society's Lots on York street, for a long period of years, at a ground rent of $50 per annum. The house was erected by him, or by the person from whom he bought or received it, and as there appeared to be no lease or contract, for the occupancy of the Society's land, he was considered, and I believe considered himself, as a tenant at will. No issue, however, was ever made with him, and from respect to his advanced age, he was never disturbed, though the ground rent was not more than half the legal interest on the estimated value of the half lot. Under these circumstances, though, it may be that the house, both in Law and Equity, should revert and belong to the Society, on whose land it stands, the Board of Managers have thought it proper and agree to allow the heirs of Mr. Starr $500 for the improvements. This seemed to the Board liberal, yet to have done otherwise might have savored of oppression. It is better for them than the removal of the buildings, relieves any apparent hardship in the case, and gives the Society at once an increase of annual income of $250.

The late Mr. Henry Haupt, I am credibly informed, bequeathed among other legacies, the sum of $500 to the Society, but in some way the will has been lost. His good intentions may be frustrated by the inability to establish the will on the part of the executor, Mr. George S. Frierson. I hope it may not be so, but even if it is, I trust that so thoughtful an act on his part in his hours of feebleness and sickness may be appreciated by the Society, and this example not be lost upon others.

I submit with this the Treasurer's Account, showing a balance of $46 63 in the Treasury of the Society; also a statement of the sources of our income, and the details of our expenditure. The total of the latter is $4,945 90, showing the cost of maintaining our boys (the average number for the year having been about 30,) not far from $165 each. The income appears to have been $3,981 99, showing a deficiency of $963 91 which has been made up by special contributions.

At the time of my last report there were twenty-five boys in the charge of the Society, since which there have been 19 admitted, and four withdrawn by parents or guardians—none having been of a suitable age to bind out. The present number under your care is 40.

We have now reached the maximum number that we can shelter, even if our pecuniary ability were adequate to support more, and as many as can be thoroughly instructed by one teacher.

It may reasonably be asked by you, why with an inadequacy of income your managers have continued to enlarge the operations of the Society. The answer is, that we have had to feel our way and gain our own experience. It has been an experiment, and though our expenses *may* be beyond our income, a successful one. The salaries, cost of buildings and specific expenses, are no greater for 40 boys than for 25. The only addition to the cost is for food and clothing If the Society and the community will not sanction what we have done, we cannot go back to 25 only, we must go back to a small family of 12, which can be superintended and instructed by one person. But when you consider the advantages conferred on the community, the relief to the suffering, the good accomplished, there seems only one course to pursue. It does not seem a question of how we shall reduce our expenditures, and restrict our charities, but how we shall increase our resources, and perfect and extend our operations.

My last report showed the Society to be in debt the sum of $1,209 49. An active effort at your anniversary meeting resulted in a considerable addition to the number of members, and some donations were made to the funds of the Society. Among them was one for $175, from an unknown but liberal friend, with the promise of a like sum annually, on certain conditions. All this, however, was insufficient, and this winter a further movement was made to relieve the Society from debt, and add to its permanent funds. The appeal was not a general one, for want of time, but a generous response has been made, and thirty-seven ladies and gentlemen have contributed upwards of $2,700 Unquestionably more would have been obtained by more extended applications, but it is hoped that all interested will come forward and follow up this beginning, with such voluntary aid as they may be able to render. *Our debt is paid for the present*, and $500 has been added to the property of the Society, and about the same amount set apart for the "building fund."

You will perceive that the house occupied by the Superintendent and his family is very much decayed, and we must be providing means to erect substantial, permanent and more extensive buildings to accommodate more enlarged operations on the part of the Society. We should also steadily increase our permanent fund, so that our income may be of sufficient amount to be independent of the annual fluctuation in the number of contributing members. This should be the fixed policy of the Society. At the last anniversary meeting the suggestion to separate the offices of President and Treasurer met the approval of the Society, though it could not be finally acted upon. The Board of Managers therefore felt authorized to adopt the change, and

---

elected Mr. James M. Prentiss temporarily as Treasurer, but his other arrangements compelling him to give up the appointment it was transferred to Mr. James A. Courvoisie, who now holds it. Both these gentlemen have rendered acceptable service.

At the same meeting also, the Rules of the Society were referred to the Board of Managers for entire revision. They have performed this duty, and now submit a draft of Rules or By-Laws conformable to the altered position and operations of the Society. I hope they will be approved and promptly adopted.

With regard to "the ungranted lands in Chatham County," nothing has yet been accomplished, and without the co-operation of the Trustees of Chatham Academy, who seem quite indifferent to the matter, I fear nothing will ever accrue to the Society from them.

I submit a report from our Superintendent and farmer, Mr. Murphy. Our farm has gained somewhat in productiveness, and has added more than in any previous season to the support of the family. I hope this progress will continue—much has been done, but more remains to be accomplished.

It seems hardly needful to comment upon the state of things here. It shows for itself to those who visit Bethesda. To those who do not I will briefly state that Mr. Murphy, as Superintendent, and Mrs. Murphy, as Matron, have well performed their parts, and that all has gone on steadily and in a satisfactory manner.

Our school has been more successful than ever, and has been pronounced by those who have examined it as second to none of its class in Chatham County, or perhaps elsewhere. The Teacher of last year, Mr. Tasker, left us for the west, soon after the anniversary, as contemplated, and was succeeded by Mr. William H. Shepard, whose report I submit with this. He has proved himself very competent, and has given entire satisfaction. The boys have progressed admirably under his care, and continue to maintain a high character for deportment. They usually attend, when the weather is suitable, the Isle of Hope Church, and are indebted to some ladies and gentlemen of that District for valuable Sunday School Instruction.

The Superintendent's report shews a continuance of health, for which we should be duly grateful to the Giver of all Good. During the three years and upwards that we have occupied Bethesda, there has been, as he remarks, no occasion to call a physician to the boys under our charge. This is also an evidence of good care and judicious superintendence.

The number of members reported at the last anniversary was 260. Some have removed to other sections of the country, and others,

Robert Raiford and W. W. Goodrich, have gone "to that bourne whence no traveler returns." Some have resigned, but enough have been added to bring your present number up to 363.

I congratulate you upon the prosperous condition of the Society. It occupies a position in the affections and interest of the community, which insures its vigorous continuance and maintenance. To the Board of Managers I owe many thanks for hearty co-operation and kind assistance at all times. You owe an acknowledgement to them for the principal cost of an addition to the sleeping accommodations of the boys, and among them to Wm. T. Thompson, J. R. Sneed, Esq., the Rev. John Pierpont, Jr., and Mrs Perla S. Solomons, for valuable books, and to others for many tokens of friendship. I close with this my term of service as your President. Its remembrance will be full of pleasant associations, and I am thankful to you for your confidence, and for the encouragement and the very many kind expressions I have received from members of the Society. I have retained the post longer than I intended, and as long as it was one of doubt or embarrassment. All is now progressing well, "though the poor ye have always with you," and there is no rest from duty. A good work has been begun, and God has so far favored it. It is for you, with His help and blessing, to continue it. Without these you will work in vain.

May God bless and prosper the Union Society.

JOS. S. FAY.
President.

SUPERINTENDENT'S REPORT.

BETHESDA, April 17, 1858.

To Mr. Joseph S. Fay, President of the Union Society:

Dear Sir—At your request, I make the following statement of the stock belonging to the Society, and of produce raised on the place during the past year:

We have 1 pair of Mules, worth	$350
2 Horses "	175
35 head of Cattle, large and small, at $8	280
125 " " Hogs, " " " at $2	250
Farming Utensils, worth	150

$1,205

We lost last season (died and strayed) 11 head of cattle, and among them, some of our best cows.

Last year we had under cultivation 50 acres of land, in corn, peas, potatoes. (sweet and irish) oats, beans, sugar cane, turnips and melons. We raised as many garden vegetables as could be used on the place. We hauled out and applied during the course of the season 452 two-horse loads of manure; made 612 panels of new fence, repaired 919 panels of old. Our fencing is now, for the most part, in good order.

I consider that the place is improving yearly, and the use of so much dressing on the land tells upon the product. On one piece of 1½ acres of light land which would without manure produce about 12 bushels of corn to the acre, we raised 152 bushels, or nearly 34 bushels per acre, in consequence of a free use of compost made in the cowpen of marsh mud and grass. I find deep ploughing also very beneficial in the relief afforded, from the effects of drought.

According to my estimates, we raised in all last year, about

600 bushels corn, peas, &c., worth 85c.	$510 00
300 bushels sweet potatoes, at 50c.	150 00
1060 pumpkins, at 6c.	63 60
We have killed pork and beef for the use of the place, 2395 lbs. net. at 10c.	239 50
We have sold pork, cattle, calves and hides.	259 57
We have raised forage enough for our own use, worth.	150 00

$1372 67

The boys work cheerfully, and many of them are very handy in the various departments of farm work. Indeed, all our labor except that which is too heavy, is accomplished by them. They usually do the most of their work in the afternoon, thereby avoiding the morning dews and having the benefit of the afternoon sea breeze.

In addition to field work, the boys assist in washing and ironing, scouring, milking, together with all the small work about the place.

We have morning and evening prayers, and on the Sabbath the boys attend the Sabbath School and worship at the Isle of Hope Church.

For the most part we have been favored in health, and have had no occasion to call a Physician on the place for the three years that the boys have been at Bethesda.

As for the management, we endeavor as much as possible to control them by appealing to their feelings and by relying upon their respect for themselves and those connected with the institution. We encourage them by relying upon their respect for themselves and those connected with the institution. We encourage them by allowing each boy a small piece of ground, upon which to raise corn, for which we

pay them double the market value and a premium for the largest pro⁴
duct. This stimulates their efforts and they frequently, after regular
working and play hours, are seen tending their crops by torch-light.

Mr. Shepard, the teacher, is of great assistance to me with the
boys when at work, enabling me to accomplish much more than I
otherwise would be able to do. All of which is respectfully submitted.

S. Z. MURPHY, Superintendent.

TEACHER'S REPORT.

To the Managers of the Union Society.

Gentlemen—With the exception of a little over three months, a
portion of five days per week has been spent in school. Our session
has been from 7 to 12 o'clock, A. M , during the summer and autumn,
and from 8 o'clock, A. M., to 1 o'clock, P. M., during the winter and
spring, with, in each case, one half hour's recess. Also, from two to
three hours each evening, is spent by the greater portion of the school
in reading and study, where they are free to communicate with each
other and their teacher, in the preparation of their lessons, or, to listen
to any remarks their exercises may call forth or an opportunity may
offer, to impress a truth, or lead the mind to greater action. Sabbath
School lessons are studied Saturday evenings. In all our efforts in
mental culture the improvement of the heart is kept in view.

For the increased number of pupils our school room is far too small,
and we are forced to sacrifice comfort and convenience in our limited
space.

We feel warranted in saying, not boastingly, that, considering their
advantages, a more intelligent class of boys cannot be found; and we
feel that our exertions, for the improvement of their minds, have
been amply rewarded in the interest all have manifested in their
studies, in their exertions to gratify their teacher, and in their advancement; still our motto ever is "Excelsior."

Two or three of the more advanced usually have charge of some in
the elements of reading and spelling, and thereby I can devote more
time to the more advanced classes, and all make greater progress. We
make singing a daily and general exercise, which is entered into with
much spirit; most of them are natural singers, and only require cultivation. We devote part of an evening one week in practicing singing with the larger boys, and part of an evening of the next week,
alternately, in a juvenile debating society, which affords pleasure as
well as profit. Subjects for discussion are usually chosen, of which
all have learned, or may learn from our library, and thus they are led
to chose profitable reading, and facts become fixed in their minds.

We have a library of about 380 volumes, many of which are in a
style to attract and interest youth, to which the many and interesting
little readers have daily access.

The latter part of the year, a few of the larger boys have been
drawn out of school each week, the same boys every fifth week, to
assist on the farm, which makes their amount of schooling about 2½
months per year less than the smaller boys, or about 7 months schooling per year, though many smaller boys are more advanced than many

23

large ones. Those which would most derange the classes have always been chosen by the Superintendent, who, with the Matron, have ever sought to promote the interests of the school, and through their kind and efficient care, seldom a boy is out of school on account of sickness.

Before closing these remarks we would present our most earnest thanks to those officers of the Society, who have stimulated to greater exertion by the awarding of prizes, and who have manifested so kind an interest in our welfare and improvement.

Respectfully presented,
WM. H. SHEPARD, Teacher.

BETHESDA, April 23d, 1858.

Summary.

The following represents the number of boys in school, including the Superintendent's sons, and their present attainments, as taken collectively.

Whole number in School,*			40
"	"	who Read and Spell,	32
"	"	who study Mental Arithmetic,	9
"	"	who Cipher,	16
"	"	who study Primary Geography,	17
"	"	who study Geography and Map Drawing,	6
"	"	who study Grammar,	7
"	"	who study Physiology,	2
"	"	who practice Declamation,	25
"	"	who write Compositions,	6

*This includes Mr. Murphy's children.

Current Income and Expenditure of the Union Society, for year ending April, 1858.

Income.

Received for annual subscriptions,	$1,260 00	Bethesda
" rents, less repairs and insurance,	1,964 95	
" Dividends,	95 00	
" interest,	17 50	
" Support of boys from guardians,	375 00	
" Sales farm produce,	269 54	
	3,981 99	
Deficiency made up by donations,	963 91	
	$4,945 90	

Expenditure.

Anniversary expenses,		$113 58
Addition to house sleeping rooms,		97 33
Insurance on buildings,		75 00
Repairs, Carpenter work,		38 00
Lumber,		57 97
Furniture (10 new bedsteads, &c.,)		129 35
Dry Goods for clothing, &c.,		406 56
Making clothing for boys,		160 13
Provisions and groceries,		888 38
Meal and grist,		91 53
Corn, peas, rice, flour, &c.,		286 30
Hats,		33 78
Shoes,		97 46
Medicine, Garden Seed, &c.,		81 11
School books, stationery, &c.,		105 53
Table cutlery, &c.,		22 95
Glassware and crockery,		43 27
Household expenses, sundry,		62 63
Hardware, stove pipe and repairs,		45 06
Farm utensils, tools, &c.,		99 38
Repairs, wagon,		20 83
Outfit for boys apprenticed Jan. 1857,		82 37
Labor and Servant hire,		457 35
Servants' clothing,		31 75
An old horse,		50 00
Salaries—Mr. and Mrs. Murphy,	$1,000	
Mrs. Chitty,	85	
Mrs. Spencer,	24	
Mr. Shepard,	235	
Mr. Tasker, *present,*	25	
		1,369 00
		$4,945 90

SUMMARY FROM TREASURER'S ACCOUNT CURRENT.

Total Expenditure this year, as per Treasurer's report, as published in
  printed "Proceedings of the 108 Anniversary"............$6,615 89
Added to Permanent Investments................ $500 00
Invested as a Building Fund,.................... 510 00
                               ————— 1,010 00
Leaving Balance in hand...................................... 46 63
                               $7,672 52

Receipts from all sources,............................$4,930 52
Donations from 37 persons,............$2.712 00
Subscriptions...... .... 30 00
                   ————— 2,742 00
                               ————— $7,672 52

(The By Laws of the Union Society reported by the Board of Managers are omitted here, this being the first reading.)

Thomas Purse moved to accept the By-Laws as reported, put the same in operation for one year, and then take a final vote thereon. Adopted unanimously.

ELECTION OF OFFICERS.

The Society then went into an election of officers for the ensuing year, (Joseph S. Fay, Esq., the present President, and Edward G. Wilson, Esq., the present Secretary, declining re-election,) and upon counting out the ballots the following result appeared, viz:

ROBERT D. WALKER, elected President.
JOHN M. COOPER, elected Vice President.
JOHN T. THOMAS, elected Secretary.
JAMES A. COURVOISIE, elected Treasurer.
FREDERICK MYERS, } elected Stewards.
FREDERICK W. SIMS, }

The President having declared the result of the elections the Society adjourned, and with the ladies and other visiters partook of refreshments.

The Society and visiters then proceeded to the grove, the place prepared for the annual address.

The exercises were opened with prayer by the Rev. Reddick Pierce, after which an appropriate address was delivered by the Rev. W. H. Potter.

The exercises were closed by a benediction by the Rev. W. H. Potter.

The members of the Society then returned to the School Room when the following resolutions were read and unanimously adopted:

By Frederick W. Sims, seconded by William R Symons.

RESOLVED, That the thanks of this Society be tendered to the late President, Joseph S. Fay, and to the late Secretary, Edward G. Wilson, for their long and faithful service as officers of this Society.

By William Battersby, Esq.

RESOLVED, That the thanks of this Society be tendered to W. T. Thompson, J. R. Sneed, Rev. John Pierpont, and to Mrs. Perla Sheftall Solomons (a descendant of one of the founders of the Society) for valuable books.

By Joseph S. Fay, Esq.

RESOLVED, That the thanks of the Society be tendered to Messrs. Wadley and the late Board of Managers for their contribution towards the addition to the house made by them.

By F. W. Sims.

RESOLVED, that the thanks of the Society are due and hereby tendered to the Rev. W. H. Potter for his beautiful and appropriate address, and that a copy be requested to be placed in the archives of the Society.

By Edward G. Wilson.

RESOLVED, That the thanks of the Society be and the same are hereby tendered to those members of the Society and others who made the very handsome donations to the funds of the Society set forth in the Treasurer's accounts submitted this day.

By William T. Thompson.

RESOLVED, That the Board of Managers be instructed to have published in pamphlet form the report of Ex-President Fay with the other reports, and the address of Rev. W. H. Potter, and that the cost be raised by voluntary subscription of the members of the Society.

(Here follows list of Beneficiaries, 40 in number.)

The President appointed the following Board of Managers, viz:

Abraham A. Solomons,   Emanuel Heidt,
Benjamin Whitehead,   James Wallace McAlpin,
John Gammell,   Wallace Cumming,
John Scudder,   James H. Demund,
William R. Symons.

The Society then adjourned.

EDWARD G. WILSON,
Secretary.

ANNIVERSARY SONG,

(Sung at the 106th Anniversary, April 23d, 1856, instead of the Ode, as stated by mistake on page 161.)

AIR.—"HOME AGAIN."

Here again, here again,
    Beneath these shades we meet;
A year has pass'd, how free from pain,
    Within this calm retreat!
The days of youth, how slow they fly
    When Hope, impatient, paints
The future with a cloudless sky,
    The present, all restraints.
        Happy youth! Happy youth!
        Its cares, like April show'rs;
        To age is left to feel the truth,
        Joys fade like summer flow'rs.

Age alone, Age alone,
  Press'd on life's hurried race,
Can tell how deeply sin and wrong,
  The lines of sorrow trace.
It learns to pity other's woe—
  It feels that earth has given
No peace, no Joys, like those that flow
  From hopes laid up in heav'n.
    Happy age! Happy age!
      Whose steps now blameless roam,
    Along life's fitful, changing stage, ·
      Still drawing nearer home.

Then let youth early learn,
  That life is not a play—
That good and gay may have their turn,
  But good must rule the day.
Age an example has to give,
  Of patience and of love,
That youth from it may learn to live,
  That life which dawns above.
    Happy youth! Happy age!
      Each has its calling due,
    To write its record on the page
      Of useful and of true.

        .

~~~~~~~~~~~~~~~~~~~·

*Items of expenditure for tuition, &c., from Journal 3 not embraced in
extracts on pa●●92 to 96.*

1802. DISBURSEMENTS FOR CHILDREN TO CASH.   Dr.
Dec. 20. For this sum paid Wm. F. Port for tuition....$24.00
          Paper, Ink and Quills................... 2.00——26.00
1803.
April 23. For this sum paid Mrs. Lydia M. Myers,
            for tuition......................   6.00
          CONTINGENT EXPENSES TO CASH.   Dr.
  " 24. For this sum paid Peter S. Laffitte, for
            services as Secretary for one
            year, ending 23d instant......   60.00
  " 28.   Do. James Johnston for printing
              3 qrs Summons................. 4.00
            Do. Lyon & Morse for publishing
              four advertisements, from
              26th Jan'y to 7th instant.... 3.75—— 7.75
June 3.   Do. John Lawson, Steward, being
              so much expended on the last

Ann. more than the amount rec'd from members for Anniversary expenditures........... 106.08

DISBURSEMENTS FOR CHILDREN DR. TO CASH.

June 16. Do. Wm. F. Port, for tuition, paper, ink and quills.............. 25.62

CONTINGENT EXPENSES DR. TO CASH.

" 28. Do. Hazen & Kimball for posting the accounts of the Society, and for two Account Books as per receipt...................... 158.00

July 8. Do. Seymour, Woolhopter & Stebbins for printing for the Society from the year 1799 to the 23d April, 1803, inclusive, as per accounts and receipts............................ · 36.52½

DISBURSEMENTS FOR CHILDREN. Dr. to Cash.

Sept. 19. Do. paid Schooling 16.00
Paper, ink and quills........... 37½——16-37½

Nov. 4. Do. John Lawson, for clothing.... 26.50

Dec. 19. Do. Paid tuition..................... 9.00

1804.

Feb. 16. For this sum paid John Lawson for D. & C. Gugel's account of clothing for —— Randolph....... ..... 21.00

March 22. Do. Wm. F. Port, for tuition........ 10.50

April 2. Do. G. Tufts & Co., for 1 pair shoes for Randolph............. 75

CONTINGENT EXPENSES TO CASH. Dr.

July 2. For this sum paid Peter S. Laffitte for one years' salary to 23d April last, 60.00

" 18. Paid the Stewards, being so much expended on the last Anniversary, more than was received from the members...................... 52.62½
Paid Lyon & Morse for printing............ 2.75
" Seymour & Woolhopter, do.............. 3.50——58.87½

DISBURSEMENTS FOR CHILDREN. Dr. to Cash.

Dec. 27. For this sum p'd Wm. F. Port, for schooling children......................... 67.50

Do.	Mr. Lawson for clothing.......	9.00——76.50

1805.
March 30. Paid Mr. Port for schooling...............   37.50
1806.   CONTINGENT EXPENSES TO CASH.   Dr.
April 23. Paid James Johnston for printing.........   8.00
     "   James Hely,   "   ".............   2.00
     "   Lyon & Morse.........................   4.25
     "   Ann Scrimger bal. on Ann. Dinner 45.25
     "   Joseph Prescott for two wands......   1.50
     "   Seymour & Woolhopter for print'g.   3.75
     "   Thos. Dechenean for advertising a
        Bank Note which delivered to the
        President.................................   2.50——67.25
1808.
April 23. Paid J. Johnston for printing.............. 12.00
     "   Adam Cope (Steward) a balance due
        him on the Anniversary Dinner... 33.75
     "   J. F. Everett for printing............   4.00
     "   Seymour & Woolhopter, for do......   2.75——52.50
1809.
April 24.   "   McLean & Barnes....................   6.00
     "   Everett & Evans.....................   4.75
     "   Jas. Johnston, printing.............. 33.75——44.50
       Peter S. Laffitte paid him 17th Oct.
       last.....................................   20.00

(The following entry appears in Journal 3, folio 134.)
1810.
April.   Cash.   Dr.
    To Bonds and Notes received from *Orphan House Estate.**
Feb. 23. Rec'd of C. Odingsells on account his bond.600.00
Mar. 2.   "   Jas. Johnston,   "   "   "   485.02~1085.02
         (And in Ledger 4, folio 202.)
1814.   VOLUNTARY CONTRIBUTIONS.   Dr.   Cr.
April 23. By cash received from sundry persons....   70.00

(*This is all that appears upon any book in possession of the Society, in reference to the *Orphan House Estate.* In looking for Acts and Records relative to it or to Bethesda, the following have been found. See pages of Acts and Schedule which follow.)

An act to explain an act, entitled "An act to establish an academy in the county of Chatham, and for vesting certain property in Selina, countess dowager of Huntingdon.

1. WHEREAS there is in this state a considerable property, real and personal, known and distinguished by the appellation of Bethesda College or Orphan House estate, originally intended for an academy, and devised in trust by the late rev. George Whitefield for literary and benevolent purposes, to Selina, countess dowager of Huntingdon, and the same was, in and by an act, entitled " An act to establish an Academy in the county of Chatham, and for vesting certain property in Selina, countess dowager of Huntingdon," vested in her accordingly: *And whereas,* the said Selina, countess dowager of Huntingdon, was a British subject, and is, since the passing of the said act, departed this life, whereby the said trust is concluded, and the heirs of the said Selina being likewise British subjects and non-residents, are incapable of receiving or executing the same, and it therefore becomes necessary for the legislature to explain their intention respecting the premises, as well to effect the end for which the same was devised, as to remove all doubts, in and concerning the same: *Be it enacted by the Senate and House of Representatives of the state of Georgia in General Assembly met,* That the true intent and meaning of the said act was, and the same shall be construed to have been a vesting of the said Bethesda College or Orphan House estate in the said Selina, in trust for benevolent and literary purposes, only during her natural life and no longer.

2. *And be it further enacted,* That the said property, both real and personal, called Bethesda College or Orphan House estate, as aforesaid, shall from and after the passing of this act, be under the inspection of thirteen trustees, a majority of whom shall have power to employ such professors and tutors, and to establish such rules and regulations for admission into and the governance of the said college, and to employ such overseers and managers for the working the said estate to advantage, and to do all other, and further acts and things in and concerning the same as they may think necessary and beneficial for carrying the original intention of the aforesaid institution into full effect, to hold the same, and the powers hereby vested to the said trustees and their successors in office for ever.

3. *And be it further enacted,* That the trustees hereby appointed, shall be and they are hereby declared a body corporate, and as such shall be authorized to use a common seal, and shall be liable to sue and be sued *Provided,* That no action shall be brought against the said trustees for the term of two years after the passing of this act.

4. *And be it further enacted,* That George Houston, William Stevens, William Gibbons, Senr., Joseph Habersham, Joseph Clay, Junr., William Gibbons, Junr., John Morell, Josiah Tattnall, Junr., John Milledge, James Whitefield, Junr., George Jones, Jacob Waldburger, and James Jackson, shall be, and they are hereby appointed trustees for the purposes hereby intended; and in case of vacancy, either by death, resignation or other means, the said trustees or a majority of them, shall ballot for three persons, out of whom his excellency the governor shall select one to fill the same.

5. *And be it further enacted,* That the said trustees, or a majority of them, shall once in every year, well, truly and faithfully account for and have their accounts,

21

receipts and expenditures, in and concerning the premises, audited, and the same with a copy of their proceedings, laid before the governor for public information.

WILLIAM GIBBONS,
Speaker of the House of Representatives.

NATHAN BROWNSON,
President of the Senate.

EDWARD TELFAIR, *Governor.*
December 20, 1791.

AN ACT *to authorize the Trustees of the Orphan House or Bethesda College, in the county of Chatham to sell certain unproductive lands, and to reduce the number of Trustees of the said Institution.*

WHEREAS, it appears by the memorial of the Trustees of the Orphan House, in the county of Chatham, that it is expedient to sell and dispose of certain unproductive lands, belonging to the said Institution.

SEC. 1. *BE it therefore enacted by the Senate and House of Representatives of the State of Georgia, and it is enacted,* That it shall and may be lawful to, and for the Trustees of the said Orphan House or College, or a majority of them, to sell and dispose of, at public or private sale, the following tracts of land: (that is to say) one thousand acres in the former Parish of St. Patrick, now county of Glynn, situate and being on the south branch of Turtle River, bounded at the time of survey, on all sides by vacant lands; also five hundred acres in the former Parish of St. David, now county of Glynn, bounded to the north-east by the Altamaha river, to the north by a Carolina survey for Henry Laurens, and on every other side by vacant land; and also five hundred acres in the same Parish of St. David, and county of Glynn, bounded eastwardly by the Altamaha, north-west by land laid out for Henry Monroe, and to the south by land vacant, which said several tracts of land, were granted to the Reverend George Whitefield, for the endowment of the said Institution, of which he was the founder, and to make and execute good and sufficient titles to the purchaser or purchasers of the said land, in whole or in part, in fee simple or otherwise, as to the said Trustees shall seem most beneficial and advantageous; and to apply as well the monies arising from such sale or sales, as the rents, issues and profits of those other lands appertaining to the said Institution, known by the name of Bethesda, Euphrates, Nazareth, Huntingdon, Habersham, or by whatever other name or names such lands may be called or known, to the use, benefit and advantage of the said Institution, according to the intention of the founder, and the laws of the State relative thereto.

AND WHEREAS, from the difficulty of convening a majority of the present Trustees, it is rendered expedient to reduce the number.

SEC. 2. *BE it therefore enacted,* That the present Trustees shall continue and remain until by death or otherwise, the number shall be reduced to nine, and that in the meantime, a majority of the existing number shall constitute a board, and be competent to do and perform all the business of the said Institution. And from and after the reduction of the said Trustees to the number nine, the said nine, or a majority of them, shall constitute a board, and be competent to business as aforesaid, and that when and so often as a vacancy shall happen amongst the said nine members, such vacancy shall be filled as heretofore by the governor.

187

SEC. 3. *And be it further enacted,* That all acts heretofore passed, so far as the same are contrary hereto, be and the same are hereby repealed.

ABRAHAM JACKSON,
Speaker of the House of Representatives.
JARED IRWIN,
President of the Senate.

Assented to, December 3, 1804.
JOHN MILLEDGE, Governor.

AN ACT *to authorize the president of the trustees of the Bethesda college, the president of the Union society, the president of the board of managers of the Savannah poor house and hospital society, the chairman of commissioners of the Chatham academy, and the mayor of the city of Savannah, to dispose of the property of the Bethesda college or orphan house estate, for the uses herein mentioned.*

WHEREAS, It has been suggested that from the loss by fire of one of the wings of the college, the injury of the other, as well as the destruction of the buildings on the plantation by the hurricane, and which inundated the rice lands with salt water so as to render them unproductive, with other casualties, have rendered this property by no means advantageous, or the original intention of the institution in its present situation capable of being carried into effect. To the end thereof, that the said property may be useful, and applied as nearly as possible to the original intention of the said institution.

SEC. 1. *BE it therefore enacted by the Senate and House of Representatives of the State of Georgia, in General Assembly met, and by the authority of the same,* That it shall and may be lawful for the president of the trustees of Bethesda college for the time being; the president of the Union society in Savannah, for the time being; the president of the board of managers of the Savannah poor house and hospital society, for the time being; the chairman of commissioners of the Chatham academy, and the mayor of the city of Savannah, for the time being, or a majority of them, to sell and dispose of all the real and personal property of the said Bethesda college or orphan house estate, on the most advantageous terms that may be obtained for the same, and to make titles to the purchasers thereof; and after the trustees of the orphan house estate shall have retained a sufficiency to pay any just debts that may be due and owing from the said orphan house estate, and also retained a sufficient sum to pay any debts that may be in litigation until decision at law on such claims, when such sum retained shall be applied agreeably to such legal decisions, to apply the nett proceeds as follows, that is to say: one-fifth of such nett proceeds to the uses of the Savannah poor house and hospital society; and the remainder of such nett sum, one-half thereof to the Union society in Savannah, and the other half to the Chatham academy, to aid their funds for the instruction of youth generally.

SEC. 2. *And be it further enacted,* That the aforesaid herein authorized persons shall, after carrying this act into execution, file their proceedings in the executive office of this State for public information.*

SEC. 3. *And be it further enacted,* That the commissioners of the Chatham Academy shall, in consequence of this donation, support and educate at least five orphan children from its funds, as soon as it shall receive the property herein vested in said institution.

---

*Application having been made to the Executive Department through Mr. W. T. Thompson, one of the Managers, for a copy of said "proceedings," the letter on next page from Mr. T. M. Bradford, was received in reply.

Sec. 4. *And be it further enacted*, That nothing in this Act shall be construed to defeat the responsibility of the present trustees of the Bethesda college, under an act passed in December, 1791.

Sec. 5. *And be it further enacted*, That this act shall be held a public Act.

BENJAMIN WHITAKER,

Speaker of the House of Representatives.

HENRY MITCHELL,

President of the Senate.

Executive Department, Georgia, Assented to, 22d December, 1808.

Jared Irwin, *Governor.*

LAND AND GENERAL AGENCY OFFICE, }
Milledgeville, Aug. 11, 1859. }

Mr. W. T. Thompson.

Dear Sir: Your letter of the 8th inst., addressed to P. Thweatt, Esq., was received by him, and as every moment of his time is taken up in the examination of the Tax Digests which have been recently returned to his office, he handed to me your letter with a request that I would attend to it.

Yesterday and part of the day before, I have devoted to the examination of the books and papers in the Executive office, to endeavor to find the "proceedings" to which you allude; but I have been unsuccessful. I went through the whole of the Index Book of Packages, and examined every package having any thing from Savannah or Chatham county—all returns from Academies, Poor Schools, Colleges, &c. I then went through a large number of packages of "Miscellaneous Papers;" and I then examined all the small books, as I supposed it possible the return may have been made in a small book. In all this tedious and laborious search I found nothing with the name of *Bethesda* on it, except one return, made by Judge Wil. Stephens, dated 28th Oct., 1801, containing proceedings "appropriating two thousand dollars for repairing and completing North wing," &c. This report appears to have been filed for information, &c. If the report to which you allude, was ever sent up, it has been placed where it ought not to be, or I certainly would have found it.

After spending so much time about it, I regret that I have been unsuccessful. If the recorded proceedings of the Society show in what year these "proceedings" took place, and you desire it, I will make further search.

Very respectfully,   T. M. BRADFORD.

SCHEDULE of debts apportioned to the Savannah Poor House and Hospital Society from the debts arising from the sale of Bethesda or Orphan House Estate.

1809. March 15. Amount received by Poor House and Hospital in purchase of negroes, exclusive of the one-fourth cash payment.......................... .... $1,270 00

Bond and mortgage of			W. G. Porter, Security......		832 00
"	"	"	Peter Miller,	"	180 00
"	"	"	Moses Sheftall,	"	400 00
"	"	"	Thomas Jones,	"	472 50
"	"	"	William A. Moore,	"	1,088 00
"	"	"	John D. Mongin,	"	870 00
"	"	"	John H. Deubell,	"	1,335 00
"	"	"	William Cocke,	"	202 50

$6,650 00

Upon a division had this day of the debts proceeding from the sales of Bethesda or Orphan House Estate, according to the Act of Assembly passed the last session of the Legislature, amongst the Union Society, the Chatham Academy, and the Savannah Poor House and Hospital, the above proportion was taken and accepted by the President of the Board of Managers of the Savannah Poor House and Hospital Society. Therefore, we the subscribers, Commissioners appointed by the said Act of the Legislature, hereby assign, transfer and set over unto the said President of the Board of Managers of the Savannah Poor House and Hospital Society and his successors in office, and assigns for the use of said Savannah Poor House and Hospital Society, the said bonds and mortgages, and all right, interest and title thereto belonging, hereby giving and granting full power and authority to the said President of the Board of Managers of the Savannah Poor House and Hospital Society and his successors in office or assigns to receive, sue for and recover the said different debts and amount, and upon receipt and payment of the said debts or either of them, good and sufficient receipts and discharges to be given for the same, by the said President of the Board of Managers of the Savannah Poor House and Hospital Society or his successor in office or assigns. Dated at Savannah this seventh day of August, in the year of our Lord one thousand eight hundred and nine.

W. B. BULLOCH, *President Union Society,* [L.S.]
CHARLES HARRIS, *Chairman C. A.* [L.S.]
JOHN P. WILLIAMSON. *Mayor C. S.* [L.S.]

Witnesses:
J. CUYLER, N. P.
C. POPE.

Recorded 6th November, 1809 in County Records Book C. C. folio 325.

Cash Account Kept by President Sheftall—1815, '16, '17.

This is the only record the Society has of this period. The book in which it is contained is about the size and style of a child's copy book, and was given to the Society together with a loose sheet containing the resolution of thanks which follow, by Mr. Lizar Solomons.

UNION SOCIETY.

—:o:—

1815.			DR.	CR.
April 23.	To balance due on old account. examined and passed.		75	
" 24.	" cash paid H. Williams, late Secretary, rec't. No. 1.		145.00	
" 27.	" " deposited in Bank		287.00	
May 2.	" " " " "		21.50	
" 4.	" " paid over to the Secretary		5.00	
	By cash on 23d April, received in Society			225.38
" 1.	" " received of Thomas Mendenhall			16.50
" 1.	" " received of James Hunter			4.50
" 3.	" James Powell			4.00
	R. W. Habersham for Judgment obtained against			
	Judge Stephens			205.50
				$455.88
4.	" cash paid Ann Christie, per rec't.	No. 2	168.00	
23.	" " " J. J. & F. Blanchard, rec't.	No. 3	19.50	
24.	" " " May & Lewis,	No. 4	11.25	
"	" " " Votee,	No. 5	5.00	

June	6.	" " "	Williams & Seymour,	No. 6	90.00	
	23.	" " "	Ann Christie,	No. 7	181.50	
	26.	" " "	Chatham Academy,	No. 8	119.00	
	29.	" " "	Hoag & Ames,	No. 9	5.00	

				$1058.50
	29.	" amount brought forward	1058.50	
		By amount brought forward		455.88
July	19.	By cash received of C. Treasurer on account of two Exchange shares up to Jan'y. 1st, 1815		60.00
		To cash paid R. H. Pettygrue, rec't, No. 10	49.00	
Aug.	15.	By cash received of Js. M. Wayne on a judgment against Jos. Scott, deposited in Bank		57.00
	16.	By cash received of Js. M. Wayne on account of Stulz & Gibson's bond		200.00
	15.	To cash paid Ann Christie, rec't. No. 11	96.00	
	16.	" " " J. Fisher, No. 12	2.50	
	17.	" " R. H. Pettigrue, 13	35.00	
	26.	" " E. S. Kempton, 14	4.00	
Sept.	1.	" " R. H. Pettigrue, 15	9.99½	
Nov.	3.	By cash received of Jno. B. Norris, Sheriff, on judgment against Levi Sheftall interest, cost &c. included,		142.00
	6.	By cash received of J. Cuyler on jugdment against P. Deveaux		100.00
		To cash paid at Bank and took up note, No. 16	240.00	
Dec.	15.	By cash of Js. Morrison, on a judgment against Jno. Detten cost &c		74.00

				$1088.88
	"	To cash paid Stebbins & Mason, rec't. No. 17	43.68½	
	"	" " " Jno. Douglas, 18	5.00	

				$1543,68½
	"	" amount brought forward	1543.68½	
		By amount brought forward		$1088.88
1816.				
Feb'y.	13.	To cash paid Hoag & Ames, rec't. No. 19	4.00	
	15.	" " " Eaton & Johnson, 20	4.00	
	29.	By cash received of G. Glen acting Secretary being by him received of Densler, on rent account		70.00
		To cash paid Ann Christie, rec't. No. 21	70.00	•
March	25.	" " " Wm. T. Williams, rec't. No. 22	21.50	
		By cash received of Wm. B. Bulloch on a judgment against estate John Glass 22d June 1815 omitted to be credited deposited in Bank		297.25
April	9.	To cash paid E. S. Kempton's acc't 23d	4.00	
Omitted.				
1815.				
May	2.	To cash paid G. Glen on Dinner account	41.87½	
Aug.	16.	To cash paid at Bank take up note	160.00	

1816.

April 17. To cash paid at Bank per balance on note due...... 74.76

                                                                       1923.81 1456.13

29. By cash received of R. W. Habersham amount of
Jos. Tatnal's and J. Howell's Estate bond principal
and interest............................... 331.50

                                                                       $1787.63

19. To amount brought forward.....................1923.81
By amount brought forward.................... 1787.63

22. To cash paid balance of Mrs. Christie's account..... 142.00
By cash received of Js. M. Wayne on balance of
James Johnson and Jno. Wood's Bond, principal
and Interest................................. 1235.00

" To cash paid Js. Marshall Cashier P. Bank balance
due by Building Committee.................. 575.67

" To cash paid Chatham Academy................. 105.00

                                                                       $3022.63

Settled April 23d, 1816.

April 23. By balance due Society on settlement
this report of Committee..................... 593.64
By cash received from sundry persons in Society, this
day 268.87½

April 26. To cash paid F. Densler, Steward balance on Dinner
account,   rec't. No. 1..... 55.00

May 1. To cash paid May & Lewis,   rec't. No. 2..... 10.25
" " " A. Low & Co.   3..... 2.75
" " " D**** Gresham & Co.   4.... 20.62½
3. " " " Jno. Tanner   5..... 14.37½
4. " " " E. S. Kempton,   6..... 3.75
4. " " " Hoag & Ames,   7..... 3.00
9. By cash of H. McCall........................... 62.00
" " of Wm. Gaston......................... 10.00
" " of R. Habersham....................... 10.00
" " of Jos. Habersham Jr., excused him $1.50
cash..................................... 13.00
21. By cash of J. P. Williamson for estate Jno. Williamson... .... 4.00
" " of Petite DeVilliers.................... 6.00
• 23. To cash paid Ann Christie board, &c.,   No. 8..... 131.00
" " " " " for clothing,   9..... 5.31¼
June 20. To cash paid Jno. Hunter, Committee of Repairs for
lumber, &c.   No. 10..... 48.59

                                                    $294.65¼ 917.51½

" By amount brought forward..................... 917.51½
" To amount brought forward.................... 294.65¼
" By cash received of Jno. J. Robert, C. Tr., one years'
interest on 2 Exchange Shares up to January 1st
1816.. 24.00

	21.	By cash received of G. Glen, for the following acs. viz: Geo. Low, $6.00; Es. J. Powell, $4; Alex. Habersham, $11.00; Jos. Habersham, $7.00....			18.00
		Jno. Lawson, $4.00........................			4.00
	"	By cash received by self of R. Isaacs............			61.50
	"	" " of A. Low..................			60.50
	1	To cash paid P. D. Woolhopter, being balance due him on his account,	No. 11.....	5.25	
	"	Paid E. S. Kempton per receipt	No. 12.....	5.00	
	21.	By cash received of J. M. Wayne on bonds of Stulz & Gibson and Jonathan Norton..			845.00
	26.	To cash paid P. D. Woodhopter, rec't. No. 13.....		6.25	
		By cash of Peter Deveaux's account.............			16.00
July	8.	" " received of J. Cuyler on Bond of P. Deveaux agreeable to resolution of U. S...............			180.43¼
					2136.95¼
	10.	To cash paid Brown & Green, lumber rec't. No. 14.	123.000		
				$434.15¼	
	10.	To amount paid brought forward...............	434.15¼		2136.95¼
	16.	To cash paid H. Gibert. rec't. No. 15.....		6.50	
	"	" " " Jno. Hunter, 16.....		21.50	
	19.	By cash received of Jno. H. & G. Ash, 2 years rent of lot No. 2 and 3, Percival Ward, up to the 4th of June, 1816..............................			200.00
Aug.	7.	To cash paid R. W. Habersham, T. C. a. per rec't. No. 17.......................................		119.00	
	8.	To cash paid T. V. Gray, rec't. No. 18.....		62.50	
	12.	By cash received of W. Davis on judgment against W. Lewden................................			215.50
	15.	To cash paid Mrs. Christie, rec't. No. 19.....		96.00	
	22.	" " " " " rec't. 20.....		7.87½	
Oct.	23.	" " " T. V. Gray, 21.....		62.50	
Omitted.					
Sept.	21.	Cash paid E. S. Kempton, rec't. No. 22.....		5.00	
Nov.	9.	" " Hoag & Ames, " 23.....		5.00	
	9.	" " Abm. Stevens. 24.....		5.62½	
	11.	" " Gillett & Milne, 25.....		8.12½	
	"	" " May & Lewis, 26.....		22.62½	
	15.	" " Ann Christie, 27.....		117.50	
	16.	" " Hoag & Ames, 28.....		5.00	
	"	" " E. S. Kempton, 29.....		3.00	
				$981.90¼	2552.45¼
		To amount brought forward..................		$981.90¼	2552.45¼
"	19.	To cash paid P. & J. Barrie, rec't. No. 30.....		8.04	
		" " " May & Lewis, No. 31.....		21.62½	
	26.	By cash of R. W. H. on a judgment against Es. J. Clay, Jr..................................			322.14
Dec.	2.	To cash paid J. Carr in advance one quarter's schooling ten boys, No. 32.....		80.00	
	13.	To cash paid Jno. Hunter, Building Committee per rec't. No. 33.....		200.00	

193

1817.

Jan'y. 13. To cash paid John Hunter, Building Committee.
rec't. No. 34.....530.00
14. Cash paid John Douglas, 35..... 5.62½
Feb'y. 11. " " Eaton Johnson, 36..... 3.37½
" " Wm. T. Williams. 37..... 59.07
12. " " T. V. Gray, Sec'ry.. 38..... 62.50
15. " " Ann Christie, 39....120.00
" " P. D. Woolhopter, 40..... 5.25
18. By cash received of J. Cuyler on judgment against
Ex'ix Jno. Glass............................... 225.59
March 3. To cash paid Jno. Carr, No. 41..... 92.66
13. " " " John Hunter, 42.....300.00
31. " " " J. Morrison, advertising lands for sale,
rec't. 43..... 6.75

$2476.79¼ 3100.18¼
April. To amount paid brought foward...............$2476.79¼
By this amount received brought forward........ 3100.18¼
5. To cash paid Jno. Douglas shoes rec't. No. 44..... 7.87½
7. By cash received in Society this day............ 166.50
10. To cash paid Jno. Hunter, B'ding Com'tee, 45.....400.00
17. " " advanced for Dinner.................. 30.00
April 21. " " paid Eaton, Johnson & Co.. Shoes, No. 46.. 1.25

2915.92 3266.68¼
To balance carried down......................... 350.76

$3266.68 3266.68

By balance brought down.......................$ 350.76
E. E.
Savannah, 23d April, 1817.

April 23. By balance in hand this day..... .... 350.76
Cash received in Society this day......., ... 231.75
" of John Lawson.............. .... 7.50
24. To cash paid T. V. Gray, act'g for Stewards, No. 1, 11.50
25. By cash of P. Deveaux, annual contribution.... 4.00
28. To cash paid T. V. Gray, Sec'y, No. 2..... 62.50
29. By cash received of D. B. Mitchell............. 46.00
May 2. To cash paid S. Hollis. rec't. No. 3..... 50.00
" " " Way & Baker, 4..... 45.50
5. " " " Jonas Harrison & Co. 5..... 26.12½
" " " R. May, 6..... 1.18½
13. " " " Jonas Harrison & Co. 7..... 4.50
14. " " " Way & Baker, 8..... 7.06½
' By cash received of J. M. Wayne, Esqr., the bal.
of Stulz & Gibbons' bond.................... 679.72
15. To cash paid Ann Christie, board, &c. 9.....192.50
20. " " " John Carr, Teacher. 10..... 83.00

25

July	5.	John Douglas.	11...	1.00	
	"	' A. Stevens.	12....	6.75	
	23.	' T. V. Gray, Sec'ry	13.....	38.50	

			$530.12½	1319.73
	23.	To amount pd away brought forward.... ....530.12½		
		By this sum rec'd and brought forward..........		1319.73
Aug.	11.	To cash paid Jno. Carr, (tuition) rec't. No. 14.... 83.00		
	18.	Cash paid Robert Christie (board, &c.) No. 15....180.00		
	20.	To cash paid Jno. Hunter, Building Com., No. 16..240.00		
	28.	" " " Wm. Starr's account, No. 17........ 10.00		
Nov.	12.	By cash of C. Treasurer, on Exchange Shares up		
		to January 1st, 1817......................		24.00
	17.	By cash of H. Densler for 6 quarters rent of half		
		of lot No. 3.............		60.00
		To cash paid Jno. Carr, Teach'g, board, &c., rec't.		
		No. 18...................................260.72		
Dec.	1.	By cash received Es. Francis Courvoisie........		90.73
		To cash paid T. V. Gray, Sec'ry, quarters salary.		
		No. 19.................................. 62.50		

Omitted.

Nov.	24.	To cash paid A. Low & Co.,	No. 20.... 45.43	
Dec.	5.	Cash paid Jno. Carr's bill for making clothes, 21.... 22.00		
	7.	By cash collected at the Presbyterian Church, in-		
		cluding T. V. Gray's due bill for 20 dollars.....		370.75
	9.	By cash received of Ths. Young, Esqr., this		
		amount of legacy left by Ths. Young, dec'd, prin-		
		cipal.......................... .... ⎰		428.57
		£100 in dollars............................ ⎱		
		Interest on the above for 9 years........... ...		308.52
		By cash a donation from Miss Campbell........		5.00

			$1439.77½	2607.30
	14.	To this amount paid brought forward...... ..1439.77½		
		By this amount received and brought forward....		2607.30
		By this amount collected this day at the Episcopal		
		Church.... . ...:...........		229.81¼
	16.	To cash paid Jno. Hunter, for building, No. 22...370.75		
	21.	By cash collected at Methodist Church..........		34.56
	24.	To cash paid Jno. Bapt*** for Coffin, rec't. No. 23.. 6.00		
	28.	By cash received of R. C. Chapel..........		38.25
	29.	To cash paid Jno. Hunter per receipt No. 24......302.62½		

1818.

Feb.	3.	By cash received of Js. Morrison, a donation from	
		an unknown hand.........................	50.00
	4.	By this amount received of R. W. Habersham on	
		judgment against P. * Jno. H. Moril..........	511.48
		To cash paid Wm. T. Williams, stationary, No. 25. 75.19	
	13.	" " " Jno. Carr, per rec't. No. 26.....411.72	
	15.	By cash received at Baptist Church.............	32.00

March 19.	To cash paid Jno. Hunter, B. C.,	No. 27.....613.20		
	" " " Jared Hotchkiss,	No. 28..... 2.50		
26.	By cash received of J. Morrison & Lloyd, on judgment against estate Jno. Eppinger, Jr........			30.87½
27.	To cash paid Mr. Carr in advance. rec't 29....100.00			
			3321.76	3534.27⅞
April 6.	By this amount received and brought forward....			3534.27¼
	To this amount paid away brought forward......3321.76			
	By this amount received this day in Society......			68.50
7.	" " " " " " " "..........			24.50
8.	" " of Lloyd & Morrison on a judgment against A. Hunter.................			75.81¼
"	To cash paid G. Relphs for Linnen. rec't. No. 30.. 18.02			
13.	" " " Moses Cleland.	31..... 21.45		
14.	" " Clark & Tillitson,	32..... 3.00		
21.	" " Betsy Beard, (work, &c.)	33..... 12.00		
			3376.23	3703.09
	To balance due carried down................ 326.86			
			3703.09	3703.09
	By balance brought down...................			$326.86

Errors excepted.

Savannah, 23d April, 1818.

Signed   MOSES SHEFTALL.

Resolution on a loose sheet of letter paper in the handwriting of Secretary Morrison, which accompanied the book containing the above, received from Mr. L. Solomons.

On motion of JAMES M. WAYNE, Esq.—

Resolved, "Unanimously that the thanks of this Society be presented to Doctor MOSES SHEFTALL, for his faithful and constant exertions to advance the interest of this Society during the three last years of his Presidency."

Extract from the Records of the Union Society, at a quarterly meeting, April 23, 1818.   JAMES MORRISON, Sec'ry.

MEETINGS OF THE SOCIETY, &c.

1774, 1st Monday in January, at the house of Peter Tondee.

Wm Gibbons, Sec.

1775, April 24th, 23d being Sunday, at same place at 8 o'clock, A. M.

David Zubly, ⎰ Stewards.
N. W. Jones, ⎱

" " Advertisement for a person to school the children. " "

1784, April 21—At the house of Richard Donavan Murray.

David Montaigut, Sec.

1784, April 23—At the same place, at 9 A. M., to choose officers, and celebrate the Anniversary. Dinner to be on table at 3 o'clock.

David Montaigut, Sec.

1785, Feb'y. 14—At the house of Mr. Allison, at 6 P. M., Special business.

David Montaigut, Sec.

1786, April 24—At the Coffee House, 9 A. M., to choose officers and celebrate the Anniversary. Dinner at 3 P. M.

David Montaigut, Sec.

Wm. Pierce, Ben. Lloyd, Stewards.

1786, June 5, Members in arrears earnestly requested to pay to the President by 1st Monday in August.

David Montaigut, Sec.

1786, Sept. 14. A certified copy of the Act of Assembly, passed 14th July, 1786, for incorporating this Society, being read,

Resolved, That the thanks of this Society be given to the Hon. William Gibbons, Esquire, Speaker of the House of Assembly, Major John Habersham, William Pierce, and George Walton, Esquires, Members of the House of Assembly, and the Honourable Benjamin, Andrew and William Gibbons, jun. Esquires, of the Executive Council; members of this Society, and all other members of the Legislature who supported the said law in the different stages thereof; and that this resolution be published in the next Gazette.

David Montaigut, Secretary.

1787, April 23—At the Coffee House, 9 A. M. to choose officers, pay arrearages and celebrate Anniversary.

David Montaigut, Sec.

UNION SOCIETY.

The Members of this Society are desired to meet at the Coffee House in Savannah, on Monday, the 23d instant, at nine o'clock in the forenoon, to choose officers for the ensuing year, pay off their arrears, and celebrate the Anniversary of this Society.

David Montaigut, Secretary.

Savannah, April 2d, 1787.

—:o:—

ON THE UNION SOCIETY.

Welcome the worthy President,
And welcome all, I say,
You meet to keep and celebrate
Anci'nt Saint George's day.

The founders of this Society—
Wisdom their plan had laid;
Benevolence their sole design—
'Twas the distressed to aid.

The unlearnt, hopeless orphan youth—
O virt'ous Institution!—
They took them in, and had them taught,
To forward their promotion.

Those who survive remember, then,
Their plan improve and cherish,
Never to let the helpless youth
For want of learning perish.

Then will your worthy names resound
Thro' all the world around,
And they with grateful thanks repeat
The benefits they found.

God Grant you length of happy days,
Old age and time may prove,
Friendship in heart and mind may reign
In Unity and Love.

1788, April 23—At the Coffee House, 9 A. M., to choose officers, pay off arrears, and celebrate Anniversary. Those who had not attended for some time past, particularly requested to notify the President whether they considered themselves any longer members or not.

David Montaigut, Sec.

1789, April 23—At Coffee House, 9 A. M., to choose officers, pay off arrears and celebrate Anniversary. D. M. Sec.

1790, April 5—Notice given to those who have been admitted members and who have neglected to pay their admission money, and subscribe the Rules, to do so by the Anniversary, or they will no longer be considered members. D. M. Sec.

1790, April 23d—At Brown's Coffee House, 9 A. M., to choose officers, pay arrears and celebrate Anniversary D. M., Sec.

1799, Jan. 7—At the Filature, "precisely at sun set"—quarterly
meeting.   Peter S. Laffitte, Sec'ry.

1800, Jan. 7—At the City Hall, "precisely at sun set"—quarterly
meeting.   Peter S. Laffitte, Sec.

1800, July 7—At the City Hall, "precisely at 8 P. M."—quarterly
meeting.   Peter S. Laffitte, Sec.

1801, Jan. 5—At the City Hall, "precisely at 6 P. M."—quarterly meeting.   Peter S. Laffitte, Sec.

1801, April 23—At the City Hall, "precisely at 9 A. M. to
transact the business of the day, and celebrate the Anniversary."
                                           Peter S. Laffitte, Sec.

1801, July 6—At the City Hall, "precisely at 6." P. M.—quarterly meeting.   Peter S. Laffitte, Sec.

1802, April 5—At the City Hall, "precisely at 10 A. M."—quarterly meeting, preparatory to the Anniversary.
                                           Peter S. Laffitte, Sec.

1803, Jan. 27—At the City Hall, "precisely at 6 P. M."—extra
meeting.   Peter S. Laffitte, Sec.

1803, April 23—At the City Hall, "precisely at 10 A. M."—to
transact the business of the day, and celebrate the Anniversary. Dinner
at half-past 3 o'clock.   Peter S. Laffitte, Sec.

1804, April 23—At the City Hall, "precisely at 10 A. M."—to
transact the business of the day, and celebrate the Anniversary.
                                           Peter S. Laffitte, Sec.

1805, April 23—At the City Hall, "precisely at 8 A. M."—to
transact the business of the day, and celebrate the Anniversary. A
charity sermon will be preached by the Rev. Mr. Clay, in the Baptist
Church, at 12 o'clock.   Peter S. Laffitte, Sec.

1806, April 7—At the City Hall, "precisely at 9 A. M."—quarterly meeting preparatory to the Anniversary.
                                           Peter S. Laffitte, Sec.

"Those persons who are desirous of joining this institution will
take notice, that agreeable to the rules, unless application is made at
the above period, they will not be admitted at the Annual Meeting."
                                           Peter S. Laffitte, Sec.

1806, April 23—At the City Hall, "precisely at 9 A. M."—to
transact the business of the day, and celebrate the Anniversary. Sermon at 12 M., by the Rev. Mr. Best, in the new Presbyterian
Church, St. James' Square.   Peter S. Laffitte, Sec.

Officers elected—Gen. D. B. Mitchell, President, Wm. B. Bulloch,
V. P., Peter S. Laffitte, Sec., Adam Cope and Edward Harden,
Stewards.

1807, April 6—At the City Hall, 10 A. M.—quarterly meeting preparatory to the Anniversary.　　　Peter S. Laffitte, Sec.

"Those persons who are desirous of joining this institution will please take notice that agreeable to the rules, unless application is made at the above period, they will not be admitted at the Annual Meeting."

1807, April 23—At the City Hall, " precisely at 9 A. M."—to transact the usual business and celebrate the Anniversary. A Sermon at 12 M., by the Rev. Mr. Kollock, at the new Presbyterian Church, St. James' Square.　　　Peter S. Laffitte, Sec.

1808, April 4—At the Filature, precisely at 9 A. M.—quarterly meeting preparatory to the Anniversary.
　　　　　　　　　　　Peter S. Laffitte, Sec.

1808, April 23—At the City Hall, precisely at 9 A. M.—to transact the usual business, and celebrate the Anniversary. A sermon at 12 M., by Rev Mr. Holcombe, in the Baptist Church, New Franklin Square.　　　Peter S. Laffitte, Sec.

From the Savannah Republican, April 28th, 1808.

On Saturday, the 23d Instant, the Union Society of this city, met at the City Hall, and celebrated their fifty-eighth Anniversary. At 12 o'clock, they went in procession to the Baptist Church, where a handsome discourse was delivered by the Rev. Mr. Holcombe, from the following words: "He that has mercy for the poor, happy is he"—from thence they returned to the City Hall, admitted eight new members, and at four o'clock, sat down to an elegant dinner provided by Mrs. Gunn, and spent the remainder of the day as usual, in harmony and good order.

OFFICERS ELECTED FOR THE ENSUING YEAR.

WM. B. BULLOCH, Esq., President.
WM. DAVIS, Esq., Vice President.
PETER S. LAFFITTE, Secretary.
Mr. ROBERT HABERSHAM. } Stewards.
Mr. JAMES BILBO,

John Lawson, Jeremiah Cuyler, John M. Berrien, Esqrs., Committee to superintend the education of children schooled upon the bounty of the Society.

From the Savannah Republican, April 25th, 1809.

The fifty-ninth Anniversary of the Union Society was celebrated on Monday last, the 24th instant. An appropriate discourse was delivered in the Presbyterian Church, by the Rev. Mr. Kollock, at the request of the Society, which concluded with an affecting address to the seventeen boys, educated and supported on the bounty of the institution. The members of the Society partook of a well provided dinner at the Filature, and spent the day in great harmony.

The following persons were elected to the offices of the Society for the ensuing year :

WILLIAM B. BULLOCH, re-elected President.
WILLIAM DAVIS, re-elected Vice President.
JOHN N. BRAILSFORD, re-elected Secretary.
THOMAS SCHLEY, } Stewards.
ROBT. J. HOUSTON. }
JOHN M. BERRIEN, }
JOHN P. WILLIAMSON, } School Committee.
MORRIS MILLER. }

UNION SOCIETY.

The members of the Union Society, are desired to convene at the Filature, on Monday, the 23d instant, precisely at ten o'clock, in the forenoon, to transact the usual business of the day, and celebrate their anniversary.

J. N. BRAILSFORD, Sec'ry.
April 21st, 1810.

1810, April 23—At Filature, precisely at 10 A. M.—to transact the usual business of the day and celebrate their Anniversary.

John N. Brailsford, Sec.

1810, July 2—At the City Hall, 7 P. M.—quarterly meeting.

John N. Brailsford, Sec.

1810, Oct. 1—At the City Hall, 7 P. M,—quarterly meeting.

John N. Brailsford, Sec.

1811, April 23—At the Filature, 10 A. M.—to transact the usual business of the day, and celebrate their 61st Anniversary.

John N. Brailsford, Sec.

1811, July 1—At the City Hall, 7 P. M.—quarterly meeting.

John N. Brailsford, Sec.

1811, Oct. 7—At the City Hall, 7 P. M.—quarterly meeting.

Griffin L. Lampkin, Sec. P. T.

1812, Jan. 2—At Filature, "Monday morning next," at 6 o'clock. Quarterly meeting. Griffin L. Lampkin, Secretary.

1812, April 23—At Filature, precisely at 10 A. M.—to transact the usual business and celebrate 61st Anniversary.

Griffin L. Lampkin, Secretary.

From the Savannah Republican, 30th April, 1812.

The following gentlemen were chosen officers of the Union Society, for the ensuing year, at their Anniversary meeting on the 23d Instant.

WILLIAM B. BULLOCH, President.
JAMES JOHNSTON, Vice President.
GRIFFIN L. LAMPKIN, Secretary.
FREDERICK S. FELL, } Stewards.
D. M. McCONKY. }

From the Savannah Republican, Jan'y. 5th, 1813.

NOTICE.

The meeting of the Union Society which was to have taken place last evening, is postponed until this evening, the 5th instant, at 7½ o'clock, in consequence of a large number of the members not being able to attend.

The members are requested to be punctual in their attendance, as business of much importance will be brought before the Society.

G. L. LAMPKIN, Sec'ry.

1813, April 23d.—At the Georgia Hotel, 10 A. M.—to transact the usual business and celebrate their Anniversary.

G. L. Lampkin, Sec.

From the Savannah Republican, April 24th, 1813.

UNION SOCIETY.

Yesterday, being the 63d Anniversary of the Union Society, they assembled at the usual hour, at the Georgia Hotel. At 12 o'clock they formed in procession, and preceded by the youths educated by their bounty, repaired to the Baptist Church, where an elegant and appropriate discourse was delivered by the Rev. Mr. Johnston, from St. Luke, 6th chapter and 36th verse. *"Do good, and lend; hoping for nothing thereby, and your reward shall be great."* They then returned from whence they came, and after going through the business of the day, sat down at 4 o'clock, to an excellent dinner, provided for them by Mr. Bunch. The day closed in good humor, harmony, and social converse. The following gentlemen were chosen officers for the ensuing year:

JOHN M. BERRIEN, re-elected President.

JAMES JOHNSTON, Vice President.

G. L. LAMPKIN, Secretary.

STEELE WHITE, }
JOHN KELL,   } Stewards.

P. D'VILLERS,   }
OLIVER STURGES, } School Committee.
WM. PARKER,   }

1813, Oct. 4th—At the Exchange, 7 P. M.—quarterly meeting.

G. L. Lampkin, Sec.

1814, Jan. 3.—At the Exchange, 7 P. M.—quarterly meeting.

G. L. Lampkin, Sec.

1814, Jan. 6.—At the Exchange, 7 P. M.—adjourned meeting.

G. L. Lampkin, Sec.

1814, April 23.—At the Exchange, 10 A. M.—to transact the usual business of the day, and celebrate the 64th Anniversary.

G. L. Lampkin, Sec.

1814, July 11.—At the Exchange, 8 P. M.—quarterly meeting.
H. W. Williams, Sec.

1814, Oct. 8.—Members requested to meet at the Exchange on Monday evening next. H. W. Williams, Sec.

1815, April 24.—At the Exchange, 10 A. M.—65th Anniversary. Dinner at half-past 3. Business of importance to be laid before the Society. Members will come prepared to settle their accounts. H. W. Williams, Sec.

From the Savannah Republican, April 25th, 1815.

UNION SOCIETY.

Yesterday being the 65th Anniversary of the Union Society, they assembled at the usual hour, at the City Hall, after going through the business of the day, sat down at 4 o'clock, to an excellent dinner, provided for them by Mr. Bunch. The day closed in good humor, harmony and social converse. The following gentlemen were chosen officers for the ensuing year:

MOSES SHEFTALL, President.
EDWARD HARDEN, Vice President.
JOHN WALLACE, Secretary.
RAYMOND DEMERE, } Stewards.
FREDERICK DENSLER, }

1821, April 23.—At Society's Hall, 10 A. M.—71st Anniversary. A sermon will be delivered by the Rev. Mr. Capers.

L. Mason, Sec.

From the Savannah Republican, April 24th, 1821.

UNION SOCIETY.

The 71st Anniversary of the Georgia Union Society was celebrated yesterday. The members assembled at the usual hour at their Hall, and after going through the business, a spirited address was delivered to them, and the youths educated and supported upon their bounty, by Mr. Carr, a member of the Society. At 3 o'clock, they partook of a well provided dinner, and the day closed with that harmony and sociability which ever distinguish cordial and benevolent hearts.

The following gentlemen were elected officers for the ensuing year:

R. W. HABERSHAM, President.
W. C. DANIEL, Vice President.
L. MASON, Secretary.
Dr. MOSES SHEFTALL, }
JOS. GEORGE, }
JOHN LEWIS, } Managers.
JOSIAH PENFIELD, }
JACOB SHAFFER, }

1822, April 23.—At Society's Hall, 10 A. M.—72d Anniversary

L. Mason, Sec.

From the Savannah Republican, April 24th, 1822.

UNION SOCIETY.

The 72d Anniversary of the Georgia Union Society was celebrated yesterday. The members assembled at the usual hour at their Hall, and after going through the business of the Society, they repaired with the youths educated by their bounty, to the Episcopal Church, where an eloquent and impressive discourse was pronounced by the Rev. Mr. Cranston. At 3 o'clock they partook of a well provided dinner, and the day was closed with harmony and sociability. The following gentlemen were elected officers for the ensuing year :

STEELE WHITE, President.

JAMES EPPINGER, Vice President.

L. MASON, Secretary.

GEORGE W. COLE, }
ISAAC D'LYON, } Stewards.

The President elect, appointed the following gentlemen to constitute the Board of Managers for the ensuing year:

JOHN F. LLOYD, WM. SMITH, S. M. BOND, MICHAEL BROWN, JOS. C. HABERSHAM.

1823, April 23.—At Society's Hall, 10 A. M.—73d Anniversary.

L. Mason, Sec.

From the Savannah Republican, April 24th, 1823.

UNION SOCIETY.

Yesterday was the seventy-third Anniversary of this benevolent institution. About fifty members assembled at the Society's Hall, from whence they moved in procession to the Episcopal Church, *the use of which had been kindly granted on the occasion*, where divine service was performed by the Rev. Mr. Carter, and an eloquent and impressive oration was pronounced by Thomas U. P. Charlton, Esq., a member of the Society. The Society then returned to the Hall, where the following gentlemen were elected officers for the ensuing year :

THOMAS POLHILL, President.

JAMES S. BULLOCH, Vice President.

L. MASON, Secretary.

G. W. ANDERSON, }
CHARLES HARTRIDGE. } Stewards.

The President elect appointed Mich'l Brown, Wm. Smith, James Eppinger, G. W. Coe, and S. C. Schenk, a Board of Managers.

At 4 o'clock the Society sat down to an excellent dinner, which had been provided by Messrs. Nesler & Griggs, at the Exchange, and the day closed with that harmony and sociability which ever distinguish cordial and benevolent hearts. This Society is the oldest of the kind in our State—its object is benevolence in the education and support of orphans. It surely then should meet the decided support of every good citizen.

1824, April 23.—At Society's Hall, 10 A. M.—74th Anniversary.

L. Mason, Sec.

From the Savannah Republican, April 24th, 1824.

UNION SOCIETY.

The seventy-fourth Anniversary of this valuable institution, was yesterday celebrated in the usual manner. A discourse was pronounced by the Rev. Mr. How, and the following officers were appointed for the succeeding year:

WM. DAVIES, President

JOHN C. NICOLL, Vice President.

L. MASON, Secretary.

HUGH ROSE. } Stewards.
L. GORDON, }

MANAGERS.

GEO. W. COE, S. C. SCHENK, WM. SMITH, GEORGE GLEN, G. W. ANDERSON.

1825, April 23d.—At Sunday School Room, Academy, 10 A. M. 75th Anniversary. L. Mason, Sec.

From the Savannah Republican, April 25th, 1825.

UNION SOCIETY.

The seventy-fifth Anniversary of the Georgia Union Society, was celebrated in this city on Saturday last. The members assembled at the usual hour, at their Hall, and after going through the business of the Society, they repaired with the youths educated by their bounty, to the Lutheran Church, where an impressive discourse was pronounced by the Rev. Mr. Mealy. At 3 o'clock they partook of a well provided dinner, and the day was closed with harmony and good fellowship. The following gentlemen were elected officers for the ensuing year:

JOHN C. NICOLL, President.

ALEX. TELFAIR, Vice President.

L. MASON, Secretary.

W. W. GORDON, } Stewards.
THOS. CLARK, }

MANAGERS.

GEO. W. ANDERSON, GEO. GLEN, S. C. SCHENK, JACOB SHAFFER, NORMAN WALLACE.

1826, April 24th,—At Society's Hall, 10 A. M.—76th Anniversary.

L. Mason, Sec.

From the Savannah Republican, April 24th, 1826.

UNION SOCIETY.

The seventy-sixth Anniversary of the Georgia Union Society, (falling on Sunday,) was this day celebrated in the usual style. The members assembled at 10 o'clock A. M., at their Hall, and after going through the business of the Society, they repaired with the youths educated by their bounty, at 12, to the Lutheran Church, where an address was delivered by M. Myers, Esq., a member of the Society; previous to which, an appropriate prayer was offered up to the throne of Grace, by the Rev. Mr. Mealy. The following gentlemen were re-elected officers for the ensuing year:

JOHN C. NICOLL, President.
ALEX. TELFAIR, Vice President.
L. MASON, Secretary.
GEO. H. JOHNSTON, } Stewards.
SOLOMON COHEN. }

BOARD OF MANAGERS.

NORMAN WALLACE, GEORGE W. ANDERSON, JACOB SHAFFER, FRANCIS SORREL, MORDECAI MYERS.

1827, April 23d.—At their Hall, Academy, 10 A. M.—77th Anniversary.

L. Mason, Sec.

From the Savannah Republican, April 24th, 1827.

THE 77TH ANNIVERSARY OF THE GEORGIA UNION SOCIETY, was celebrated yesterday in this city, in the usual style. The members assembled at 10 o'clock, at their Hall, and after going through the business of the Society, they repaired with the youths educated by their bounty, at 12, to Christ Church, where an address was delivered by the Rev. Mr. Carter. The following gentlemen were elected officers for the ensuing year:

JOHN C. NICOLL, President.
GEORGE GLEN, Vice President.
L. MASON, Secretary.
J. DE LAMOTTA, } Stewards.
JAMES JOHNSTON. }

BOARD OF MANAGERS.

GEO. W. ANDERSON, JACOB SHAFFER, HUGH ROSE, FRANCIS SORREL, M. MYERS.

1828, April 23.— At the Hall, 10 A. M.—78th Anniversary.

L. Mason, Sec.

The regular and continuous minutes of the Society begin April 1st, 1828. These notes of meetings, proceedings, &c., have been gleaned from the newspaper files only for those periods during which no minutes appear—viz: previous to 1791, from 1798 to 1813, and from 1820 to 1828. They were obtained through Mr J. F. Cann, and were copied for him from the old files in the possession of the Georgia Historical Society and in the office of the Savannah Republican, by Mr. Lemuel Mallery. Neither this matter nor that received from Mr. L. Solomons on pages 189 to 195, was received in time to be printed in regular order.

Anniversary discourses and addresses have been delivered before the Society as far as can be ascertained, as follows:

1805.	By Rev. Jos. Clay, (Charity Sermon), in the Baptist Church.	
1806.	Rev Mr. Best,	New Pres. Church, St. James' Sq.
1807.	Rev. Henry Kollock,	" " " "
1808.	Rev. Mr. Holcombe,	Baptist Church, New Franklin Sq.
1809.	Rev. Henry Kollock,	Presbyterian Church.
1813.	Rev. Wm. B. Johnston,	Baptist Church.
1817.	Rev. Mr. Cranston,	Episcopal Church.
1818.	Rev. Dr. Kollock,	Presbyterian Church.
1819.	Rev. Mr. Carpenter,	
1820.	Rev. Mr. Carpenter,	
1821.	Rev. Mr. J. Carr, 'a member,' Society's Hall.	
1822.	Rev. Mr. Cranston,	Episcopal Church.
1823.	T. U. P. Charlton, Esq.	Episcopal Church.
1824.	Rev. Sam'l B. How,	Presbyterian Church.
1825.	Rev. S. A. Mealy,	Lutheran Church.
1826.	M. Myers, Esq.	Lutheran Church.
1827.	Rev. Walter Carter,	Christ Church.
1828.	Rev. George White,	Lutheran Church.
1829.	Rev. Edw'd Neufville,	Episcopal Church.
1830.	Rev. Geo. W. Bethune,	Lutheran Church.
1831.	Mr. Robert Birch,	Methodist Church.
1832.	Rev. George White,	Lutheran Church.
1833.	Rev. Willard Preston,	Presbyterian Church.
1834.	Col. Howell Cobb,	Christ Church.
1835.	Robt. M. Charlton, Esq.	Unitarian Church.
1836.	Rev. Mr. Scott,	Indep't Presby'an Church.
1837.	Rev. John L. Jones,	Baptist Church.
1838.	Rev. S. A. Mealy,	Presbyterian Church.
1839.	Dr. W. B. Stevens,	Unitarian Church.
1840	H. K. Preston, Esq.	Unitarian Church.
1841.	Rev. Mr. Harrington,	Unitarian Church.
1842.	No Address.	
1843.	No Address.	
1844.	Rev. J. B. Gallagher,	First Presbyterian Church.
1845.	No Address.	
1846.	Rev. J. B. Ross,	First Presbyterian Church.
1847.	Rev. N. Aldrich,	Lutheran Church.
1848.	Rev. J. H. Robert,	Second Baptist Church.
1849.	Rev. A. J. Karn,	Lutheran Church.
1850.	Rev. J. P. Tustin,	Second Baptist Church.
1851.	Rev. Thos. Rambaut,	First Baptist Church.
1852.	Rev. L. Pierce,	Trinity Me. Epis. Church.
1853.	Rev. John Pierpont,	Unitarian Church.
1854.	No Address.	
1855.	Robt. H. Griffin, Esq.	Bethesda.
1856.	Hon. Francis S. Bartow,	Bethesda.
1857.	Rev. Geo. H. Clark,	Bethesda.
1858.	Rev. W. H. Potter,	Bethesda.
1859.	Col. A. R. Lawton,	Bethesda.

Record of the Beneficiaries of the Union Society as far as could be ascertained.

No.	Names.	Age.	Admitted.	Remarks.	Died.
1.	Henry Lyon		November 24, 1785	Son of John Lyon, deceased; bound an apprentice to a carpenter.	
2.	Jeremiah Lyon		Ditto	" " " " " " " "	Dead.
3.	John Peter Oates		Ditto	Son of Jacob Oates, deceased; bound apprentice to a carpenter.	Died.
4.	Robert Strange		Ditto	Son of Mr. Strange, a revolutionary soldier; bound apprentice to a cabinet maker.	[1817.
5.	Peter Chambers		Ditto	Son of Peter Chambers, deceased; removed to his relations.	
6.	William Dews	23,	January 1786	Son of Robert Dews; bound an apprentice to a cooper.	
7.	Matthew Roche	24,	February 1786	Son of Matthew Roche, dec'd member of this society	
8.	Ann Roche	24,	"	Daughter " " " " " } removed to their relations.	
9.	Catharine Kirick	4,	January 1787	" of Adam Kirick, deceased, removed to her relations.	
10.	John Adam Kirick	14,	September 1787	Son of Adam Kirick,	Dead.
11.	Nancy Bidulph	14,	"	Daughter of Stephen Bidulph, deceased; gone to her parents.	
12.	William Evans	25,	January 1788	Son of Randall Evans, deceased.	Dead.
13.	Martha Chambers	12,	November 1787	Daughter of Peter Chambers, deceased.	Dead.
14.	William Wright	5,	February 1788	Son of Benjamin Wright, deceased; bound to a carpenter.	
15.	Abraham Hayes	7,	April 1788	bound to a tailor.	
16.	William Smith	15,	July	bound to a sadler.	
17.	Sarah Gwin	22,	"	Daughter of George Gwin; gone to her parents.	
18.	William Toxey	15,	September 1789	bound to a merchant.	
19.	David Curtis	18,	November	bound to a carpenter, 15 March, 1790.	
20.	Isaac Laroche	1,	February 1790	Son of Isaac Laroche, deceased.	
21.	John Warnock	23,	April 1791	" " John Warnock, deceased; withdrawn 4 August, 1794.	
22.	John Riley	"	"	" " John Riley,	
23.	Sarah Hershman	"	"	Daughter of John C. Hershman, deceased; * * * * * * with her mother.	
24.	Marlow Prior	23,	April 1791	Son of John Prior.	
25.	John Prior	4,	June 1792	Son of John Prior.	
26.	John W. Jones	13,	August	Mary Ann Jones.	
27.	Elizabeth Hayes	4,	February 1793	Daughter of John Hayes; gone to her friends.	[Aug. 7, 1795. Died.
28.	Jacob Hershman	29,	April	Son of John C. Hershman, deceased.	
29.	Martha Jones	1,	July	Daughter of Mary Jones; refused to accept the bounty of the Society.	
30.	Mary Stoner	1,	"	" " Peter Stoner } refused to continue with the Society, 7 Oct'r, 1794.	
31.	Sarah Stoner	1,	"	" "	

No.	Names.	Admitted.	Age.	Remarks.	Died.
32.	Patsey Henry........	January 6, 1794		Daughter of James Henry, withdrawn by her mother.	
33.	Mary Lavender........	April 23, 1794	13 yrs.	" Benjamin Lavender; withdrawn 4th August, 1791.	
34.	Betsey Hall........	"		" Talmadge Hall, deceased } gone to their friends.	1794.
35.	Lotty Hall........	"		" " " " }	
36.	Mary Cameron........	June 2, "	12 yrs.	Step daughter of Absalom Ball, deceased	
37.	David Murray Washington July	7, "	12 yrs.	Son of John Washington.	
38.	Benjamin Alter........	August 4, "	12 yrs.	" " Ulrick Alter, deceased.	
39.	David Nesler........	"	9 yrs.	" " Adam Nesler.	
40.	James Buely........	November 3, 1794		" " Mary Buely.	
41.	John Gilbert........	April 23, 1799	8 yrs.	" " John Gilbert.	
42.	George Wells........	Unknown.		A poor orphan now in the care of Mrs. Jenkins.	
43.	Malsey Kitchen........	June 1, 1795		Daughter of John Brown; gone to her friends.	
44.	Mary Brown........	February 1, 1796		Son of William Gilbert, deceased.	
45.	Henry Gilbert........	April 22, 1799			
46.	Abraham Gilbert........	"			
47.	Thomas McLean........	"	9 yrs.	Son of Catharine McLean; bound apprentice to Lyon & Morse, printers, 7 years.	
48.	William Patterson........	" 1801			
49.	Thomas Patterson........	" 1801			
50.	John Randolph........	15, 1804	9 yrs.	Bound to Everett & Evans, printers, 12th Feb'ry, 1808, for 7 years; since bound [to F. S. Fell for 3 years.	
51.	Joseph Rawl........	17, 1804			
52.	William Norton........	Unknown.			
53.	Joseph Glover........	Time unknown.		Bound to Capt. P. B. Hathaway, mariner, 2d Jan'ry, 1811, for 3 years.	
54.	Charles Gugel........				
55.	William McMurrain........	Sept'r. 6, 1801	10 yrs.	Son of Elizabeth McMurrain.	
56.	John Hutchinson........	Unknown.			
57.	——— Bourcher........	April 23, 1805		Child of Adrian Bourcher.	
58.	William Cahill........	Oct'r. 3, 1807			
59.	William Randolph........	Unknown.			
60.	Wil'm W. Womack........	June 3, 1807	13 yrs.	Bound to Thomas Stewart, tinplate worker, 17th June, 1809, for 7 years.	
61.	John Campbell........	Unknown.			
62.	Harriet S. Mulreyne........	March 5, 1808	13 yrs.	Daughter of Jane Mulreyne; returned to her friends.	
63.	Jesse J. Jerrey........	" 5, "	11 yrs.	Son of Margaret Casco.	
64.	Daniel A. Baas........	June 7, 1779	11 yrs.	Son of Samuel and Rebecca Baas.	

No.	Names.	Admitted.	Age.	Remarks.	Died.
65.	George Michael Durr.....	Aug't 1, 1805	9 yrs.	Son of Elizabeth Hoffman.	
66.	John M. Webb.	Oct'r 9, 1805	7 yrs.	Jane Winn, guardian: bound to Jas Washington, sadler, for 8 years, Ap. 30, 1810.	
67.	William A. Thompson....	Jan'ry 9, 1806	9 yrs.	Son of Ann Thompson.	
68.	Joseph R. Thompson....	Jan'ry 9, 1806	7 yrs.	" " bound to Jas Davenport, carp'r, Nov. 12, 1811, for 8 yrs. 3 mos.	
69.	William F. Simpson.....	Aug't 29, 1806	10 yrs.	Son of Susannah Simpson: bd to Jos. Kitchen, sadler, June 17, 1811, for 6 yrs. 11 ms.	
70.	Nicholas Harbock......	May 1, 1807	12 yrs.	Dr. M. Sheftall, Guardian.	
71.	Mary Magdalen Gromet..	Feb'y 20, 1807	7 yrs.	Daughter of Mary M. Gromet: returned to her friends.	
72.	Samuel Ashton........	June 3, 1807	10 yrs.	Son of Hannah Ashton.	
73.	Michael Harbock.......	May 1, 1807	13 yrs.	Dr. M. Sheftall, guardian; bd to F. S. Fell, printer, Mch 13, 1813, for 2 yrs. 5 mos.	
74.	Roger Shaw..........	May 30, 1807	9 yrs.	Son of Elizabeth Shaw.	
75.	Judith S. Gromet......	Feb'y 12, 1807	9 yrs.	Daughter of Mary M. Gromet; returned to her friends.	
76.	William Wiley........	June 12, 1807	8 yrs.	Son of Elizabeth Womack.	
77.	John Shaw...........	June 15, 1807	6 yrs.	" Elizabeth Shaw.	
78.	William Ashton.......	Jan'y 16, 1808	13 yrs.	" Hannah Ashton.	
79.	Joseph Eppinger	May 30, 1808	6 yrs.	} Son of Elizabeth Wilton; bd to P. DeVillers, merchant, Aug. 24, 1813; } 1820 for 9 years—now with J. H. Ash, carpenter.	
80.	John W. Roley........	Mch 10, 1808	13 yrs.	Son of Mary Johnston.	
81.	William S. Mulreyne....	Feb'y 1, 1809	8 yrs.	" Jane Mulreyne.	
82.	William R. Parker.....	May 1, 1809	7 yrs.	" Ann Parker.	
83.	Leslie McCullough.....	Oct'r 19, 1809	11 yrs.	" Mary Mitchell.	
84.	Thomas H. Mulreyne...	Sept'r 18, "	8 yrs.	" Jane Mulreyne.	
85.	Robert S. Burgess.....	Feb'y 18, "	12 yrs.	" Sophia S. Burgess.	
86.	Howell Cobb.........	May 1, "	14 yrs.	Jeremiah Cuyler, guardian: bound to F. S. Fell, printer, Mch 13, 1813, for 3 yrs.	
87.	Thomas Bryan........	May 1, "	9 yrs.	Jeremiah Cuyler, guardian.	
88.	Edmund Walsh.......	April 13, 1810	11 yrs.	Son of Mary Walsh.	
89.	James Fountain.......	July 13, "	12 yrs.	" Mary Fountain.	
90.	Augusto Masolle......	May 5, "	8 yrs.	" Marie Masolle.	
91.	Joseph Marshall.......	Oct'r 22, "	11 yrs.	Elizabeth Shaw, guardian.	
92.	Thomas Walsh........	April 30, "	8 yrs.	Son of Mary Walsh; bound to F. S. Fell, printer, June 23, 1813, for 6 years.	
93.	Mario Masolle.........	May 5, "	11 yrs.	Daughter of Mario Masolle: returned to her friends.	
94.	George Norris.........	Aug't 22, "	13 yrs.	Son of Elizabeth Norris.	
95.	John B. Brown........	May 22, "	12 yrs.	" Ann Brown.	
96.	James Gillon.........	Aug't 10, "	11 yrs.	" Margaret Driscoll.	Oct. 21, 1810.

No.	Names.	Admitted.	Age.	Remarks.
97.	Philip J. Shealy or Charly.	Feb'y 22, 1810	9 yrs.	E. F. Campbell, guardian; bound to John R. King. See min: June 1, 1819.
98.	Joseph Peranger.	Jan'y 11, 1811	8 yrs.	Martin Martz, grandfather.
99.	Thomas Bradley.	Dec'r 4, "	8 yrs.	Mary Bradly, guardian.
100.	John Bolinger.	M'ch 16, "	10 yrs.	Son of Mary Bolinger; b'd to Silas Cooper, painter & gilder, June 11, '14, for 7½ ys.
101.	Stephen Thos. Walsh.	May 27, 1811	4 yrs.	Edmund Walsh, Guardian; bound to J. F. Herb, blacksmith, July 8, 1818, for 6 ys.
102.	John F. W. Duresseau.	M'ch 14, 1811	7 yrs.	Mary S. Duresseau, mother; b'd to Jno. R. King, tailor, Ap. 24. 1817, for 7 ys 9 ins.
103.	Hezekiah Wright.	Jan'y 25, 1811	8 yrs.	Son of Christianna Wright.
104.	Gabriel Lewis.	May 25, 1811	8 yrs.	" Sarah Mitchell; b'd to Jno. R. King, tailor, June 11, 1814, for 5 ys. 8 mos.
105.	William Bolinger.	M'ch 16, "	12 yrs.	" Mary Bolinger. Died at the house of Mr. Carr, Dec. 12, 1817
106.	James C. Johnston.	" 23, "	7 yrs.	Solomon Zitrour, guardian; bound to S. & C. Schenk.
107.	Charles A. Martin.	Aug't 25, 1815	12 yrs.	Son of Melinda Bartlett.
108.	James S. Hoffman.	" 24, "	9 yrs.	" Eliz'th Hoffman: b'd to Miles Jones, stone cutter, July 17, '18, for 9 ys. 6 ms. 1920
109.	Alexander Marlome.	Unknown.		Bound to John M. Harney, painter; Presidents report June 1, 1819.
110.	Charles Harden Stillwell.	Sept'r 18, 1816	11 yrs.	Son of Sarah E. E. Stillwell.
111.	Charles Blakely Mullen.	July 3, "	8 yrs.	" Eleanor Mullen; returned to his friends.
112.	William F. Shearer.	May 26, "	12 yrs.	" Catharine Shearer; bound to his brother, Trespar, a blacksmith.
113.	John Edward Thomas.	May 10, 1817	11 yrs.	Stephen Britton, guardian; bound to —— Young, house carpenter.
114.	James Tracey.	" "	14 yrs.	Mary Pearer, mother.
115.	Joseph W. Gibbons.	July 31, "	7 yrs.	Mary R. Gibbons, mother.
116.	Thomas A. Steel.	Unknown.		Bound to Lyon & Morse, printers, June 15, 1803, for 6 years and 10 mos.
117.	Anthony Suares.	"		" Crane & Baker, bricklayers, April 21, 1817.
118.	Jacob Fulk.	"		" Silas Cooper, painter & gilder, Aug. 26, 1815, for 4 yrs and 3 mos.
119.	Daniel Phillips.	Jan'y 21, 1818	12 yrs.	} Orphans of a Welsh family; bound to Jacob Shaffer, sadler.
120.	Benjamin Phillips.	" "	10 yrs.	} Taken by Mrs. Fitzgerald, and to be provided for by her, 1818.
121.	William Phillips.	" "	5 yrs.	
122.	John David Howell.	Jan'y 2, 1817	8 yrs.	Sarah Ann Howell, mother; bound to J. B. Berthelot, Dec. 4, 1821.
123.	Thomas William Howell.	Sept'r 1, 1817	8 yrs.	" " " Peter Drege.
124.	Richard Shop.	Oct'r 6, 1818	10 yrs.	Samuel M. Bond, guardian.
125.	William Middleton.	Jan'y 5, 1819	14 yrs.	John Bogue, guardian; bound to Dr. A. DeLaRoche.
126.	Daniel L. Dent.	" "		Son of Mrs. Frances Dent; with Russell, printer.
127.	John McLagrun.	M'ch 2, 1819	9 yrs.	An orphan, from the hospital.
128.	Henry Hatfield.	April 23, "		Son of Mr. and Mrs. Hatfield; parents dead; bound to H. Tuppet.
129.	Pierce Prendergast.	"	13 yrs.	An orphan; bound to Wm. Robertson, printer.

No.	Names	Admitted	Age	Remarks	Died.
130.	Lawrence Shop.......	Dec'r 4, 1821	10 yrs.	An orphan, bound to Isaiah Davenport, carpenter.	
131.	Abner Townsend......	1822	10 yrs.	" "	
132.	Lewis Trevoyer.......	"	8 yrs.	" "	
133.	Edward Tillinghast......			Apprenticed to G. R. Hendrickson, Druggist, April 23, 1839.	
134.	Alfred Mills........	1828 or 9		" I. W. Morrell, furniture store, and manufactory, Nov. 12, 1830.	
135.	Joseph Young........	1822	6 yrs.	Given up to his mother, Aug. 1, 1839; she refusing to bind him.	
136.	Joseph Wilson........	1822	4 yrs.	Father living; sent to Mr. Connolly, Jefferson county; died in up country.	
137.	Edward G. Wilson......	1823	2 yrs.	" " bound to R. W. Pooler, Esq., Clerk of the Sup. Court C. C. Jan. 14, 1834.	
138.	James Wilson........	"		" " " " I. W. Keating, to learn the trade of a mason, Sept. 2, 1833.	
139.	Robert Trout.........	"	1½yrs.	Orphan; bound to Shafer & Little, to learn the trade of a sadler; (minutes of Sept. 1, 1830, says given up to Mrs. Gilden at her earnest solicitation.)	
140.	Robt. L. Tillinghast......	1829 or '30		May 23, 18?2, given up to his relations in South Carolina, with assurance of being provided for.	
141.	Joseph Cooper........	Sept. 8, 1829	12 yrs.	Jan. 11, 1836, to J. R. Thompson, to learn the carpenter's business or trade.	
142.	John Trevoyer........	June, 1832		July 8, 1833, bound to Dougald Ferguson, cabinet maker—afterwards with Wm. Warner, carriage maker.	
143.	Thomas Newton........	"		Jan. 14, 1834, reported bound to John Robinson, to learn the blacksmith's trade.	
144.	Charles Lynch........	May 22, "	11 yrs.	bound to D. B. Brower, wheelwright in Bulloch county, April 23, '37.	
145.	Charles Groves........	June 18, "	7 yrs.	Bound to G. W. Keating, to learn the trade of a mason, Minutes Feb. 4, 1834.	
146.	Benj. Franklin Ridge...	Oct. 8, "	7 yrs.	Orphan; given up to H. F. Willink, March 15, 1839.	
147.	William H. Ladson ...	8, "	5 yrs.	Mother living; sent to Elizabethtown, N.J., to learn cabinet maker's trade, Feb. 12, '37.	
148.	Joseph H. Ladson	"	7 yrs.	" bound to B. Snider, dry goods merchant; Sept. 12, 1840; Min July 26, '41.	
149.	Michael Riley........	"	9 yrs.	Orphan; placed with Michael Dillon, as a clerk, April 22, 1837.	
150.	James Henry Bailey....	June 1, 1833	13 yrs.	taken by Lutheran Church, Savannah, Sept. 18, 1842.	
151.	John G. Denny.......	July "	12 yrs.	Died in the spring of 1836.	
152.	James Henry Brogan ..	Aug? 6, "	10½yrs.	apprenticed to Wm. Waite, painter; March 15, 1838.	
153.	David Emanuel.......	April 7, 1834	12 yrs.	returned to his uncle who promised to take care of him, April 22, 1835.	
154.	Berry James.........	19?, "	1 yrs.	with D. S. Little, saddler and harness maker, March 15, 1838.	
155.	Leander Moore.......	May 15, "	6 yrs.	bound to Wm. Thomas, pilot, Nov. 26, 1846.	
156.	George Brogan.......	April "	10½yrs.	Bound to the Society by his mother and taken away by her to the North, July, '36.	Died in spring of 1836
157.	Robert Hall Still......	18, 1836	12 yrs.	Orphan; bound to James P. Dent, pilot, for 6 years, August 14, 1838.	
158.	William Wallace Mahew..	4, "	12 yrs.	Bound to the Society by his mother: bound to Geo. Betts, painter, May 20, 1839.	
159.	Wm ? Smith........	May 18, "	14 yrs.		

No.	Names	Admitted		Age	Remarks.	Died.
160.	John Smith	May 18,	"	11 7-12	Bound to the Society by his mother; b'd to W. H. Bulloch, printer, May, 1839.	1836
161.	Edward Godfrey	April 6,	1835	10½ yrs.	Nov. 9, 1842. Given up to his mother. [See minutes, April 23.]	
162.	John Harrison	June 30,	1836	12 yrs.	B'd to Society by father; placed with W.H. Bulloch, printer, March 18, 1835.	
163.	Charles Donaho	" 30,	"	8 yrs.	by Inferior Court of Effingham county: runaway Feb. 21, 1838.	
164.	Allen Stephens	Aug't 24,	"	8 yrs.	bound to J. V. Conerat, merchant. Oct. 19, 18.	
165.	John Williams	Jan'y 16,	1837	10½ yrs.	absconded : Ap'l 28, 1839.	
166.	William C. Harrington	" "	1837			
167.	John Campbell	April 15,	1835		Bound to James Kennedy, cabinet maker: Minutes March 15, 1838	
168.	Thomas West	Feb. 22,	1836	11 yrs.	Feb. 21, 1838. Runaway	
169.	Thomas Clifford	M'ch 15,	1838	9 yrs.	Bound to D. Ferguson, cabinet maker, Oct. 9, 1841.	
170.	Benjamin H. Spencer	" "	"	9½ yrs.	Left May 20, 1843. Record of Mr. John Haupt. Now a Pilot.	
171.	William Henry Judah	" "	"	6½ yrs.	July 24, 1843. Bound to Alvin X. Miller, machinist.	
172.	Edward Jessup Judah	" "	"	8 yrs.	Left April 28, 1847. Mr. Haupt's record.	
173.	John H. Blackburn	Sept. 11,	1839	5 yrs.	Feb. 20, 1850. Bound to printer's trade, Republican office.	
174.	George Blackburn	" "	"		March 10, 1851. Bound to book-binder's trade, to John M. Cooper & C.	
175.	David James Judah	" "	"	10 yrs.	June 18, 1847, placed with W. H. Bulloch, printer, on trial.	
176.	Robert V. Thomas	" "	"		Left Jan. 14, 1815. Mr. Haupt's record.	
177.	Samuel Davies	Sept. 12,	1840		June 18, 1811. Given up to his mother.	
178.	William Davies	June 18,	1841		Left Sept. 29, 1811. Mr. Haupt's record.	
179.	Mar'n Ensworth Pritchard	April 5,	"			Died Oct. 11, 1843
180.	Francis Oliver Wells	May,	1842		May 28, 1845 ; given up to his mother.	
181.	William L. McKendree	April 26,	1844		Feb. 9, 1845 taken away by their mother: Mr. Haupt's record.	
182.	Robert McKendree	Dec. 10,	"		" 26, 1846	
183.	Thomas J. kirk	Feb. 14,	"		May 1, 1849, put to the bricklayer's trade.	
184.	Edward Clark	Oct'r. 22,	1844		Dec. 17, 1844, taken away by his mother.	
185.	Michael Kirk	June 11,	1845			
186.	William A. Sturdevant	Oct'r 16,	"			Came sick: died Oct. 10, 1846
187.	William Wray	Nov. 16,	1846		Nov. 30, 1847, given up to his grandmother.	" " Dec. 14, "
188.	Thaddeus E. Fisher	July 19,	1817		July 6, 1851. Withdrawn, by his mother.	
189.	Augustus M. Fisher	" "	"			Died Oct. 29, 1849
190.	Thomas J. Sanders	Nov. 11,	"		Feb. 1851, put to the printer's trade.	
191.	Oven Brittle	" "	"		Jan. 22, 1855, removed from Mr. Haupt's to Bethesda : runaway Jan. 27, 1855.	
192.	William H. H. Young	Dec. 10,	"		Nov. 2, 1852. Given up to his relations.	

No.	Names.	Admitted.	Age.	Remarks.	Died.
193.	Joseph Wingate	April 24, 1848		Sept. 21, 1848. } given up to their mother, who returned with them to South	
194.	Elias P. Wingate	April 24, 1848		" " " } Carolina.	
195.	Joseph E. Compass	Nov. 17, "		Jan'y 27, 1854, bound to Dougald Ferguson, cabinet maker.	
196.	Edward R. Law	" 19, "		Oct. 27, 1849, returned to his mother.	
197.	John W. Thompson	May 25, 1849			Dec. 25, 1850.
198.	Joseph J. Suger	Nov. 8, "		March 19, 1853, absconded. Re-admitted Feb. 15, 1854. See below.	
199.	John Hart	" 8, "		Nov. 22, 1852, given up to go to the bricklayer's trade.	
200.	James W. Leonard	Feb. 4, 1850		March 22, 1850. Given up to his mother.	
201.	William L. Wilson	May 28, "		April 22, 1851. Given up to go to the printer's trade.	
202.	Alexander K. Wilson	"	8¼ yrs.	Jan. 22, 1855, taken from Mr. Haupt's to Bethesda; Jan. 13, 1857, placed with Jno. M. Cooper & Co., and a few months after bound to L. S. Bennett & Co.. Carriage makers and blacksmiths.	
203.	John Wreutz	July 15, "		Left Sept. 18, 1852. Mr. Haupt's record.	
204.	Jeremiah Manning	June 23, 1851		April 1, 1854, placed with Verstille & Kempton, merchants, with the consent and wish of his mother.	
205.	Richard H. Manning	" "	7 yrs.	Sept. 4, 1854, given up, and help afforded to go back to Columbus, Ga.	
206.	Ewen Mortimer	Oct. 1, "	10 yrs.	Taken from Mr. Haupt's to Bethesda Jan. 22, 1855: Orphan.	
207.	Wm. Henry Sagurs	Dec. 2, "	8 yrs.	" Jan. 13, 1857, bound to J. M. Cooper & Co., printers.	
208.	Charles A. Sagurs	" 18, "	10 yrs.	" " " book binders.	
209.	Robt. A. Beasley	Jan. 25, 1853	12 yrs.	" " Jan. 17, 1855; withdrawn by his mother in 1856.	
210.	Geo. Washington Cole	M'ch 24, "	5½yrs.	" " 22, " b'd to Sturtevant, carpenter. Feb. 19, '56.	
211.	Jacob Rohr	April 28, "	3 yrs.	" " " } Orphans.	
212.	Frederick Rohr	" "		" " " }	
213.	Marion Besinger	June 20, "		Dec. 28, 1853, withdrawn by mother.	
214.	Joseph Besinger	" "		July 18, 1853.	
215.	James E. Beasley	July 20, "	6½yrs.	Taken from Mr. Haupt's to Bethesda, Jan. 17, '55, withdrawn by mother, 1856.	
216.	George Gwyn	Sept. 6, "		Nov. 28, 1854, withdrawn.	
198.	Joseph J. Singer	Feb. 15, 1854	13 yrs.	Taken from Mr. Haupt's to Bethesda, Jan. 22, '55, June 13, '55 bound to W. T. Thompson, printer.	
217.	Henry H. Manning	M'ch 31, "		Sept. 4, 1854, given up and help afforded to go back to Columbus, Ga.	
218.	William S. Clark	Jan'y 24, 1855	9 yrs.	Dec. 4, '58, withd'n and b'd to Jno. M. Cooper & Co., booksellers and stationers.	
219.	Josiah T. Clark	" "	5 yrs.	Orphan.	
220.	Samuel Miller	Feb. 29, "	5 yrs.	Jan. 8, 1857, taken away by his mother.	

No.	Names.	Admitted.	Age.	Remarks.	Died.
221.	John O'Keefe...........M'ch 6, 1855		4 yrs.	Orphan.	
222.	Matthew Dotson.... .....M'ch 6, "		13 yrs.	Aug. 27, 1855, absconded.	
223.	Cornelius A. Long.......April 3, "		10 yrs.	Fatherless.	
224.	Chas. H'y. Rod's Thorpe. " 11, "		11 yrs.	Dec. 25, 1855, sent to his mother in Charleston, by her urgent request.	
225.	Daniel Towles........... " 23, "		5 yrs.		
226.	Corn's Wash'n Carpenter.June 13, "		12 yrs.	Aug. 10, 1855, absconded.	
227.	Julius Ceasar Alf'd Heidt. " 23, "		7 yrs.	Fatherless.	
228.	Francis John Hunt...... " "		12 yrs.	Nov. 10, '58, given up and placed with H'y Lathrop & Co., dry goods merchants.	
229.	Albert J. Carolan......July 31, "		10½yrs.	Fatherless.	
230.	Jacob Bennett Trumps...Aug. 22, "		7 yrs.	"	
231.	Geo. Emanuel Trumpler.Nov. 7, "		7½yrs.	"	
232.	Sylvester Syntis.........Dec. 10, "		11 2-3	Fatherless.	
233.	Thomas Smith...........Feb. 20, 1856		10 yrs.	Motherless.	
234.	Patrick O'Brine.........M'ch 15, "		12 yrs.	March 9, 1857, placed with Dr. B. G. D. Moxley, Virginia, Agriculturist.	
235.	Edward Wall............April 7, "		5 10-12	Fatherless.	
236.	Thomas Mulligan.......June 25, "		9 yrs.	Orphan, b'd by brother; June 29, 1856, absconded	
237.	Henry Ennis............. " 25, "		5 yrs.	Motherless.	
238.	Rand'ph Sp'g Williamson.Sept. 10, "		9½yrs.	Jan. 8, 1858, taken away by his mother.	
239.	Lewis Endres...........Feb. 18, 1857		12½yrs.	Motherless.	
240.	Albert Hunt...........M'ch 5, "		11½yrs.	Fatherless.	
241.	Charles V. Baker....... " "		6 yrs.	Fatherless.	
242.	Rufus E. Thompson.... " "		9 yrs.	Motherless.	
243.	John Crawford......... " "		10 yrs.	Fatherless.	
244.	Wm. Jacob Friend..... " 18, "		9½yrs.	Fatherless.	
245.	Joseph Lopez..........April 10, "		5 yrs.	Fatherless.	
246.	Thomas Wallace Robins. " 23, "		8½yrs.	Fatherless.	
247.	James Shepard.........May 23, "		7 yrs.	Motherless.	
248.	Archibald Barber.... ...June 22, "		7 yrs.	Motherless.	
249.	James Bird Harris...... " 24, "		8½yrs.	Fatherless.	
250.	Wm. Henry Adams.....July 17, "		6 4-12	Fatherless.	
251.	Millard Zachariah Benton.Sept. 25, "		6 yrs.	Orphan.	
252.	Albert Risley Spencer....Dec. 27, "		10 5-12 yrs.	Jan. 14, 1858, given up to his mother.	
253.	John Ward.............Jan. 19, 1858		11½yrs.	Fatherless.	

9

No.	NAMES.	ADMITTED.	AGE.	REMARKS.	DIED.
254.	Thomas Ward...........	" "	9¾yrs.	Fatherless.	
255.	William Gavan..........Jan.	22, 1858	12 yrs.	Fatherless.	
256.	John O'Hara...........Feb.	8, 1858	10½yrs.	March 15, 1858, given up to his mother.	
257.	Jno. Lafayette Robertson.....M'ch	29, "	10 10-12	Fatherless.	
258.	Wm. Wh. Johnston "	29, "	6½yrs.	Fatherless.	
259.	Stephen Lewis Harmon... "	29, "	7 yrs.	Came to Society dropsical and otherwise diseased, of which he died, Aug. 14,'58	
260.	George Street.......April	10, "	11½yrs.	Fatherless.	
261.	Wm. Capers Street...... "	"	9¾yrs.	Fatherless.	
262.	Wm. McKeon........... "	"	12¾yrs.	Jan. 30, 1859, given up to his father.	
263.	Charles Sandburg........ "	23, "	6 yrs.	Father a Swede, about to die when son was admitted—died soon after.	
264.	John Donovan.........Dec.	9, "	11¾yrs.	March 5, 1859, given up to his mother, Mrs. Catherine Lee.	
265.	William Montgomery.....M'ch	1, 1859	8 yrs.	Orphan.	
266.	Thomas Sullivan.......... "	22, "	11 2-3	"	
267.	Milton Streeter Jones.....Apr.	22, 1859	12 yrs.	Fatherless.	
268.	Richard Arnold Hunt....M'ch	26, "	14 3-12	Orphan—on pay. Rules exclude boys over 14.	

Record of officers and members of the Union Society, as far as could be ascertained.

FOUNDERS OF THE INSTITUTION IN 1750.

BENJAMIN SHEFTALL, RICHARD MILLEDGE, PETER TONDEE, and two others, whose names have not come down to us.

OFFICERS.

1774. * * * , Pres't; * * * , Vice-Pres't; Wm. Gibbons, Sec'ry; Wm. Young, Henry L. Bourquin, Stewards.
1775. * * * , Pres't; David Zubly, Jr., N. W. Jones, Stewards.
1776.
1777.
1778.
1779.
1780.
1781.
1782.
1783.
1784. David Montaigut, Sec'ry.
1785.   "   Wm. Pierce, Benjamin Lloyd, Stewards.
1786. Wm. Stephens, Pres't, Leonard Cecil, V.P.   David Montaigut, Sec; James Bulloch, George B. Spencer, Stewards.
1787.   "   "   "
1788.   "   "   "
1789.   "   "   "
1790. Noble W. Jones, Pres., Joseph Clay, V. P.   "   Justus H. Scheuber, Ass't Sec; W. H. Spencer, Steward.
1791.   "   James Port, Sec.; Francis Courvoisie, John Eppinger, Stewards.
1792. Joseph Clay, Pres., Joseph Habersham, V. P.   Justus H. Scheuber, Sec.; Edward Lloyd, James B. Young, Stewards.
1793. Joseph Habersham, Pres., William Stephens, V.P.   "   James Port, Isaac Fell, Stewards; Daniel Course, elected Aug. 5, 1791, in room of I. Fell, absent from the State.
1794.   "   "   Justus H. Scheuber, Sec.; Peter S. Laffitte, George Throop, Stewards.
1795. Wm. Stephens, Pres., Mordecai Sheftall, V. P.   "   Matthew McAllister, John Berrien, Stewards.
1796.   "   Geo. Jones, V. P.,   Peter Samuel Laffitte, Sec.: John D. Dickinson, Frederick Herb, Stewards.

NOTE.—The Society originated with a Club formed by *five* gentlemen, in the year 1750. The names of three only of them, Benjamin Sheftall, Richard Milledge and Peter Tondee, have come down to us. They organized themselves as the St. George's Society, proposing for its leading object the education of orphan children. Its first President has not been ascertained. Its first Secretary was Peter Gandee, a teacher of youth. In 1756 it was incorporated, and its name changed to that of the Union Society—*Address of Dr. Preston, April, 1858.*

OFFICERS.

Year	Officers	Secretary / Stewards / Committee
1797.	George Jones, Pres., J. B. Young, V. P.	Peter S. Laffitte, Sec.; Robert Mitchell, Robert Watts, Stewards.
1798.	" " " "	" " David Gugel, Isaac Benedix, Stewards; Thos. M. Woodbridge, Milledge, School Committee, and Matthew McAllister, School Committee.
1799.	James P. Young, P.	" "
1800.	Matthew McAllister, P.	" "
1801.	"	" " Edward White, Steward.
1802.	Joseph Habersham, "	Thomas Pitt, Sec.;
1803.	"	Peter S. Laffitte, Sec.; John Lawson, Steward.
1804.	Charles Harris, P., Wm. B. Bulloch, V. P.	"
1805.	" " " "	"
1806.	Gen. David B. Mitchell, P.,	Adam Cope, Edward Harden, Stewards.
1807.	" "	April 23, Journal 3, "paid Mr. Petit balance due him on Anniversary Dinner, $65," probably a Steward.
1808.	Wm. B. Bulloch, P., Wm. Davis, V. P.	Robert Habersham, James Bilbo,* John Lawson, Jeremiah Cuyler, John M. Berrien, School Committee.
1809.	" " " "	John N. Brailsford, Sec.; Thomas Schley, Robert Houston, Jno M. Berrien, John P. Williamson, Morris Miller, School Committee.
1810.	William Davies, P., Jno. McPherson Berrien, V.P.,	"
1811.	" "	Joseph Maxwell, Robert W. Habersham, Stewards.
1812.	Jno. McPherson Berrien, P., James Johnson, V.P.	Frederick S. Fell, D. M. McConkey, Stewards.
1813.	" "	Griffin L. Lambkin, Sec.; Steele White, John Kell, Stewards, P. DeVillers, Oliver Sturges, Wm. Parker, School Committee.
1814.	James Johnston, P.	Henry W. Williams. Sec.
1815.	Dr. Moses Sheftall, P., Edward Harden; V. P.	John Wallace, Sec.; George Glen, Sec. from Jan. 10, 1816; Raymond Demere, Frederick Densler, Stewards; John Bolton, resigned Jan. 10, 1816, Frederick Herb appointed in his stead; Jas. Hunter, Jas. M. Wayne, Geo. Glen, Geo. Myers, Board of Managers.
1816.	"	T. V. Gray, Sec.; (June 10, 1816); F. Densler, Stewards; Moses Cleland, Hunter, Herb, James B. Read, Densler, Managers.
1817.	Dr. Moses Sheftall, P., Jno. Hunter, V. P.	T. V. Gray, Sec.; Cleland, Steele White, Jas. Morrison, Herb, Jas. Eppinger, Managers.
1818.	John Hunter, P., James Bilbo, V. P.	James Morrison, Sec.; Cleland, Herb, Jos. A. Scott, Eppinger, Dr. Moses Sheftall, Managers.
1819.	" "	" Cleland, Herb, John Lewis, Ebenezer S. Rees, Sheftall, Managers.
1820.	" "	Lowell Mason, Sec.; Sheftall, Cleland, Joseph George, Lewis, Managers.
1821.	Richard W. Habersham, P., Dr. W. C. Daniel, V.P.	" Sheftall, George, Lewis, Josiah Penfield, Jacob Shaffer, Managers.

* Elected Stewards, as per notice in Savannah Republican, April 24, 1805—Adam Cope, a Steward, as per Journal 3, folio, 100, "$83 75 paid him balance due him on Anniversary dinner." The names of Stewards do not appear in the minute book of the Board of Managers—May 4th, 1815, to May 24, 1822. No minutes at all from 1820 to '22.

OFFICERS.

Year	President / Vice-President	Secretary	Stewards and Managers
1822.	Steele White, P., James Eppinger, V. P.	Lowell Mason, Sec;	George W. Coe, Isaac D'Lyon, Stewards; John F. Lloyd, Wm. Smith, S. M. Bond, Michael Brown, J. C. Habersham, Managers.
1823.	Thomas Pollill, P., James S. Bulloch, V. P.	" "	George W. Anderson, Charles Hartridge, Stewards; Brown, Smith, James Eppinger, Geo. W. Coe, S. C. Schenck, Managers.
1824.	William Davies, P., John C. Nicoll, V. P.	Lowell Mason, Sec;	Hugh Rose, L. Gordon, Stewards; Coe, Schenck, Smith, George Glen, Geo. W. Anderson, Managers.
1825.	John C. Nicoll, P., Alexander Telfair, V. P.	"	W. W. Gordon, Thomas Clark, Stewards; Anderson, Glen, Schenck, Jacob Shaffer, Norman Wallace, Managers.
1826.	" "	"	George H. Johnston, Solomon Cohen, Stewards; Wallace, Anderson, Shaffer, Francis Sorrel, M. Myers, Managers.
1827.	George Glen, V. P.	"	J. DeLamotta, James Johnston, Stewards; Sorrel, Anderson, Myers, Hugh Rose, Shaffer, Managers.
1828.	" "	W. W. Wash, Sec;	John W. Anderson, T. M. Driscoll, Stewards; Shaffer, Sorrel, Anderson, Mordecai Myers, Rose, Managers.
1829.	" "	"	Robert Hutchison, C. B. Carter, Stewards; Board of last year re-appointed Managers.
1830.	Alexander Telfair, V. P.	"	John Low, William King, Stewards; Board of last year re-appointed Managers.
1831.	Geo. W. Anderson, P., Francis Sorrel, V. P.	"	William P. Bowen, William Patterson, Stewards; John C. Nicoll, Myers, Shaffer, Norman Wallace, Ralph King, Managers.
1832.	Francis Sorrel, P., Norman Wallace, V. P.	"	Anthony Barclay, John Stevens, Jr., Stewards; Shaffer, John W. Anderson, Elias Fort, Wm. Patterson, Moses Cleland, Managers.
1833.	" "	"	J. Curwin, Wm. R. Gaston, Stewards; J. C. Nicoll, Patterson, Shaffer, Anderson, Anthony Barclay, Managers.
1834.	" "	"	M. H. McAllister, John Day, Stewards; Barclay, Nicoll, Anderson, Shaffer, William Duncan, Managers.
1835.	" "	"	John B. Gaudry, H. W. Mercer, Stewards; Nicoll, Shaffer, Duncan, Thomas Purse, Anderson, Managers.
1836.	Thos. Purse, P., William Duncan, V. P.	"	William H. Bulloch, William H. Miller, Stewards; Nicoll, Anderson, Shaffer, Joseph W. Jackson, Charles S. Henry, Managers.
1837.	" "	Sam'l C. House, Sec;	John M. Cooper, Matthew Hopkins, Stewards; Anderson, Dr. R. D. Arnold, Henry, Joseph R. Thompson, Benj. Snider, Managers.

OFFICERS.

1838. " " Dr. R. D. Arnold, V. P. Ewd. G. Wilson, Sec.: Dr. A. Y. Nicoll, George S. Harding, Stewards; Anderson, Henry, Snider, W. F. Crabtree, Jr., Thompson, Managers.

1839. " " " " I. K. Tefft, Joseph S. Fay, Stewards; Old Board re-appointed Managers.

1840. Dr. R. D. Arnold, P., W. F. Crabtree, V. P. " " Joseph S. Fay, Dr. Philip Minis, Stewards; Thompson, Anderson, Snider, Henry, Octavus Cohen, Managers.

1841. " " " " Joseph L. Shaffer, Henry K. Preston, Stewards; Old Board re-appointed Managers.

1842. " " Jno. W. Anderson, V. P. " " George Haas, Francis S. Bartow, Stewards; Snider, Wm. Hale, Solomon Cohen, A. A. Smets, Joseph Felt, Managers.

1843. Solomon Cohen, P. " " John G. Falligant, Young S. Pickard, Stewards; Snider, Hale, Aaron Champion, Matthew Hopkins, Felt, Managers.

1844. " " " P. B. Prendergast, John G. Falligant, Stewards; Champion, L. Baldwin, Hale, Felt. Snider, Managers.

1845. " " " Michael Prendergast, Michael Reilly, Stewards; Thomas Purse, Felt, Hale, Felt. Snider, Baldwin, Managers.

1846. " " " Michael Reilly, George White, Stewards; Purse, Snider, Michael Prendergast, Felt, Baldwin, Managers.

1847. " " " Rev. George White, Wm. H. Bulloch, Stewards: Felt, N. B. Knapp, Purse, Snider, Dr. R. D. Arnold, Managers.

1848. " " " Robt. H. Griffin, Abraham Minis, Stewards; Snider, Jno. Murchison, Dougald. Ferguson, Wm. H. Bullach, David Bell, Managers.

1849. " " " Griffin and Minis, Stewards; Snider, Murchison, Bell, Knapp, S. B. Williams, Managers.

1850. " " " Joseph S. Fay, Alexander R. Lawton, Stewards; Edward Padelford, Murchison, Thomas Purse, A. Minis, A. A. Smets, Managers.

1851. " " " Lawton and Fay, Stewards; Old Board re-appointed, Managers.

1852. " " " Fay and Lawton, Stewards; Smets, Purse, Minis, Robert D. Walker, A. R. Wright, Managers.

1853. Edw. Padelford, P.* " " Edwin Parsons, Jas. T. Webb, Stewards; Solomon Cohen, Walker, Minis, Wright, Smets, Managers.

*Resigned May 14, '53 and Joseph S. Fay, elected.

OFFICERS.

1854. Joseph S. Fay, P., Abraham Minis, V. P., " John L. Cope, James H. Johnston, Stewards; Cohen, Walker, John R. Johnson, Wright, Smets, Managers.

1855. " " " " " Daniel H. Baldwin, James M. Prentiss, Stewards; Johnson, Wright, Walker, Francis G. Dana, William Battersby, Managers.

1856. " " " " " James H. Demund, James W. McAlpin, Stewards; Charles Green, Francis S. Bartow, John M. Cooper, Chas. Van Horn, Charles F. Mills, Managers.

1857. " " Robert D. Walker, V. P., " William Hone, James B. Foley, Stewards; Cooper, Jno. R. Johnson, Battersby, Wm. M. Wadley, Geo. W. Wylly, Managers.

1858. Robt. D. Walker, P., Jno. M. Cooper, V. P., Jno. T. Thomas, Sec.; Jas. A. Courvoisie, Treas. Frederick Myers, F. W. Sims, Stewards; A. A. Solomons, E. Heidt, Benj. Whitehead, Jas. W. McAlpin, John Gammell, Wallace Cumming, John Scudder, Jas. H. Demund, W. R. Symons, Managers.

HONORARY MEMBERS:

A. A. SUARES, Esq., elected July 29, 1833. Col. HOWELL COBB, elected April 23d, 1834.
Dr. JOHN T. POSEY, elected April 23d, 1850.

MEMBERS:

(Who have been, are, and when, as far as could be ascertained.)

A few names appear more than once, but at different dates, indicating a renewal of membership, and are given thus in accordance with the records.

1772. Allman, Philip
     Anderson, James
1786. Andrew, James
1795. Armour, John
1794. Anciaux, John
     Anciaux, Nicholas
1806. Alger, James
     Allen, Alexander M.
1808. Ansley, Benjamin
1809. Armstrong, James
1819. Akin, Fleming
1822. Anderson, George W.
     Auze, Joseph
1828. Anderson, John W.
1832. Anderson, James
     Arnold, Dr. R. D.
1838. Ash, George A.
1850. Allen, R. A.
1852. Arnold, Charles S.
1855. Allen, Robert E.
     Anderson, Edward C.
1856. Alexander, Peter W.
     Adams, Richard W.
1858. Adams, William B.
     Anderson, Young J.
1859. Adams, George W.
     Atkinson, Henry
     Axson, Rev. I. S. K.
     Alexander, W. E.
1768. Belcher, William
1772. Bulloch, Archibald
     Box, Philip
     Butler, Elisha
     Bowen, Samuel
     Bryan, Hugh
     Bryan, Jonathan
1774. Bourquin, Henry L.
1786. Bulloch, James
     Bowen, Oliver

1790. Bryan, William
     Bond, Venables
     Beacroft, Samuel
1793. Berrien, Major John
     Bolton, Robert
1796. Benedix, Isaac
     Belcher,* William
     Brailsford, John N.
1802. Brown, John
     Bryan, Joseph
     Bulloch, William B.
1803. Blount, Stephen
1806. Berrien, John M.
     Ball, Frederick
     Bourke, Thomas
     Brickel, John
     Bilbo, James
1808. Bulloch, Archibald S.
1809. Barnes, William B.
1810. Boyle, James
1812. Bunch, Samuel G.
1813. Bolton, John
1818. Bulloch, John J.
     Bulloch, Jas. S.
     Bond, Samuel M.
1819. Bogne, John
     Bruen, Joseph
     Bruen, John H.
     Brown, Michael
1821. Bacon, Joseph
1822. Broom, Thomas R.
1823. Belcher, William
1828. Bliss, Elias
     Brown, Charles
1829. Baker, Rev. Daniel
1831. Bowen, William P.
     Birch, Robert
     Bulloch, N. W. J.
1832. Barclay, Anthony

---

* Son of William Belcher, admitted 1768.

1832. Bryan, S. J.
1833. Bayard, N. J.
       Burroughs, Joseph H.
       Barnsley, Godfrey
       Beaulard, John A.
       Bell, David
1834. Bourquin, Edward
1835. Boston, John
       Bulloch, William H.
1837. Branch, J. H. S.
1838. Butler, Gilbert
       Bulloch, George J.
       Baldwin, Loami
       Bird, Lewis
       Bartow. F. S.
       Bennett, Amasa F.
1850. Battersby, William
1852. Baldwin. Daniel H.
1853. Brundidge, J. H.
       Brooks, J. P.
       Brunner, Isaac
       Bunker, Edward H.
1854. Baldwin. Joseph H.
1855. Bartow, Francis S.
       Brigham, Henry
       Bradley, Richard
       Burke, Joseph
       Berg, S.
       Brautley. W. F.
       Bailey, F. W.
1856. Behn, Philip H.
       Bell, Samuel P.
       Boston, John
       Bryan, Joseph
       Bulloch, William J.
       Borchert, Anton
       Basinger, William S.
       Blois, Alfred J. J.
1857. Belden, William
       Blair, Francis
       Bonaud, Augustus
       Bacon, E. H.
       Bransby, Thomas
       Brown, Dominick
1858. Barron, James A.
       Bourquin, D. G.
       Bryan, M. M.
       Bourquin, Edward
       Barnum, N. K.
       Bulloch, Dr. W. G.
       2

1858. Blois, Theodore
       Bogart, William S.
       Brunner, Valentine
       Bennett, A. F.
       Bryan, Henry
1859. Bennett, William H.
       Bliss, Frederick
       Bliss, Alfred
       Burns, William
       Bulloch, W. H.
       Butler, Osceola
       Banks, Dr. W. H.
       Backer, A.
       Butler, James M.
       Baker, F. B.
       Buckner, Milton J.
       Battersby, Joseph
       Butler, Alexander F.
       Bogardus, H. S.
       Butler, Worthington C.
       Branch, John S.
       Bell, Henry Stiles
1772. Cochran, Jonathan
       Cramer, Christopher
1786. Cecil, Leonard
       Clay, Joseph
1790. Courvoisie, Francis
       Cumming, Thomas
1793. Course, Daniel
       Clay, Jr., Joseph,
1794. Cunningham, John
1795. Cowling, Slaughter
1802. Cuthbert, S. J.
       Cuyler, Jeremiah
1805. Charlton, T. U. P.
       Cope, Charles
1806. Cope, Adam
       Cumming, John
1807. Clark, Joseph H.
1808. Cleland, Moses
1810. Cooper, Lewis
       Cuthbert, Alfred
1818. Carr, John
       Cohen, Isaac
1819. Carnochan, John
       Cutter, Jonas
       Crane, John
       Clark, Thomas
1822. Coe, George W.
       Cooper, William

1822. Cope. George L.
1825. Cumming, George B.
Cuyler, Dr. W. H.
1826. Cohen, Solomon
1828. Carter, C. B.
1832. Charlton, Robert M.
1833. Corbett, Samuel D.
Curwen, J.
1835. Cohen, Octavus
Crabtree, Jr., William
1837. Cooper, John M.
Champion. Aaron
1838. Clark, W. P.
Cohen, Octavus
Clifford, J. A.
Cuyler, R. R.
1839. Cohen, Solomon
1840. Cooper, Peter G.
1842. Constantine, Bernard
1849. Cohen, Moses S.
1850. Cumming, Montgomery
Crowder, William
1851. Clark, William P.
Cope, John L.
1852. Connerat, Joseph V.
Cope, Jr., George L.
1855. Curran, P.
Cunningham, John
Cope, James E.
Clarke, T. B.
Clark, Isaac S.
Crane, H. A.
1856. Cohen, Moses A.
Cooke, John G.
Clark, Rev. G. H.
Cohen, Octavus
Crowder, William
Courvoisie, James A.
Carleton, Grenville E.
Cornwell, F. W.
Cumming, Wallace
Cuyler, George A.
Carruthers, Jos. S.
Claghorn, Jos. S.
Couper, William A.
Cheever, George H.
Chaplin, William F.
Connery, Charles H.
Christie, Luke
1857. Cumming, Montgomery

1857. Camp. Daniel B.
Carter, J. H.
Cranston, Uriah
Crosby, Joseph M.
Cox, William
Collins, J. P.
Cotton, William B.
1858. Casey, C. C.
Cohen, Jr., Solomon
Cunningham, T. M.
Charlton, W. O.
Curran, P.
Cannon, Luke
Caughey, Robert J.
1859. Charlton, John D.
Cooper, John
Cullen, William
Chisholm, Walter S.
Couper, Hamilton
Cohen, Jacob
Catherwood, S. C.
Chick, T. C.
1786. Deveaux, Peter
Demere, Raymond
1795. Dickinson, John D.
1803. Dechenaux, Thomas
1805. Davies, William
Davidson, George H.
1807. Dillon, John
1810. Davis, Joseph J.
1812. Dufaure, J.
1813. Densler, Frederick
1814. Demere, Raymond P.
1819. Daniell, William C.
1822. Davidson, John
DeLyon, Isaac
1825. DeLyon, Abraham
De LaMotta, Jr., Jacob
1828. Driscoll, T. M.
DeLyon, Sr., A.
Dews, John I.
1832. Duncan, William
1834. Day, John
1835. Demere, Raymond P.
1837. Dillon, Michael
Dillon, Michael O.
1838. Dowell, Thomas
De LaMotta, E.
Davis, William H.
Drysdale, Alexander

1840. DeLyon, Levi S.
1849. Dunning, Ralph
1852. Denslow, D. B.
Demund, James H.
1855. De LaMotta, Jr., Jacob
Davis, John H.
Delannoy, John D.
Dana, Francis G.
Dickson, Samuel D.
1856. Dickerson, H. J.
Davis, George W.
Davidson, William M.
Daniell, William S.
Dickson, William G.
Dawson, A. H. H.
1857. Dunning, Ralph
Dupon, Stephen F.
1858. DeLyon, Levi S.
Deitz, John G.
Donnolly, Robert B.
1859. Davis, William L.
Dean, George M.
Dure, George A.
Davenport, Hugh M.
Durward, William
Doe, J. F.
1772. Eppinger, John
Ewen, William
Evans, William
Elliott, Gray
1806. Enoc, George
1809. Everitt, John F.
1810. Eppinger, Jr., John
1811. Evans, John J.
1816. Eppinger, James
1855. Epping, Carl
1856. Einstein, Abraham
1858. Elliott, Rt. Rev. Stephen
1859. Ernst, James
Echols, Abner A.
Eckman, S. H.
Evans, W. E.
1772. Farley, Samuel
1786. Fields, James
1790. Fahm, Frederick
Fell, Isaac
1809. Flyming, F. T.
1810. Fritot, Charles E.
1811. Fell, Frederick S.
1814. Fahm, Jacob

1818. Furth, Dr. Louis M.
1819. Faries, George G.
1825. Foster, Jr., A.
Fort, Elias
1828. Footman, R. H.
1829. Fay, Samuel Howard
1835. Freeman, Henry H.
1838. Felt, Joseph
Falligant, John G.
Falligant, L. N.
Ferrill, John C.
Ferguson, D.
1839. Fay, Joseph S.
1840. Folsom, James M.
1853. Florence, W. Z.
1855. Fleming, William R.
Foley, James B.
Falligant, John G.
1856. Frierson, George S.
Ferrill, John C.
1857. Fawcett, Alexander
Falligant, Joseph E.
Freeman, Albert
1858. Foote, Emerson
Felt, Joseph
Fay, Calvin
Freeman, Henry C.
Finlayson, John
Ferguson, William
Ferguson, J. D.
Fairchild, L. J. B.
Feay, William T.
Footman, R. H.
1859. Foote, William G.
Ford, Martin J.
Freeman, Milo S.
Fullerton, Allan
Fraser, John C.
Footman, Joseph C.
Foley, John
Farrell, William H.
Freeman, G. C.
Fleming, William M.
Ferrill, John Oliver
1772. Gwinnett, Button
Goldwire, Benjamin
1774. Gibbons, William
1786. Gibbons, Jr., William
1790. Gibbons, Joseph
1796. Gibbons, John

1796. Gugel, David
    Grommet, John
    Glass, John
1806. Gray, John J.
    Grant, Joseph
1807. Gugel, Christian
    Gebere, Peter
1809. Grimes, John
    Gugel, Daniel
1810. Gaston, William
    Glen, George
1811. Gugel, John C.
    Griggs, Samuel
1812. Gray, Tobias V.
    Gindrat, John
1818. Gale, Worthington
1819. George, Joseph
    Guerard, Peter
1822. Girodon Lewis
1825. Gordon, W. W.
    Greene, H. D.
1830. Guilmartin, John
1832. Gaudry, John B.
    Gardner, John
1833. Gaston, W. K.
1834. Guerard, Robert G.
    Gordon, Austin R.
1835. Gardner, Stephen
    Ganahl, Joseph
    Green, Charles
1848. Griffin, Robert H.
1853. Garrard, W. W.
    Gammell, John
    Garmany, George W.
1855. Gordon, George A.
    Giles, William B.
    Guerard, John M.
    Gallic, John B.
1856. Gowdy, Hill
    Greiner, Charles A.
    Gordon, George
    Gladding, William H.
    Goodrich, W. W.
    Greenough, Joseph Fay
    Goodwin, William T.
    Ganahl, Joseph
    Godfrey, Rev. James E.
1858. Gray, George S.
    Gemenden, George
    Goodwin, Theodore A.

1858. Gue, Francis E.
    Gibson, Robert T.
    Gordon, Charles
    Grady, William
1859. Godfrey, Dr. J. E.
    GrosClaude, F.
    Goodwin, Robert M.
    Graybill, J. H.
    Giles, John L.
    Gallager, M. J.
    Geiger, Abram H.
    Galloway, David H.
1772. Horton, Nicholas
    Herb, Frederick
1774. Habersham, Major John
1786. Habersham, James
    Habersham, Joseph
    Handley, George
    Herb, Frederick
1790. Houstoun, Sir George
    Herb, John
1795. Herb, Frederick
    Howell, John
1796. Hunter, William
    Hull, George J.
1802. Harris, Charles
    Horskins, Zachariah
    Houstoun, James E.
    Holmes, John
    Handley, George
1803. Harden, Edward
1806. Habersham, Robert
1807. Habersham, Alexander
1808. Houstoun, Robert J.
1809. Herb, George
    Habersham, John
    Hunter, Alexander
    Habersham, Richard W.
1810. Hall, Henry
    Harral, George
    Henry, Jacob P.
1811. Howard, Charles
1813. Hunter, John
    Hunter, James
    Hartridge, J. E.
1814. Hersman, Jacob
    Habersham, Jr., Joseph
1818. Hollis, Silas
    Howe, Asahel
    Herbert, Moses

1819. Habersham, Joseph C.
Howard, Benjamin
Hall, Durham T.
Hayden, Charles H.
1822. Hartridge, Charles
1825. Higgins, C. A.
Hoyt, C. H.
Heinemann, F. W.
Howe, S. B.
1826. Henry, J. P.
Henry, Charles S.
Harris, S. L. W.
1828. Huguenin, J. D.
Harris, Stephen
House, Samuel C.
1829. Hutchison, Robert
1832. Houstoun, Patrick
Huntington, George
1834. Hall, George
1835. Harper, Henry
Haas, George
1837. Hopkins, M.
Herb, William
Harmon, A.
1838. Hogg, James E.
1838. Hunter, George W.
Henderson, E.
Hart, L.
Hale, William
Harding, George S.
Hand, B. E.
1842. Howell, John B.
Howard, Dr. J. G.
1850. Hardee, N. A.
Holcombe, Thomas
1853. Hunter, William
1855. Hartridge, Algernon S.
Hertz, Edwin E.
Hone, William
Headman, F. W.
Hartridge, Julian
Heidt, Rev. E.
Holland, W. F.
Hodgson, W. B.
1856. Hardee, Benjamin H.
Hills, Stephen,
Harding, George S.
Hunter, William P.
Hough, Edward C.
Habersham, A. T.

1856. Hasbrouck, J.
Hall, George
Hamilton, Charles F.
1857. Hutton, John S.
Harden, Edward H.
Henderson, David S.
Henderson, James M.
Henderson, William
Herderson, Thomas
Habersham, William Neyle
Houstoun, Patrick
1858. Harrison, George Paul
Humphreys, Milton
Hamilton, Luke M.
Hood, Jason P.
Halsey, Samuel P.
Hogg, John B.
Hitchcock, J. H.
Houstoun, Miss Mary
Hardee, Charles S.
Hopkins, M. H.
Hartridge, Alfred L.
Hall, Charles A.
Hamilton, M.
Haupt, William L.
Hutchings, Rev. T.
1859. Habersham, Fred A.
Hines, J. Steel
Heidt, James E.
Hamilton, S. P.
Harriss, Dr. Juriah
Harris, Lewis F.
Harden, Thomas H.
Hale, William
Hamlet, John R.
Henderson, Amos
Holst, C. M.
Harriss, R. Y.
Henderson, M. Y.
Hudtwalcker, J. N.
Haywood, Alfred
Hastings, Charles
1808. Isaac, Robert
1819. Irvine, Alexander
1837. Ingersoll, John
1855. Ingersoll, John
1774. Jones, Dr. Noble W.
1794. Jones, George
1795. Jones, James
1796. Jackson, Ebenezer

1856. Lachlison, Robert
1857. Lawrence, Dr. S. A. T.
    Levy, S. Yates
    Lovell, Edward
    LaRoche, James A.
    Lamar, A. R.
    Lefils, Daniel F.
    Lodge, C. L.
    LaRoche, Oliver A.
1858. Landershine, C. P.
    Lovell, Nathaniel
    Lawton, E. P.
    Linville, H. H.
    Lathrop, J. L.
    Lewis, John N.
    Lippman, Joseph
    Lloyd, Thomas E.
1859. Lancaster, J. S. F.
    Lathrop, J. S.
    Long, William E.
    Lawson, Robert R.
    Lattimore, William
    Legriel, Edward C.
    Lillibridge, O. M.
    Lefler, A.
    Lamar, George W.
    Lachlison, Jr., James
1750. Milledge, Richard
1784. Murray, Richard Donavan
    Montaigut, David
1785. Martin, John
1786. Morel, John
    Milledge, James
1790. Morel, Peter H.
    McCredie, Andrew
    Millen, George
    Moore, James
    Millen, Stephen
    Milledge, John
1794. Miller, Joseph
    Montfort, Robert
    McAllister, Matthew
1796. Mitchell, David B.
    Mitchell, Robert
    Milledge, Philip
    Moore, John
    McCall, John
    McKinnon, John
    McIntosh, James
    Mitchell, James Brydie

1796. McCaule, Rev. Thomas H.
1802. Miller, Peter
1803. Morel, John H.
1805. Miller, Morris
1806. McGee, James
    Moore, William A.
1807. Mounger, Edwin
1808. Miller, John
    Mendenhall, Thomas
1809. Mendenhall, John W.
    Maxwell, William
    Minis, Isaac
    McKinne, Joseph P.
    Maxwell, Joseph
1810. Mein, William
    McLeod, Norman
    McConky, D. M.
1811. Myers, Jr., George
1812. Morris, James E.
    McLeod, Murdoch
1813. McCall, Hugh
1816. Morel, Thomas N.
1816. Morrison, James
1818. Mason, Lowell
    Morel, John
    McLeod, Donald
1819. Maurel, Charles
    Morrall, John
    McNish, John
    Miller, Jacob
    Mitchell, Peter
    McHenry, James
1825. Myers, M.
    Marshall, W. P.
    McIntire, C.
1826. Morel, John H.
    McNeil, John
1828. Mackay, W.
    McKinnon, W. N.
    Millen, John
1829. Mills, Charles F.
1830. Morrell, I. W.
1832. McAlpin Henry
    Merriman, Charles P.
1833. Mongin, John D.
1834. McAllister, M. H.
    Moore, George W.
1835. Miller, Andrew T.
    Murchison, John
    Mercer, H. W.

1835. Miller, W. H.
1837. Morel, William
1838. Mayer, Jacob R.
Moye, O,
McIntyre, Andrew
Mallery, John
1839. Minis, Dr. Philip
1848. Minis, Abraham
1850. Moore, A. K.
Myers, Levi J.
1851. Marsh, Mulford
1852. Mills, Thomas R.
McMahon, John
1854. Mills, Charles F.
1855. Mortmollin, John S.
Miller, Thomas R.
Morse, Horace
Miller, A. N.
Myers, Frederick
Moore, John B.
Mills, Thomas R.
May, William H.
1856. McAlpin, James W.
Marsh, Isaac M.
Mackay, William
McAlpin, Angus
Minis, Isaac
Mills, James G.
Miller, William H.
Morrell, I. W.
Mallette, John D.
McAlpin, Donald W.
1857. Mallette, D.
Miller, E.
McCulloh, Anthony
1858. Molina, M.
Martin, E. H.
Morel, Bryan M.
Minis, Mrs. D.
Mitchell, Walter H.
Mortimer, Capt. John H.
Marshall, George S.
Murphy, S. Z.
McGee, Eli K.
Marshall, Thomas B.
Mendell, E.
Millen, M. B.
Munnerlyn, J. K.
McIntire, Robert
1859. Millar, W. D. R.

1859. Mills, N. C.
Mallon, Bernard
Moore, B. Frank
Miller, Samuel S.
McFarland, Dr. J. T.
Mayers, Serenus
Magill, C. A.
Millen, John M.
Moorehouse, Mrs. R. L.
Mitchell, Henry
Morgan, J. H.
McFarland, W. S.
McRae, F.
Myers, Octavus C.
Millar, Charles C.
Montmollin, Jr., John S.
1793. Noel, John Y.
1795. Norment, William
1796. Netherclift, Thomas
1810. Nichols, E.
1812. Nichols, Abm.
1819. Neff, William
Nicoll, John C.
1835. Neufville, Rev. Edward
1838. Nicoll, Dr. A. Y.
Norris, James A.
Newman, W.
Nevitt, John W.
1850. Neyle, G. N.
1856. Neely, T. W.
Norris, J. A.
Nichols, George S.
1858. Norton, John R.
Neidlinger, J. S.
Norton, T. S.
Norris, John S.
1859. Nichols, James S.
Nichols, George N.
Nelson, Andrew
1790. Oddingsells, Charles
1803. Oates, John P.
1832. Oemler, A. G.
1838. Olmstead, Jonathan
O'Driscoll, W. C.
1855. O'Driscoll, W. C.
Ogden, F. J.
1856. Owens, John W.
1856. Owens, George S.
O'Byrne, Dominick A.
1857. Olcott, William H.

1857. Olcott, Daniel G.
1858. Oliver, John
Owens, Mrs. George W.
Owens, Miss Mary W.
Oemler, Dr. A.
1859. Orme, Dr. F. H.
Osmond, Jesse
O'Sullivan, Charles E.
1772. Pryce, Charles
1774. Pierce, William
1790. Pendleton, Nathaniel
Port, James
1797. Pitt, Thomas
1805. Petit de Villers, Francis D.
Powell, James
Port, William F.
1808. Parker, William
1812. Polock, David
Pinder, Joseph W.
1813. Penfield, Josiah
1816. Proctor, George V.
1819. Polhill, Thomas
Ponce, Dimas
Palmes, George F.
1820. Petty, Lazarus
1825. Parkman, S. B.
Porter, Anthony
1826. Potter, James
1831. Patterson, William
1833. Padelford, Edward
Purse, Thomas
1834. Potter, Thomas F.
Pooler, Robert W.
1835. Porcher, James
Philbrick, Samuel
Pickard, Y. S.
1839. Pyncheon, E. E.
1840. Preston, Henry K.
Prendergast, Michael
1843. Pendergast, P. B.
1851. Palmes, George F.
1852. Parsons, Edwin
1854. Prentiss, James M.
1855. Powell, M.
Padelford, Jr., Edward
1856. Poullain, Philip
Parsons, George
Porter, Anthony
Palmer, Samuel
Purse, Edward J.
1858. Padelford, Dr. George P.

1858. Potts, S. O.
Palmer, S. B.
1859. Parsons, Charles
Postell, John
Preston, W. F.
Phillips, W. S.
Pond, Thomas G.
Pollard, T. J.
Pritchard, W. R.
Pinder, Joseph W.
Parker, Dr. Orrin C.
Pelot, Joseph F.
Parker, William F.
Phillips, Clavius
1858. Quint, Jacob
1772. Roche, Matthew
Rad, John
Roche, Jr., Matthew
Ring, Christopher
1786. Richards, John
1790. Rester, Frederick
Ruppert, John
Rees, David
1794. Rice, Thomas
1795. Rentz, John
Roberts, Joseph
1797. Roberts, John H.
1802. Robertson, James
1806. Read, Dr. James Bond
Roma, Francis
1807. Rutherford, Nathaniel G.
Roe, Alexander S.
1810. Rodman, Thomas W.
Ralston, John
Roberts, Edmund
Roe, Walter
1818. Roberts, John J.
Rees, Ebenezer S.
1819. Reed, Elias
1822. Rose, Hugh
Rowland, John T.
1825. Rockwell, C. W.
1828. Roe, Charles
1832. Reid, John H.
Roser, Henry
Ryerson, Jr., Thomas
1834. Roach, William
1838. Roberts, Hiram
Remshart, William
Reynolds, L. O.
1845. Reilly, Michael

3

Members of the Union Society.

1859.

Adams, George W.
Adams, Richard W.
Adams, William B.
Allen, Robert A.
Allen, Robert E.
Alexander, William E.
Anderson, Edward C.
Anderson, George W.
Anderson, Capt. John W.
Anderson, Young J.
Arnold, Dr. Richard D.
Atkinson, Henry
Axson, Rev. I. S. K.
Bacon, Maj. Edwin H.
Backer, Abraham
Bailey, Capt. Francis W.
Baker, Francis D.
Baldwin, Daniel H.
Baldwin, Joseph H.
Banks, Dr. William H.
Barnum, Noah K.
Barron, James A.
Bartow, Capt. Francis S.
Basinger, William S.
Battersby, William
Battersby, Joseph
Beach, Eben C.
Bee, Barnard E.
Behn, Maj. Philip H.
Belden, William
Bell, David
Bell, Samuel P.
Bell, Henry Stiles
Bennett, Alexander F.
Bennett, William H.
Berg, Sigismund
Blair, Francis
Bliss, Frederick
Bliss, Alfred
Blois, Alfred J. J.
Blois, Theodore
Bogardus, Henry S.
Bogart, William S.
Borchert, Anton
Boston, John
Bourquin, David G.
Bourquin, Edward
Bradley, Richard

Branch, John L.
Bransby, Thomas
Brantley, Gen. William F.
Brigham, Henry
Brooks, Capt. Jourdan P.
Brown, Marmaduke D.
Brown, Nathan B.
Brunner, Isaac
Brunner, Valentine
Bryan, Joseph
Bryan, Henry
Buckner, Milton J.
Bulloch, Dr. William G.
Bulloch, William J.
Bulloch, William H.
Burke, Joseph
Burns, William
Butler, Gilbert
Butler, Worthington C.
Butler, James M.
Butler, Alexander F.
Butler, Osceola
Camp, Daniel B.
Canon, Luke
Carleton, Grenville E.
Carter, James H.
Carruthers, Joseph S.
Casey, Christopher C.
Catherwood, Samuel C.
Caughey, Robert J.
Chaplin, William F.
Charlton, William O.
Charlton, John D.
Cheever, George H.
Chick, Thomas C.
Chisholm, Walter S.
Christie, Capt. Luke
Claghorn, Capt. Joseph S.
Clark, Rev. George H.
Clark, William P.
Cohen, Isaac
Cohen, Moses A.
Cohen, Moses S.
Cohen, Octavus
Cohen, Solomon
Cohen, Jr., Solomon
Collins, Joseph P.
Connerat, Joseph V.

Connery, Charles H.
Cooke, John G.
Cooper, John
Cooper, John M.
Cope, George L.
Cope, James E.
Cornwell, Frederick W.
Couper, William A.
Couper, Hamilton
Courvoisie, James A.
Cox, William
Crane, Heman A.
Cranston, Uriah.
Crowder, William
Cumming, George B.
Cumming, Montgomery
Cumming, Wallace
Cunningham, John
Cunningham, Thomas M.
Curran, Patrick
Cuyler, Dr. William H.
Cuyler, Richard R.
Cuyler, George A.
Dana, Francis G.
Daniell, William S.
Davenport, Hugh M.
Davidson, William M.
Davis, George W.
Davis, William H.
Davis, William L.
Dawson, Andrew H. H.
Dean, George M.
Deitz, John G.
Delannoy, John D.
DeLyon, Hon. Levi S.
Demund, James H.
Dickson, Samuel D.
Dickson, William G.
Dickerson, Capt. Henry J.
Doe, Jacob F.
Donnolly, Robert B.
Dupon, Stephen F.
Dure, George A.
Durward, William
Echols, Abner A.
Eckman, Samuel H.
Einstein, Abraham
Elliott, Rt. Rev. Stephen

Epping, Carl
Ernst, James
Evans, William E.
Fairchild, Lewis J. B.
Falligant, John G.
Farrell, William H.
Fawcett, Alexander
Fay, Joseph S.
Fay, Calvin
Feay, William T.
Felt, Joseph
Ferguson, John D.
Ferguson, William
Ferrill, John C.
Ferrill, John O.
Finlayson, John
Fleming, William R.
Fleming, William M.
Foley, John
Footman, Robert H.
Footman, Joseph C.
Foote, William G.
Ford, Martin J.
Fraser, John C.
Freeman, Albert
Freeman, Henry C.
Freeman, George C.
Freeman, Milo S.
Frierson, George S.
Fullarton, Allan
Gallager, Dr. Mahlon J.
Gallie, Capt. John B.
Galloway, David H.
Gammell, John
Ganahl, Joseph
Garmany, George W.
Garrard, William W.
Geiger, Abraham H.
Gemenden, George
Gibson, Richard T.
Giles, William B.
Giles, John L.
Gladding, William H.
Godfrey, Rev. James E.
Godfrey, Dr. James E.
Goodwin, Theodore A.
Goodwin, William T.
Goodwin, Robert M.
Gordon, George A.
Gordon, Charles
Gowdy, Hill
Grady, William
Gray, George S.
Graybill, James H.
Green, Charles
Greiner, Charles A.
GrosClaude, Frederick
Gue, Francis L.
Guerard, John M.

Habersham, Robert
Habersham, William N.
Habersham, Alexander T.
Habersham, Frederick A.
Hackett, Elisha L.
Hale, William
Hall, Charles A.
Hall, George
Halsey, Samuel Parkman
Hamilton, Charles F.
Hamilton, Luke M.
Hamilton, Marmaduke
Hamilton, Sam'l Prioleau
Hamlet, John R.
Hardee, Noble A.
Hardee, Benjamin H.
Hardee, Charles S.
Hardin, Edward H.
Harden, Thomas H.
Harding, George S.
Harriss, Dr. Juriah
Harriss, Robert Y.
Harris, Lewis F.
Harrison, Gen. George P.
Hartridge, Julian
Hartridge, Algernon S.
Hartridge, Alfred L.
Hasbrouck, Jonathan
Hastings, Charles
Haupt, William L.
Haywood, Alfred
Heidt, Rev. Emanuel
Heidt, James E.
Henderson, James M.
Henderson, David S.
Henderson, Thomas
Henderson, Amos
Henderson, Moses Y.
Henderson, William
Hertz, Edwin E.
Hines, J. Steel
Hitchcock, James H.
Hodgson, William B.
Hogg, John B.
Holcombe, Thomas
Holland, William F.
Holst, Christian M.
Hood, Jason P.
Hone, William
Hopkins, Matthew H.
Hough, Edward C.
Houstoun, Patrick
Houstoun, Miss Mary W.
Hudtwalcker, J. N.
Humphreys, Milton
Hunter, William P.
Hunter, William
Hutchison, Robert
Hutchings, Rev. Thomas

Hutton, John S.
Jackson, Hon. Henry R.
Jacobs, Peter
Jaudon, William A.
Jencks, Ebenezer
Jesse, John D.
Johnson, George O.
Johnson, John R.
Johnson, Dr. Warren
Johnston, James H.
Johnston, Joseph
Jones, John T.
Jones, John
Jones, Jr., Charles C.
Jones, George J.
Karn, Rev. Aaron J.
Kelly, John J.
Kibbee, John F.
Kine, William
King, William
King, Francis H.
King, Capt. Nicholas
King, McLeod
Knapp, Col. Noah B.
Knapp, Edwin
Lachlison, Robert
Lachlison, Jr., James
Lama, John
Lamar, Capt. Chas. A. L.
Lamar, George W.
Lancaster, John S. F.
Landershine, Charles P.
LaRoche, Oliver A.
LaRoche, Isaac D.
LaRoche, James A.
Lattimore, William
Lathrop, Jere S.
Lathrop, James W.
Lathrop, Henry
Lathrop, Harvey W.
Lathrop, Dwight
Lathrop, Edward S.
Lawrence, Dr. Sam'l A. T.
Lawton, Edward P.
Lawton, Col. Alexander R.
Lefils, Daniel F.
Letler, Dr. Albert
Legriel, Edward C.
Levy, Jacob C.
Levy, S. Yates
Lewis, John N.
Lillibridge, Oliver M.
Lincoln, William W.
Linville, Henry H.
Lippman, Joseph
Lloyd, Thomas E.
Lodge, Charles L.
Long, William E.
Lovell, Edward

Lovell, Nathaniel
Low, Andrew
Luce, Alonzo B.
Lyon, Noble
McAlpin, Angus
McAlpin, James W.
McAlpin, Donald M.
McCulloh, Anthony
McFarland, Dr. John T.
McFarland, William S.
McGee, Eli K.
McIntire, Robert
Mackay, William
Magill, Charles A.
Mallett, David
Mallette, John D.
Mallon, Bernard
Marsh, Isaac M.
Marshall, George S.
Marshall, Theodore B.
Martin, Dr. Edward H.
May, William H.
Mayer, Serenus A.
Mendell, Emanuel
Mercer, Hugh W.
Millar, Charles C.
Millar, Wm. D. R.
Miller, Alvin N.
Miller, William H.
Miller, Samuel S.
Millen, Hon. John M.
Millen, Macpherson B.
Mills, Charles F.
Mills, Capt. James G.
Mills, Thomas R.
Mills, Nathaniel C.
Minis, Abraham
Minis, Mrs. D.
Mitchell, Col. Walter H.
Mitchell, Henry
Molina, Manuel
Montmollin, John S.
Moore, John B.
Moore, B. Frank
Moorehouse, Mrs. R. L.
Morel, Bryan M.
Morrell, Isaac W.
Morgan, Joseph H.
Morse, Horace
Mortimer, Capt. John H.
Munnerlyn, James K.
Murchison, John
Murphy, Simeon Z.
Myers, Frederick
Myers, Octavus C.
Neely, Thomas W.
Nelson, Andrew
Neidlinger, James S.
Nevitt, John W.

Nichols, George S.
Nichols, James S.
Nichols, George N.
Nicoll, Hon. John C.
Norris, John S.
Norris, James A.
Norton, John R.
Norton, Thaddeus S.
O'Byrne, Dominick A.
O'Driscoll, William C.
O'Sullivan, Charles E.
Oemler, Dr. Armenius
Olcott, William H.
Olcott, Daniel G.
Oliver, John
Orme, Dr. Francis H.
Osmond, Jesse
Owens, George S.
Owens, John W.
Owens, Miss Mary W.
Owens, Mrs. George W.
Padelford, Edward
Padelford, Jr., Edward
Padelford, Dr. George P.
Palmer, Samuel
Palmer, Samuel B.
Palmes, George F.
Parker, William F.
Parker, Dr. Orrin C.
Parsons, Edwin
Parsons, George
Parsons, Charles
Pelot, Col. Joseph F.
Phillips, Clavius
Pinder, Joseph W.
Pollard, Thomas J.
Pond, Thomas G.
Porter, Maj. Anthony
Potter, James
Potts, Stephen O.
Poullain, Philip
Powell, Martin
Prentiss, James M.
Pritchard, Col. William R.
Purse, Thomas
Purse, Edward J.
Quint, Jacob
Rahun, Gen. John W.
Read, Dr. James B.
Read, Capt. John P. W.
Reid, Francis W.
Reilly, Michael J.
Reeves, Capt. Thomas
Remshart, Capt. Daniel
Remshart, William W.
Remshart, William
Richardson, John
Richardson, Mrs. John
Richardson, John A.

Richmond, Henry A.
Ripley, Joseph B.
Robinson, Charles E.
Rockwell, Col. William S.
Rogers, Cornelius D.
Rogers, John S.
Rogers, William
Rogers, Rev. Charles W.
Rogers, William R.
Rose, Charles
Rose, William
Ross, Van R. G.
Rothchild, Henry
Rowland, John C
Russell, Philip M.
Russell, Waring
Ryan, John
Saussy, Joachim R.
Saussy, Robert
Scattergood, George W.
Schenck, Capt. George R.
Schley, Dr. James M.
Schley, Philip T.
Schley, John
Scranton, Daniel T.
Scranton, Henry H.
Screven, Capt. John
Scudder, Ephraim
Scudder, John
Selkirk, James M.
Selleck, Clarence H.
Shaffer, George W.
Sims, Frederick W.
Slone, John
Smets, Alexander A.
Smedberg, James R.
Sneed, James R.
Snider, James I.
Solomons, Abraham A.
Solomons, Joseph M.
Solomons, Moses J.
Sorrel, Francis
Sorrel, George Moxley
Soullard, Edward A.
Staley, John A.
Starr, William
Stebbins, Charles
St. Croix, George do
Stevens, Thomas F.
Stevenson, Capt. John
Stewart, Daniel H.
Stibbs, Henry
Stiles, Hon. William H.
St. John, George A.
Stoddard, John
Stone, Francis M.
Stoneback, William
Sutcliffe, George
Swift, Edward

Symons, William R.
Symons, John F.
Symons, John J.
Taylor, John C.
Taylor, William S.
Tebeau, Lewis C.
Tefft, Israel K.
Thiot, Charles H.
Thomas, John T.
Thomas, Joseph
Thomas, William A.
Thompson, William T.
Thompson, James C.
Tilden, Barnard G.
Tinsley, William B.
Tison, William H.
Torlay, Alfred F.
Tucker, Capt. John F.
Tufts, Martin
Tupper, Frederick A.
Tupper, Frederick
Turner, Thomas M.
Valleau, William N.
Vanhorn, Charles
Villalonga, John L.
Vroom, William L.
Wade, Edward C.
Wadley, William M.
Waldberg, Jacob
Waldhauer, David

Walker, Col. Robert D.
Wallace, Norman
Wallace, Robert G.
Walsh, Thomas J.
Ward, Hon. John E.
Waring, George H.
Waring, Joseph F.
Warner, William
Warnock, James G. M.
Washburn, Joseph
Washburn, Henry K.
Way, William I.
Wayne, Thomas S.
Wayne, Richard A.
Webb, George S.
Webb, James T.
Weber, Christian
Webster, Joseph W.
Webster, Amos E.
Weed, Henry D.
Wells, Lewis W.
West, Dr. Charles W.
Wetter, Augustus P.
Wheaton, John F.
White, James W.
White, Gen. William P.
White, Charles J.
Whitehead, Benjamin
Whitehead, George A.
Wight, Sheldon W.

Wilbur, Aaron
Wilder, John
Wilder, John R.
Wilder, Mariner A.
Wilmot, Samuel
Wilson, Charles
Wilson, Edward G.
Wilson, Alexander K.
Wiltberger, William H.
Williams, Stephen B.
Williamson, John
Willink, Sen., Henry F.
Willis, Dr. Francis T.
Willis, Wylly F.
Winkler, Zachariah N.
Withington, Edward O.
Withington, James E.
Wood, Samuel A.
Woodbridge, Wylly
Wray, William
Wright, William
Wright, Allen R.
Wylly, George W.
Wylly, Robert E.
Yonge, Philip
Zeigler, William
Zeigler, Solomon
Zittrouer, James A.
Zogbaum, William D.

HONORARY MEMBERS.

ANTHONY A. SUARES, Elected July 29th, 1833.
Col. HOWELL COBB, Elected April 23d, 1834.
Dr. JOHN F. POSEY, Elected April 23d, 1859.

OFFICERS—1859.

ROBERT D. WALKER, President.
JOHN M. COOPER, Vice President.
JOHN T. THOMAS, Secretary.
JAMES A. COURVOISIE, Treasurer.

BOARD OF MANAGERS.

JOHN GAMMELL,
JAMES WALLACE McALPIN,
JAMES H. DEMUND,
WILLIAM T. THOMPSON,
EMANUEL HEIDT,
FREDERICK MYERS,
FREDERICK W. SIMS,
JULIAN HARTRIDGE,
STEPHEN S. DUPON.

STEWARDS.

CORNELIUS D. ROGERS.
JOHN F. WHEATON.

BETHESDA,

Its Founders, &c. A Historical Sketch,

BY J. F. CANN.

As WHITEFIELD well and properly deserves to be called the Father of Bethesda, it is but right and proper, notwithstanding his life and character may be familiar to all, that we should introduce this brief and imperfect sketch with a few remarks in reference to him. Southey describes him as a man something above the middle stature, well proportioned, though about the time he visited Georgia, slender, and remarkable for a native gracefulness. His complexion was very fair, his eyes small and lively, of a dark blue color; in recovering from the measles, he had contracted a squint with one of them. but this peculiarity rather rendered the expression of his countenance more remarkable. than in any degree lessened the effect of its uncommon sweetness. His voice excelled both in melody and compass, and its fine modulations were happily accompanied by that grace of action which he possessed in an eminent degree, and which has been said to be the chief requisite of an orator. It is said further of him by another, that in 1735, while a student at Oxford, he was rendered so uncomfortable by the society into which he was thrown, that he frequently would remain in his study until his limbs became benumbed with cold.

But finally, his companions, seeing in him, I have no doubt the germs of the future man, left him to take his own way. It seems he had heard of the Methodists before he came to Oxford, and naturally inclined to adopt their doctrines; but from his humble condition he was deprived of the acquaintance of the leader of the Methodist sect, Charles Wesley, until, a pauper attempting suicide, Whitefield sent a poor woman to inform Wesley of the fact, enjoining upon her not to tell who sent her—which injunction was violated and Wesley for the first time learning the whereabouts of him of whom he had heard, at once invited him to breakfast, and thus was formed an acquaintance which rapidly grew into a firm and abiding friendship. From this moment Whitefield became allied with the Wesleys and others of the Methodist sect, and this doubtless led to his visiting this country, and to his name being the foundation stone of Bethesda, as will appear in its history. One word in reference to his preaching, and we come at once to the subject of the sketch.

It is said he preached five times a week to such congregations that it was with great difficulty that he could make his way along the crowded aisle to the pulpit: some hung upon the rails of the organ-loft, others climbed upon the leads of the Church, and altogether made the building so hot with their breath, that the steam would fall from the pillars like drops of rain. When he left Bristol, he was obliged to start at mid-night to avoid being escorted by horsemen and coaches. At London on Sundays, persons would often go before day-break in order to get seats, and frequently so great was the rush to hear him, that officers were stationed at the doors to preserve order.

THE PAST AND PRESENT HISTORY OF BETHESDA.

The name "Bethesda" signifying "House of Mercy," was adopted by the founders of the institution, better known perhaps as the "Whitefield Orphan House," because it seemed to express the intention and desire of those who first conceived the idea. In tracing its history from its very origin, we find it first existing in the minds of Oglethorpe and Wesley, having been conceived and discussed by them. When Whitefield had determined to visit the colony of Georgia, among the very first suggestions or disclosures made to him by Oglethorpe and Wesley, was the statement that they had in contemplation the establishment of a school for orphans.

The following extract from a letter written by Whitefield, fully attests the origin of the institution.

BETHESDA, in Georgia,
March 31st, 1745-6.

"Some have thought that the erecting such a building was only the produce of my own brain, but they are much mistaken: for it was first proposed to me by my dear friend, the Rev. Mr. Charles Wesley, who with his Excellency General Oglethorpe, had conceived a scheme for carrying on such a scheme before I had any thoughts of going abroad myself." It would have been an easy matter for Whitefield to have appropriated to himself the entire credit of having conceived and executed the noble design, but unselfishness was one of the brightest of his many excellent qualities.

The peculiar circumstance connected with Whitefield's decision to visit Georgia, and his first voyage, are matters of no ordinary interest.

He says: "When I had been in London about a month, letters

came from the Messrs. Wesley and the Rev. Mr. Ingham, their fellow-laborer, an Israelite indeed, from Georgia; their accounts fired my soul, and made me long to go abroad for God, too. But having no outward call, and being, as I then thought, too weak in body even to undertake a voyage at sea, I endeavored to lay aside all thought of going abroad. But my endeavors were all in vain; for I felt at times such a strong attraction in my soul towards Georgia, that I thought it almost irresistible. I strove against it with all my power, begged again and again, with many cries and tears, that the Lord would not suffer me to be deluded, and, at length, opened my mind to several dear friends." We are told, by his own statement, that his friends advised him not to go abroad; but Georgia seemed to hang on his mind like a "prophetic burden;" and when Wesley returned to England, and told him that he had come solely to secure more help in Missionary labor, Whitefield partially determined to go. He addresses Wesley in reference to his necessary support, and receives the reply: "Food to eat, raiment to wear, and a house to lay your head in, such as our Lord had not, and a crown of glory that fadeth not away." Upon hearing this, says Whitefield, "my heart leaped within me, and, as it were, echoed to the call." He immediately consulted the Bishop of London and the Trustees of Georgia, including Oglethorpe, who was at that time in England, and finally determined fully and positively to go.

From the account given of his farewell visits, and the eagerness of the vast crowds wherever he went to hear him preach, we are enabled to read, in part at least, the future greatness of the man.

But the point of peculiar interest in these visits, is the fact that, while he was so busily engaged in preaching, as well as taking, as many thought, a final farewell of his numerous friends and companions, *he was collecting* funds for the poor children of the colony, whom he had never seen, and of whose destitution he had heard but little. It is said that he collected for the schools then established in and about Savannah, a thousand pounds; and, besides this, procured over three hundred pounds for the poor persons of the colony.

He sailed December 28th, 1737, aged twenty-three; and while the incidents connected with his voyage have no special bearing upon his mission here, they are, nevertheless, of so memorable a character, that we cannot forbear mentioning one or two striking occurrences. It is said that he began exhorting and preaching the very moment all was quiet and the vessel was in full sail. One writer, in speaking of it, says that such a spectacle was never witnessed since Paul's

memorable voyage to Rome—that he turned the chief cabin into a
cloister, the deck into a church, and the steerage into a school-room,
reading prayers and preaching twice each day to the soldiers and
sailors, and increased these services on the Sabbath. The Hon.
Mr. Habersham, who accompanied Whitefield, and of whom we shall
have occasion to speak more fully, particularly as we advance with
this sketch, took special charge of the children, and formed them
into a sort of school, and spent his time in teaching and interesting
them.

On the 5th of May, the Whitaker anchored off Tybee, and Whitefield, we are told, took a final farewell of the crew in a sermon which
touched the hearts of all, and made them grieve to part with him.

Coming to this city—then almost a wilderness—the very first
object that claimed his attention was the condition of the children,
especially those who were orphans. Seeing the great need of immediate aid, we find him taking the money he had collected in
England, providing a home for the poor outcasts, and placing them
under proper superintendence and care.

While he had determined to establish an orphan house adapted to all
the purposes contemplated, yet, such was the destitution of the poor,
uncared-for children, that immediate steps must be taken. He hired
a house, obtained servants, and though the fact is nowhere stated, as
far as we are aware, we judge, from what occurred afterwards, that he
placed them under the charge of Mr. Habersham. Having thus
provided for the temporary support and instruction of the children,
he, at once, zealously set himself about collecting funds to establish
the Orphan House. He returned to England, was cordially received
by the Trustees of Georgia, who, at the expressed wish of the
colonists, offered him a salary to labor in Savannah; but this he
declined by requesting that, instead of paying him, they would grant
him a tract of land on which he might erect an Orphan House.

The Trustees at once acceded to his request, and donated him five
hundred acres of land for that purpose, which, as perhaps, many
know, was originally the portion belonging to the Bethesda estate

This act, on the part of the Trustees, served to fire Whitefield with
still greater zeal and fervor in the work ; and he traversed England
for the sole purpose of collecting funds. In less than one year, he
collected more than one thousand pounds, and with this amount in
hand, he left England for the colony, August 14th, 1739, attended
by eight men and three children. One of the men, a Mr. Periam,
a Minister of London, came out as a subordinate to Bethesda, where

he afterwards died, leaving two sons, who were received into the school as pupils.

Immediately, on Whitefield's arrival, the grant of land was formally donated as follows :

"June 2d, 1739, sealed a grant of five hundred acres of land to the Rev. George Whitefield, in trust for the use of the house to be erected and maintained for the receiving such children as now are, and shall hereafter be, left orphans in the Colony of Georgia, in pursuance of the direction of the Common Council, held the 30th of July, 1739."

After receiving this grant, and arranging other necessary matters, we find him making a tour through the northern States, with a view of collecting more money to carry forward the enterprise.

During this absence, we have it particularly mentioned, that the children were left under the guardianship of Mr. Habersham; for it is said, that he (Mr. H.) selected out the five hundred acres, and commenced to enclose and cultivate it during Whitefield's absence; that the latter, on his return, was somewhat dissatisfied with the arrangements made for the orphans, and immediately hired a house at a large rent, opened an infirmary, and received, at different times, about twenty-four orphans. It may not be out of place, just here, to devote a few lines in reference to Mr. Habersham, so often mentioned in connection with the early history of Bethesda. He was born at Beverly, in Yorkshire, 1712, accompanied Mr. Whitefield to Georgia only from motives of warm friendship for Mr. W., and his deep love for the missionary work. He presided over the Orphan House at Bethesda until 1744; he was married by the Rev. Mr. Whitefield to Mary Bolton, at Bethesda, on the 25th of December, 1740, by whom he had ten children, three of whom, sons, survived him, and were conspicuous in the cause of American liberty. He became President of the Colony of Georgia in 1769—mingled in the struggle for independence, but did not live to see the glorious result, as he died at New Brunswick, New Jersey, August 28th, 1775, where he had gone in search of health.* Returning to the subject of our sketch, we would remark, that while Whitefield's mind seemed intent upon the one grand object, viz.: the establishment of his Orphan House, we find a large Tabernacle erected at this time in London, capable of seating some four thousand people, chiefly through his immediate instrumentality. But the dawn of his full hope appeared on the 25th of March, 1740, when was laid the first brick of the main building of the Orphan House, or, as then named by him, Bethesda—

a " House of Mercy." This building was built of wood, and measured seventy by forty feet; and yet, within these small dimensions, it is said, Whitefield accommodated about one hundred persons, consisting of forty children, the rest servants and workmen.

When Whitefield had laid this first brick, and carried on the work to the completion of the main building, he lifted a prayer to God, which the history of the Institution, from that time to this, so strikingly proves to have been answered, that I cannot forbear inserting it; " Blessed be God, I have not been disappointed of my hope. Set thy Almighty fiat to it, Oh! Gracious Father, and for thine own name sake, convince us more and more that thou wilt never forsake those who put their trust in thee." But all the funds had been expended in the erection of this building, and Whitefield was again obliged to solicit aid. We cannot better describe the course pursued, than by making the following extract from Stephens' History of Georgia, vol. 1st, page 351 : " In August, having, in the meantime, made a tour northward, as far as New Jersey, in which he had collected, in money and provisions, over £500, he sailed for New England, and went as far east as Boston, preaching everywhere as he journeyed, and gathering carefully all collections for his Orphan House. He received upwards of £700 in goods, provisions, and money for the Georgia Orphan House." After returning to Bethesda, and remaining a few days to arrange necessary matters, he again set sail for Europe, leaving the whole affair in the hands of Mr. Habersham, whose administration was very successful. The general arrangements of the Institution at this time are minutely described in the following language, by a young man from Boston, who visited Bethesda in 1741 : " The house contained sixty-eight children, the whole family numbering eighty-four persons, besides nineteen laborers, employed about the premises.

The routine of family duties were as follows : The bell rings in the morning at sunrise to wake the family. When the children arise, they sing a short hymn, pray by themselves, go down to wash, and by the time they have done that, the bell calls to public worship, when a portion of Scripture is read and expounded, a psalm sung, and the exercises begin and end with prayer. They then breakfast, and afterwards some go to their trades, and the rest to school.

At noon, they all dine in the same room, and have comfortable and wholesome diet provided. A hymn is sung before and after dinner. Then, in about a half an hour, to school again; and between whiles find time enough for recreation. A little after sunset, the

bell calls to public duty again, which is performed in the same manner as in the morning. After that, they sup and are attended to bed
by one of their masters, who then prays with them, as they often do
privately." In the year 1742, the Institution was subjected to many
severe and dangerous trials; but in the language of Whitefield,
" the Orphan House, like the burning bush, flourished unconsumed."

The Spanish invasion—the unfavorable reception the Institution
met with from many who should have acted differently—greatly
endangered its success; but Whitefield, with a never-tiring zeal and
undaunted courage, only labored the more diligently, determining
" to be sold a slave to serve the gallies, rather than his orphan family
should want." On returning from Europe, he found the number of
children had so greatly increased, that in a short time he made another voyage, to renew his efforts in their behalf. It will be seen
from the following extract in what condition he found Bethesda on
his return. " Many boys have been put out to trades, and many girls
put out to service. I had the pleasure the other day to see three
boys at the house in which they were bred—one of them out of his
time, a journeyman, and the others serving under their masters. One
that I brought from New England, is handsomely settled in Carolina ;
and another from Philadelphia, is married, and lives very comfort-
ably in Savannah. We have lately begun to use the plough, and
next year, I hope to have many acres of good oats and barley. We
have nearly twenty sheep and lambs, fifty head of cattle, and seven
horses.

We hope to kill a thousand weight of pork this season. Our
garden is very beautiful, and furnishes us with every sort of greens.
We have plenty of good milk, eggs, poultry, and make plenty of
butter weekly.

A good quantity of wool and cotton has been given me; and we
hope to have sufficient spun and woven for the next winter's clothing. The family now consists of twenty-six persons. Two of the
orphan boys are blind—one is little better than an idiot. I have two
women to take care of the household work, and two men and three
boys employed about the plantation and cattle. A set of Dutch
servants has lately been sent over. A valuable young man from New
England is my schoolmaster, and in my absence performed duty in
the family.

Georgia is very healthy—not above one, and that a little child, has
died out of our family since it removed to Bethesda." The fore-

going is taken from a letter written by Mr. Whitefield, describing the condition of the Orphan House during the years 1745-6.

Shortly after this, his health became so much enfeebled, that he was advised to make a trip to the Bermudas, and while there made collections for his school; but his health not being improved, instead of returning home, he made another voyage to Europe. He spent the years 1748-9 as Chaplain to Lady Huntingdon, of whom we shall speak more fully and particularly hereafter. During this time, he neither forgot, nor neglected the interests of Bethesda, but was in constant correspondence, keeping himself acquainted with the condition and wants of his orphan children. In 1750, we find Whitefield laboring in England, with a view to make Bethesda a College, where all the advantages of a liberal education could be enjoyed. Could he have succeeded in accomplishing this noble effort, doubtless, we should have had to-day, at our very doors, an institution equal, in every respect, to Yale or Princeton. In 1751, he made a very unexpected visit to this country, bringing with him several orphans; but finding the Institution in a highly prosperous and encouraging condition, he almost immediately returned to Europe, resuming his place in the household of Lady Huntingdon.

In 1754, he visited Bethesda, found every thing satisfactorily progressing, made a trip to the North for the purpose of securing more assistance, but his health again failing, he hurried back, and in the early part of 1755, again embarked for Europe. While there, the Governor of Georgia consulted with him concerning Bethesda. Whitefield urged him to visit the school, assuring him that " Mrs. Crane, the wife of the steward, would well provide for him." On Nov. 22d, 1755, Whitefield returned to Bethesda, buoyant with the hope of the speedy establishment of a first-class college, as appears from the following : " Peace and plenty reign here; all things go on successfully. God hath given me great favor in the sight of the Governor, Council, and Assembly. A memorial was presented for an additional grant of land, consisting of two thousand acres. It was immediately donated. Both houses addressed the Governor on behalf of the intended college. A warm answer was given, and I am now putting every thing in repair, and getting every thing ready for that purpose.

His Excellency dined with me yesterday, and expressed his satisfaction in the warmest terms.

The auditing the accounts, and laying the foundation for a college, hath silenced enemies and comforted friends. The finishing this affair confirms my call to England at this time."

But it was a call to disappointed hope—fruitless labor—a very different result from what his many encouragements had led him to anticipate, or even for a moment to suspect. It must have been a severe shock to his generous ambition and zealous labors—when, after petitioning his Majesty for a College Charter after the plan of the one already granted to Princeton, N. J., his prayer should have been refused. How many, after expending so much time, means and labor for no personal emolument, but for the benefit, in a great measure, of those who indirectly caused its defeat, would have given up, and refused ever to have any more to do with the Institution.

But how differently did Whitefield act. He did not allow himself to be daunted; because, forsooth, the longing desire of his heart could not be satisfied. He gave up the thought of a charter, but determined, if possible, to make Bethesda an Academy similar in arrangement to one then established in Philadelphia, which bore a very high character.

In 1769, he again visits Bethesda, and reports: "Everything exceeds my highest expectation; it is good for me to be here." During this year, two wings were added to the main building, Governor Wright laying the corner-stone March 25th, 1769. We find in the Georgia Gazette, the following: "Savannah, January 31st, 1770. Last Sunday, his Excellency the Governor, Council, and Assembly, having been invited by the Rev. Mr. Whitefield, attended divine service in the chapel of the Orphan House Academy." This notice goes on to state, that Whitefield preached from the text—"For who hath despised the day of small things," setting forth the difficulties encountered during the thirty years existence of the Institution, its present prosperity, and prospect of future usefulness. The two wings which had just been added were one hundred and fifty feet each in length, giving accommodations for a much larger number.

The company were highly delighted with the many and tasteful improvements that had been made, and expressed themselves pleased with the plan of operations.

Mr. Whitefield had remained this time at Bethesda, some five months or more, giving personal and continual attention to all the affairs of the Institution; but the care was too arduous for him, and with impaired health and a fast declining constitution, he made a trip North—only to be arrested by illness, at Newburyport, Massachusetts, where he died September the 30th, 1770.

No language can describe the sorrow which, like a dark, thick cloud, overshadowed the hearts, not only of the poor orphan ones at

2

Bethesda, and of the people of the colony, but also the hearts of thousands in this country and in Europe.

As long as the Gospel of Christ shall be respected among men, as long as education shall have a friend, and the poor one to feel for them, Whitefield's name and memory shall be cherished. When the fatherless and motherless shall be cast out and left uncared for, the shadow of Whitefield shall shelter them; and his prayers, long since registered in Heaven in their behalf, shall secure for them the tender care and protection of the Father of the fatherless. Few in this country or in Europe felt more deeply the severe stroke than Lady Huntingdon, with whom Whitefield had been long and intimately associated as Chaplain, confidential friend, and spiritual adviser.

Their efforts, desires, and feelings, in reference to the great work of doing good, fitted them to be companions in their Master's cause, and made it exceedingly felicitous for Whitefield, that, in his last benediction to his orphan children, he could commit them into the hands of one whose "life was hid in Christ." The following extract from his Will, shows the manner and form in which he committed Bethesda to the care of Lady H.; and in case of her demise before his own, he names the next one in every way best fitted for the trust:

"I will and bequeath the Orphan House in Bethesda, and likewise all the buildings, land, books and furniture belonging thereto, to that lady elect, that mother in Israel, that mirror of true and undefiled religion, the Right Honorable Selina, Countess of Huntingdon; and in case she should be called to enter upon her glorious rest before my decease, to Honorable James Habersham, a merchant of Savannah."

It is said the death of Whitefield and the care imposed by this trust, weighed so heavily upon Lady Huntingdon's mind, and so sensible was she of the necessity of divine aid, that she appointed a day of fasting and prayer to be observed by the chapels under her patronage. Just here, we must again beg the privilege of dropping the subject-matter of this sketch, while we take a brief glance at the life of Lady Huntingdon, whose name and acts form a conspicuous part of the remaining history of Bethesda. Selina Shirley, second daughter of Earl Ferrars, was born in Chartley, August 24, 1707. Almost from infancy, it is said, her life was marked by a wonderful seriousness; sober and thoughtful, she avoided playmates, and had no disposition or desire whatever to mingle in children's gayeties. The secret quiet of her closet, or solemn walks in the graveyard, had far sweeter and holier charms for her.

From her history, we can but believe that the seeds of a deep, earnest and abiding piety were planted very early in her tender heart; and as she grew in knowledge and experience, these seeds of right-cousness budded forth into fair and full maturity. At the age of twenty-one, she married Theophilus, Earl of Huntingdon, and thus became still more involved in the fashionable life of the nobility.

Her associates were such persons as the Duchess of Marlborough, Lady Mary Wortley Montague, Margaret, daughter of the Earl of Oxford, Whitefield, Wesleys, Romaine, Doddridge, and others of like celebrity. Although she had, by birth and marriage, every temp-tation to haughtiness and frivolity, yet, an humble meekness, a noble generosity, a heart abounding with pity and commiseration for all oppressed or in sorrow, were the distinguishing features in her character. Her Redeemer's name and glory seem to have been her constant thought and effort; every energy of her soul, every pulsation of her heart, acted in holy harmony to the accomplishment of this great result. In a discourse, written by Doddridge, on Christian can-dor and unanimity, dedicated to Lady Huntingdon, he speaks of her "as an eminent example of Christian candor and unanimity, and of every other virtue and grace which can support and adorn it." There are sev-eral individual cases specially mentioned, which are happy illustrations of her deep interest in the temporal and spiritual welfare of others. When Doddridge's health began to fail, and there seemed to be nothing that would benefit him but a journey, to make which he had not the means, Lady H. offered to supply all the funds needed, and thus, doubtless, was instrumental in preserving, for many years, the life of that great and good man.

When a Mr. Allen and Col. Williams were sent to England to solicit aid for Princeton College, they carried letters of introduction to Lady H., who received them most cordially, and assisted them greatly, both by personal contribution and by her influence.

In 1760, Sansom Occum, an Indian preacher, visited London to secure funds for Rev. Dr. Wheelock's school for the education of Indian youth at Lebanon, Connecticut. As was natural, he excited very great attention, and was a source of interest to many. Lady H. took an active part in helping him to make collections, and by her aid and influence, he obtained seven thousand pounds in England, and two or three in Scotland. To follow this wonderful woman through all her journeyings in England; tell of the many young men she was instrumental in establishing in the ministry; to point out the difficulties she met with, and the obstacles she overcame in the erection of from seven to ten chapels, together with the schools she had in operation, and the college she had instituted at Trevacca; to record all the private and public acts of this woman, would require a volume.

Her name is rich in all that can adorn and beautify the female character.

The year 1770 was a memorable one in her history. Although unconscious of the dark cloud hanging over her, she set apart the first day of this year as one of special prayer, that God would be her guide and protector. The afflictions and sad events of the year, her after history proves, were but the verifications of the encouraging truth—"Whom the Lord loveth, he chasteneth." This year a spirited controversy took place between Wesley and Whitefield, in reference to the doctrine of election. A conference was appointed, which agreed to annul the doctrine. This so much offended Lady H., that she forbid any one holding such views to be a student at her institution.

The matter assumed a very serious aspect; but, finally, by the arrangement of friends, Wesley and Lady H. made to each other satisfactory explanations, and all was finally and happily adjusted between them. It was a matter deeply painful to Lady H., that Benson, her head teacher at the College, took grounds against her; and Fletcher, who had been a friend to her, wrote an article defending Wesley's views, which appeared after the matter had been amicably settled. The deep family afflictions through which she passed, added to the news of Whitefield's death, almost crushed her loving spirit.

As we have said, when she learned that he had bequeathed the care and responsibility of Bethesda to her, she at once set apart a day for fasting and prayer, that she might be fitted for the duty. Her first step was to obtain all information concerning the past working of the institution, and its present condition. She found the number there to be sixteen children, nine workmen, and seventy-five negroes. The few children and great number of laborers, may be accounted for by the fact, that the two wings were at this time being added to the main building.

Lady H. immediately sent over her own housekeeper to manage the domestic affairs, the Rev. Mr. Crosse, the same who had been acting under Whitefield, was continued as teacher, and Mr. Piercy made President and general agent.

About this time she projected a mission to this country making

Bethesda head-quarters, and in order to act prudently, she advised with many in reference to the expediency of such a design. It was determined to make the experiment—and in October, 1770, quite a number of students from the College, under her patronage, were selected and set apart for the work. They landed here after a voyage of six weeks—repaired at once to the Orphan House, and in a few days entered upon their labors. In a letter written by lady H., she says: "The province of Georgia has made proposals to build a Church at their own expense and present me with it—that the College of Georgia, (Bethesda,) may have their ministry, in that part, honored. My last letters from America, inform me that our way seems open to the Cherokee country, and in all the back settlements we are assured the people will build us Churches, at their own expense and present them to us, to settle perpetually for our use. I cannot help thinking that the Lord will have *me* there before I die if only to make coats and garments for the poor Indians." Lady H. never was permitted to visit this country, yet, doubtless much is due to this noble christian woman, for active exertions in spreading knowledge and truth among the earliest settlers of the Colony.

She seemd to prosecute her noble purposes with an energy, devotion and interest, akin to that manifested by Whitefield.

But her plans and efforts, in reference to the Orphan House, were suddenly arrested by the destruction of the buildings by lightning. When the news of this calamity reached her she said: "Though we may be disappointed God the Judge of all is not defeated. I cannot wish it for one moment to be otherwise." It was this abiding confidence in "Him who doeth all things well," that enabled this christian woman to triumph over so many difficulties. This misfortune lessened the zeal and interest of many who up to this period had been active supporters of the Institution.

By liberal contribution of her own private means and the assistance of others, she soon restored buildings capacious enough to accommodate the few pupils now in attendance.

The Institution never regained its former vigor. Piercy returned to England which left the children without proper attention. No one could be obtained who would take a lively interest in their welfare. Finally lady H. succeeded in securing the services of the Rev. David Phillips, from England, and under her own patronage and his superintendance, she had issued in the Georgia Gazette, the following notice:

14

TO THE PUBLIC.

Bethesda College, near Savannah, instituted by the late Reverend George Whitefield, Chaplain to the Right Honorable the Countess Dowager of Huntingdon, is to be opened the 24th instant, under the patronage of her Ladyship, whose warm zeal to promote the happiness of mankind, in spreading religion and learning in this State, is above praise, and by whose authority and appointment the Reverend David Phillips, late from England, anxious to carry her Ladyship's pious designs into the fullest execution, solicits the attention of such Ladies, Gentlemen and Guardians of youth, as are desirous of sending young gentlemen for instruction in every branch of useful and polite Literature, comprehending *English gramatically, Writing, and the use of Figures, and every branch of the Mathematics, the use of the Globes, Latin, Greek, and French,* including Board, Washing, &c., on the following terms, viz: Thirty guineas per annum for each student, without distinction of age, or class of education. Punctuality is expected in four quarterly payments. A line for admission to the Rev. David Phillips, Superintendent, or to Rev. Benjamin Lindsay, Rector of Christ Church, Savannah, Classical Tutor of said College, will have immediate attention from

Their devoted, much obliged, humble servant,

DAVID PHILLIPS.

N. B. Every student is expected to bring his bedding complete, which will be returned on his leaving College. Public notice will be given, in the Gazette of this State, for the reception of Orphan Children, on the original benevolent plan, immediately on the estate being productive for that purpose.

The Trustees of the Academy of the county of Chatham, not having it yet in their power to carry into effect the trust reposed in them by the Honorable the Legislature, and being sensible of the utility of the above design, do recommend to the parents and guardians of youth, an attention to encourage an institution which has for its object the promotion of learning.

By order of the Board of Trustees.

JOHN HABERSHAM,
President, pro. tem.

Savannah, June 3d, 1788.

Notwithstanding the many and serious difficulties occasioned by the destruction of the building and the invasion of the Royal troops during the revolution, we see by the foregoing notice the result of the indomitable perseverance and christian zeal of lady H., as well as the condition of the institution at her death, which occurred June 17th, 1791, aged eighty-four. The Countess of Huntingdon died, as she lived, in the full hope of a blessed immortality.

At her death, the school was discontinued, the estate reclaimed by the State Legislature, and the management of it committed to a Board of Trustees.

The Board took no active steps towards the completion of the buildings and other necessary measures for the organization of the School for some ten years, as will appear from the following extracts:

ORPHAN HOUSE.

The Trustees of the Orphan House Estate, are requested to meet the President of the Board, on Monday next, at 12 o'clock at noon, at the Court house in the city of Savannah.

By order of the President.

J. WHITEFIELD, Sec'ry.

Oct. 22d, 1793.

—

ORPHAN HOUSE.

The Trustees of Bethesda College, or Orphan House Estate, are requested to attend at the house of Mr. John Carson, on Monday, the 24th instant, at 11 o'clock of the forenoon, on business of importance to the Trust.

By order of the President.

J. WHITEFIELD, Sec'ry.

Feb. 18th, 1794.

—

BETHESDA COLLEGE.

The Trustees are notified to meet, at the plantation on Saturday next, the 1st of February, at ten o'clock.

Jan. 30th, 1800.

—

BETHESDA.

Annual Meeting of the Trustees on Saturday next, at Bethesda.

1st May, 1800.

—

As we have stated, for some time after the Estate was reclaimed by the State Government and entrusted to a Board of Trustees, little or nothing was done toward the re-opening of a school, until the year 1801, when we find the following account of their proceedings:

BETHESDA, 6TH MAY, 1801.

At a Meeting of the Trustees, the following Resolutions were agreed to, and ordered to be published :

Resolved, That a sum be appropriated for the purpose of repairing and completing the North Wing of Bethesda College, and that the President of the Board, Mr. Morel, and Mr. William Gibbons, or any two of them, be a committee to contract with suitable persons to undertake the same, and to require and take sufficient security for the completion thereof, within a reasonable time.

That as soon as a room convenient for the purpose of a School, and a room for the residence of a tutor, shall be completed, the english reading, writing, and arithmetical school, of the Trust, shall be removed thereto.

That the salary of such tutor shall be at the rate of five hundred dollars *per annum,* and that the President be authorized to engage such tutor.

That all applications for the admission of orphans on the free grounds of the Institution, shall be made through one of the members of the Trust, who shall vouch for the indigence of such orphan, and for his or her being a proper object of charity ; and the member's name so vouching shall be entered on the minutes, together with the Orphan's name, on the day of admission.

That children of poor parents, vouched for in like manner, shall be admitted only so far as respects schooling *gratis,* unless it shall appear to the Trust that such parents are in so distressed a condition as not to be able to maintain such children, in which case they may be admitted on the free grounds of the Institution, as in the case of real orphans.

That all other children whose parents may wish them educated at Bethesda may be admitted into the said school, at and after the rate of three dollars per quarter for reading and spelling, four dollars per quarter for writing, and five dollars per quarter for ciphering ; and, as soon as sufficient accommodations are provided, may be admitted as boarders on such terms as the Trust may hereafter see fit, giving the preference of such admission to board, to such children as may enter the school prior to such accommodations being completed.

That the monies arising from schooling such children shall be appropriated for the payment of the tutor's salary.

That the President be authorized to purchase such books, as may be adapted to the use of such school.

And, in order to induce parents to place their children at the said school, and to exhibit the intentions of the Trust to establish an early and complete seminary of learning at Bethesda.

Resolved, That, as soon as the North Wing shall be repaired, the Trust will immediately take steps to repair the South Wing, and to engage a Professor as Principal of the College, with qualified teachers of the Latin, Greek and French languages, the Mathematics, Natural Philosophy, and such other sciences as are usually taught in the respective Colleges of the United States, and will procure a complete apparatus for such sciences, and a library for the use of the students.

Extract from the minutes.

W. B. BULLOCH, Sec'ry.

BETHESDA.

The Trustees are notified to meet at the College precisely at 11 o'clock on Saturday next, being the Annual Meeting.

29th April, 1802.

BETHESDA.

Annual meeting of the Trustees, at the College on Saturday the 5th instant, at 10 o'clock.

May 1st, 1804.

This extract from the minutes of the Board, shows the institution again in a prosperous condition, and possessing every facility to make it rank among the first in our State.

But these efforts were soon defeated, and Bethesda College and Orphan House left only to live in name. A dreadful fire broke out in 1805, destroying one of the wings and so injuring the other parts of the building as to render repair impossible. Moreover, the out-buildings were so seriously damaged by a hurricane as to render them valueless.

The Trustees were unable to build, and indeed they could not again establish a school, as the rice land had been inundated by the hurricane and rendered wholly unproductive. They therefore advised the Legislature to dispose of the property and distribute the proceeds among the benevolent institutions in Savannah. *See Act to dispose of Bethesda, assented to Dec. 22d*, 1808.

BETHESDA COLLEGE.

The Trustees are requested to meet at the Plantation, on Monday next at Ten o'clock.

March 11th, 1809.

3

ORPHAN HOUSE ESTATE.

Purchasers at the above sale, yesterday, are hereby notified, that the Commissioners will attend at the house of the Hon. William Stephens, in Broughton street, at eleven o'clock, to-morrow morning, for the purpose of granting titles and receiving payment and securities. The negroes will then be ready for delivery.

March 14th, 1809.

Thus ends the history of Bethesda, otherwise called the White-field Orphan House, which had been for nearly three quarters of a century, a house of mercy to hundreds of fatherless children, and now

"Bethesda's gate is still
No cries its porches fill."

In the year 1854, the Board of Managers of the Union Society, an Institution very similar in its purposes and operations to Bethesda, purchased one hundred and twenty-five acres of the ancient Bethesda estate, which included the original locality of the Whitefield Orphan House.

They at once erected suitable buildings, and in January of 1855, removed from Savannah, the boys under their charge, to this place.

This site, we are told by Mr. Fay, late President of the Union Society, was selected "at a higher price than that at which some other place might have been obtained and perhaps above its market value, from the fact that upwards of a century ago it had been consecrated to the same noble purpose."

Does not this act on the part of the Board of Managers, together with the history and present condition of modern Bethesda (or the Union Society) seem clearly an answer to the prayer of Whitefield, when in 1740 he uttered the petition "Set thy Almighty fiat to it, Oh, Gracious Father and for thine own name's sake, convince us more and more that thou wilt never forsake those who put their trust in thee."

The similarity in the present produce of the land, the rules and regulations of the Society, the general management of the institution, the daily routine of duties for the boys, compared with those of the Whitefield Orphan School make in reality as well as in name,

"A new Bethesda here."

After the many and eloquent addresses that have been delivered from time to time, before the Union Society, giving full and graphic descriptions of its general history and operations, it would be presumption in me to attempt to add anything. The annual reports, the published extracts from the minutes, the list of officers, members and pupils, the present prosperous condition of the school, its excellent management and the deep interest and active part taken in it, by many of our citizens, clearly indicate that the star of Bethesda which descended into Whitefield's grave, has arisen with undimmed glory to light once more with its holy rays, the sorrowful heart of the orphan.

"Here orphan tears are stayed,
Here orphan prayers are prayed.
Here nameless blessings craved,
　　For orphan Hearts."

"Bless those, Oh God, who bless
The poor and fatherless,
　　With loving care!
Though here no angel wings
Wave o'er Bethesda's springs,
Receive, thou King of Kings,
　　The orphan's prayers."

HON. JAMES HABERSHAM.

——: o :——

After having completed the history of Bethesda, I discovered from letters placed in my hands by Mr. Robert Habersham, the grandson of the subject of these remarks, that the brief notice given in the sketch, did great injustice to his sacrifices, zeal and personal devotion to the institution. He was in reality its life and support from the first formation in Savannah, until long after its removal to Bethesda.

Mr. Habersham came to this country much against the advice and wishes of his family and friends.

In a letter to his uncle after his arrival here, he mentions the unwillingness manifested by his family, and states that to give them reasons for such a step would be unsatisfactory, as they concern only God and himself.

The wealth and honor of earth were placed on the one hand before him, on the other, the service of Christ, and without giving his friends a single reason, he decided to take up his cross and follow Christ.

Setting sail with Whitefield, December, 1737, he spent the time on the voyage, in teaching and instructing the children. Immediately on his arrival, Whitefield and himself gathered all the poor and orphan children they could find, and organized a school, thus forming the germ of the future Bethesda. The expenses involved in the beginning soon consumed the little they had collected previous to leaving England. Whitefield decided to return, to secure further aid, leaving the entire charge of the school to Mr. Habersham. The latter was obliged to teach, and at the same time, to make provisions for feeding and clothing the children, and hence in a letter addressed to Mr. Whitefield, he states, "Our affairs have sometimes been so pressing upon me that, had not God, in a particular manner, supported me by his presence, I must have sunk."

In another place, he speaks of being obliged to retrench expenses in every way,—"even to the substitution of coffee for green tea, because it was cheaper."

About September of 1738, he received letters from Whitefield, acquainting him that the Trustees had donated five hundred acres of land for the Orphan House. He also received directions about obtaining boards and other necessary materials, so that on Whitefield's arrival, they can select the location and commence building without delay. Mr. Habersham's reply dated Savannah, Nov'r 29th, 1738, contains so full an account of the affairs of the school at that time, that I quote it almost entire.

"About three months ago, your letters dated in June, came to hand, wherein you mention my getting boards, &c., ready without any further direction. As you supposed I had received yours, as above, upon which I endeavored to procure boards, &c., but found upon further inquiry, that no stuff could be cut unless I knew the lengths, without great loss. Withal, I could not tell where you would build, so that I turned my thoughts another way, to forward your generous undertaking.

I knew that you designed to procure five hundred acres of land for the use of your Orphan House, and I applied and got possession of a good tract. This I did by the advice of friends and personal reasons, which then appeared strong to us. We thought it the best thing I could do, indeed, I had but money sufficient to carry me on a little way in such a large charge. But God has enabled me by the help of my friends to go with it much farther than I thought it possible.

Blessed and adored be His holy name. I am glad that I went about it, though it has been a great fatigue to me, because it will save you great trouble. I am about eighty pounds sterling in debt, and have laid out thirty pounds more I had by me, upon the particular thing, in all about one hundred and ten. You will see when you come, a fair and clear account of this and all my other expenses since you left me, in a very particular manner, and I trust to your satisfaction, but if I have done wrong, I have only to say that I intended well. The land is situated in an open place upon the salts, and in ye midst of ye settlements and likewise upon ye main about nine miles from town and I believe is very convenient for fish. It appears to me to be ye best place that I have seen for the Orphan House itself. But that you'll be a judge of when you come. I have bought forty head of cattle, sows and poultry and horses enough and now am about getting the whole five hundred acres fenced in. As much land is already cleared as I intend at present, being enough for peas, &c. and conveniences absolutely necessary, likewise there is a good hut erected, so that I have got almost all done, which will be wanted till you come. The stock are now daily increasing and in a few months part of it will be useful, whereas had this undertaking been deferred till you come it would have been some months before you could have had milk or any other produce of it. This will fully appear when it comes to be fully explained to you. All my friends agree that the preparing stuff for a house is even more after I have received your directions impracticable, there being no lengths mention'd in the inventory, no, not in any part of it, besides I cannot see yet any place very near the town proper for such an expensive building and ye stuff must be prepared upon or very near the place you intend to build upon or the charge will be prodigiously increased. Upon the land I have possession of there is cedar enough to build twenty houses an advantage not to be overlooked, being a very durable wood. You will find I dont doubt, most, if not all ready to work upon building when you arrive, that there will be no delay, when but few would come to split rails and fall trees. These and many other reasons appear to me and my friends here strong enough to justify my conduct. But why should I multiply reason to you who I know rather look at the intention than the event of an action. I believe it would be in my power at any time by ye sale of ye live stock, wholly or very near to clear my debts, or I might improve it to a personal advantage in case any accident should befall you.

I do not, I do not indeed my loveliest best friend, in the heart suppose you will blame my conduct, in this particular, but I think myself answerable to you for all my actions of this nature, especially as I shall make it your concern."

In about one year from the time the five hundred acres were selected all was in readiness for removing the children. From a letter written to Mr. Whitefield, by Mr. Habersham dated Oct. 21st, 1740, we judge they were in very straightened circumstances, and anxious to get into the country where expenses would be lighter.

He says—"Upon the maturest consideration we have unanimously agreed as soon as possible to go down to Bethesda. * * *

By having the family together it will much lessen our expenses and we can be much better pursuing the spirit of the institution."

Evidently from this letter and from another dated only nine days later, they were making active exertions to get to Bethesda at the earliest possible moment—for in the last dated Oct. 30th, 1740, he states—

"On Monday I intend moving with the family to Bethesda. It must be, though it is contrary to our dear friend's desire (referring to Whitefield)—"Legem non habit necessitas." On Monday, Nov. 3d, 1740, the children were moved and from this date, properly begins the history of Bethesda, as a school for providing for and instructing orphan children. Writing to a lady friend, from Bethesda, Nov. 7, he states, "blessed be God our family are well settled at the place where we have long desired to be."

To show what meagre circumstances they were in, when they removed, we quote again from this same letter—"We have one hundred and fifty souls with the workmen to feed every day, and at this time have not one ounce of flesh kind by us."

It is astonishing to see to what destitution they were sometimes reduced. Mr. Habersham himself says: "It is truly wonderful to see how nearly one hundred and fifty souls are daily fed by the invisible hand of God, frequently we are without necessary food."

About this time when poverty was staring them in the face—most bitter calumnies were circulated against Whitefield and the institution, and though for a while they lessened the confidence of some, yet eventually served to advance the interest in the school. Mr. Habersham writing to Mr. Whitefield, who had again gone to England, concerning the false charges, begs him not to notice them, as God will make them result only in good to all concerned.

In the midst of their poverty and this malicious effort to injure the character of Whitefield, and impede the progress of the school— there occurred a great religious awakening among the children, the workmen and the servants.

Mr. Habersham in giving an account of this to Whitefield says, "most, if not all the boys appear to be under some concern, little as well as great." * * * * "I observed them retire next day in the woods and sing and pray together." * * * * "We all went and saw twenty-five or thirty dear lambs on their knees before God, some pleading the promises and others calling on Jesus." * * * "One or two of the workmen have, I hope, closed with Jesus for salvation, and one or two more are in a fair way. Some of our own servants want to learn to read." He speaks of this work of grace as continuing through more than a year, the result being to the glory of God in the conversion of many immortal souls.

Before the spring they had cleared some twenty acres of land and planted potatoes, rice, corn, peas, &c. The personal labor Mr. Habersham bestowed upon the grounds, while at the same time, he bore the entire responsibility of the school, is worthy of note. He taught, superintended the buildings which were in course of erection, provided workmen and materials, attended to the clearing of the land and supervised the household affairs. The burden of these labors and cares must have been heavy for a young man not yet twenty-eight; and yet, this with what Whitefield endured, shows us what trial, discouragements, and distresses were suffered for ancient Bethesda.

Things finally grew more prosperous, the land together with the fine stock, they were able to keep on hand, began to yield sufficient for their support. The only difficulty was to obtain bricks to complete the main building, to get workmen at moderate wages, and to secure good help in the house; but these difficulties were finally all removed.

Mr. Habersham remained in charge of the institution until sometime after his marriage. He then went into business in Savannah, and became one of the most prominent merchants in the place.

He was chosen to fill several responsible positions, and at the time of his death, was acting Governor of the colony.

He continued contributing much by his counsel, influence and means to advance the interest of Bethesda. When it was under the patronage of Lady Huntingdon, we find that Mr. Habersham loaned at times large sums of money to the Countess for the use of the institution.

Mr. Habersham was a man of rare talent and ability, and one needs but to read his many deeply interesting letters to be persuaded of his fervent piety.

His love for Mr. Whitefield seems to have been "passing the love of woman"—no expression of endearment seems to have been too strong, too tender to lavish upon his friend—no labor, no suffering was too hard to bear when demanded by Whitefield's welfare. And with a still higher enthusiasm and devotion, he gave himself to the service of his God. In his beautiful humility and unselfishness, thinking only of doing good to others, he unconsciously won for his name a prominent place among those of Oglethorpe, Whitefield and Lady Huntingdon.

ANNIVERSARY ADDRESS,

APRIL 23, 1823, BY THE

HON. THOMAS U. P. CHARLTON.

———◆•••◆———

Accustomed, as I am, to public debate, and, in some measure, to the feelings of self-possession so requisite to a proper
or impressive discharge of the duties expected from every one
in my present situation,—with all these supposed advantages,
I can with great sincerity, declare that on no similar occasion
did I rise to address an assembly, composed as this is, with
greater reluctance, or with more unaffected sensations of diffidence. I say with reluctance, because my mind has ceased
to find any gratification in these presentations; but the reluctance has been greatly diminished by the considerations of the
respect and esteem I owe and feel to the medium through
which I have been solicited to address you, and that I am
permitted to do so in a temple dedicated to the Almighty,
whose portals are, or ever should be, opened to every voice
raised in commendation of good works, or the true spirit of
religious or civil liberty; for, under our form of government,
the existence of the one must essentially depend upon the vigorous health of the other. He who denies the proposition,
may, in all charity, receive the appellation of Christian; but
he rears a banner under which I, as one, would never consent
to enlist as a patriot citizen.

I rise, also, with unaffected sensations of diffidence; and
my reasons will appear extremely obvious from the facts and
explanations I shall now afford.

Anterior to 1779, we know not what was the rule as to the
person who was expected to deliver an anniversary address, and

from that year to 1804, the minutes of the society are equally silent, for no person is designated as having performed that duty. In 1804, the resolution was agreed to, that "at every anniversary the President request some minister of the gospel to preach a sermon."

In 1805, a sermon was preached by the Rev. Mr. Clay; in 1806, by Rev. Mr. Best; in 1807, by Rev. Dr. Kollock; in 1808, by Rev. Mr. Holcombe; in 1809, by Rev. Mr. Johnston; in 1813, by Rev. Mr. Johnston.

At the anniversary of 1814, the rule requiring a minister of the gospel, was so far abrogated as to authorize the President to make his election between a minister of the gospel and this society.

In 1817, a sermon, after an interval of four years, was preached by the Rev. Mr. Cranston; in 1818, by Rev. Dr. Kollock; in 1819, by Rev. Mr. Carpenter; in 1820, by Rev. Mr. Carpenter; in 1821, by Rev. Mr. Carr.

Thus it appears, from 1805, to 1822, the last anniversary, a minister of the gospel has always been solicited to perform the duty which now devolves upon me. I am the only one of the laity, from 1804, or for aught that is recorded in your minutes, from the organization of this society, in 1750, to the present anniversary, who has been called upon to address you. Is not this an appalling circumstance? Is it in any way calculated to inspire confidence into the feelings of any member of this community upon whom the choice of the Union Society might have fallen?

Sirs and Gentlemen of the Union Society, what expositions or illustrations can ye expect from me? What benefits can be derived from my efforts as your orator on this day, when the learning of a Clay and a Best are arrayed against me: when fresh within your recollections is the unsophisticated piety of such men as Holcombe, Johnston, Carpenter and Carr? Only five years have rolled over, when, for the last time, the Union Society was addressed by that highly gifted man, the Rev. Dr. Kollock. Under any aspect we may consider him, who can be more entitled to our respect, our love, our admiration: our respect for his piety, our love for his benevolence, our admiration for his great and splendid attainments? Whoever heard his eloquence, and caught not a spark from the fire of his genius? It seemed as if the lips of this christian Isaiah had been touched by a coal from the altar! And then, you have heard (and only one year hath rolled over since you heard him) the pious, meek, the classical and philanthropic, Cranston: I say, with all the emphasis that can be thrown upon the term—the philanthropic Walter Cranston! I knew him well; and I belive that all the doctrines, as a minister of the gospel, promulgated from this tribune of the church, were felt by him in the true charity of primitive faith. His heart and his hand were ever in unison with the heavenly annuncia-tion: "Peace on earth, and good will towards all men." In-deed, the practical operations of his benevolence evinced, to all who knew him, that the last tear in the treasury of his feeling soul, and the division of the last resource in the exchequer of his temporal circumstances, were ever at the disposal of the unhappy—the afflicted—the poor.

With such predecessors in this discharge of duty, there is still a cheering consolation left me: that the subject on which I have to address you is one which paralyses the attacks of criticism; and therefore, whether ill, or well, disposed of, there can certainly be no feelings of acrimony or contempt towards me, the object of this Society's selection.

The heart is only concerned in the topics of this day's dis-cussion, and in appealing to that alone, though the pulsations may be stronger in one bosom than another, yet bearing on the same objects—the amelioration of the condition of dis-tressed fellow-creatures—and for that purpose, the organization of a society, almost coëval with the colonization of this State. I say the throbbings and pulsations of every bosom in this assembly must partake of the same character, and, thank God, be divested of all those sectional and sectarian feelings which would be more or less excited in the discussion of any other subject—save that of CHARITY. Charity! it is a God-like at-tribute, for Jesus wept! The eternal and incarnate Deity, by *His* tears demonstrated, that commiseration for human suffer-ings of body or of mind, has its source, in heaven. It is dem-onstrated that, in the degree we promote the views of affec-tionate charity, in that ratio we approximate to the image of

Him who made us; and do we not imitate the all-glorious example of Him who made us?

How brilliant, how permanent, how lasting, is the fame, the character, the reputation, of a benevolent man! Contrast it with the fame and character of a candidate for public distinctions—for political honors. Whatever may be the object in the vista of his ambition—a creed, official station—no matter what the course may be through which he may seek to ascend, and firmly seat himself on the proud height of popular gratitude,—the tempests through which his barque must struggle; the machinations with which his strong or honest spirit must contend; the perversions to which his most righteous motives may be subjected; the missiles thrown at him in every step of his arduous progress, by the accursed hands of envy, malice and jealousy; the uncertainty, under such a combination of circumstances, of attaining to the object of his integrity or his ambition; and, when attained, the lacerations, anxieties and pains, through which he may have arrived at the consummation of his wishes, more than counterbalance, in the estimation of a moral mind, the honor or the dignity which proclaims victory to his efforts. Should those efforts terminate in disappointment, the incensed and goaded spirit rises up in rebellion against the very doctrines and measures which, until then, it had advocated with pious zeal; and the alleged ingratitude of the community is the poor, but natural, apology for the acknowledged apostacy. That firmness of soul, that conviction of the purity of conduct and of action, which remains unshaken amid all the vicissitudes of public life, which grapples with its vexations, and preserves its equanimity, its fortitude, and, I may add, its orthodoxy, in every shifting scene of prosperity or adversity,—how seldom is the whole found among that horde of candidates soliciting distinction, and striving, with martyr-like fervency, to catch the mantle of a little brief authority, and thus to extricate themselves from the common and vulgar ranks of the great mass of society.

If this picture affords any features that can be recognized, the philosopher must look with pity upon it, and every one who views it critically, and in detail, must exclaim under the influence of nature's emotions: "It is not to be envied."

With the benefits of my experience, I know it is not. Happiness is not necessarily, or, indeed, usually, associated with the public honors most of us are so anxious to obtain; for no dignity emanating from human institutions can guarantee permanent fame, or even secure much more than those evanescent plaudits which hail the first triumph of a favorite aspirant, and then, in the next moment, to be shouted before the car of some other who has rudely pushed this favorite from his seat of honor.

Not so with the man whom Charity has recorded in the fair pages of her volume! His fame will live in future ages, fresh in the memory of millions, when the names of kings, emperors, statesmen, and thousands who have had their public strut and fleeting official consequence, shall have fallen into oblivion, or only to be found in musty chronicles for the amusement of the antiquarian; Howard will be remembered in all ages, because he was benevolent: they will be forgotten or contemned, because not a ray of redeeming charity has darted its light of immortality through the gloom which hovers over their vices and their follies. The man whom Charity has adopted as her own, can feel none of those bitter sensations which agitate the breast of the successful, or unsuccessful, candidate for public honors. No retrospect can poison the possession of his elevated rank in society: *he* has no injuries to repair in ascending the ladder of popular applause; *he* never blasted, by the operation of a malignant passion, the hopes and prospects of a disinterested patriot; *he* never knew, or practiced, the subtleties of an intrigue which dashed with gall the cup of a virtuous citizen, because that citizen was an obstacle in the path of his ambition; he, in short, has no recollections to agonize his heart or to disturb those placid and lasting enjoyments, which spring, Minerva-like, armed, full grown and enlightened, from the head of Charity. He steps forward from the ranks of his fellow-citizens, in the possession of the proudest gift a human being can aspire to—the love of his fellow-man; and we see his brow encircled with an honor the most dazzling that a human being, accountable to his Maker, can wish for—a wreath woven by the hand of Charity.

Permit me to illustrate this feeling of the heart by further contrasts. What is patriotism? In this free country the word patriotism is identified with devotedness to civil liberty, and the rights of man. Not so, elsewhere. In other regions, patriotism is a devotedness to country, its institutions, and its sovereign: that country may be Russia—the institutions, absolute power, Cossacks and the Greek Church—the sovereign an autocrat; or it may be Austria—her stupid despotism, a bigoted catholicity, and an emperor; or it may be Turkey—there the Koran, a harem, and the Grand Seignor; or Thibet—there, idolatry, and the Grand Lama. Thus, a principle calculated to grace the triumphs of a righteous cause when consecrated by the voice of Liberty, is rendered an auxilliary, powerful and irresistable, to the great destroying of man's glory, his rights and his happiness.

What is heroism? In its legitimate import it is a fearless defiance of all perils in the cause of virtue: it is a moral Curtius, rushing to the gulph of destruction, and, by the self-immolation, adding ten-fold vigour to some sacred principle. But heroism may also mean a dauntless contempt of all perils in any cause: it may be, in the cause of a tyrant, and the Decius sacrifice intended to protract his existence and his dynasty, when the Io Peans of Liberty would joyously hail the utter extinction of both.

What is military glory? Legitimately, in this free country, it is a chief, leading to victory the warriors of the republic against foreign myrmidons, sent to destroy our lives, and to subvert our institutions: it is that glory which has been acquired, and can only be acquired, under the Star-spangled Banner, so long as the Lord of Hosts, of battles, and of freedom, permits it to waive over e'en the last bulwark of this great federal democracy. But alas! it may mean the mere glory of victory: the progress of an Attilla, whose track of desolation is marked with the blood of God's creatures: or a successful conspiracy of tactics, bravery and steel, against human liberty and independence. Its illustration may, perhaps, be soon found in the march of holy and legitimate cohorts against the nascent regeneration of the gallant Spaniards.

What is martyrdom? It is the death of Stephen. "He kneeled down, and cried with a loud voice, Lord, lay not this sin to their charge. And when he said this, he fell asleep." A soul thus taking its departure, with the aspirations of forgiveness on its lips, is martyrdom. But how often has the appellation been given to fanatical and Juggernaut sacrifices on the altars of absurd, metaphysical and impious tenets, abhorred by true religion, and leading, without the mercy of heaven, to that condemnation a misguided zeal had intended to obviate!

Thus, the noblest passions of our nature, calculated, in the excellency of their original purity, to assimilate men to angels, in their corruption and abuses, sink men to the level of demons.

Is it so with Charity? Does that feeling of the heart, upon which the Almighty, himself, smiles with complacency,—is it ever subject to mutations? Can the obliquities of education, or the vacillating opinions of man, change one feature in its heavenly aspect?

Ladies,—I say its heavenly aspect, because it resembles yours, in the full meridian of all your fascinating attractions. The personification of this virtue is a female: a beautiful female, at that time of life which developed the ripened charms of a Cornelia: and at that period when, asked by a belle of Rome for a sight of her jewels, she presented her two sons— and those sons the Gracchi as the richest casket that could belong to a matron of the republic. My portrait of Charity will betray Cornelia's years. I cannot consent to have her too young; for the exquisite tenderness and susceptibility of a youthful female heart might be too lavish and indiscriminating in the distribution of its bounties. Now, look at my heroine: she is seated; in the back-ground, ye may see the halt, the blind and the aged, who, by their positions and apparent tranquility, seem to have forgotten their infirmity, under the recent alleviations administered by her hand. Nearer, is a group of dejected widows: dejected because unfortunate; but manifesting, in their looks, that Charity had wiped away the bitterest tears of their affliction, and dispelled all their future apprehensions of want and misery. Nearer still, some in her very lap, others clinging to her bosom, and others at her feet, with ruby lips, and eyes uplifted to her benignant countenance,

seeming to wait with infantile anxiety for their turn of affectionate caresses. These are fatherless children : the children
of that group of widows, to whom Charity now, with one of
those gracious smiles, such as ever plays around her balmy
lips when gently removing the icy pressure of poverty from
the heaving breast of some deserted and wretched creature :
with such a smile she now beckons to that group of widows,
inviting them to approach and partake, with her, of the joy,
the felicity, and cheerfulness of these their protected offspring.

This, ladies, is my portrait of Charity. I regret, for your
sakes, the pencil I have wielded had not been dipped in the
colors of an abler master ; but I have the vanity to believe
it has some striking features of resemblance ; and, at all events,
I have the consolation to know that it can, at any time, be
rendered more perfect, when one of you, as the representative
of my beauty, shall do me the honor of a sitting. I shall not
for a moment hesitate in the selection of an object. She may
be at times found among the members of the Female Asylum
—an institution where Charity delights to sojourn, and over
which she has shed some of her sweetest benedictions.

Gentlemen of the Union Society—to this queen of all our virtues, you erected a temple, in the year 1750. The plan was
projected by some three or four persons, of as many different
religious persuasions, and it was baptized " Union," to designate the amalgamation of creeds, thus giving it existence.
The object of the society has ever been the maintenance and
education of distressed male ophan children. The proceeedings
of your society, the names of its officers, and all the other facts
connected with its rise and progress, from 1750 to 1779, are
lost. Among the outrages of the War of the Revolution, the
spoliation or destruction of your archives, between these periods, was one. The re-organization of your Society, in 1779,
is thus stated, in an extract from the minutes, dated 23d April,
1779, and is eminently interesting to us all:—

" By the unhappy fate of war, the members of the Union
Society are some made captives, and others drove from the
State ; and by one of the rules of said Society it is ordered
and resolved, that so long as three members shall be together,
the Union Society shall exist : and there being now four mem-

bers present, who being desirous as much as in them lies, notwithstanding they are CAPTIVES, to continue so laudable an
institution, have come to the following *Resolve*, to wit: To
nominate and appoint officers for said Society for the ensuing
year, as near and as agreeable to the rules of the Society as
they can recollect, the rules being lost or mislaid."

The four persons present on that occasion were, Mordecai
Sheftall, Josiah Powell, John Martin and John Stirk; and
the following persons chosen officers for the year: Josiah
Powell, *President;* Mordecai Sheftall, *Vice President;* John
Martin, *Secretary:* Matthew Roach, Levi Sheftall, *Constables.*

Thus, amid the perils of that tempest which threatened to
sweep before it the liberties of this extended republic, four
patriots, then in captivity for devotedness to that sun of freedom which now diffuses its beams of light and glory around
us, animating with warmth and vigor the breasts of millions of
exulting citizens,—at such an epoch, when most of the gentler
feelings were scared to their recesses,—under the recollection
of a rule, that when three of this Society shall have been gathered together in the name of Charity, there would she be in the
midst of them,—under such circumstances did these captive
patriots re-organize your institution. Life was breathed into
it in the year 1750, eighteen years after the colonization of
this State, and twenty-six years before the declaration of independence proclaimed it a republic. It owed its origin to a
feeling of benevolence which identifies all creeds and all persuasions; and which draws no line of demarcation between the
descendants of Abraham or the followers of Jesus. It views
man as a creature formed by the same Creator, destined to
travel through this vale of tears as a member of God's great
earthly family, and responsible to Him not for conscientious or
abstract differences of faith, but for that hard-heartedness which
expels from the human bosom the love of our neighbor and
of mankind. Systems of faith have no lineal or collateral
consanguinity with this feeling of benevolence; for "Though
1 have all faith, so that I could remove mountains, and have
not Charity, I am nothing." So says St. Paul, and so say we
all. Hence, this Society was called Union; and Charity, who
stood near, heard the baptismal annunciation—shouted her ap-

2

probation—and consecrated it with her choicest blessings. The deep foundations on which your edifice was built have withstood the peltings of the pittiless storms of seventy-three years; and during that long period, evolving catastrophes and events the most portentous in the annals of the world, the rains have descended on it, the winds have beaten against it, and it retains its primitive strength, because it was built on a rock of Charity. This society has remained unshaken, unassailed, by any commotions which have agitated the minds of men, or distracted their systems of religion or of government. It has kept on in that meek and humble course which is never impeded by the electrical shocks of the passions, and acquiring strength in its progress, is still animated with the hope that it may last as long as Charity is suffered to manifest her good works under the fostering protection of American benevolence.

Gentlemen, in my special address to you, that the Charity I have attributed to you "vaunteth not itself, is not puffed up." I have, therefore, one or two facts in reserve, which speak a volume of panegyric, and will silence me in reference to our noble selves.

One hundred and twenty-nine children, since the revolutionary War, have been supported and educated on the bounty of this Society. How many more from 1750 to 1779 we have no records to inform us; but twenty, within that period is something better than a hypothetical calculation. Thus, certainly, one hundred and twenty-nine orphans, and conjecturally, if you please, one hundred and forty-nine, have taken their stations in society under the benevolent auspices of this Society.

Fellow-citizens,—The Union Society hath given this number of citizens to the republic, and sent them forth with minds imbued with the principles of piety and the elements and benefits of a practical education. The Union Society snatched them from the thraldom of ignorance, and it saved them from the temptations, the expedients and the crimes of poverty. Where are the hearts that would not beat with sensations of delight in the reflection that many, very many, of the objects of this Society's charity are now enjoying the honorable distinctions of upright, valuable and intelligent citizens, with perhaps numerous descendants around them taught to hail and reverence the Union Society, as the benificent creator of the noble and affecting spectacle. A Society thus distinguished for its antiquity and good works is surely entitled not only to the warmest tribute of your esteem, but to your warmest and sincere patronage. Will ye not solicit membership? Believe me, it is no inconsiderable honor; for the roll before me discloses the names of officers who have presided over the destinies of the Society, whom patriotism, benevolence and wisdom will always delight to honor. Some are patriots of the Revolution, and others their respectable descendants. To fill the stations such men have occupied cannot be an inferior object of ambition to any virtuous citizen. Believe me, when I tell you again, that perhaps one of the most tranquil consolations you will have left when the spirit is about to take its leave for "another and a better world," on a voyage to that "house not made with hands, eternal in the heavens," will be that you have contributed to the exodus of these dear boys, or their successors, from the bondage of ignorance and poverty, and rendered them as you are, happy husbands—fathers—patriot citizens. Looking down the vista, there is still a more exhilerating prospect, and it is not beyond the wide circumference of contingencies: it is, that one of these boys, or their successors, may take the helm of the republic, and in steering the mighty and gallant ship through the ocean of civic virtue, draw down upon the Palinurus, the homage of this country's love—the admiration of the world.

In conclusion, accept my thanks, gentlemen, for the patience and kind attention bestowed upon my crude and, in many particulars, unpremeditated remarks; and for this indulgence and politeness, I tender you, also, and this audience, the homage of my respectful salutations.

AN ADDRESS

DELIVERED BEFORE

THE UNION SOCIETY,

APRIL 23, 1834,

—BY—

COL. HOWELL COBB.

GENTLEMEN OF THE UNION SOCIETY:

Your kindness and partiality have imposed upon me a duty I feel wholly incompetent of performing; but which I am prompted to undertake from the relationship I bear you, and from a knowledge, that however far below the expectation that has been formed, I may fall, your known hospitality will be ready to excuse me.

I am aware that nothing but the novelty of being addressed by a *former* beneficiary, has placed me before you; and I beg you to believe, that nothing but the knowledge of a heavy debt of gratitude, has prompted me to the undertaking, and a belief that it would be improper to refuse, at least, undertaking, anything you might request.

We have not met for the purpose of commemorating any blazoned event of history, ancient or modern; or to admire, as we detail, the achievements of some warrior; nor yet to offer, in sacrifice, adulation at the shrine of political ambition. We have no such fanciful and superficial duty before us: ours is a duty of a higher, deeper, nobler sort: it is to commemorate an event fraught with *benevolence* and *philanthropy*, which, if it has no bright page of history to relate it, deserves, far more, a place there than many of its recitals, which otherwise would not be known to have had an existence.

There are periods in all human institutions, in the lives of individuals, and the histories of societies, that seem naturally calculated to invite retrospection. Embracing this, as that period in your history, let me ask, what, eighty-four years ago, formed your society, and during that extensive period, has kept it together? Our history, as a people, dates some of its most important events during that time: indeed, from the subjects of a crown we have become the citizens of a republic. Since we have been citizens of that republic, the horizon of our political atmosphere has, more than once, been darkened by a gathering storm; clouds highly charged with *electricity*, threatening every moment to disgorge themselves upon us; thunderings moved the earth beneath us; lightnings rent the air around us; winds lent their strength and fury to the scene to make it more terrific; the angry elements combined, seemed to threaten a general devastation; amidst all this, like the stately pedestal, around whose base the whirlwinds scowl in rapid motion, you have remained steady and undisturbed. It is quite natural to ask, why is this so? Many associations have been formed since yours, that seemed not to want zeal, enterprise or an object, but which have languished and become extinct, whilst yours gains strength by age,—becomes more and more useful and better appreciated, as it is understood: the answer to all this is found on understanding the *cardinal* virtue that first associated you, and now keeps you together—BENEV-OLENCE, the soul of your community; like the principle of gravitation, draws everything to the centre, however remote it may be from it.

Benevolence first united you, has, so far, and I think always will, keep you united. This virtue is practiced upon by you in a manner entirely different from its usual exercise; usually, a recompense, a reward, some return or other is required or expected; but you *cannot* require, *cannot* expect, and know that you *never will* receive a return. Who are the objects of your anxiety, solicitude and care? Not the wealthy; not the great; not the known. If it were so, perhaps a return *might* be made you: the poor, ignorant, helpless, destitute, friendless orphan boy, is him for whom you search, and whose wretchedness and destitution you relieve. I stand before this enlightened assembly a witness, in your favor, of these truths.

This high virtue, as acted upon by you, presents more for admiration than at first view appears: it sees further, examines closer, is more sensitive, untiring and sleepless in the pursuit of the objects of your care, than in any other pursuit. Ordinarily, its office seems to be performed when it relieves upon application; but with you the object is sought for, and its situation is such as almost to forbid the idea of success; yet, your efforts are continued, and only abate after such a scrutiny as denies the existence of that peculiar species of wretchedness you relieve, within the scope of your operations. These are not figurative or hyperbolical expressions; they are not opinions given, and sentiments uttered, to please and flatter on one hand, or divert the attention on the other,—but established truths, of which I speak from experience. With a full knowledge of that weight of obligation I am now and shall always remain under to you, there is no one, I am sure, in this concourse that will forbid me the gratification of saying, I thank you, kind gentlemen, for what I am. It will always afford me the highest pleasure to say, that to your goodness to me, at an unprotected time of life, I am indebted for any usefulness I may be of amongst my fellow-men.

I should be an intruder upon your understanding if I were to say, from a knowledge of the good you have done, go forward; that principle that impels you is entirely prospective, and needs no such resort as an *impetus* to future action. You *will* go forward; you *will* search out other *abandoned* orphans; you *will* continue to them your care, as you did to me, and are now doing to those before me; and I hope if any of *them* should be called upon to perform the duty assigned me this day, they may be able to acquit themselves better, and more to your expectations.

If, in the fields of honor in which I have been permitted to tread, I have been enabled to glean anything worth having, to you, gentlemen of the Union Society, am I indebted for my success, and to you do I most cheerfully offer it.

To you, my young friends, who are *now* the beneficiaries of the Union Society, I conceive it a part of my task to address a few words. The want of a father's care, perhaps, a mother's too; the want of other relatives, able and *willing* to supply your wants and relieve you from the distresses incident to your situations, has thrown you upon the charity of a society;

which society has kindly undertaken, as far as it can, to supply you. You should look upon the present, as it certainly is, the most interesting period of your lives that has yet passed. Improve every opportunity of benefiting yourselves, that you are favored with. Remember that whatever is done for you, is gratuitous on the part of the donor. Whatever claims you could have had upon a father, death has deprived you of by a removal of that parent. You are now indebted to strangers for whatever care may be bestowed upon you.

There are three periods or points in your lives that are fraught with more than ordinary interest, as at them you will, probably, form those connections that will mark your future usefulness or worthlessness in society. The first of these is the time at which you were taken into the care of the Union Society: had it not been for *its* vigilence, *you* would have remained in that same forlorn and destitute situation in which it found you. That period has passed, however, and I advise you to remember, as connected therewith, what you are and what you would have remained, had it not been for the voluntary act of the society. Your legitimate inheritance appeared to be poverty and ignorance.

Placed as you now are, under circumstances so much more favorable, you should be extremely careful to appreciate properly the motives of your benefactors, and endeavor to gain and secure their approbation. All that you can expect is to receive the rudiments of an English education; this, however, may be looked upon as the key of the mind that unlocks its inner appartments and developes its powers. Be attentive to the studies assigned you; be kind, conciliating and obedient to those under whose immediate care you are placed. I was placed with an old lady,* now no more, who made me obedient by her kindness. Her religious examples and admonitions, received at the time of life to which I now allude, made an impression on my mind which time cannot efface. She required it as a part of my duty to attend divine worship on the sabbath: this duty, though at first irksome, afterwards became pleasant: I could not at first perceive *my* interest in things that appeared to be dressed in melancholy, which I took seriousness,

* Mrs. Ann Christie.

3

then to be; but when I did discover *my* interest in these important matters, the object of the good old matron was no longer a mystery. The burning truths so finely depicted, in strains of the most fervid eloquence, as they were by him* whose ministry I attended, fastened upon my mind a charm that now affords me the most pleasant reflections.

The second period of your simple history, that is of more than ordinary importance, is that at which you will be apprenticed out to learn some of the mechanic arts. Expect nothing more than this. At the time of which I now speak, many of those restraints that now surround you, will be removed; new associations will be formed; other companions sought for, and much will depend upon the choice you may make. I was unfortunate in my selections; and, although I ultimately succeeded in dissolving them, yet I found it a task very nearly superior to my ability. In the community in which you reside, you never will want for virtuous associates, if you will have them. Let it be your constant object, therefore, to contract such friendships as will further you in the pursuit of virtue. Do not put the less estimate upon yourselves, because of the obscurity of your origin, or because of your being mechanics. We have no advantages of noble parentage in our country, and all well regulated communities must have their mechanics.

> "Honor and wealth from no condition rise,
> Act well your part, there *all* the honor lies."

One of our countrymen, whom the world honors, was, himself, an obscure printer boy. To know that there once lived, such persons as Cæsar, Pompey and Hannibal, who made themselves distinguished by their feats in arms; that Solon and Lycurgus, were conspicuous as legislators; that there was a philosopher, though a pagan, renowned for his virtues, called Socrates; that Alexander the Great, carried his arms further in conquest, than any of his predecessors; that Demosthenes and Cicero, chained in rapture admiring crowds, at their oritorical displays,—we must resort to ancient history. To understand the harmony of the solar system; that our globe is ninety-five millions of miles from the sun; that it revolves on

---

* Dr. Henry Kollock.

its axis, from west to east, at the astonishing rate of sixty-eight thousand miles an hour, performing, periodically, a revolution round the sun,—we must consult the works of the learned. The military captain, who proudly struts, lord of the tented field, has his deeds recorded in letters of blood and fields of carnage; these, as soon as the brief day of life is passed, are snatched from oblivion by the preservation of the record in the libraries of the learned, which then become their depositories. It is not so with our Franklin: his fame needs no book to preserve it: no·trumpet to proclaim it; a different renown is his. The learned and unlearned, of every age and country, know and speak his praise, and it will remain imperishable as long as the iron rod is a conductor of electricity. Our countryman was not possessed of a mind distinguished for one particular faculty of greatness above another, but for a mind that grasped everything that presented itself to it, and reduced all to a mathematical and systematic precision. *All of you may not be Franklins*; it does not require you should be, to be useful citizens; but with this illustrious example before you, say not that you cannot become distinguished. In whatever avocation you may be employed, set, as a model, him that has attained the most conspicuous height in it, and determine to place yourself by his side. Let no misfortune repulse, or failure deter you from this accomplishment; let every failure be but the signal for renewed effort. The pinnacle of Fame is only reached in this way. Her front presents a precipice but few attempt to scale, and is only scaled by untiring exertion. If you never accomplish this object, yet your efforts will be well repaid; for when the time of life arrives at which your struggles end, you will be astonished to see, that without the facilities possessed by the rich, how far you have outstripped many of them. Remember, if you are not permitted to drink at the fountain head, there are many important points of the stream below, at which you may approach it.

The last period that I look upon, as containing interest and danger, and which may properly be accounted the vestibule of life, is that at which your apprenticeship ends. You then withdraw yourselves from the guardianship of the society, and take your place amongst men. You will now find it necessary to have a closer watch over your conduct, for habits now formed, will stick to you during your whole lives. Search for associates known for their virtues: be temperate and industrious; be not over-anxious to become conspicuous for anything but virtue; above all, do not form, too suddenly, connections with any political party. Look to the Constitution of your country, as the great bulwark of its liberties, and do not place *immutable* reliance in *any* party leader, however vociferous of his tenets he may be. These items of advice are given you with all the sincerity that can actuate the bosom of an elder brother. If you observe and follow them, you will deserve and receive the approbation of your benefactors, which is the highest reward you need want. If you, however, pursue a different course of conduct, you will prove yourselves unworthy their esteem and regard, and the sequel will show that you had better been left to grovel where first they found you.

My task is now performed. I have spoken of those generous sentiments and noble virtues that characterize the Union Society, of the City of Savannah, and addressed some remarks to its *immediate* beneficiaries. During the performance of that duty, propriety required that nothing should be said calculated to divert the attention from the object then in view; this being over, I surely cannot be denied a moment's indulgence in those reflections my present situation naturally inspires.

A return to your city, my friends, after an absence of seventeen years—the spot of my nativity, and where was spent my juvenile days—is calculated to awaken and revive the recollection of events over which time and distance had drawn an oblivion. Every step that I take, every object I see, every movement I make, arouses the recollection of some event of by-gone days, all serving to convince me that amongst you is located the remembrance of scenes that must always remain dear to my heart. In looking about me, I see the countenances of many that are familiar; on enquiry for others, I am answered, "they are dead." I go around and through your city, visit its public works and improvements, and in all, find much for gratification and instruction. Lastly, I visit your Cemetery. O! it would be sacrilege to omit that; those I miss amongst the living, an inscription tells me are deposited there. That consecrated spot contains those, the recollection of whom, is dear to me; an affectionate and indulgent mother, of whom death robbed me at the early age of five years, a brother and a sister sleep there. *These reflections, with their concomitants, spring up in the mind, strike along every cord of the heart, rush to its centre and fill it with emotions that are only expressed in tears.*

AN ORATION

THE UNION SOCIETY,

APRIL 23, 1835,

—BY—

HON. ROBERT M. CHARLTON.

Almost a century hath passed away, since the foundations of the Society, whose Anniversary we have met this day to celebrate, were first established. Since *then*, the ever changing tide of time hath rolled onwards, bearing with it MAN, and the proud monuments of his grandeur. Nations have flourished and decayed; kings have ascended their thrones of greatness, and descended from them to their graves. War hath slain its millions, and Pestilence, its tens of millions; and yet, amid all these convulsions of art and nature, our humble and obscure Society hath continued to flourish, undiminished in its numbers, and undying in its enthusiasm.

In turning our attention back to the time when this Association was first instituted, feelings both of pleasure and melancholy will intrude themselves upon our minds. When we find individuals stepping aside from the busy scenes of life, casting away the trammels of self-interest, and devoting themselves to the promulgation of a secret and yet wide spread benevolence, it speaks volumes in behalf of the doctrine that there is an innate principle of charity in the human heart, which though it may be hidden by the clouds of passion or of interest, does exist, and will continue to dwell there, coeval with man's existence. And yet, when we recall to our recollection, that the hearts that nourished and carried into effect the principles of this Society; that the donor and the recipient; that those who gave, and they who received, have all, all fallen beneath the stroke of time, and have co-mingled with their native dust, the shadow of melancholy casts its darkness around our hearts like the cloud across the summer sun, bidding us remember that the hour will quickly come, when we too, must leave this ever changing and inconstant life, " be laid with our fathers, and see corruption."

> " For come he slow, or come he fast,
> It is but death, that comes at last."

> " All that is bright, must fade,
>   The brightest, still the fleetest ;
> All that was sweet, was made,
>   But to be lost, when sweetest.
> Stars that shine and fall,
>   The flower that droops in springing,
> These, alas, are types of all
>   To which our hearts are clinging."

But even this is not without its moral. When we behold the loftiest genius, the wealthiest individual, the brightest form of beauty, changed in an instant into a cold, inanimate, loathsome mass of corruption, it teaches our hearts to expand towards the afflictions of others, and to provide an asylum for those, to whom our affections yearn, and upon whom our hopes are concentrated; who, though now radiant in beauty, happy in the sports of childhood, and bright in the sunshine of their parents' affections,—to-morrow may be the houseless children of want, with affliction for their only parent, and poverty for their only inheritance.

Of all the afflicting and isolated situations in which it pleases God to cast the lot of feeble man, there is none more heart rending and desolate, than that of *the Orphan*. The hapless *Widow*, whose beloved partner has been torn away by the cruel hand of death, whose hopes are desecrated, and whose affections blighted by the blow, may, when the healing balsam of time hath been poured upon her wounds, and the angel of consolation whispered kindly unto her, find refuge from the coldness of the world, and the heaviness of anxious sorrow, in the affections of another heart; and the broken and withered blossom may again flourish in beauty and cheerfulness. The *parent*, the child of whose heart hath fallen a victim to life's eternal foe, just as the morn, whose dawning gave glorious promise, was bursting into the resplendent glory of the noon day, may mourn in bitterness of heart and weariness of spirit; but even he may gather hope, when he sees other joys springing around him, and learn to tear his affections from the dear departed one, to those who have come after him. Alas, to whom shall the *Orphan* turn—to whom shall he look for kindness and consolation? Shall time, that buries all other sorrows, bear with it, also his? Shall he find in another bosom, the ardent attachment, the overflowing affection, the ever ready succor that he has been accustomed to? Is there one, who lingers upon his steps, who gladdens at his smile, who sorrows at his tears, who cleaves unto him in darkness and brightness, in pain and pleasure, amid the smiles of joy and the bitter pangs of loathsome sickness? Alas, there is not *one!* The flower may wither and yet bud again; the stream may dry up, beneath the burning fervor of the summer sun, and yet again sparkle and bubble under its milder influence; the brightness of the day may fade beneath the darkness of the night, but the darkness shall again flee at the dawning of the morrow; but the flower of hope is withered and forever, the stream of joy exhausted and vanished, and the day of pleasure lost in the eternal night of misery, to *him* whose parents have passed away from this scene of life, leaving him without a home or refuge. Aye, but there is a refuge, a shelter where pain and misery may not enter, a haven where Poverty with its thousand ills, and Oppression with his iron heel, dare not intrude,—the home of the weary and the broken hearted, the bruised and blighted spirit—the *grave!*

Of all the virtues of the human character, there is none more exalted and noble than that of *Charity.* The man whose feelings are alive to the sufferings and misfortunes of his fellow beings, whose heart is ready with its sympathy, and whose hand prepared with its succor, has a redeeming spirit within him, whose influence will purify his soul from the errings incident to human frailty, and the vices natural to mortal depravity. It is the filtering stone of all the imperfections of our nature, which suffers all the purer principles to pass onwards with the current of our life, but throws back the grosser and more selfish passions; and he that possesses the true spirit of genuine charity, though he may have wandered, aye, fled from the straight path of strict morality, is not, and cannot be, the irreclaimable, lost and forsaken being, spoken of in the Holy Scriptures. He is still thousands of moral miles ahead of the being whom it would be sacrilege to call a man, and flattery to designate as a brute; whose whole existence, from the helplessness of infancy to the feeble tottering of decrepid age, from the cradle to the sepulchre, has been past without the offering of a single sympathy, or the boon of a single comfort towards his fellow travelers on the road to death. What though he may have worshiped no false Gods, committed no murder, borne no false witness against his neighbor, nor taken from him that which belonged to him; still he hath neglected those duties imposed upon him alike by the precepts of holy writ and the principles of morality. I am speaking of the true spirit of genuine Charity: that which finds its way into the chamber of the dead and dying—which lurks amid the by-ways of existence—which comes amid the watches of the night and under the veil of darkness—which letteth not the left hand know what the right hand doeth—which " does good by stealth and sighs to find it fame;" not that illegitimate and purse-proud spirit, which is to be found vaunting itself in the high ways and most frequented places in the noon-tide, with the trumpet of ostentation sounding its approach, and the criers on the house-tops proclaiming, " Look, he giveth!"—it is the secret, hidden gift—the kind and parental offering—the fostering and unpretending affection; *these* are the attributes of that virtue, which is first on the list of human perfections. Pardon me for saying, that of this character is the Society of which we are members. The fatherless child, who enters the threshold of our Association, and who learns within its portals to forget his afflictions and to look onwards to brighter days and better circumstances; who is reared up in the path of virtue, honor and integrity, goes forth amid the busy ranks of men and pursues his course of usefulness and prosperity with no blush of shame upon his cheek, no bitter reproach upon his feelings; and when he truns to bless the Institution that has thus reared and protected him, that has administered to his

4

sufferings and to his necessities and carried him through the bitter trials of helpless orphanage, he seeks in vain to bestow that benediction upon any particular individual; he knows not the hands that have thus succored him, the hearts that have thus felt for him; he only knows that from the kindness of those who constitute the Association, he has received those blessings; but a veil of impenetrable darkness covers all things else from his observance.

My young friends, upon whose path affliction hath too quickly cast its shadow, whom the evils and sorrows of life have already encompassed—it is to you that I must now address myself. True it is, that the morning of life, which to others hath been bright and beautiful, to you hath come clouded with storms and darkened by sorrows and afflictions. True it is, that he whom God sent to nourish and protect you, hath been stricken by the hand of death, ere yet the task of duty and affection had scarce commenced, and the bosom that nourished and the heart that cherished you are withering amid the silence of the tomb. Too soon have the endearing smiles of a mother ceased to animate and inspire you; too quickly has the care and protection of a father been removed from you forever; but be ye not dispirited; think not that God, your maker hath deserted you; believe not that you have been selected as the victims of care and anguish, whilst others are revelling in the sports of childhood and in the sunshine of joy and happiness; do not thus upbraid your Creator; rather lift your voices in praise and thanksgiving to Him, that when the hour of your affliction came; when all those who were knit to you by the bonds of nature had been snatched away from you, and your young hearts quailed beneath the shock; when poverty was casting its blight around you, and the snares of danger and of vice, were fast compasing your souls, *then*, even *then*, when the prospect seemed most gloomy, the danger most terrible, He raised around you friends, kind, generous, affectionate friends, who snatched you from the evils that surrounded you; and whilst they gave sustenance to your bodies, also bestowed that education and instruction, necccessary to sustain you through life, in honor and usefulness. Banish from your hearts, then, the idea that you have been the selected victims of misfortune. Alas, my young friends! you know not what life is. **If** you imagine that it is ever unsullied by cares or sorrows, look around you : look out upon the world, and tell me, is there one amongst the countless millions that exist there, whose heart hath never sickened at the approach of anguish? Why doth the form of beauty droop; the smile of loveliness vanish; the warrior's spirit quail? Why doth *he*— the calm, the quiet philosopher—who has abandoned all the idle pleasures of the world in the pursuit of wisdom, now desert, in its turn, the page of learning, and sit with downcast look and tearful eyes? Why : because the hand of sorrow hath grasped them ; because the rod of affliction hath stricken them, and the shadows incident to human existence have compassed them around. And is it indeed true: can nothing arrest the progress of that tyrant, whose coming spreads desolation around him? Do the brightest hours of pleasure, the loftiest walks of genius, lead but to the grave? Let the habiliments of woe that meet your gaze wheresoever you turn, and the monuments of sorrow which each moment is erecting around you, whilst they answer the enquiry, also instruct and purify your minds.

But do not misunderstand me. I do not come here to dispirit and dishearten you. Nay : it is my duty to encourage your hopes, and to inspire you with new desires and feelings. It is too true that the path of life is often a rugged and a dangerous one; and that each traveler upon it must encounter privations and difficulties. But is it not so always? It has its sunshine as well as its storm: its pleasures, as well as its sorrows ; and he that progresses onwards with a determination to discharge his duty to God and man, will always be entitled to his own respect, and the honor of his associates. Be it your task to walk thus fearlessly. Remember that in this free and happy country, there is no post of honor, no station of usefulness, no rank in society, to which the humblest individual, possessing the proper requisites, may not aspire ! You cannot have forgotten a shining example that has been but recently held up before you; and whilst it proves that honor and esteem ever await the exertions of talent and virtue, it should inspire you to fresh trials and renewed efforts. Now, then, whilst your hearts are yet untrammelled by the temptations of vice and pleasure: whilst kind friends and competent instructors are yet surrounding and ministering to you, you should endeavor to improve your minds and your dispositions ; so that, when a few brief years shall have passed away, you may enter upon the busy scenes of life, armed with virtue, courage and intelligence, to combat against the attacks of vice and sorrow. Prepare yourselves for the encounter ; and may the God of the afflicted and the desolate, of the fatherless and the widow, bring you safely through the temptations of this world, to that eternal home, " where the wicked cease from troubling, and the weary are at rest."

Gentlemen of the Society : *much* has been done in the cause in which we are engaged, but *more* remains to be done. The husbandmen have sown the seed, but they may not yet rest from their labors. It has been said, that there is no stationary existence, that all things must either advance or retrograde, that they must either progress, acquiring strength, beauty and vigor, or they must recede into darkness, destruction and decay. If the principle be a general one, our Society cannot hope for an exemption from its application. The question then is, shall we advance in the great and glorious cause of Charity, or shall we abandon it now and forever? Shall we go on, diffusing benevolence, aiding the distressed, shedding light unto those around whom the darkness of ignorance and misery is fast gathering, or shall we recede to the haunts of selfishness and apathy, leaving vice, ignorance and immorality, united together in an unholy alliance, to blight and wither the intellect and enervate and destroy the body? *This* is the question : will not your hearts answer it for me ? Let each of us then arouse our faculties, and increase our exertions ; let no man believe that his efforts will be unavailing, " every atom has its shadow," and the tallest mountains are formed from almost invisible particles of matter. And then when we have done this, and the irrevocable fiat hath gone forth, and the angel of death comes to summon us before that judge who knoweth every secret of our hearts, and hath recorded every vice and virtue of our nature : at that dread time, when the soul looks back with fear and sorrow, through the long vista of years, and marks the various and manifold transgressions it has committed, and the hours it has wasted and misapplied—*one* ray of light will, at least, break in upon that moment of darkness ; one consolation shed its balmy influence upon the trembling and departing spirit : the consolation that amid all its errors, it has never turned away from the supplications of the weary and heavy laden ; and that it has welcomed, with outstretched arms and ready succor, those upon whom the clouds of affliction had cast their deepest shadow, and their darkest influence. What prouder name would ye leave as an inheritance to your children? What nobler epitaph could ye have inscribed upon your monuments?